# HIDDEN RECORDS
## of the
# LIFE OF JESUS

# HIDDEN RECORDS
## of the
# LIFE of JESUS

*An introduction to the New Testament Apocrypha, and to some of the areas through which they were transmitted, namely, Jewish, Egyptian, and Gnostic Christianity, together with the earlier Gospel-type records in the Apocrypha, in Greek and Latin texts, translations, and explanations*

## by JACK FINEGAN

Pilgrim Press          Philadelphia / Boston

συναγάγετε τὰ περισσεύσαντα κλάσματα, ἵνα μή τι ἀπόληται

—John 6:12

# Preface

In relation to the painstaking and detailed labor of textual criticism Hans Lietzmann once remarked that it stood under the sign of the saying in John 6:12, "Gather up the fragments left over, that nothing may be lost." [1] The same saying is equally relevant to work on the New Testament Apocrypha. These are scattered and, in many cases, long-lost fragments of early Christian tradition. Many of the manuscripts which contain the records have literally been buried for many centuries in the sands of the ancient past. To recover the records, fit the pieces together again, and understand their place in the tradition, is possible only through the labors of many people, those who find the manuscripts as well as those who read, translate, and interpret them.

My own interest is primarily in any fragments of this sort which may deserve consideration along with the four Gospels of the canonical New Testament as witnesses to the tradition about the life of Jesus, and this book is intended for others who may share this interest. The materials of this sort, i.e., specifically apocryphal Gospel-type materials, have been brought together in Italian by P. Giuseppe Bonaccorsi, *Vangeli Apocrifi* (1948), in Spanish by Aurelio de Santos Otero, *Los Evangelios Apocrifos* (1956), and in German by Wilhelm Schneemelcher and others in the third edition of Edgar Hennecke's *Neutestamentliche Apokryphen*, Vol. I, *Evangelien* (1959). The last book became available in English translation edited by R. McL. Wilson, *New Testament Apocrypha*, Vol. I, *Gospels and Related Writings* (1963), only after I had completed most of the work on my own volume. I am of course indebted to these as well as

---

[1] Hans Lietzmann, *Zur Würdigung des Chester-Beatty-Papyrus der Paulusbriefe*. Sonderausgabe aus den Sitzungsberichten der preussischen Akademie der Wissenschaften, phil.-hist. Klasse. 1934, XXV, 11.

to the large number of other works cited in the Literature throughout this volume.

Above all, however, I have endeavored to base what is said, both in the introductory sections and in the textual sections, upon the original sources, and these are cited throughout. The present book corresponds with Bonaccorsi and Santos in the fact that it gives Greek and Latin texts in the original languages, as Schneemelcher does not. As far as Coptic texts are concerned, only translations and summaries are presented, but I am glad to be able to say that all of these materials have been read by Dr. Pahor Labib, former Director of the Coptic Museum in Old Cairo, and he has certified that "everything is correct." My book is alone, I think, in providing photographs of all the oldest fragments of papyrus and parchment on which are Greek apocryphal texts with which we are concerned. It corresponds with all three of the other books mentioned in that it gives attention to the definition of "apocryphal" in distinction from "canonical." It provides, I think, more introductory information than the other three books about Jewish, Egyptian, and Gnostic Christianity (since many Apocrypha come to us through these areas), information which is elsewhere presumably taken for granted but which is actually not too widely known. As far as the apocryphal text-material is concerned, some is presented which is not in the other three books, either because it has only recently become available or for some other reason; and all of the text-material has been independently organized according to principles which appear logical to the present writer and which will be evident from the Table of Contents and from explanations in the book. The actual text-material selected for presentation is undoubtedly less in total amount than in the other three collections. Some of the principles of selection will be explained more fully in the course of the book.

In brief it may be said here that the total amount of material now available in this field is very great, but much of it would surely be recognized by almost all readers as belonging to those realms of imaginative amplification which are unmistakably legendary, or to those areas of thought which are clearly mythological. Materials of these sorts have their own values, and we will work through considerable portions of such, in order to become familiar with their character and to neglect no area of possible interest. But our chief concern is still with the question of whether in all the material there is any which deserves consideration alongside the canonical Gospels as witness to the earliest tradition about Jesus. The material presented is that in which, it seems, there is the greatest likelihood of finding fragments of early, extracanonical tradition about Jesus, if such fragments are to be found anywhere.

The Table of Contents, List of Tables, and List of Illustrations, give an outline of the material which is to be found in the book. The List of Ancient Sources identifies the early church writers and their writings which are frequently cited. The Abbreviations, shown in their own lists, are intended to assist in making the presentation compact. The Literature is shown at relevant points throughout the book.

Jack Finegan

# Contents

## II. TEXTS

### A. Quotations

### B. Manuscripts

# LIST OF ILLUSTRATIONS

# LIST OF TABLES

# LIST OF ANCIENT SOURCES

*Literature:* Johannes Quasten, *Patrology.* 3 vols. 1950–60; W. Schneemelcher, ed., *Bibliographia Patristica.* 1959ff.; Berthold Altaner, *Patrology.* 1960.

Athanasius. Bishop of Alexandria. A.D. 295–373. *Festal Letters,* Eng. tr. NPNFSS IV.

Augustine, Aurelius Augustinus. Bishop of Hippo in North Africa. A.D. 354–430. Latin text *Sancti Aurelii Augustini Hipponensis episcopi opera omnia,* 11 vols. Paris 1836–39; Latin text and French tr. *Oeuvres completes de Saint Augustin,* 34 vols. Paris 1872–78; Eng. tr. NPNF I–VIII.

Barnabas, Letter of. Because of its opposition to the OT (9:4) this letter cannot have been written by Barnabas, the companion of Paul, to whom tradition ascribes it. Because of its allegorical character it may have been written in Alexandria. The destruction and building again of the Temple are mentioned (16:3-4), and if the reference is to the building of the Temple by Hadrian in 130, the date of the writing would be shortly after that. It is found in Codex Sinaiticus immediately after the Revelation of John (§34). Greek text PAO; Greek text and Eng. tr. LCL; Eng. tr. ANF I.

Chrysostom, John Chrysostom. b. at Antioch between 344 and 354, preacher in Antioch 386–97, made patriarch of Constantinople in 398, d. in exile in 407. Eng. tr. NPNF IX–XIV.

Clement of Alexandria, Titus Flavius Clemens. Christian scholar. d. before A.D. 215. *Stromata* ($\Sigma\tau\rho\omega\mu\alpha\tau\epsilon\hat{\imath}s$ = "Carpets"), Greek text ed. Otto Stählin, GCS II 3d ed. 1960, III 1909; Ger. tr. *Bibliothek der Kirchenväter* XVII, XIX, XX 1936–38; Greek Text and Eng. tr. in part LCL; Eng. tr. ANF II.

Clement of Rome. Irenaeus (*Against Heresies* III 3, 3) and Eusebius (*Ch. Hist.* III 15) name him as the third successor of Peter as head of the church at Rome. Origen (*Commentary on John* VI 54 [36] GCS Origenes IV 163) and Eusebius identify him with the friend of Paul in Phl 4:3. Eusebius puts the beginning of his office in the twelfth year of Domitian and the end (*Ch. Hist.* III 34) in the third year of Trajan, i.e., he was head of the Roman church from A.D. 92 to 101. In Rome the Basilica of San Clemente is supposed to stand on the foundations of his house. Two letters of Clement to the church at Corinth are mentioned by Eusebius (*Ch. Hist.* III 38) and are preserved in Codex Alexandrinus, Codex Hierosolymitanus (A.D. 1056), and a Syriac NT manuscript (A.D. 1170) in the Cambridge University Library. The First Letter (1 Clem) was written by Clement about A.D. 96. The so-called Second Letter (2 Clem) was not used by the ancients, as far as Eusebius could ascertain. It was probably written in Corinth between 120 and 140 (Lightfoot), although some think in Rome c. 170 (Harnack). Greek text, PAO; Greek text and Eng. tr., Joseph B. Lightfoot, *The Apostolic Fathers.* Part I, S. Clement of Rome, 2 vols. 1890; Kirsopp Lake, *The Apostolic Fathers,* LCL, I, 1912; Eng. tr., ANF I (1 Clem); Edgar J. Goodspeed, *The Apostolic Fathers.* 1950.

Cyprian, Thascius Caecilius Cyprianus. Bishop of Carthage. b. between 200 and 210 probably at Carthage. Became bishop of that city in 248/249. Martyred in 258. Latin text ed. G. Hartel, CSEL III 3 vols. 1868–71; Eng. tr. ANF V.

Cyril of Alexandria. Patriarch of Alexandria in 412. d. 444. Wrote exegetical, polemical, and apologetical works, and letters and sermons. Greek text MPG 68–77.

Cyril of Jerusalem. Probably b. in Jerusalem c. 315. Became bishop of Jerusalem in 347/348, and at that time gave a series of twenty-four catechetical lectures in the Church of the Holy Sepulcher. Eng. tr. NPNFSS VII.

Epiphanius. b. c. 315 in the vicinity of Eleutheropolis near Gaza in Palestine. c. 335 visited the monks of Egypt, then founded a monastery at Eleutheropolis in Palestine and headed it for thirty years. In 367 became bishop of Salamis (Constantia) on the island of Cyprus. Was opponent of Origen and friend of Jerome. Jerome (*Against Rufinus* III 6 NPNFSS III 522) called him *papa Epiphanius* πεντάγλωττος, "bishop Epiphanius the five-tongued," since he knew Hebrew, Greek, Syriac, Coptic, and Latin. *Ancoratus* ('Αγκυρωτός) or "The Firmly-Anchored Man," written in 374; and *Panarion* (Πανάριον) or "Medicine Chest" (designed as an antidote for those bitten by the poisonous snakes of heresy, also cited as *Haereses*), written in 374–77; Greek text ed. K. Holl, GCS 25, 31, 37. *De mensuris et ponderibus* (Περὶ μέτρων καὶ σταθμῶν) or "On Weights and Measures," written in 392, a Bible dictionary treating canon and versions of the OT, measures and weights in the Bible, and geography of Palestine, Eng. tr. of the complete Syriac version, ed. James E. Dean, SAOC 11, 1935.

Eusebius of Caesarea, Eusebius Caesariensis, Eusebius Pamphili. Church historian. A.D. 263–339. *Chronicle* (Χρονικοὶ κανόνες), published c. 303, translated into Latin and continued to 378 by Jerome; tr. from Armenian, J. Karst, GCS XX 1911; Jerome's version, ed. R. Helm, GCS XLVII (Eusebius VII) 2d ed. 1956. *Praeparatio evangelica* (Εὐαγγελικὴ προπαρασκευή), written between 312 and 322, ed. K. Mras, GCS XLIII 2 vols. 1954–56; *Demonstratio evangelica* (Εὐαγγελικὴ ἀπόδειξις), probably written immediately after the preceding work, ed. I. A. Heikel, GCS XXIII 1913; *Theophany* or "Divine Manifestation," draws on the *Praeparatio* and *Demonstratio* and was probably written c. 333, ed. H. Gressmann, GCS III 2, 1904. *Church History* ('Εκκλησιαστικὴ ἱστορία), to the victory of Constantine over Licinius (324), ed. E. Schwartz, GCS IX 3 vols. 1903–9; Kirsopp Lake, LCL I–II 1926–32; A. C. McGiffert, NPNFSS I. *Onomasticon* (Περὶ τῶν τοπικῶν ὀνομάτων), topographical dictionary written probably before 331, ed. E. Klostermann, GCS Eusebius III 1, 1904.

Hegesippus. Christian writer against the Gnostics. Probably a Jew by birth, he came to Rome under Pope Anicetus (c. 154–66). Returning home, he wrote five books of *Memoirs* ('Υπομνήματα) c. 180, which are quoted by Eusebius.

Hippolytus. A presbyter at Rome in the early part of the third century. He came into conflict with Pope Callistus (217–22) and was elected head of a schismatic group, but was reconciled to the main church before he died. In the persecution under Maximinus Thrax both he and Pope Pontianus were exiled to Sardinia where Hippolytus died (235). One reference makes him a pupil of Irenaeus. He wrote voluminously in Greek. A broken seated marble statue of him, which was probably erected at his burial place on the Via Tiburtina, was rediscovered in 1551 and placed in the Lateran Museum. It contains an incomplete list of his writings, and his Easter tables. His major extant work, written after 222, was in ten books, called Κατὰ πασῶν αἱρέσεων ἔλεγχος, or *Refutatio omnium haeresium,* "Refutation of All Heresies"; the first four books, on Greek philosophy, are called *Philosophoumena.* Greek text, L. Duncker and F. G. Schneidewin, *S. Hippolyti . . . Refutationis Omnium Haeresium librorum decem quae supersunt.* 1859; BHP 5, 6; GCS 26; Eng. tr. ANF V.

Ignatius. Eusebius (*Ch. Hist.* III 22, 36) says that he was second bishop of Antioch, after Evodius, and that under Trajan (98–117) he was taken to Rome and thrown to the wild beasts. En route he wrote seven letters to the churches at Ephesus, Magnesia, Tralles, Philadelphia, Smyrna, and Rome, and to Bishop Polycarp (d. 156) of Smyrna. The letters are preserved in Greek. About 380 the text was enlarged, and this longer recension is extant in Greek and Latin. There is also a Syriac version of the shorter form of three of the letters. Greek and Syriac texts, Joseph B. Lightfoot, *The Apostolic Fathers.* Part II, S. Ignatius, S. Polycarp, 3 vols. 2d ed. 1889; Greek texts PAO; Greek text and Eng. tr., Kirsopp Lake, *The Apostolic Fathers,* LCL, I, 1912; Eng. tr., ANF I; Edgar J. Goodspeed, *The Apostolic Fathers.* 1950.

Irenaeus. b. between 140 and 160 in Asia Minor, probably in Smyrna, where he heard Polycarp. Later a priest and (177/178) bishop in Lyons in Gaul. Wrote in his native Greek. *Against Heresies* ("Ελεγχος καὶ ἀνατροπὴ τῆς ψευδωνύμου γνώσεως, "Refutation and Overthrow of the Falsely Called Knowledge"), Greek text (of the first book) BHP V; Eng. tr. ANF I.

Jerome, Eusebius Hieronymus. Latin church scholar. b. A.D. c. 347. Active in Rome 382–85 under Pope Damasus. Settled at Bethlehem in 386. d. A.D. 419 or 420. Latin text CCSL LXXII 1959, etc. Eng. tr. NPNFSS III, VI.

Josephus, Joseph ben Mattathias, Flavius Josephus. Jewish historian. A.D. c. 37—after 100 (*War,* 75–79; *Antiquities,* c. 94; *Life,* c. 100; *Against Apion,* c. 100). Greek text ed. B. Niese, 6 vols. 1888–95; Greek text and Eng. tr. LCL 1926ff.

Justin Martyr. d. A.D. c. 165. Born of a pagan Greek family at Flavia Neapolis (Nablus) in Palestine, he studied philosophy, became a Christian, wrote in defense of Christianity, and was beheaded at Rome under the city prefect, Junius Rusticus. Of his writings, two *Apologies* and the *Dialogue with Trypho* survive. Greek text BHP 3–4; Eng. tr. ANF I.

Lactantius. Lucius Caecilius Firmianus Lactantius. 260–330. Teacher of Latin rhetoric at Nicomedia under Diocletian. Having become a Christian, he was compelled to resign his position in the persecution. Later (c. 317) was called by Constantine to Treves as tutor for his son, Crispus. Author of *The Divine Institutes,* written in 304–13, and other works. Eng. tr. ANF VII.

Marcion was born at Sinope (Sinob) in Pontus on the Black Sea, and became a wealthy shipowner. Excommunicated by his father, the bishop of Sinope, Marcion came to Rome under Antoninus Pius, about 140, and was excommunicated here too in July 144. He then founded his own church, communities of which existed for many centuries. Polycarp (quoted by Irenaeus, *Against Heresies* III 3, 4) called him "the firstborn of Satan." Justin Martyr says (*Apology* I 26, cf. 58) that he misled many of every nation. Irenaeus (*Against Heresies* I 28, 1) classes him with the Gnostic Encratites (§103) and says (I 27, 1) that he developed the doctrine of Cerdo, who took his system from the followers of Simon (§§100f.). Cerdo, who was in Rome in the time of Hyginus (136–40), "taught that the God proclaimed by the law and the prophets was not the Father of our Lord Jesus Christ." In the interest of similar doctrine Marcion mutilated the Gospel according to Luke and dismembered the Letters of Paul. Tertullian wrote his longest work *Against Marcion*, and this is the chief source for knowledge of Marcion since the latter's own volume of *Antitheses* has been lost.

Melito. Bishop of Sardis in Lydia. A.D. c. 180. Eusebius (*Ch. Hist.* IV 26) places him under Marcus Aurelius, and mentions and quotes from a number of his writings.

Nicephorus, Callistus Xanthopulus. Church historian at Constantinople in the fourteenth century. His *Church History*, in eighteen books, is of some value as incorporating an anonymous church history of the tenth century, as using some older sources such as the *Ch. Hist.* of Eusebius, and as preserving some apocryphal material. Greek text MPG 145–47.

Origen, Origenes. Christian scholar and theologian. b. A.D. c. 185 probably at Alexandria. Head of the catechetical school at Alexandria, A.D. 203–31. Moved to Caesarea in Palestine in 232. d. c. 253 at Tyre. Greek text GCS 12 vols.; Eng. tr. ANF IV, IX.

Paulinus of Nola was born at Bordeaux in 353, was a pupil and friend of the Roman rhetorician, Ausonius, adopted a monastic life, became bishop of Nola in 409, and died in 431. He wrote poems, and letters to Augustine, Sulpicius Severus, and others. Latin text MPL 61; CSEL XXIX–XXX (1894).

Philo, Philo Judaeus. Hellenistic Jewish philosopher. c. 20 B.C.–A.D. 54. Many writings. Greek text and Eng. tr. LCL 1929ff.

Socrates. Lawyer in Constantinople. b. c. 380, d. after 439. Continued the work of Eusebius with a *Church History* which covers the time from 305 to 439. Eng. tr. NPNFSS II.

Sozomen. Lawyer at Constantinople. Author of *Church History*, written between 439 and 450, which deals with the period from 324 to 425. Eng. tr. NPNFSS II.

Tatian, the son of pagan parents in Syria, was probably converted in Rome, where he was a pupil of Justin Martyr. He returned to the East about 172, and was associated with the Gnostic Encratites (§103). Out of more numerous writings only his *Oration to the Greeks* (ANF II) and *Diatessaron* are extant.

Tertullian. Latin Christian writer at Carthage. b. A.D. c. 160, d. after A.D. 220. Latin text CCSL I, II 1954; Latin text and French tr. SC; Eng. tr. ANF III, IV.

Theodoret of Cyrus. b. Antioch c. 393. Became bishop of Cyrus, a small town east of Antioch, in 423. d. c. 466. His *Church History* was written in 449–50 and covers the period from 325 to 428. Greek text ed. L. Parmentier, GCS XIX (1911), 2d ed. GCS XLIV (1954); Eng. tr. NPNFSS III. *History of Heresies* (αἱρετικῆς κακομυθίας Ἐπιτομή, *Haereticarum fabularum compendium*), written about 453, Greek text MPG 83, 335–556.

# LISTS OF ABBREVIATIONS

## 1. Old Testament

| | | | |
|---|---|---|---|
| Gen | Genesis | Ec | Ecclesiastes |
| Ex | Exodus | SS | Song of Solomon |
| Lev | Leviticus | Is | Isaiah |
| Num | Numbers | Jer | Jeremiah |
| Dt | Deuteronomy | Lam | Lamentations |
| Jos | Joshua | Ezk | Ezekiel |
| Jg | Judges | Dan | Daniel |
| Ru | Ruth | Hos | Hosea |
| 1 S | 1 Samuel | Jl | Joel |
| 2 S | 2 Samuel | Am | Amos |
| 1 K | 1 Kings | Ob | Obadiah |
| 2 K | 2 Kings | Jon | Jonah |
| 1 Ch | 1 Chronicles | Mic | Micah |
| 2 Ch | 2 Chronicles | Nah | Nahum |
| Ezr | Ezra | Hab | Habakkuk |
| Neh | Nehemiah | Zph | Zephaniah |
| Est | Esther | Hag | Haggai |
| Jb | Job | Zec | Zechariah |
| Ps | Psalms | Mal | Malachi |
| Pr | Proverbs | | |

## 2. Old Testament Apocrypha

| | | | |
|---|---|---|---|
| 1 Esd | 1 Esdras | Bar | Baruch |
| 2 Esd | 2 Esdras | Ep Jer | Epistle of Jeremy, or |
| Tob | Tobit | | Letter of Jeremiah |
| Jth | Judith | Thr Ch | Song of the Three Children |
| Ad Est | Additions to Esther | Sus | Susanna |
| Wisd | Wisdom of Solomon | Bel | Bel and the Dragon |
| Ecclus, | Ecclesiasticus, or the | Pr Man | Prayer of Manasses |
| or Sir | Wisdom of Jesus the | 1 Macc | 1 Maccabees |
| | Son of Sirach | 2 Macc | 2 Maccabees |

## 3. Pseudepigrapha

| | | | |
|---|---|---|---|
| Apc Bar | Apocalypse of Baruch | Jub | Jubilees |
| Asc Is | Ascension of Isaiah | Ps Sol | Psalms of Solomon |
| Asm M | Assumption of Moses | Sib Or | Sibylline Oracles |
| En | Enoch | 12 P | Testaments of the Twelve Patriarchs |

## 4. New Testament

| | | | |
|---|---|---|---|
| Mt | Matthew | Lk | Luke |
| Mk | Mark | Jn | John |

| Ac | Acts | Tit | Titus |
|---|---|---|---|
| Rom | Romans | Phm | Philemon |
| 1 Cor | 1 Corinthians | Heb | Hebrews |
| 2 Cor | 2 Corinthians | Jas | James |
| Gal | Galatians | 1 Pet | 1 Peter |
| Eph | Ephesians | 2 Pet | 2 Peter |
| Phl | Philippians | 1 Jn | 1 John |
| Col | Colossians | 2 Jn | 2 John |
| 1 Th | 1 Thessalonians | 3 Jn | 3 John |
| 2 Th | 2 Thessalonians | Jd | Jude |
| 1 Tim | 1 Timothy | Rev | Revelation |
| 2 Tim | 2 Timothy | | |

### 5. Apostolic Fathers

| Did | Didache, Teaching of the | 2 Clem | 2 Clement |
|---|---|---|---|
| | Twelve Apostles | Shep | Shepherd, Shepherd of |
| Barn | Letter of Barnabas | | Hermas |
| 1 Clem | 1 Clement | Smyr | Smyrnaeans, Letter of |
| | | | Ignatius to the |

### 6. Books and Periodicals

AAA    *Acta apostolorum apocrypha.* ed. C. Tischendorf, 1851. Vol. 1 ed. R. A. Lipsius 1891; vols. 2, 1 and 2 ed. M. Bonnet 1898 and 1903; 3 vols. reprinted 1959.

ANF    Alexander Roberts and James Donaldson, eds., rev. by A. Cleveland Coxe, *The Ante-Nicene Fathers, Translations of the Writings of the Fathers down to A.D. 325.* 10 vols. 1885–87.

ASV    *American Standard Version.*

BACC    Alfred J. Butler, *The Ancient Coptic Churches of Egypt.* 2 vols. 1884.

BHP    ΒΙΒΛΙΟΘΗΚΗ ΕΛΛΗΝΩΝ ΠΑΤΕΡΩΝ ΚΑΙ ΕΚΚΛΗΣΙ-ΑΣΤΙΚΩΝ ΣΥΓΓΡΑΦΕΩΝ, *Bibliothēkē hellenōn paterōn kai ekklesiastikōn syngrapheōn.*

BVA    P. Giuseppe Bonaccorsi, *Vangeli Apocrifi.* 1948.

CAP    R. H. Charles, ed., *The Apocrypha and Pseudepigrapha of the Old Testament in English with Introductions and Critical and Explanatory Notes to the Several Books.* 2 vols. 1913.

CBQ    *The Catholic Biblical Quarterly.*

CCKÄ    Maria Cramer, *Das christlich-koptische Ägypten einst und Heute, Eine Orientierung.* 1959.

CCSL    *Corpus Christianorum, Series Latina.*

CSEL    *Corpus scriptorum ecclesiasticorum latinorum.*

DACL    *Dictionnaire d'archéologie chrétienne et de liturgie.* 1924ff.

DB    *Dictionnaire de la Bible.*

DJD    *Discoveries in the Judaean Desert.* 1955ff.

| | |
|---|---|
| EI | *The Encyclopaedia of Islam.* |
| FAWR | Jack Finegan, *The Archeology of World Religions.* 1952. |
| FHBC | Jack Finegan, *Handbook of Biblical Chronology.* 1964. |
| FLP | Jack Finegan, *Light from the Ancient Past, The Archeological Background of Judaism and Christianity.* 2d ed. 1959. |
| GBT | Lazarus Goldschmidt, *Der babylonische Talmud.* 9 vols. 1899–1935. |
| GCS | *Die griechischen christlichen Schriftsteller der ersten Jahrhunderte.* Deutsche Akademie der Wissenschaften zu Berlin. |
| GGSB | Robert M. Grant, *Gnosticism, A Source Book of Heretical Writings from the Early Christian Period.* 1961. |
| HDB | James Hastings, ed., *A Dictionary of the Bible.* 4 vols. 1898–1902. |
| HSNTAE | Edgar Hennecke's *Neutestamentliche Apokryphen in deutscher Übersetzung.* 3d ed. by Wilhelm Schneemelcher. Vol. I, *Evangelien.* 1959. |
| HTR | *The Harvard Theological Review.* |
| HZNT | *Handbuch zum Neuen Testament.* |
| IDB | *The Interpreter's Dictionary of the Bible.* |
| JBL | *Journal of Biblical Literature.* |
| JBR | *The Journal of Bible and Religion.* |
| JE | Isidore Singer, ed., *The Jewish Encyclopedia.* 12 vols. 1901–5. |
| JEA | *The Journal of Egyptian Archaeology.* |
| JTS | *The Journal of Theological Studies.* |
| JUSJ | Joachim Jeremias, *Unknown Sayings of Jesus.* 1957. |
| KJV | *King James Version.* |
| KT | *Kleine Texte für Vorlesungen und Übungen.* |
| LCGP | Pahor Labib, *Coptic Gnostic Papyri in the Coptic Museum at Old Cairo.* Vol. I, 1956. |
| LCL | *The Loeb Classical Library.* |
| LXX | The Septuagint. Henry B. Swete, ed., *The Old Testament in Greek According to the Septuagint.* I, 4th ed. 1909; II, 3d ed. 1907; III, 3d ed. 1905. Alan E. Brooke, Norman McLean, and others, eds., *The Old Testament in Greek.* 1906ff. Alfred Rahlfs, ed., *Septuaginta, id est Vetus Testamentum Graece iuxta LXX interpretes.* 2 vols. 1935. *Septuaginta, Vetus Testamentum Graecum auctoritate Societatis Litterarum Gottingensis editum.* 1931ff. |
| MPG | Jacques Paul Migne, *Patrologiae cursus completus. Series graeca.* |
| MPL | Jacques Paul Migne, *Patrologiae cursus completus. Series latina.* |
| Moffatt | James Moffatt, *The Bible, A New Translation.* |
| NPNF | Philip Schaff, ed., *A Select Library of the Nicene and Post-Nicene Fathers.* First Series. 14 vols. 1886–89. |
| NPNFSS | Philip Schaff and Henry Wace, eds., *A Select Library of Nicene and Post-Nicene Fathers of the Christian Church.* Second Series. 14 vols. 1890–1900. |

| | |
|---|---|
| NT | New Testament. |
| NTS | *New Testament Studies.* |
| OP | *The Oxyrhynchus Papyri.* |
| OT | Old Testament. |
| PAO | *Patrum apostolicorum opera, textum ad fidem codicum et graecorum et latinorum adhibitis praestantissimis editionibus,* ed. Oscar de Gebhardt, A. Harnack, T. Zahn. Editio tertia minor. 1900. |
| PEQ | *Palestine Exploration Quarterly.* |
| RA | Alfred Resch, *Agrapha.* 1889, rev. ed. 1906. |
| RB | *Revue Biblique.* |
| RSV | *Revised Standard Version.* |
| SAOC | *Studies in Ancient Oriental Civilization.* Oriental Institute. |
| SBT | I. Epstein, ed., *The Babylonian Talmud* (Soncino Press). 1935ff. |
| SC | *Sources Chrétiennes.* |
| SEA | Aurelio de Santos Otero, *Los Evangelios Apocrifos.* 1958. |
| ST | *Studia Theologica.* |
| SWDCB | William Smith and Henry Wace, *A Dictionary of Christian Biography.* 4 vols. 1877–87. |
| TEA | C. Tischendorf, *Evangelia Apocrypha.* 1876. |
| TL | *Theologische Literaturzeitung.* |
| TU | *Texte und Untersuchungen zur Geschichte der altchristlichen Literatur.* |
| VC | *Vigiliae Christianae.* |
| VT | *Vetus Testamentum.* |
| ZKG | *Zeitschrift für Kirchengeschichte.* |
| ZNW | *Zeitschrift für die neutestamentliche Wissenschaft und die Kunde der älteren Kirche.* |
| ZRGG | *Zeitschrift für Religions- und Geistesgeschichte.* |

## 7. Miscellaneous

| | | |
|---|---|---|
| b. | | born |
| c. | *circa* | about, around |
| cf. | *conferre* | compare |
| chap., chaps. | | chapter, chapters |
| d. | | died |
| ed., eds. | | edited, editor, editors |
| et al. | *et alii* | and others |
| f., ff. | | following |
| n. | | note |
| p., pp. | | page, pages |
| pl. | | plate |
| tr. | | translated, translation |
| v., vv. | | verse, verses |

## 8. Arbitrary Signs

[ ]    square brackets mark portions missing from a text and, upon occasion, supplied by the editor

( )    round brackets mark letters or words supplied to fill out an abbreviation in a text, or to express the sense in a translation

⟨ ⟩    angled brackets mark portions supplied in a text from some parallel or as required by the context

{ }    braces mark superfluous letters or words

. . .    dots indicate missing letters in a text, or omitted portion in a translation or quotation

# Introduction

The Gospel according to Luke begins (1:1) with the statement that "many have undertaken to compile a narrative of the things which have been accomplished among us"; and the Gospel according to John concludes (21:25) with the remark that "there are also many other things which Jesus did; were every one of them to be written, I suppose that the world itself could not contain the books that would be written." The Gospels according to Luke and according to John were themselves two of the four Gospels which were accepted as "canonical," i.e., authoritative and normative, in the early church. By the middle of the second century Lk and Jn appear as the third and fourth of the Gospels (undoubtedly following Mt and Mk as the first and second) in the partially preserved list of canonical books of the NT known as the Muratorian Fragment. Likewise by around A.D. 180 Irenaeus declares that as there are four regions of the world and four principal winds so, too, the church has four pillars, namely, the four Gospels, fittingly symbolized by the four living creatures of Ezk 1:10, the lion (Jn), the calf (Lk), the man (Mt), and the eagle (Mk).

This conviction that the four Gospels which have been preserved in the canonical NT are authoritative and adequate has, of course, persisted and prevails properly throughout the church today. Nevertheless the canonical NT itself contains at least one saying of Jesus which is outside of the four Gospels and entirely independent of them. This is the saying, "It is more blessed to give than to receive," which was quoted by Paul in his address to the Ephesian elders, according to Ac 20:35. Such a saying is not found in the four Gospels, yet is eminently in accord with the spirit of the sayings of Jesus which are given in the four Gospels. Whether Paul had learned this saying from an oral or written source it is not necessary here to inquire; it is evident that early Christian tradition preserved material about Jesus which, at least to the extent of this saying of Jesus, was additional to what was incorporated in the four Gospels which became canonical.

While the saying given by Paul is preserved in the canonical NT, inasmuch as it was included in the Book of Acts, the statements of Lk (1:1) and Jn (21:25) quoted at the outset make it probable that there also existed materials about Jesus which were put down in written documents which were never incorporated in the canonical NT at all.

The existence, at a relatively early date, of orally transmitted and of written-down materials about Jesus other than those contained in the canonical NT is, of course, not purely hypothetical. Writers of the early church, whose own works we possess, quote sayings of Jesus not found in the NT; and various noncanonical manuscripts, found at different times and often preserved only in fragments, give sayings and narrate deeds of Jesus.

In contrast with the writings which are accepted as canonical, materials of the sort just described are commonly called "apocryphal." As will be explained more fully in the Prolegomena, the Greek adjective ἀπόκρυφος means "hidden," and the neuter plural ἀπόκρυφα means "hidden things." An ἀπόκρυφος βίβλος is, therefore, a "hidden book." In the area of early Christianity, apocryphal books are actually mentioned first in connection with certain groups which professed to be the custodians of secret doctrines. They therefore kept hidden the books in which these doctrines were contained. From this usage it became customary to designate as apocryphal those books which might have been included in the canonical Bible but were not. As far as the OT is concerned, it is the books which are found in the Greek translation known as the Septuagint (LXX), but are not included in the Hebrew canon, which are ordinarily called the Apocrypha. The adjective apocryphal is sometimes also used in reference to the books which are more technically (although not altogether satisfactorily) called the Pseudepigrapha. As far as the NT Apocrypha are concerned, these are for the most part books which in name, form, or content make some claim to be of the same sort as the books in the NT canon. That is to say, they are or make some claim to be Gospels, Acts, Letters, or Revelations. Here we are concerned only with apocryphal materials which have some relationship to the kind of materials which are found in the canonical Gospels. These include sayings which purport to be those of Jesus, whether found in isolation or in collections, and accounts which profess to tell of things done by or in connection with Jesus. All of this we may designate as apocryphal records, or hidden records, of the life of Jesus.

The example of the saying of Jesus quoted by Paul and recorded in Ac 20:35, which accords in general with the spirit of the sayings of

Jesus in the canonical Gospels, raises the hope that in the apocryphal material about Jesus, even though it was not included anywhere in the canonical NT, there might at least occasionally be found something deserving of attention along with the canonical material. The subject matter is so important that no effort should be spared to find anything whatsoever that does actually contribute to authentic knowledge of Jesus. At the same time the first explicit occurrence of "apocrypha" among groups which the main church regarded as heretical, and the conviction of a churchman such as Irenaeus that the four canonical Gospels provide a completely adequate basis for the church and that, as he said, it was not possible for these to be more or fewer than four in number, may serve as warning not to expect too much from even the most assiduous search.

On that search we now embark. First we will investigate more fully the distinction indicated above between "canonical" and "apocryphal" and, for proper perspective, will necessarily do this in regard to both the OT and the NT. After that we will recognize that many of the NT Apocrypha have come down through Jewish Christian, Egyptian Christian, and Gnostic Christian channels and, since these are relatively little-known areas, will bring together some information about Jewish Christianity, Egyptian Christianity, and Gnosticism. Then we will describe at some representative and important points the actual process of discovery, some of it even quite recent, through which long-lost Apocrypha have come to light. Presentation of these matters will constitute the Prolegomena of this volume. After that, under the heading of Texts, the "hidden records of the life of Jesus" will themselves be set forth, with sufficient description to show what is known of where they come from and, it is hoped, sufficient discussion to provide initial guidance for such further study of them as the reader may desire to make. In the case of manuscripts something of their external features and arrangement, and the way they are divided and cited in modern editions, will also be explained to assist those who wish to work directly with these sources.

# I. Prolegomena

# 1 / Apocrypha

*Literature:* George F. Moore, "Apocrypha," in JE I 1–6; Frank C. Porter, "Apocrypha," in HDB I 110–23; C. T. Fritsch, "Apocrypha," in IDB I 161–66.

§1. In the customary usage of the present time, Apocrypha may be defined as books which raise some claim to be like the writings which are in the biblical canon, but which are not themselves in that canon, at least not fully in it, and are perhaps wholly outside it. Since this definition is phrased in terms of non-canonicity, it is necessary to explain the origin of the word "canon" as well as of the word "apocrypha."

§2. The Hebrew word קנה and the Greek κάνη mean "reed," and κανών therefore means "measuring reed" or "measuring rod." A measuring rod may represent a standard or rule. Thus 4 Macc 7:21 speaks of walking "by the whole rule of philosophy" (πρὸς ὅλον τὸν τῆς φιλοσοφίας κανόνα), and Gal 6:16 wishes peace and mercy for "as many as shall walk by this rule" (ὅσοι τῷ κανόνι τούτῳ στοιχήσουσιν). Compare also §163 for another example of this usage. In the church, therefore, that which was κανών or κανονικός was that which embodied the standard and the rule. Since the collection of holy Scriptures which was made and accepted in the church constituted above all the ruling and normative standard of Christian teaching and practice, it was the most important possible κανών. This manner of speaking went over into Latin, where κανών became *canon*. *Canon* was used synonymously with *biblia*. *Biblia* meant the "books" par excellence, and when the plural noun *biblia* was taken as a singular form, the name "Bible" emerged.[1] From Greek and Latin the word canon was, of course, adopted directly into English. As synonymous with the

---

[1] FLP 395.

divine Scriptures of the OT and the NT, the word canon is used for the first time unmistakably by Athanasius in his *Festal Letter* XXXIX (NPNFSS IV 552), written before Easter A.D. 367. In this place he lists the books of the OT, counted as twenty-two in number after a Hebrew manner of reckoning (§6), and the books of the NT, comprising exactly the twenty-seven which have been recognized ever since.

§3. The word apocrypha is also derived from the Greek. In Greek ἀπό means "from" and κρύπτω means "to hide"; hence ἀποκρύπτω means "to hide from" or "to hide away." Accordingly the adjective ἀπόκρυφος signifies "hidden" or "concealed," and the neuter plural τὰ ἀπόκρυφα means "the hidden things." Thus 1 Macc 1:23 speaks of "the hidden treasures" (τοὺς θησαυροὺς τοὺς ἀποκρύφους), and Sir 23:19 mentions "hidden places" (ἀπόκρυφα μέρη), while Sir 39:3 says, "he will seek out the hidden things (i.e., meanings) of proverbs" (ἀπόκρυφα παροιμιῶν ἐκζητήσει). From Greek these words passed into Latin as *apocryphus* and *apocrypha*, and hence into English as "apocryphal" and "apocrypha."

§4. In etymology, then, "apocryphal books" (ἀπόκρυφα βιβλία) are really "hidden" books rather than noncanonical books as such. In the earlier centuries when the canon was still in process of formation, Christian writers used words other than "apocryphal" to designate books which were questioned or excluded from the approved list. Thus Eusebius (*Ch. Hist.* III 25), for example, contrasted with the books which he regarded as "acknowledged" (ὁμολογούμενοι), those which were "disputed" (ἀντιλεγόμενοι) and those which were "spurious" (νόθοι). At the same time when early Christian writers first mention apocryphal books they refer to books actually kept in the secret or restricted possession of various groups which were peripheral to the main church, groups which made a point of being the custodians of esoteric doctrines not lightly to be divulged. Thus, for example, Clement of Alexandria (*Stromata* I 15, 69, 6 GCS Clemens Alexandrinus II 44; ANF II 316) says that "those who follow the heresy of Prodicus" boast of being in possession of the "secret books" (βίβλους ἀποκρύφους) of Zoroaster. Such books were often of a nature to be repudiated by the main church, hence the word apocryphal came to have an unfavorable connotation and meant not only books which were kept "hidden" by their possessors but also books which were of an undesirable character. Thus Irenaeus (*Against Heresies* I 20, 1) speaks of the heretical Marcosians as having "an unspeakable number of apocryphal and spurious writings" (ἀμύθητον πλῆθος ἀποκρύφων καὶ νόθων γραφῶν); and Tertullian (*On Modesty* X 12) says that the book known as the Shepherd of Hermas had been judged by every ecclesiastical council to be "among apocryphal and false (writings)" (*inter apocrypha et falsa*).

# 2 / Old Testament Apocrypha

*Literature:* R. H. Charles, *The Apocrypha and Pseudepigrapha of the Old Testament.* 2 vols. 1913; Edgar J. Goodspeed, *The Apocrypha, An American Translation.* 1938; Edgar J. Goodspeed, *The Story of the Apocrypha.* 1939; Charles C. Torrey, *The Apocryphal Literature.* 1945; Robert H. Pfeiffer, *History of New Testament Times with an Introduction to the Apocrypha.* 1949, 231–522; Jean-Paul Audet, "A Hebrew-Aramaic List of Books of the Old Testament in Greek Transcription," in JTS New Series 1 (1950), 135–54; Peter Katz, "The Old Testament Canon in Palestine and Alexandria," in ZNW 47 (1956), 191–217; Gaalyahu Cornfeld, ed., *Daniel to Paul.* 1962, 68–92; Jack P. Lewis, "What Do We Mean by Jabneh?" in JBR 32 (1964), 125–32; Albert C. Sundberg, Jr., *The Old Testament of the Early Church.* 1964; and see also §13 (LXX), §18 (Vetus Latina), and §24 (Vulgate).

§5. The canon of the Hebrew Bible as it exists today was probably well established in the period of the Tannaim, the Jewish "teachers" active in the years approximately 10 to 220 of the Christian era. In the process, deliberations at the Council of Jamnia about the year 90 are generally supposed, although on not too extensive evidence, to have been specially important. 2 Esd 14 (CAP II 622–24), written probably about the beginning of the second century of the Christian era,[1] contains a legend according to which the Law was burned (v. 21) (presumably at the destruction of Jerusalem by Nebuchadrezzar) but was rewritten under inspiration (vv. 39f.) by Ezra in forty days of dictation to five men (vv. 42f.). In all, Ezra wrote ninety-four books at this time: twenty-four were to be made public for both the worthy and the unworthy to read; seventy were to be kept and given only to the wise among the people (vv. 44-46). At the immediate moment the point is that the publicly known divine Scriptures comprised twenty-four books. Likewise in the Talmud and Midrash the

---

[1] Goodspeed, *The Apocrypha* 39.

OT is regularly called "the twenty-four holy Scriptures." [2] A Baraita found in *Baba Bathra* 14b (SBT IV 3, 70f.) gives the sequence of the books and thereby makes it possible to see how the number of twenty-four was arrived at. The five books of the Law (Gen, Ex, Lev, Num, Dt) are not enumerated but must be assumed, and may have been listed in the original source, since in the immediately ensuing discussion of the authors of the various books it is stated that "Moses wrote his own book," which must refer to the Mosaic authorship of the Torah. As it stands, the excerpt begins: "Our Rabbis taught: The order of the Prophets is, Joshua, Judges, Samuel, Kings, Jeremiah, Ezekiel, Isaiah, and the Twelve Minor Prophets." Continuing to the last division of the canon, the passage goes on: "The order of the Hagiographa is Ruth, the Book of Psalms, Job, Proverbs, Ecclesiastes, Song of Songs, Lamentations, Daniel, and the Scroll of Esther, Ezra, and Chronicles." As so arranged, then, there were five books in the Law, eight in the Prophets, and eleven in the Writings, a total of twenty-four. The book of Ezra undoubtedly includes Nehemiah,[3] and in our present reckoning Samuel, Kings, and Chronicles are each counted as two books, while the twelve Minor Prophets are also counted separately. Therefore in the same framework we would reckon five books of Law, twenty-one books of Prophets, and thirteen books of Writings, for a total of thirty-nine, the number found in our OT.

§6. Josephus, writing *Against Apion* (I 8 §38, cf. Eusebius, *Ch. Hist.* III 10) around A.D. 100, makes it quite as plain as does 2 Esd 14 (§5) that there was then an agreed-upon list of scriptural books, but he gives a different total number and a different grouping. "Our books," he writes, "those which are justly accredited, are but two and twenty." These were grouped, according to his immediately following comments, as five books of Moses, thirteen books of the Prophets, and four books of "hymns to God and precepts for the conduct of human life." The total number of twenty-two books, as compared with twenty-four (§5), was almost certainly arrived at by combining Jg and Ru, and Jer and Lam. These were natural combinations, and the total thereby obtained coincided in what was undoubtedly considered a significant way with the total number of letters in the Hebrew alphabet (§8). As for the groupings, the five books of Moses were of course Gen, Ex, Lev, Num, and Dt; while

---

[2] CAP II 624 n. to v. 45; JE III 142f.
[3] SBT IV 3, 72 n. 1.

the four books of hymns and precepts for human conduct were probably Ps, SS, Pr, and Ec. The thirteen books of the prophets would then probably have been (1) Jos, (2) Jg + Ru, (3) S, (4) K, (5) Ch, (6) Ezr + Neh, (7) Est, (8) Jb, (9) Is, (10) Jer + Lam, (11) Ezk, (12) the Twelve Minor Prophets, and (13) Dan. Again, exactly our thirty-nine individual books are accounted for.

§7. Early Christian writers also give lists of the books of the OT which contain exactly the same items. The oldest list is given by Melito of Sardis (A.D. c. 180) in the Preface of his *Extracts from the Law and the Prophets Concerning Our Savior and Our Entire Faith.* As quoted by Eusebius (*Ch. Hist.* IV 26, 12–13), this "catalogue of the acknowledged books of the Old Testament" comprised the books shown in Table 1.

§8. Eusebius (*Ch. Hist.* VI 25) also gives us the catalogue of the OT Scriptures of Origen. This was found in Origen's exposition of the first Psalm, written while he was still in Alexandria (before A.D. 232). Origen states that the Hebrews have twenty-two canonical books and notes that this number corresponds with the number of letters in the Hebrew alphabet (§6). He explicitly confirms that Jg and Ru were combined in one book, and Jer and Lam in another. His list, reproduced in a portion of our Table 2, is of special interest because he transliterates in Greek the Hebrew names of the books, as well as naming them in their customary Greek forms. The list of Athanasius published in A.D. 367 (*Festal Letter* XXXIX NPNFSS IV 552), already referred to (§2), also explicitly numbers twenty-two books, but arrives at the total by counting Ru separately and omitting Est (which is mentioned later, outside the canon [§20]). Athanasius also includes the Letter of Baruch along with Lam and Jer in one book. His list of the twenty-two books runs: (1) Gen, (2) Ex, (3) Lev, (4) Num, (5) Dt, (6) Jos, (7) Jg, (8) Ru, (9) 1–2 K, (10) 3–4 K, (11) 1–2 Ch, (12) 1–2 Ezr = Ezr-Neh, (13) Ps, (14) Pr, (15) Ec, (16) SS, (17) Jb, (18) the Twelve Minor Prophets, (19) Is, (20) Jer-Lam-Bar, (21) Ezk, (22) Dan. Finally Jerome, in his *Preface to Samuel and Kings* (*prologus galeatus*) (NPNFSS VI 489f.) (§22), also explains that as there are twenty-two letters in the Hebrew alphabet, "so we reckon twenty-two books, by which, as by the alphabet of the doctrine of God, a righteous man is instructed in tender infancy"; gives a list of five books of Moses, eight of the Prophets, and nine of the Hagiographa, to total twenty-two; but further notes that the number is raised to twenty-four if Ru and Lam are reckoned separately. As Origen transliterates the Hebrew names of the books into Greek, so Jerome does into Latin, and his list is also reproduced in

TABLE 1

*The Books of the Old Testament According to Melito of Sardis*

| | |
|---|---|
| Γένεσις | Genesis |
| Ἔξοδος | Exodus |
| Ἀριθμοί | Numbers |
| Λευιτικόν | Leviticus |
| Δευτερονόμιον | Deuteronomy |
| Ἰησοῦς Ναυῆ | Jesus Nave = Joshua the son of Nun |
| Κριταί | Judges |
| Ῥούθ | Ruth |
| Βασιλειῶν τέσσαρα | four books of Kingdoms (= 1–2 S, 1–2 K) |
| Παραλειπομένων δύο | two books of Chronicles |
| Ψαλμῶν Δαυίδ | Psalms of David |
| Σολομῶνος Παροιμίαι ἡ καὶ Σοφία | Proverbs of Solomon which is also his Wisdom (cf. *Ch. Hist.* IV 22, 9) |
| Ἐκκλησιαστής | Ecclesiastes |
| Ἆισμα Ἀισμάτων | Song of Songs |
| Ἰώβ | Job |
| Προφητῶν Ἡσαίου | the prophets Isaiah |
| Ἰερεμίου | Jeremiah |
| τῶν δώδεκα ἐν μονοβίβλῳ | the Twelve in a single book |
| Δανιήλ | Daniel |
| Ἰεζεκιήλ | Ezekiel |
| Ἔσδρας | Esdras = Ezr-Neh |

a portion of our Table 2. In that table, for convenient reference, we give the canon divisions and book names from the Hebrew, and the corresponding materials in Greek from Origen, in Latin from Jerome, and in English.

§9. In the last centuries of the pre-Christian era the Hebrew Bible was translated into Greek in Alexandria, Egypt. *The Letter of Aristeas*, which purports to have been written under Ptolemy II Philadelphus (285–246 B.C.), tells (46–50, 301–7; CAP II 100, 120f.) that the work was done by seventy-two elders, i.e., six from each of the twelve tribes, who were sent by the high priest in Jerusalem, were quartered

# TABLE 2

## The Hebrew Canon of Scriptures with the Lists of Origen and Jerome

| NO.–DIV. | BOOKS | | ORIGEN IN EUSEBIUS, CH. HIST. VI 25 | |
|---|---|---|---|---|
| | Hebrew Name | Translation of Hebrew Name | Transliteration of Hebrew Name in Greek | Translation of Hebrew Name, or Comment, by Origen |
| **I.** תּוֹרָה νόμος Lex Torah Law | | | | |
| 1 | בראשית | "In the beginning" | Βρησίδ | ἐν ἀρχῇ |
| 2 | ואלה שמות | "Now these are the names" | Ουελεσμώθ | ταῦτα τὰ ὀνόματα |
| 3 | ויקרא | "And called" | Οὐικρά | καὶ ἐκάλεσεν |
| 4 (a) | וידבר | "And spoke" | | |
| (b) | המש הפקודים | "The fifth [part of the Pentateuch treating] of the mustered" (*Yoma* VII 1, 68b GBT II 951) | Ἀμμεσφεκωδειμ | |
| (c) | במדבר | "In the desert" | | |
| 5 | אלה הדברים | "These are the words" | Ἐλεαδδεβαρειμ | οὗτοι οἱ λόγοι |
| **II.** נְבִיאִים προφῆται Prophetas Prophets | | | | |
| 1 (a) | יהושע | Joshua | | |
| (b) | יהושע בן־נון | Joshua the son of Nun | Ἰωσοῦε βεν Νοῦν | Ἰησοῦς υἱὸς Ναυῆ |
| 2 | שפטים | Judges | Σαφατειμ | Κριταί, Ρούθ, παρ' αὐτοῖς ἐν ἑνί ("Judges and Ruth, among them in one book") |

| Name in the Greek Old Testament | JEROME, *PREFACE TO SAMUEL AND KINGS* (*PROLOGUS GALEATUS*) | | | English Name | Abbrev. |
| | Transliteration of Hebrew Name in Latin | Comment of Jerome, if any | Latin Name (Vulgate) | | |
| Γένεσις | Beresith | | Genesis | Genesis | Gen |
| Ἔξοδος | Veelle Semoth | | Exodus | Exodus | Ex |
| Λευειτικόν | Vaijcra | | Leviticus | Leviticus | Lev |
| | Vaieddaber | | | | |
| Ἀριθμοί | | | Numeri | Numbers | Num |
| Δευτερονόμιον | Elle Haddebarim | | Deutero-nomium | Deuteronomy | Dt |
| Ἰησοῦς | | | Josue | Joshua | Jos |
| | Iosue ben Nun | | Jesus filius Nave | | |
| Κριταί Ρούθ | Sophetim Ruth | "And in the same book they include Ruth, because the events narrated occurred in the days of the Judges." | Judicum Ruth | Judges Ruth | Jg Ru |

# TABLE 2 (*continued*)

| NO.–DIV. | BOOKS | | ORIGEN IN EUSEBIUS, *CH. HIST.* VI 25 | |
|---|---|---|---|---|
| | Hebrew Name | Translation of Hebrew Name | Transliteration of Hebrew Name in Greek | Translation of Hebrew Name, or Comment, by Origen |
| 3 | שמואל | Samuel | Σαμουήλ | ὁ θεόκλητος ("The called of God") |
| 4 (a) | מלכים | Kings | | |
| (b) | והמלך דויד | "The Kingdom of David" (implied by Origen) | Οὐαμμελχ Δαβίδ | Βασιλεία Δαβίδ |
| 5 | ישעיה | Isaiah | Ἰεσσία | |
| 6 | ירמיה | Jeremiah | Ἰερεμία | Ἰερεμίας σὺν Θρήνοις καὶ τῇ Ἐπιστολῇ, ἐν ἑνί (Actually the Ep Jer was in the LXX but not in the Hebrew canon.) |
| 7 | יחזקאל | Ezekiel | Ἰεζεκιηλ | |
| 8 (a) | שנים עשר הנביאים | The Twelve Prophets | The Book of the Twelve Minor Prophets is omitted, no doubt by accident, in Eusebius' copy of Origen's list. | |
| (b) | תרי עשר | The Twelve | | |
| (1) | הושע | Hosea | | |
| (2) | יואל | Joel | | |
| (3) | עמוס | Amos | | |
| (4) | עבדיה | Obadiah | | |
| (5) | יונה | Jonah | | |
| (6) | מיכה | Micah | | |

| | JEROME, *PREFACE TO SAMUEL AND KINGS (PROLOGUS GALEATUS)* | | | | |
|---|---|---|---|---|---|
| Name in the Greek Old Testament | Transliteration of Hebrew Name in Latin | Comment of Jerome, if any | Latin Name (Vulgate) | English Name | Abbrev. |
| Βασιλειῶν πρώτη ("Kingdoms") Βασιλειῶν δευτέρα | Samuel | "Which we call First and Second Kings" | Regum 1 Regum 2 | 1 Samuel 2 Samuel | 1 S 2 S |
| Βασιλειῶν τρίτη Βασιλειῶν τετάρτη | Melachim | "And it is far better to say *Malachim*, that is Kings, than *Malachoth*, that is Kingdoms. For the author does not describe the Kingdoms of many nations, but that of one people." | Regum 3 Regum 4 | 1 Kings 2 Kings | 1 K 2 K |
| Ἡσαΐας | Isaias | | Esaias | Isaiah | Is |
| Ἰερεμίας | Ieremias | | Jeremias | Jeremiah | Jer |
| Θρῆνοι | Cinoth | | Threni, Lamentationes | Lamentations | Lam |
| Ἐπιστολὴ Ἰερεμίου | | | | (Letter of Jeremiah) | (Ep Jer) |
| Ἰεζεκιήλ | Ezechiel | | Ezechiel | Ezekiel | Ezk |
| οἱ δώδεκα προφῆται τὸ δωδεκαπρόφητον | There Asar | | Liber duodecim prophetarum | The Book of the Twelve Prophets | |
| Ὡσηέ | | | | Hosea | Hos |
| Ἰωήλ | | | | Joel | Jl |
| Ἀμώς | | | | Amos | Am |
| Ὀβδίας | | | | Obadiah | Ob |
| Ἰωνᾶς | | | | Jonah | Jon |
| Μιχαίας | | | | Micah | Mic |

TABLE 2 *(continued)*

| NO.–DIV. | BOOKS | | ORIGEN IN EUSEBIUS, *CH. HIST.* VI 25 | |
|---|---|---|---|---|
| | Hebrew Name | Translation of Hebrew Name | Transliteration of Hebrew Name in Greek | Translation of Hebrew Name, or Comment, by Origen |
| (7) | נחום | Nahum | | |
| (8) | חבקוק | Habakkuk | | |
| (9) | צפניה | Zephaniah | | |
| (10) | חגי | Haggai | | |
| (11) | זכריה | Zechariah | | |
| (12) | מלאכי | Malachi | | |
| III. כתובים ἁγιόγραφα Hagio- grapha Writings | | | | |
| 1 (a) | תהלים | Praises | | |
| (b) | ספר תהלים | Book of Praises | $\Sigma\varphi\alpha\rho\theta\epsilon\lambda\lambda\epsilon\acute{\iota}\mu$ | $\mathrm{B}\acute{\iota}\beta\lambda os\ \Psi\alpha\lambda\mu\widehat{\omega}\nu$ |
| (c) | מזמור לדוד Ps. 3:1, etc. | "A Psalm of David" | | (מזמור $= \Psi\alpha\lambda\mu\acute{os}$) |
| 2 (a) | משלי | Proverbs | | |
| (b) | משלי שלמה | The Proverbs of Solomon | | $\Sigma o\lambda o\mu\widehat{\omega} vos$ $\Pi\alpha\rho o\iota\mu\acute{\iota}\alpha\iota$ |
| (c) | מלות | "Sayings" (implied by Origen) | $\mathrm{M}\epsilon\lambda\acute{\omega}\theta$ | |
| 3 | איוב | Job | $\mathrm{'I}\acute{\omega}\beta$ | |

| | JEROME, *PREFACE TO SAMUEL AND KINGS (PROLOGUS GALEATUS)* | | | | |
|---|---|---|---|---|---|
| Name in the Greek Old Testament | Transliteration of Hebrew Name in Latin | Comment of Jerome, if any | Latin Name (Vulgate) | English Name | Abbrev. |
| Ναούμ | | | | Nahum | Nah |
| Ἀμβακούμ | | | | Habakkuk | Hab |
| Σοφονίας | | | | Zephaniah | Zph |
| Ἀγγαιος | | | | Haggai | Hag |
| Ζαχαρίας | | | | Zechariah | Zec |
| Μαλαχίας | | | | Malachi | Mal |
| | | | Liber Psalmorum | | |
| Ψαλμοί | | "*David*, whose writings they divide into five parts and comprise in one volume of Psalms (*uno Psalmorum volumine*)" | Psalmi | Psalms | Ps |
| Ψαλτήριον (Cod. Alex.) | | | | Psalter | |
| Παροιμίαι | | | Liber Proverbiorum | Proverbs | Pr |
| | Misle | "Solomon, in three books, *Proverbs*, which they call *Misle*, that is *Parables* (*Proverbia, quae ille Misle, i.e., Parabolas appellant*)" | Proverbia | | |
| Ἰώβ | Iob | | | Job | Jb |

# TABLE 2 (*continued*)

| NO.–DIV. | BOOKS | | ORIGEN IN EUSEBIUS, *CH. HIST.* VI 25 | |
|---|---|---|---|---|
| | Hebrew Name | Translation of Hebrew Name | Transliteration of Hebrew Name in Greek | Translation of Hebrew Name, or Comment, by Origen |
| 4 | שיר השירים | Song of Songs | Σὶρ Ἀσσιρίμ | οὐ γὰρ ὡς ὑπολαμβάνουσί τινες, Ἄσματα Ἀσμάτων ("Not, as some suppose, Songs of Songs") |
| (5) | רות | Ruth | | (See under II, 2 Judges) |
| (6) (a) | איכה | How | | (See under II, 6 Jeremiah) |
| (b) | קינות, Jer. 7:29, etc. | Lamentations | | קינות = Θρῆνοι |
| 5 (7) | קהלת | The Preacher | Κωέλθ | |
| 6 (8) | אסתר | Esther | Ἐσθήρ | |
| 7 (9) | דניאל | Daniel | Δανιηλ | |
| 8 (10) | עזרא נחמיה | Ezra, Nehemiah | Ἐζρᾶ | Ἔσδρας πρῶτος, δεύτερος, ἐν ἑνί, Ἐζρᾶ, ὅ ἐστι, βοηθός ("Esdras, First and Second in one, Ezra, that is, an assistant") |
| 9 (11) | דברי הימים | "Things of the days" | Δαβρηϊαμείν | |

5 + 8 + 9 = 22
5 + 8 + 11 = 24

| | JEROME, *PREFACE TO SAMUEL AND KINGS* *(PROLOGUS GALEATUS)* | | | | |
|---|---|---|---|---|---|
| Name in the Greek Old Testament | Transliteration of Hebrew Name in Latin | Comment of Jerome, if any | Latin Name (Vulgate) | English Name | Abbrev. |
| Ἄσμα Ἀσμάτων | Sir Hassirim | "The Song of Songs, which they denote by the title *Sir Assirim*" | Canticum canticorum | Song of Songs | SS |
| | | (See under II, 2 Judges) | | Ruth | Ru |
| | | (Assumed under II, 6 Jeremiah) | | | |
| | | | | Lamentations | Lam |
| Ἐκκλησιαστής | Coheleth | | Ecclesiastes | Ecclesiastes | Ec |
| Ἐσθήρ | Esther | | Esther | Esther | Est |
| Δανιήλ | Daniel | | Daniel | Daniel | Dan |
| Ἔσδρας β′ | Esdras | "Esdras, which itself is likewise divided amongst Greeks and Latins into two books" | Esdras | Ezra, Nehemiah | Ezr, Neh |
| παραλειπομένων ("Omitted things") πρώτη παραλειπομένων δευτέρα | Dibre haiamim | "That is, words of days (*verba dierum*), which we may more expressively call a Chronicle (*chronicon*) of the whole of sacred history, which among us is called Paralipomenon 1 and 2" | Chronica | 1 Chronicles 2 Chronicles | 1 Ch 2 Ch |

on the island of Pharos, and accomplished their task in seventy-two days. This undoubtedly romanticized account may be influenced by the tradition (Ex 24:9) that Moses was accompanied by seventy elders when he went to the mountain to receive the Law. At any rate the version was known as the *Interpretatio iuxta septuaginta seniores* or, more briefly, the *septuaginta* or Septuagint, i.e., the "Seventy," the title being abbreviated as *οἱ ο′* or LXX. In the Prologue to Ecclesiasticus the grandson of Jesus ben Sirach states that he came to Egypt in the thirty-eighth year of Euergetes (= 132 B.C.; CAP I 293) and mentions the law, the prophecies, and "the rest of the books," as existing in translation. Therefore all or virtually all of the Jewish Scriptures must have been in Greek by this time.

§10. In the first century of the Christian era the LXX was widely popular among Hellenistic Jews, and was normally quoted by both Philo and Josephus. Hellenistic Jews and Gentiles who were converted to Christianity also naturally used the Scriptures in the LXX translation, and most of the scriptural quotations in the NT appear to be from the LXX.[4] Thus the LXX of the Jews became the Greek OT of the Christian Church. Use of this version by the Christians, however, made the LXX less acceptable in Jewish circles, and other Greek versions were prepared by Jewish or Jewish Christian (§51) scholars. Of these the best known are those of Aquila, of Theodotion, and of Symmachus, all probably made in the second century of the Christian era. The Christian scholar Origen undertook to establish what we would call a critical text of the LXX and to show its relation to the Hebrew. For this purpose he prepared a very large work to which he devoted many years of his life. It was known as the *Hexapla* (*τὰ ἑξαπλᾶ*), or "sixfold" Bible. In it he arranged in six parallel columns (1) the Hebrew text of the OT in Hebrew characters, (2) the Hebrew text transliterated in Greek characters, and after that the Greek translations of (3) Aquila, (4) Symmachus, (5) the LXX, and (6) Theodotion. The version of Aquila was most like the Hebrew, therefore was put next to it; that of Symmachus was still based on the Hebrew, but was not so close to it, consequently came next; and the version of Theodotion was based on the LXX rather than the Hebrew, accordingly followed the LXX. In the fifth column added signs showed the relationship of the LXX to the Hebrew: an obelus (÷) marked what was additional in the Greek text as compared with the Hebrew; an asterisk (*) marked what was supplied

---

[4] Crawford H. Toy, *Quotations in the New Testament.* 1884.

in the Greek text from one of the other translations, usually that of Theodotion. According to Eusebius (*Ch. Hist.* VI 16), Origen also discovered three other Greek translations, one in Nicopolis near Actium in Greece, one in a jar in Jericho, and one in some other place. These translations were added to the *Hexapla* in the Psalms. Coming after the four prominent translations they were known simply as the fifth, sixth, and seventh (*quinta*, *sexta*, and *septima*), and must have made a work at this point of no less than nine parallel columns. Eusebius also says that Origen later arranged a *Tetrapla* (ἐν τοῖς τετραπλοῖς ἐπικατασκευάσας) which was an edition of Aquila, Symmachus, and Theodotion, with the LXX. It would seem likely that this was for only those writings for which there was no Hebrew text anyway.

In his own time Eusebius (*Life of Constantine* IV 36–37) himself was asked by the Emperor Constantine to prepare fifty parchment manuscripts of the sacred Scriptures for use in Constantinople[5] and, since Eusebius was in Caesarea where Origen did his later work, it seems likely that in the OT portion the Greek text of these manuscripts would have been copied if not directly from the fifth column of Origen's *Hexapla* at least from Bible editions derived therefrom. At least as late as in the time of Jerome the *Hexapla* was still available in Caesarea, for Jerome (*Commentarioli in Ps.* I 4 CCSL LXXII 180) himself consulted it there. Later, however, the great work perished, and of it now only fragments and excerpts survive.[6] Jerome (*Preface to the Four Gospels* NPNFSS VI 488; cf. *Lives of Illustrious Men* 77 NPNFSS III 378) also mentions, disparagingly, manuscripts associated with the names of Lucian and Hesychius. Lucian was founder of the theological school at Antioch, and died as a martyr in A.D. 312 (Eusebius, *Ch. Hist.* IX 6, 3). His revision of the LXX was widely used in Syria and Asia Minor, and is quoted by Chrysostom and Theodoret. Hesychius may be the same person as the Egyptian bishop of that name who was martyred under Diocletian (Eusebius, *Ch. Hist.* VIII 13, 7). The text of his revision is quoted by Cyril of Alexandria.

§11. Of the extant manuscripts of the Greek translation of the Scriptures, relatively few have survived from among the Jews themselves, and it is to these that the designation LXX properly belongs. The earliest presently known is Rylands Papyrus Greek 458. This

---

[5] Cf. Carl Wendel in *Zentralblatt für Bibliothekswesen* 56 (1939) 165–75.
[6] F. Field, *Origenis Hexaplorum quae supersunt.* 2 vols. 1867–75.

consists of fragments of a papyrus scroll which had been used for the cartonnage of a mummy and were obtained in Egypt by Rendel Harris in 1917. The fragments contain several portions of Dt, and the date of the writing is probably not later than the middle of the second century B.C.[7] Fuad Papyrus 266 at Cairo contains part of the Song of Moses in Dt 31–32, and was probably written in the first century B.C. The divine name is written in square Hebrew characters rather than in the usual Greek translation, Κύριος. Among the Dead Sea Scrolls are these examples: p4Q LXX Lev[b] consists of papyrus fragments of Lev 2–5 in a handwriting similar to that of the Fuad Papyrus. Here the divine name appears as ιαω instead of Κύριος. 4Q LXX Num is a parchment with portions of Num 3–4, probably also written in the first century B.C.[8] p7Q LXX Ex consists of two papyrus fragments with a few lines of Ex 28, written around 100 B.C. p7Q LXX Ep Jer is a small piece of papyrus with a few words of the Letter of Jeremiah, also dating around 100 B.C.[9] 4Q LXX Lev[a] is a parchment with part of Lev 26 in a hand of the first century of the Christian era. There is also a fragmentary parchment scroll, which Bedouins brought in from an unidentified cave in 1952, which contains portions of the Minor Prophets, Mic, Jon, Nah, Hab, Zph, and Zec. It was probably written around A.D. 100 and was found in conjunction with other materials evidently deposited there during the revolt of Bar Kokhba.[10]

§12. Manuscripts of the Greek translation of the Scriptures which come from Christian sources are more numerous and extensive. Since at this point the LXX has become the OT of the Christian church these may properly be spoken of as manuscripts of the Greek OT. The oldest of these are found among the papyri. The Chester Beatty Biblical Papyri were obtained from Egypt in 1931 by A. Chester Beatty and others. They comprise eleven codices. Seven are of the OT, three of the NT, and one has part of the Book of Enoch and a homily by Melito of Sardis (§7). They must be part of the library of some early Christian church in Egypt.[11] Of the manuscripts the earliest is Chester Beatty Papyrus VI, a codex of which fifty leaves

---

[7] C. H. Roberts, *Two Biblical Papyri in the John Rylands Library, Manchester.* 1936, 9–46.

[8] P. W. Skehan in VT Supplement IV 1957, 155–58.

[9] DJD III Textes 142–43 Planches XXX 1, 2.

[10] D. Barthélemy in RB 60 (1953) 18–29.

[11] Frederic G. Kenyon, *The Chester Beatty Biblical Papyri.* 1933–41.

survive in larger or smaller pieces, containing substantial parts of Num and Dt, extending from Num 5 to Dt 34. Written not later than the middle of the second century, this is the earliest known Christian copy of part of the Greek OT and also an early example of the codex form of manuscript. Chester Beatty Papyrus VIII consists of small parts of two leaves of a codex of Jer with portions of Jer 4–5, written about the end of the second century. Chester Beatty Papyrus VII comprises fragments of thirty-three leaves of Is extending from Is 8 to 60. It is written in a beautiful hand of the first half of the third century. The manuscript was evidently owned by a Coptic-speaking Christian, for the Coptic translation of words and phrases has been written in the margin at a number of places. The Coptic does not yet have the supplementary native letters which were eventually adopted, and is a relatively early Coptic text (cf. §80). Chester Beatty Papyri IX and X comprise twenty-nine somewhat broken leaves of a codex containing Ezk, Dan, and Est, while John H. Scheide subsequently obtained an additional twenty-one almost perfect leaves of the Ezk portion of the same codex.[12] The date is in the first half of the third century. Altogether much of Ezk 11–39 is available, and much of Dan 3–8 (chaps. 5–6 follow 7–8) and Est 2–6. The manuscript contains the Song of the Three Children in Dan, and the Additions to Esther. Chester Beatty Papyrus V contains twenty-seven leaves with portions of Gen 8–46, and was probably written in the second half of the third century. The Washington Manuscript of the Minor Prophets, which was obtained in Egypt for Charles L. Freer in 1916, comprises portions of thirty-three leaves of a papyrus codex with a small part of Hos and most of Am through Mal. The date is in the latter half of the third century. The Berlin Fragment of Genesis was purchased in Egypt in 1906 by Carl Schmidt. This was a papyrus codex of thirty-two leaves of which only the first and last were lost. It contains much of Gen 1–35, and was probably written in the early fourth century.[13] Chester Beatty Papyrus IV is a codex of fifty more or less damaged leaves extending from Gen 9 to 44, and may be dated in the first half of the fourth century. Chester Beatty Papyrus XI is a complete leaf and the lower half of another, with portions of Ecclus 36–37 and 46–47. The date is the latter part of the fourth century. Chester Beatty Papyrus XII consists of fourteen leaves which begin

---

[12] Allan C. Johnson, Henry S. Gehman, and Edmund H. Kase, Jr., *The John H. Scheide Biblical Papyri, Ezekiel.* 1938.
[13] Henry A. Sanders and Carl Schmidt, *The Minor Prophets in the Freer Collection and the Berlin Fragment of Genesis.* 1927.

with the last part of the Book of Enoch (En 97–107), called in the title at the end, "The Epistle of Enoch," and continue with a homily on the Passover by Melito of Sardis (§7). The date of the papyrus is in the fourth century.[14]

§13. While the Jewish and early Christian papyri provide the earliest copies of parts of the OT Scriptures in Greek, it is only among the parchments that substantially complete copies of the Greek OT are found. Here the most important are the well-known uncial manuscripts, Codex Vaticanus (middle of the fourth century), Codex Sinaiticus (middle of the fourth century), and Codex Alexandrinus (first half of the fifth century). These are more or less complete early Christian Bibles containing both OT and NT. More exact notice of their contents will be given in §14. There are also not a few other uncials and likewise a great many minuscule manuscripts which give part or all of the OT in Greek so that, together with the papyri, there is a vast amount of evidence for this text.[15] In general Codex Vaticanus has been judged the single best extant copy. An edition of the Greek OT based chiefly upon Codex Vaticanus was issued in 1587 under the auspices of Pope Sixtus V. An English translation of this so-called Sixtine text was made by Charles Thomson, Secretary of the Continental Congress of the United States of America, and published in 1808. A new edition of this translation is given by C. A. Muses, *The Septuagint Bible* (Indian Hills, Colorado: The Falcon's Wing Press, 1954). A more precise English translation of Codex Vaticanus was made in 1844 by Lee and Brenton, and is printed along with the Greek text in *The Septuagint Version* (London: Samuel Bagster and Sons Limited).[16] A critical edition of the text of Codex Vaticanus along with variants from some other uncials is given by Swete, LXX. A critical edition based mainly on Codices Vaticanus, Sinaiticus, and Alexandrinus, with other variants, is provided by Rahlfs, LXX. More detailed critical editions are being published at Cambridge and Göttingen. *The Old Testament in Greek*, edited by Alan E. Brooke, Norman McLean, and others (Cambridge: The University Press, 1906ff.), is based on the text of Codex Vaticanus, with variants from the other chief ancient authorities. *Septuaginta, Vetus Testamentum Graecum, auctoritate Societas Litterarum Got-*

---

[14] Campbell Bonner, *The Last Chapters of Enoch in Greek.* Studies and Documents, ed. Kirsopp Lake and Silva Lake, VIII. 1937.

[15] Frederic Kenyon, *Our Bible and the Ancient Manuscripts.* 5th ed. rev. 1958, 113ff.; John W. Wevers in *Theologische Rundschau* 22 (1954), 85ff.

[16] Cf. Paul Winter in VT 8 (1958) 334f.

TABLE 3

*The Books of the Old Testament in Codex Vaticanus*

Pentateuch
| | | |
|---|---|---|
| Γένεσις | | Genesis |
| Ἔξοδος | | Exodus |
| Λευειτικόν | | Leviticus |
| Ἀριθμοί | | Numbers |
| Δευτερονόμιον | | Deuteronomy |

History
| | | |
|---|---|---|
| Ἰησοῦς | | Joshua |
| Κριταί | | Judges |
| Ῥούθ | | Ruth |
| Βασιλεῶν αʹ | = 1 Kingdoms | 1 Samuel |
| Βασιλεῶν βʹ | = 2 Kingdoms | 2 Samuel |
| Βασιλεῶν γʹ | = 3 Kingdoms | 1 Kings |
| Βασιλεῶν δʹ | = 4 Kingdoms | 2 Kings |
| Παραλειπομένων αʹ | = 1 Omitted Things | 1 Chronicles |
| Παραλειπομένων βʹ | = 2 Omitted Things | 2 Chronicles |
| Ἔσδρας αʹ | | *1 Esdras* |
| Ἔσδρας βʹ | = 2 Esdras | Ezra-Nehemiah |

Poetry and Precepts
| | | |
|---|---|---|
| Ψαλμοί | | Psalms (including an additional Psalm ἔξωθεν τοῦ ἀριθμοῦ = Ps 151) |
| Παροιμίαι | | Proverbs |
| Ἐκκλησιαστής | | Ecclesiastes |
| Ἆισμα | = Song | Song of Songs |
| Ἰώβ | | Job |
| Σοφία Σαλωμῶνος | | *Wisdom of Solomon* |
| Σοφία Σειράχ | | *Wisdom of Sirach* |

Stories
| | | |
|---|---|---|
| Ἐσθήρ | | Esther with *Additions* |
| Ἰουδείθ | | *Judith* |
| Τωβείτ | | *Tobit* |

Prophets
| | | |
|---|---|---|
| Ὡσηέ | | Hosea |
| Ἀμώς | | Amos |

| | |
|---|---|
| Μειχαίας | Micah |
| Ἰωήλ | Joel |
| Ὀβδιάς | Obadiah |
| Ἰωνᾶς | Jonah |
| Ναούμ | Nahum |
| Ἀμβακούμ | Habakkuk |
| Σοφονίας | Zephaniah |
| Ἅγγαιος | Haggai |
| Ζαχαρίας | Zechariah |
| Μαλαχίας | Malachi |
| Ἡσαΐας | Isaiah |
| Ἰερεμίας | Jeremiah |
| Βαρούχ | *Baruch* |
| Θρῆνοι | Lamentations |
| Ἐπιστολὴ Ἰερεμίου | *Letter of Jeremiah* |
| Ἰεξεκιήλ | Ezekiel |
| Σουσάννα | *Susanna* |
| Δανιήλ | Daniel with *Additions* of the Prayer of Azariah and the Song of the Three Young Men |
| Βὴλ καὶ Δράκων | *Bel and the Dragon* |

---

*tingensis editum*, edited by Alfred Rahlfs, Werner Kappler, and others (Göttingen: Vandenhoeck & Ruprecht, 1934ff.), gives an eclectic text based upon comparison of what are thought to be identifiable as the different families of manuscripts.[17]

§14. The LXX included other writings than those of the Hebrew canon (§§5–6). In part these were additions in or to the canonical books themselves, in part they were totally separate books. In the extant manuscripts the exact additional items included vary considerably. As we have already seen, in papyrus fragments of the LXX surviving from Jewish sources is a tiny bit of the Letter of Jeremiah (§11). In papyri from Christian sources the manuscripts and collections contain the Song of the Three Children, Additions to Esther,

[17] Cf. Frederic G. Kenyon, *Recent Developments in the Textual Criticism of the Greek Bible*. 1933, 88–115; *The Text of the Greek Bible*. 1949, 24–65; J. W. Wevers in IDB IV 273–78.

**TABLE 4**

*The Books of the Old Testament in Codex Sinaiticus*

---

Gen 23–24
Num 5–7
1 Paralipomenōn (= 1 Ch) 9:27–19:17
2 Esd (= Ezr-Neh) 9:9 to the end
Est
*Tob*
*Jth*
Μαϰϰαβαίων α′ = *1 Maccabees*
Μαϰϰαβαίων δ′ = *4 Maccabees*
Is
Jer
Lam 1:1–2:20
Jl
Ob
Jon
Nah
Hab
Zph
Hag
Zec
Mal
Ps (including *Ps 151*)
Pr
Ec
SS
*Wisd*
*Ecclus*
Jb

---

Ecclesiasticus, and the Book of Enoch (§12). In the great parchment codices containing the Greek OT (§13), at which we will now look more closely, there are many more books in addition to those of the Hebrew canon. Also, in comparison with the arrangement of the books in the Hebrew canon in groups of Law, Prophets, and Writings, it will be observed that the books have here been rearranged, subsequent to the Pentateuch, in a way which is evidently intended to provide a grouping more in accord with subject matter. We turn first to Codex Vaticanus. It contains a sequence of books virtually identical with the list of Athanasius (§8). The OT is almost complete. In Table 3 we show the titles and sequence of the books together with an indication in modern terminology of the categories in which they are evidently grouped. In the last column of the Table, which gives the names of the books as they are commonly known to us today, the items which are in excess of the Hebrew canon are italicized.

§15. In the case of Codex Sinaiticus considerable parts of the OT have been lost. The parts and order of what survives are shown concisely in Table 4. Greek names and full English names of books are supplied only for items not already shown for Codex Vaticanus in Table 3. Again items in excess of the Hebrew canon are italicized.

§16. In Codex Alexandrinus a table of contents at the beginning lists the books which were contained. Almost all of the OT is preserved in this manuscript. Portions of Gen 14–16 are missing, as is most of 1 Kingdoms (= 1 S) 12–14 and of Ps 49 (50)–79 (80). Prior to the Psalms is the Letter of Athanasius to Marcellinus on the Psalter, and the summary of the contents of the Psalms by Eusebius. At the end of the Psalms is not only Ps 151 but also a number of other poetic passages including the Song of Moses from Dt 32, the Song of Hannah from 1 S 2:1-10, and the Prayer of Manasseh. Also four books of the Maccabees are contained in the manuscript, which is the main authority for these books. The books are shown in order in Table 5. The Greek name is supplied for a book not already ap-

TABLE 5

*The Books of the Old Testament in Codex Alexandrinus*

---

Gen
Ex
Lev
Num
Dt
Jos
Jg
Ru
1 Kingdoms (= 1 S)
2 Kingdoms (= 2 S)
3 Kingdoms (= 1 K)

4 Kingdoms (= 2 K)
1 Paralipomenōn (= 1 Ch)
2 Paralipomenōn (= 2 Ch)
Hos
Am
Mic
Jl
Ob
Jon
Nah
Hab
Zph
Hag
Zec
Mal
Is
Jer
*Bar*
Lam
*Ep Jer*
Ezk
*Sus*
Dan
*Bel*
Est with *Ad Est*
*Tob*
*Jth*
*1 Esd*
2 Esd (= Ezr-Neh)
*1 Macc*
*2 Macc*
*3 Macc*
*4 Macc*
Ps (including *Ps 151*)
Προσευχὴ Μανασσή = *Pr Man*
Jb
Pr
Ec
SS
*Wisd*
*Ecclus*

pearing in Tables 3 and 4, otherwise the customary abbreviations are used, and again the items in excess of the Hebrew canon are italicized.

§17. The books which appear in the foregoing lists (Tables 3–5) representing Codices Vaticanus, Sinaiticus, and Alexandrinus, as in excess of the Hebrew canon, are of course not the only additional religious books produced at that time, whether in Hebrew or in Greek. In the foregoing lists a book called 1 Esdras appears, and also one called 2 Esdras, the latter being what we know as the two books of Ezra and Nehemiah. There was also another book in existence which began, "The second book of the prophet Ezra." A Greek fragment with a few verses (16:57–59) of this book was found among the Oxyrhynchus Papyri (OP 1010); otherwise the text is available only in manuscripts in Latin and some other languages. In Latin it is called 4 Esdras, but it is evident that it may also be called 2 Esdras. Other books, too, are known in various translations, such as the Book of Jubilees, and the Testaments of the Twelve Patriarchs, of which books in particular fragmentary manuscripts have recently been found among the Dead Sea Scrolls.[18] It is presumably with reference to literature of this sort that 2 Esd 14 (CAP II 624) says that Ezra wrote copies not only of the twenty-four books of the Hebrew canon but also of seventy additional books (§5). While we have perhaps not recovered as many as seventy works of this sort, we have seen that at least a considerable number of books, additional to the Hebrew canon, are preserved in the LXX and Greek OT and in writings related thereto.

§18. As the Greek OT was itself translated into other languages it tended to carry with it into those languages the additional books which were in and around itself. This was the case as the Greek OT was translated into Latin and, among the various translations, it is only with the Latin that we need to be concerned here. The Greek Bible, including both the OT and the NT, was no doubt put into Latin as early as the second century, and is quoted already by Tertullian (d. c. A.D. 220) and Cyprian (d. A.D. 258). The text of this Old Latin version (known as *Vetus Latina* or *Vetus Itala*) has to be reconstructed from the quotations of the early Latin church fathers and from scattered and almost entirely fragmentary manuscripts. The work of P. Sabatier in the eighteenth century, directed to this end, is now being carried forward by the Benedictine monks of

---

[18] J. T. Milik, *Ten Years of Discovery in the Wilderness of Judaea*. 1959, 31ff.

Beuron in Germany on a very large scale in *Vetus Latina, Die Reste der altlateinischen Bibel* (Freiburg: Verlag Herder, 1949ff.).

§19. The status of the additional books of which we have been speaking was debatable. Among the Jews the books which were additional to those of the Hebrew canon were commonly called ספרים חצונים, i.e., "external books" or "outside books." Rabbi Akiba is quoted (*Sanhedrin* X 1, 90a SBT IV 6, 602) as saying that one who reads "outside books" has no portion in the world to come, but just which books he had in mind, and whether he meant private or public reading are debatable questions. Among the Christians, where some of the additional books were found without distinction among the books of the Greek OT and the Latin OT, and where the Greek and the Latin were used directly without any particular reference back to the Hebrew, these books tended to be accepted as fully canonical. Thus Augustine, who knew Greek along with Latin, but not Hebrew, accepted Wisdom and Ecclesiasticus, for example, on the authority of ancient church usage (*The City of God* XVII 20). Following "the judgment of the greater number of catholic churches," he listed (*On Christian Doctrine* II 8) the canonical Scriptures as containing forty-four books in the OT. The number is arrived at as follows, and with the inclusion of additional books as italicized: (1) Gen, (2) Ex, (3) Lev, (4) Num, (5) Dt, (6) Jos, (7) Jg, (8) Ru, (9–12) four books of Kings (= 1–2 S, 1–2 K), (13–14) two books of Chronicles, (15) Jb, (16) *Tob*, (17) Est, (18) *Jth*, (19–20) two books of *Maccabees*, (21–22) two books of Ezra (= Ezr-Neh), (23) Ps, (24) Pr, (25) SS, (26) Ec, (27) *Wisd*, (28) *Ecclus*, (29–40) Twelve Minor Prophets, (41) Is, (42) Jer, (43) Dan, (44) Ezk.

§20. In many quarters, however, it was well remembered that the twenty-two (or twenty-four) books of the Hebrew canon (§§5–6) held a special position and, particularly where the influence of the Hebrew canon was more directly felt and where there was closer attention to the documents in the Hebrew language, there was a tendency to keep the additional books in some manner separate and at least to some extent outside the canon. Even Augustine, in his last book (*Speculum*), seems inclined to put the books additional to the Hebrew canon at the end of the OT, for he deals with Wisd, then Ec, then Tob, and then moves to Mt and the NT.[19] As we saw (§10), Origen carefully marked the LXX text in its excesses over the Hebrew. At the same time he included the Letter of Jeremiah in one

---

[19] *Sancti Aurelii Augustini . . . opera omnia* III 1 (Paris 1836), cols. 1127–54.

book together with Jer and Lam, although actually the Ep Jer was in the LXX and not in the Hebrew canon. Also at the end of his list he added: "And besides these there are the Maccabees (τὰ Μακκαβαϊκά), which are entitled Sarbēth Sabanaiel (Σαρβὴθ Σαβαναιέλ)." The meaning of this transliteration is obscure, but it may represent some such Aramaic and Hebrew title as "The Book of the House of the Princes of God." [20] As for Athanasius, having listed the canonical books in his *Festal Letter* XXXIX (§§2, 8), he then says that there are "other books besides these, not indeed included in the canon, but appointed by the Fathers to be read by those who newly join us, and who wish for instruction in the word of godliness." Then he specifically mentions Wisd, Sir, Est, Jth, and Tob, together with the Teaching of the Apostles, and the Shepherd (the last two ordinarily being related to the NT [§32]). After that Athanasius also says: "But the former, my brethren, are included in the canon, the latter being [merely] read; nor is there in any place a mention of apocryphal writings. But they are an invention of heretics. . . ." The "former" are evidently the fully canonical books, the "latter" are Wisd, Sir, etc., which are read by catechumens, and the "apocryphal writings" are the books which are yet farther afield in the possession of the "heretics."

§21. It was in Palestine, where the influence of the Hebrew canon was presumably strongest of all, and in the writings of Cyril of Jerusalem and of Jerome at Bethlehem, that the term Apocrypha was used for the first time to designate the additional books which were in excess of the Hebrew canon but were included in the Greek and Latin Old Testaments. In his *Catechetical Lectures* (IV 33 NPNFSS VII 26) delivered in the Church of the Holy Sepulcher in Jerusalem in 347/348, Cyril urged his hearers to "learn . . . from the church what are the books of the Old Testament and what those of the New Testament," and to "read the divine Scriptures, the twenty-two books of the Old Testament, these that have been translated by the Seventy-two interpreters." "And, pray," he said with earnest admonition, "read none of the apocryphal writings (τῶν ἀποκρύφων)." Since he contrasts these apocryphal writings with the twenty two books of the OT which were translated by the Seventy-two interpreters, he must be using "apocryphal" to include the portions of the LXX which were in excess of the twenty-two books of the Hebrew canon.

[20] IDB III 203.

§22. The work of Jerome in Bible translation and textual criticism is relatively well known from his own *Letters* and from his *Prefaces* to his translations. In Rome he assisted Damasus in a secretarial capacity (*Letter* 123, 10 NPNFSS VI 233), and was urged by the Pope to revise the Old Latin version (§18) which had come to have "almost as many forms of texts as there are copies" (*Preface to Four Gospels* A.D. 383 NPNFSS VI 487f.). At this time Jerome revised the Latin translation of the Four Gospels and corrected the Latin version of the Psalms by comparison with the LXX (*Preface to Pss* NPNFSS VI 492). This revision of the Psalms was adopted by Pope Damasus, is still used in St. Peter's Church in Rome, and is known as the Roman Psalter. As far as the OT was concerned, Jerome was still "willing to let that be the true translation which had apostolic approval" (NPNFSS VI 488), in other words he accepted the LXX because it was quoted in the NT (§10). Already in Rome, however, he compared Aquila's version (§10) of the OT with the Hebrew original, and worked on the revision of other OT books (*Letter* 32 A.D. 384 NPNFSS VI 46). Moving to Bethlehem in 386, Jerome continued with revision of the OT. He was now able to use the LXX text of the *Hexapla* which he consulted in Caesarea (§10), and his reproduction of the obeli and asterisks of Origen indicates increased attention to the original Hebrew. This work by Jerome was largely lost through someone's dishonesty (*Letter* 134 NPNFSS VI 280 NPNF I 544), but his translations of Job and the Psalms were preserved and the latter, being first adopted in Gaul, became the Gallican Psalter. In 391 he published his *Preface to Samuel and Kings* (NPNFSS VI 489f.), which indicated that he had started all over once again to translate the entire OT from the Hebrew, an enormous task in which he obtained the assistance of Jewish scholars and with which he was occupied until 404 (*Preface to Jos, Jg, and Ru* NPNFSS VI 489). Evidently assuming from previous experience that he would be attacked for his procedure, he called this initial *Preface to Samuel and Kings* his "helmeted introduction" (*prologus galeatus*), and set forth his principles of work at some length. Explaining that the number corresponded with the number of letters in the Hebrew alphabet, he listed the twenty-two books of the Hebrew canon, and also explained that the number could be counted as twenty-four if Ru and Lam were reckoned separately (§8). This list of the twenty-two books, with Jerome's Latin transliterations of the Hebrew names, has already been reproduced in our Table 2.

§23. With reference to this list (§22) of books, which he was even then translating from Hebrew into Latin, Jerome said in the same

*Preface to Samuel and Kings* (NPNFSS VI 490) that "what is not found in our list must be placed amongst the apocryphal writings." Then he mentioned immediately, as belonging in this category, Wisd, Sir, Jth, Tob (and the Shepherd, which is usually related to the NT); and also said, "The first book of Maccabees I have found to be Hebrew, the second is Greek, as can be proved from the very style." As far as translating these books is concerned, Jerome's *Preface to Tobit and Judith* (NPNFSS VI 494) shows that he made translations of at least these two, but also describes his work on them as done very hastily. It was the position of Jerome, therefore, that it was the books of the Hebrew canon which constituted the Scriptures of the OT; additional books found in the Greek OT and the Latin OT were Apocrypha. Additional books even beyond those limits were also Apocrypha, and here Jerome uses the word in much the original sense (§4) of "hidden" books held by peripheral groups. Thus in his *Preface to Genesis* (NPNFSS III 516) he speaks of the importance of being able to produce scriptural passages from the Hebrew, and writes: "Being ignorant of all this many follow the ravings of the Apocrypha, and prefer to the inspired books the melancholy trash which comes to us from Spain." In the *Commentary on Isaiah* 64 (CCSL LXXIII A, 735) he writes: "Certain silly women in Spain, and especially in Lusitania, have been deceived into accepting as truth the marvels of Basilides and Balsamus' treasury, and even of Barbelo and Leusiboras." These are Gnostic leaders (for Basilides see §102) and mythological figures (for Barbelo see §113), and the word Apocrypha in the *Preface to Genesis* evidently includes even Gnostic writings.

§24. In the course of time the version of Jerome was accepted so widely throughout Latin Christendom that it was called the Vulgate (*vulgata* [versio]) or "common" version.[21] It is represented by more than eight thousand manuscripts. In 1590 Pope Sixtus V issued an edition of the Vulgate which was recalled in 1592 and reissued by Pope Clement VIII. Known as the Clementine-Sixtine edition, this has remained the official text. A new critical edition is in process among Benedictine scholars: *Biblia Sacra iuxta latinam vulgatam versionem ad codicum fidem.* 1926ff. In the determination of the official position of the Roman Catholic Church toward the apocryphal

---

[21] Jerome's third translation of the Psalms was known as the *Psalterium iuxta Hebraeos*, and is found in some of the Vulgate manuscripts, but in comparison with the Roman Psalter and the Gallican Psalter (§22) this Hebrew Psalter was practically forgotten.

TABLE 6

*The Books of the Old Testament in the Vulgate*

Gen
Ex
Lev
Num
Dt
Jos
Jg
Ru
1–4 K ( = 1–2 S, 1–2 K)
1–2 Ch
1 Esd ( = Ezr)
2 Esd ( = Neh)
*Tob*
*Jth*
Est with *Ad* (10:4-16:24)
Jb
Ps (150)
Pr
Ec
SS
*Wisd*
*Ecclus*
Is
Jer
Lam
*Bar* (6 = *Ep Jer*)
Ezk
Dan with *Ad*
   *Pr Azr* and *Thr Ch* (3:24-90)
   *Sus* (13)
   *Bel* (14)
12 Minor Prophets
*1 Macc*
*2 Macc*
Appendix
   *Pr Man*
   *3 Esd* ( = *1 Esd*)
   *4 Esd* ( = *2 Esd*)

writings, Augustine's acceptance of tradition (§19) prevailed over Jerome's critical approach (§23). In 1546 the Council of Trent declared the chief apocryphal books fully canonical, and in the printed Vulgate the apocryphal writings were included in and among the other books, except for Pr Man, 1–2 Esd which were placed in an Appendix following the NT. As found in the Clementine-Sixtine edition of the Vulgate, the order of the books of the OT is as shown in our Table 6, where the apocryphal books are italicized.

§25. With Martin Luther and the Protestant Reformation, however, the more critical approach of Jerome (§23) was implemented. Following his contemporary, Andreas Bodenstein of Karlstadt (*Libellus de canonicis scripturis*. 1520; *Weliche biecher biblisch seind*. 1520), Luther collected the apocryphal books from where they were scattered in the Greek and Latin versions, and put them in a group between the OT and the NT. In his German translation of the Bible, published in 1534, the group was entitled: *Apocrypha. Das sind Bücher so nicht der heiligen Schrift gleichgehalten und doch nützlich zu lesen sind*, "Apocrypha. These are books which are not held equal to the sacred Scriptures, and yet are useful and good to read." [22]

§26. The practice of Luther (§25) was followed in many other translations of the Bible including the English. When the King James Version was published in 1611 it included between the OT and the NT those books which were in the Latin Vulgate either as a part of the OT or in the appendix (§24), but were not in the Hebrew Bible, namely, 1 Esd, 2 Esd, Tob, Jth, Ad Est, Wisd, Ecclus, Bar, Ep Jer, the Additions to Daniel (Pr Azr, and Thr Ch, Sus, Bel), Pr Man, 1 and 2 Macc, and the identical books are included as the Apocrypha in the Revised Standard Version of the Bible.

§27. Because of their inclusion in the Vulgate and in the KJV, the books just named (§26 = the italicized items in Table 6) have generally been regarded as *the* OT Apocrypha. Some of the other additional books of the time, such as Jub and XII P (§17) and others, have often been grouped together under the title "Pseudepigrapha." [23] The Greek word ψευδεπίγραφος means "falsely inscribed," or "with a false title," and *pseudepigrapha* are therefore literally "books with false titles." Dionysius of Halicarnassus (*De admiranda vi dicendi in Demosthene* 57 ed. Reiske VI [1777], 1126), for example, speaks of "pseudepigraphic orations" (ψευδεπίγραφοι λόγοι) of Demosthenes,

---

[22] William J. Kooiman, *Luther and the Bible*. 1961, 176.
[23] CAP II *Pseudepigrapha*.

meaning orations commonly ascribed to him and even published in collections of his works, but not actually of his authorship. In the Preface to his *Commentary on Jeremiah* (CCSL LXXIV 1), Jerome calls the Letter of Jeremiah a ψευδεπίγραφον. Since there are thus *pseudepigrapha* among the Apocrypha proper as well as among the other additional books, the term is really not strictly applicable to the latter alone. On this account the tendency now is to use the word Apocrypha in the broader sense too, as Jerome also did (§23), for all of the additional or "outside" (§19) books.[24] In relation to the OT, therefore, *the* Apocrypha proper, in the narrower sense of the word, are the writings which are outside the Hebrew canon but in the Latin Vulgate in the OT and in an Appendix, and in the KJV and the RSV between the OT and the NT; and the Apocrypha in the broader sense of the term are all the extracanonical books including those which have sometimes been collected under the title "Pseudepigrapha."

---

[24] Torrey, *The Apocryphal Literature*, 11; Cornfeld, *Daniel to Paul*, 74; C. T. Fritsch in IDB III 961.

# 3 / New Testament Apocrypha

*Literature:* Brooke F. Westcott, *A General Survey of the History of the Canon of the New Testament.* 6th ed. 1889, 512–20; Edgar J. Goodspeed, *The Formation of the New Testament.* 1926, 157–70; É. Amann, "Apocryphes du Nouveau Testament," in DB Supplément I cols. 460–533; Karl L. Schmidt, *Kanonische und apokryphe Evangelien und Apostelgeschichten.* 1944; M. S. Enslin, "Apocrypha, NT," in IDB I 166–69; and see also §37 n. 2 (Apostolic Fathers) and §39 (NT Apocrypha).

§28. When the Hebrew Scriptures were called the "*Old* Testament" it was implied that there was a "*New* Testament" to set alongside them. The expectation of a "new covenant" (ברית חדשה) is stated in Jer 31:31, and the establishment of a "new covenant" (καινὴ διαθήκη) is declared in 1 Cor 11:25 and other passages. The Greek word διαθήκη, which normally translates ברית in the LXX, is in turn translated *testamentum* in Latin, and hence the καινὴ διαθήκη of 1 Cor 11:25 becomes the *novum testamentum* in the Vulgate and the "new testament" in the KJV. The existence of the "new covenant" makes the former covenant the "old" one, and both the new and the old are referred to in 2 Cor 3:6, 14. Since the "old covenant" was recorded in books, namely, in the Hebrew Scriptures, it was possible to speak (2 Cor 3:14) of "when they read the old covenant" (ἐπὶ τῇ ἀναγνώσει τῆς παλαιᾶς διαθήκης), which may be translated most literally as "when the Old Testament is read aloud" (Moffatt). It has already been noted (§7) that Melito of Sardis (A.D. c. 180) spoke of and listed "the acknowledged books of the Old Testament." At about the same time another author, the unnamed contemporary of Bishop Apolinarius of Hierapolis whose work against the Montanists Eusebius (*Ch. Hist.* V 16, 3) quotes, expresses a fear "lest I might seem to some to be adding to the writings or injunctions of the word of the gospel of the new covenant" (μή πῃ δόξω τισὶν ἐπισυγγράφειν ἢ ἐπιδιατάσσεσθαι τῷ τῆς τοῦ εὐαγγελίου καινῆς διαθήκης λόγῳ). Here, the last words may be translated quite literally as "the gospel of the New Testament." Since the author wishes not to seem to add to the writings (ἐπισυγγράφειν) thereof, the καινὴ διαθήκη must be at least to some extent the NT in written form.

§29. The exact canon of the NT was determined only gradually and, as already noted (§2), it is first Athanasius (A.D. 367) who specifies precisely the twenty-seven books which have been accepted ever since. The earliest extant list is found in the so-called Muratorian Fragment. This was discovered in 1740 by L. A. Muratori in an eighth-century Latin manuscript at Milan (Codex Ambrosianus J 101 sup.) which was probably translated from the Greek. The mention of Pius, who was bishop of Rome A.D. 138–54, and the word lately (*nuperrime*) (see the text in Table 7), put the original list not long after the middle of the second century. In the list certain books are expressly repudiated while others appear which were not ultimately kept in the canon, including one book (Wisd) which has already (§26) been recognized as part of the OT Apocrypha. From the fuller text of the Muratorian Fragment, the essential list and necessary explanations are given in Table 7, with italicization of the items not ultimately retained in the canon.[1]

§30. Several of the chief passages in the writings of Origen, in which he speaks about the status of NT books, are brought together by Eusebius (*Ch. Hist.* VI 25, 3–14) after his citation of Origen's OT catalogue (§8). In the *Commentary on Mt* Origen acknowledges only four "indisputable" (ἀναντίρρητα) Gospels, namely, Mt, Mk, Lk, and Jn. In his *Commentary on Jn* he speaks of the letters of Paul, and in his *Homilies on Heb* he commends the churches which accept the Pauline authorship of Heb, although Origen himself is inclined to think that the epistle contains the thoughts of Paul in the phraseology of someone else. In the *Homilies on Heb* Origen also mentions Ac. In the *Commentary on Jn* he speaks of 1 and 2 Pet. "Peter," he says, "has left one acknowledged epistle (ἐπιστολὴν ὁμολογουμένην); perhaps also a second, but this is doubted (ἀμφιβάλλεται γάρ)." In the same place Origen speaks also of Rev and 1, 2, and 3 Jn, questioning only the genuineness of the last two epistles: "John, who has left us one Gospel . . . wrote also the Apocalypse. . . . He has left also an epistle of very few lines (ἐπιστολὴν πάνυ ὀλίγων στίχων); perhaps also a second and third; but not all consider them genuine (γνησίους)." From these passages we gather that the NT books generally "acknowledged" (ὁμολογούμενα) in the church in the time of Origen were the

---

[1] F. W. Grosheide, *Some Early Lists of the Books of the New Testament.* Textus Minores I, 1948, 5–11.

TABLE 7

*The Books of the New Testament in the Muratorian Fragment*

---

The Gospels
  Mt (missing at the beginning of the fragment)
  Mk (undoubtedly mentioned in a paragraph of which only the
    concluding words are preserved)
  Lk
  Jn

The Book of Acts
  Ac

The Letters of Paul
  1 Cor      1 Th
  2 Cor      2 Th
  Eph        Rom
  Phl        Phm
  Col        Tit
  Gal        1 Tim
             2 Tim

There is current, also, one to the *Laodiceans*, another to the
*Alexandrians*, forged in Paul's name to suit a heresy of Marcion,
and several others, which cannot be received into the Catholic
Church; for it is not fitting that gall be mixed with honey.

Other Books
  Jd
  1 Jn
  2 Jn
  *Wisd*
The Apocalypse, also, of John and of *Peter* only we receive;
which some of us will not have read in the church.

But the *Shepherd* was written quite lately in our times by
Hermas, while his brother Pius, the bishop, was sitting in the
chair of the church of the city of Rome; and therefore it ought
to be read, indeed, but it cannot to the end of time be publicly
read in the church.

But of Valentinus, the Arsinoite, and his friends, we receive
nothing at all, who have also composed a long new book of
*Psalms*, together with Basilides and the Asiatic founder of the
Montanists.

TABLE 8

*The Books of the New Testament as Seen in the Writings of Origen*

---

Acknowledged Books (ὁμολογούμενα)
> Four Gospels
> Fourteen Letters of Paul (including Heb)
> Ac
> 1 Pet
> 1 Jn
> Rev

Doubted Books (ἀμφιβαλλόμενα)
> Jas
> 2 Pet
> 2 Jn
> 3 Jn
> Jd
> *Letter of Barnabas*
> *Shepherd of Hermas*

---

four Gospels, fourteen letters of Paul (assuming inclusion of the thirteen which bear Paul's name, together with Heb), Ac, 1 Pet, 1 Jn, and Rev. This makes twenty-two books in the NT, the same number that Origen knew in the Hebrew OT (§8). "Doubted" books (ἀμφιβαλλόμενα) were, according to the passages collected by Eusebius, 2 Pet, and 2 and 3 Jn. Other passages in Origen refer to several other hooks which he appears to be willing to use, but about the acceptance of which he also appears to recognize the existence of doubts. In his *Commentary on Jn* (XIX 23 GCS Origenes IV 325) he makes a clear reference to Jas 2:17 but says, "As we read in the epistle circulating under the name of James" (ὡς ἐν τῇ φερομένῃ 'Ιακώβου ἐπιστολῇ ἀνέγνωμεν). In his *Commentary on Mt* (XVII 30 GCS Origenes X 672) he cites Jd 6 but says, "But if anyone will bring forward the Epistle of Jude" (εἰ δὲ καὶ τὴν 'Ιούδα προσοῖτό τις ἐπιστολήν). In the *Commentary on Mt* (XIV 21 GCS Origenes X 335) Origen quotes from the Shepherd of Hermas, but prefaces the quotation with these words: "And if one should dare, using a Scripture which is in circulation in the church, but not acknowledged by all to be divine" (εἰ δὲ χρὴ τολμήσαντα καὶ ἀπό τινος φερομένης μὲν ἐν ταῖς ἐκκλησίαις γραφῆς, οὐ παρὰ πᾶσι δὲ ὁμολογουμένης εἶναι θείας). Also in *Against Celsus* (I 63 GCS Origenes

TABLE 9

*New Testament and Related Books in the List of Eusebius*

---

Acknowledged Books (ὁμολογούμενα)
 Four Gospels
 Ac
 Fourteen Letters of Paul (for the inclusion of Heb cf. *Ch. Hist.*
  III 3, 5)
 1 Jn
 1 Pet
 Rev ("if it really seem proper")

Disputed Books (ἀντιλεγόμενα)
 Jas
 Jd
 2 Pet ("The so-called second Epistle we have not received as
  canonical, but nevertheless it has appeared useful to many,
  and has been studied with other Scriptures" *Ch. Hist.* III 3, 1)
 2, 3 Jn ("which may be the work of the evangelist or of some
  other with the same name")

Spurious Books (νόθα)
 *Acts of Paul*
 *Shepherd*
 *Apocalypse of Peter*
 *Letter of Barnabas*
 the so-called *Teachings of the Apostles* (τῶν ἀποστόλων αἱ λεγόμεναι
  Διδαχαί)
 Rev ("if it seem proper")
 *Gospel according to the Hebrews* (τὸ καθ' Ἑβραίους εὐαγγέλιον)

Fabrications of Heretics (αἱρετικῶν ἀνδρῶν ἀναπλάσματα)

 "the writings which are put forward by heretics under the
 name of the apostles containing *gospels* such as those of *Peter*,
 and *Thomas*, and *Matthias*, and some others besides, or *Acts*
 such as those of *Andrew* and *John* and the other apostles"

---

I 115) Origen says, "It is written in the catholic Epistle of Barnabas"
(γέγραπται δὴ ἐν τῇ Βαρνάβα καθολικῇ ἐπιστολῇ), but in *On the Principles*
(III 2, 4 GCS Origenes V 251) he cites both the Shepherd and Barna-

bas in immediate succession to the Book of Tobit, which is one of the OT Apocrypha (Table 3, etc.). As reflected in the writings of Origen, then, the books of the NT were those in Table 8. The first twenty-two were acknowledged by all; seven more were used by Origen in quite the same way as the others, but with recognition that they were doubted by many. Those not ultimately kept in the canon are italicized.

§31. Eusebius (*Ch. Hist.* III 25) also classifies the NT books according to his understanding of their status, and he does so in three main categories (§4) plus a yet additional group. In the first category are the books received by all the churches, which he calls "acknowledged" (ὁμολογούμενα), "commonly acknowledged" (ἀνωμολογήμενα), and "canonical" (ἐνδιαθηκά). In the second category are the books not received by all, which he calls "disputed" (ἀντιλεγόμενα). In the third are books which, although perhaps received by some, are actually "spurious" (νόθα). Finally, not even to be placed among the spurious books (ἐν νόθοις) are the books which are obviously the "fabrications of heretics" (αἱρετικῶν ἀνδρῶν ἀναπλάσματα). The list of Eusebius, with such explanations from his text as are necessary, is given in Table 9, and again items which did not ultimately have a place in the canon are italicized.

§32. As already noted (§§2, 29), in his *Festal Letter* XXXIX (A.D. 367) Athanasius gives for the first time as constituting the canon of the NT exactly the twenty-seven books as we have them today. He mentions also, but only as appointed for reading by catechumens, several books of the OT Apocrypha (§20) and also the *Teachings of the Apostles* and the *Shepherd*. His list of canonical books is reproduced in Table 10.

§33. In its contents Codex Vaticanus was virtually identical with the list of Athanasius in the OT (§14) and in the NT, as far as the manuscript extends, it gives exactly the same books in the same order as Athanasius. The books are the Gospels, Ac, the Catholic Letters, and the Letters of Paul as far as Heb 9:14. Lacking the original ending of the manuscript it is impossible to say certainly how it terminated, but presumably it concluded exactly as the list of Athanasius.

§34. Codex Sinaiticus contains in the NT: Mt, Mk, Lk, Jn, Rom, 1–2 Cor, Gal, Eph, Phl, Col, 1–2 Th, Heb, 1–2 Tim, Tit, Phm, Ac, Jas, 1–2 Pet, 1–2–3 Jn, Jd, Rev, the *Letter of Barnabas*, and the *Shepherd*.

§35. In its extant form Codex Alexandrinus contains in the NT: Mt (beginning at Mt 25:6), Mk, Lk, Jn, Ac, Jas, 1–2 Pet, 1–2–3 Jn,

TABLE 10

*The Books of the New Testament in the List of Athanasius*

---

Four Gospels
  according to Mt, Mk, Lk, and Jn

Ac

Seven Catholic Letters
  Jas, 1–2 Pet, 1–2–3 Jn, Jd

Fourteen Letters of Paul
  Rom, 1–2 Cor, Gal, Eph, Phl, Col, 1–2 Th, Heb, 1–2 Tim, Tit,
  Phm

Rev

---

Jd, Rom, 1–2 Cor, Gal, Eph, Phl, Col, 1–2 Th, Heb, 1–2 Tim, Tit,
Phm, Rev, and the *First* and *Second Letters of Clement.*

§36. In the foregoing lists (§§29–35) from representative Christian
authors and major NT manuscripts of the early centuries, a number
of books appear which are additional (the italicized items in Tables
7, 8, and 9 and in §§32, 34, 35) to the twenty-seven books which
obtained a permanent place in the NT canon. The Shepherd of
Hermas is mentioned in the Muratorian Fragment (Table 7), by
Origen (Table 8), Eusebius (Table 9), and Athanasius (§§20, 32),
as well as by Tertullian (§4) and Jerome (§23), and is found in Codex
Sinaiticus (§34). The Letter of Barnabas is mentioned by Origen
(Table 8) and Eusebius (Table 9), and is found in Codex Sinaiticus
(§34). 1 Clement and 2 Clement are found in Codex Alexandrinus
(§35). The Apocalypse of Peter is mentioned in the Muratorian
Fragment (Table 7) and by Eusebius (Table 9). The Teachings of the
Apostles (Didache) is mentioned by Eusebius (Table 9) and Athana-
sius (§§20, 32). The Letters of Paul to the Laodiceans and to the
Alexandrians are mentioned in the Muratorian Fragment (Table 7).
The Acts of Paul, the Gospel according to the Hebrews, the Gospels
of Peter, of Thomas, and of Matthias, and the Acts of Andrew and
of John are mentioned by Eusebius (Table 9). In another passage
(*Ch. Hist.* III 3, 2) Eusebius also mentions the Acts of Peter, and the
Preaching of Peter. Beyond this there were other authors, such as
Valentinus and Basilides, whom the Muratorian Fragment mentions

(Table 7), and other works to which Eusebius (Table 9) and others allude.

§37. Out of these additional books (§36), some of which (Barnabas, the Shepherd, 1–2 Clement) were actually copied in major NT codices (Sinaiticus and Alexandrinus), it might have been expected that at least some would have come to constitute a widely agreed-upon NT Apocrypha comparable to the Apocrypha proper of the OT (§26). This, however, was not the case. While both of the two evidently most popular works, the Shepherd of Hermas and the Letter of Barnabas, are found in Old Latin translations, neither of these nor any other of the additional books is found in the Vulgate, the KJV, or any other official version of the NT. In the Clementine-Sixtine edition of the Vulgate there is indeed an Appendix following the NT, but the books which are contained therein (Pr Man, 1–2 Esd) are books which are considered a part of the OT Apocrypha (§24), not of the NT. In fact, of the books listed in §36, some five are commonly considered to belong simply to the "Apostolic Fathers." This is a designation which applies to ten or twelve works supposed to have come from church writers who flourished in apostolic times (*qui temporibus apostolicis floruerunt*, as J. B. Cotelier said in making the first collection of them in the seventeenth century), who therefore could have known some of the original apostles or their immediate successors.[2] The five apocryphal books which are placed in the Apostolic Fathers are the following and, beyond listing them here, it will not be necessary to deal with them in detail: (1) The Teachings of the Apostles (Didache) or, more fully and precisely in accordance with the superscription of the work itself, The Teaching of the Lord to the Nations by the Twelve Apostles (Διδαχὴ κυρίου διὰ τῶν δώδεκα ἀποστόλων τοῖς ἔθνεσιν); (2) The Letter of Barnabas ('Επιστολὴ Βαρνάβα); (3) 1 Clement, or The First Letter of Clement to the Corinthians (Κλήμεντος πρὸς Κορινθίους ἐπιστολὴ α'); (4) 2 Clement, or The Second Letter of Clement to the Corinthians (Κλήμεντος πρὸς Κορινθίους ἐπιστολὴ β'); (5) The Shepherd (Ποιμήν), or The Shepherd of Hermas ('Ο Ποιμὴν τοῦ 'Ερμᾶ).

[2] J. B. Cotelier, *SS. patrum qui temporibus apostolicis floruerunt . . . opera.* . . . 2 vols. 1698; O. de Gebhardt, A. Harnack, and T. Zahn, *Patrum apostolicorum opera.* 3d ed. 1900 (abbreviated PAO); J. B. Lightfoot, *The Apostolic Fathers.* 1907; Kirsopp Lake, *The Apostolic Fathers.* LCL 2 vols. 1912–13; Edgar J. Goodspeed, *The Apostolic Fathers.* 1950; Karl Bihlmeyer, *Die apostolischen Väter.* 2d ed. Part I, 1956; *Die apostolischen Väter.* GCS 1956ff.

§38. In short, then, there are no NT Apocrypha proper in the sense of a group of books permanently occupying even a subordinate place within the NT canon and commonly printed together with the fully canonical books. There are various books, including those listed in §36, which exhibit various degrees of similarity (or dissimilarity) to the books of the NT canon, some of which have in various times and places been thought to have a right to a place in that canon. But the consensus of the main church has been to omit them from the canon, and accordingly we can describe them as the NT Apocrypha only in the broad sense of the term (§27) meaning that they are extracanonical or "outside" books. Of these "outside" books, some have found a place in the Apostolic Fathers (§37), and belong therefore to the realm of studies in that area. Of the remaining books it is those which most plainly raise the claim (§1) to be like the canonical NT books to which the designation of NT Apocrypha most properly belongs.[3] The claim may be expressed in the title or form or content of the book and, indeed, it is often the title which immediately raises the claim for, like the books of the canonical NT, many of these too are called Gospel or Acts or Letter or Revelation. Such writings are, in the broad sense of the term, NT Apocrypha. Since our concern is primarily with those portions of such writings which stand closest to the canonical NT, even if they are only isolated quotations or small fragments, we will also designate them, in the same sense, as extracanonical materials related to the NT.

§39. The first published collection of extracanonical materials expressly designated as Christian Apocrypha appears to have been that by Michael Neander in 1564 under the title, *Apocrypha: hoc est, narrationes de Christo, Maria, Joseph, cognatione et familia Christi, extra Biblia. . . .*[4] Important later editions were: J. A. Fabricius, *Codex apocryphus Novi Testamenti.* 2 vols. 1703–19; J. C. Thilo, *Codex apocryphus Novi Testamenti.* I 1832; and A. Hilgenfeld, *Novum Testamentum extra canonem receptum.* 1866. Critical editions of the major texts were published by Constantine Tischendorf in three groups: *Acta apostolorum apocrypha.* 1851; *Apocalypses apocryphae . . . supplementis.* 1866; *Evangelia apocrypha.* 1876 (abbreviated TEA); and the Acts have been newly edited, following Tischendorf, by R. A. Lipsius and M. Bonnet, *Acta apostolorum apocrypha.* 3 vols. 1959 (abbreviated AAA). A German translation of the materials, with

[3] Cf. Michaelis, *Die Apokryphen Schriften zum Neuen Testament,* XIV–XV.
[4] Schmidt, *Kanonische und apokryphe Evangelien und Apostelgeschichten,* 17.

introductions, was edited by Edgar Hennecke under the title, *Neutestamentliche Apokryphen*, in 1904, with a second edition in 1924. In 1924 Montague R. James published an English translation under the title, *The Apocryphal New Testament*, and this was reprinted with some additions in 1950. In 1952 F. Amiot published a French translation of apocryphal Gospels, Acts, Letters, and Apocalypses with the title, *La Bible apocryphe: Evangiles apocryphes* (Textes pour l'histoire sacrée). In 1956 Wilhelm Michaelis published a German translation of many of the materials entitled, *Die Apokryphen Schriften zum Neuen Testament*. In 1948 Hennecke invited Wilhelm Schneemelcher to assist him with a new edition of his work and, upon the death of Hennecke in 1951, Schneemelcher continued this project. Of the resultant third edition of Hennecke-Schneemelcher's *Neutestamentliche Apokryphen*, the first volume, *Evangelien* (abbreviated HSNTAE), appeared in 1959, and the second, *Apostolisches, Apokalypsen und Verwandtes* in 1964, with an English translation edited by R. McL. Wilson, *New Testament Apocrypha*, Vol. I, *Gospels and Related Writings*, in 1963, and Vol. II, *Writings Relating to the Apostles; Apocalypses and Related Subjects*, in 1965.

# 4 / Jewish Christianity

*Literature:* F. J. A. Hort, *Judaistic Christianity.* 1904; Joseph Thomas, *Le Mouvement Baptiste en Palestine et Syrie (150 av. J.-C.—300° ap. J.-C.).* 1935; Karl Pieper, *Die Kirche Palästinas bis zum Jahre 135.* 1938; Charles C. Torrey, "James the Just, and His Name 'Oblias,'" in JBL 63 (1944), 93–98; Hans J. Schoeps, *Theologie und Geschichte des Judenchristentums.* 1949; Klaus Baltzer and Helmut Köster, "Die Bezeichnung des Jakobus als 'ωΒΛΙΑΣ," in ZNW 46 (1965), 141–42; Jean Daniélou, *Théologie du Judéo-Christianisme.* 1958; Marcel Simon, *Les Sectes juives au temps de Jésus.* 1960; Matthew Black, *The Scrolls and Christian Origins, Studies in the Jewish Background of the New Testament.* 1961; P. E. Testa, *Il simbolismo dei Giudeo-Cristiani.* 1962; Jean Daniélou, *The Theology of Jewish Christianity,* tr. by John A. Baker. The Development of Christian Doctrine Before the Council of Nicaea, 1. 1964.

§40. A chief reason for interest in the NT Apocrypha is to see if there are materials here which will help in understanding early Christianity in general and the life of Jesus in particular. Since the first disciples of Jesus were Jews and since the original church was at Jerusalem, the very earliest Christianity is to be described as Jewish Christianity. After that, although world Christianity, as seen particularly in the missionary journeys of Paul, moved in the main westward across the Roman Empire, Jewish Christianity continued to exist in the East for centuries. While persons of Jewish background and Christian faith were undoubtedly, in many places, a part of the main church, in the East, Jewish Christianity became a distinguishable and separate entity, whose members were known particularly as Nazaraeans (Nazoraeans) and Ebionites (§§48–49). Since this area is relatively little known, and since the question will inevitably arise in relation to at least some of the Apocrypha of the possible transmission of materials in Jewish Christian circles, a brief notice may be given of the history of Jewish Christianity. As we have said, the first followers of Jesus, including the twelve apostles, were Jews, and the earliest church, centering around these apostles (Ac

1:13) and comprising in all about one hundred and twenty persons (Ac 1:15), was in Jerusalem. On the day of Pentecost the number was largely increased (Ac 2:41) and, since the converts came from among Jews and proselytes from many lands (enumerated in Ac 2:9ff.), from this time on Jews of the Dispersion as well as Jews of Palestine must have been part of the movement. Already in Ac 6:1 there is mention of Hellenists as well as of Hebrews, and the Hellenists are probably Greek-speaking Jews in contrast with Hebrew (or Aramaic)-speaking Jews. First, it appears, with Peter's conversion of the centurion Cornelius at Caesarea, Gentiles (Ac 10:45), i.e., non-Jews, were brought into the movement. Among the apostles Peter is named in first place in Ac 1:13, and in the subsequent events he takes the leading position (Ac 2:14, etc.), although John was also of some prominence (Ac 3:1). Upon his visit to Jerusalem "after three years" (Gal 1:18), Paul visited Peter and saw of "the other apostles" only James, the Lord's brother. On Paul's visit "after fourteen years" (Gal 2:9), James and Cephas and John were the reputed "pillars," and it may be noted that James is now mentioned first, although Paul recognizes that it is still Peter who is "entrusted with the gospel to the circumcised" (Gal 2:7). After his imprisonment by Herod Agrippa I in the spring A.D. 44, Peter "departed and went to another place" (Ac 12:17). At this juncture James, the Lord's brother, already mentioned in first place in Gal 2:9, presumably emerged clearly as the leader of the Jerusalem church.

§41. Eusebius (*Ch. Hist.* II 1) says that James who was called the brother of the Lord, and who was surnamed the Just on account of his virtue, was the first to be made bishop of the Jerusalem church. He quotes Clement of Alexandria as writing in the sixth book of his *Hypotyposes:* "For they say that Peter and James and John after the ascension of our Savior, as if also preferred by our Lord, strove not after honor, but chose James the Just bishop of Jerusalem" ('Ιάκωβον τὸν δίκαιον ἐπίσκοπον τῶν 'Ιεροσολύμων). Eusebius (*Ch. Hist.* II 23) also quotes Hegesippus in the fifth book of his *Memoirs* in an extended description of James. James lived as a Nazirite, drinking no wine, eating no flesh, and allowing no razor upon his head. He wore linen garments, and was so constantly on his knees begging forgiveness for his people "that his knees became hard like those of a camel." "Because of his exceeding great justice," says Hegesippus, "he was called the Just, and Oblias, which signifies in Greek 'περιοχή of the people,' and 'Justice,' in accordance with what the prophets declare concerning him" (διὰ γέ τοι τὴν ὑπερβολὴν τῆς δικαιοσύνης αὐτοῦ ἐκαλεῖτο ὁ δίκαιος καὶ ὠβλίας, ὅ ἐστιν 'Ελληνιστὶ περιοχὴ τοῦ λαοῦ, καὶ δικαιοσύνη, ὡς οἱ προφῆται δηλοῦσιν περὶ αὐτοῦ). That the righteousness or justice of James led to his being called "the Just," is plain. But the name Oblias is not known otherwise and has not been successfully explained, therefore it is also not clear how this name could be taken to signify "περιοχή of the people" in Greek, nor how it could be explained as in accordance with something which the prophets had said. By a very slight mistake, however, a scribe could have written a Λ in place of a Δ, and thus have given us the form ωBΛIAC in place of an original ωBΔAIC. In the same way, for example, the name Obed (LXX 'Ωβήδ in Ru 4:17, 21-22; 1 Ch 2:12; 'Ιωβήδ in 1 Ch 2:12 in Codex Alexandrinus) is copied in Lk 3:32 in the forms 'Ωβήλ in Codex Bezae and 'Ιωβήλ in Codices Vaticanus and Sinaiticus. Therefore the original report of Hegesippus was probably that James was called Obdias ('Ωβδίας). This can be simply a Greek transcription of the name Obadiah (עֹבַדְיָה = "servant of Yahweh"), which is found in the LXX in the forms 'Αβδιά 1 Ch 3:21, 'Αβδίας 2 Ch 17:7, 'Αβδιού 3 K 18:3 (= 1 K 18:3), etc., Ob 1:1; 'Οβδιά 1 Ch 7:3, 'Οβδίας 2 Esd 22:25 (= Neh 22:25), 'Οβδιού Ob 1:1 in Codex Vaticanus; and in Josephus 'Ωβεδίας *Ant.* VIII 13, 4f. §§329ff., IX 4, 2 §47, referring to the steward of Ahab in 1 K 18:3. Hegesippus, then, connects the name Obadiah for James with the explanation that it means in Greek, περιοχὴ τοῦ λαοῦ. The Greek word περιοχή means "circumference" and is used to translate the Hebrew מְצוּדָה, "stronghold," in 1 S 22:4 (LXX 1 K 22:4) and elsewhere, and it means "portion circumscribed" and is used for a "passage" (RSV) of Scripture, or the content thereof, in Ac 8:32. So in accordance with the first meaning just cited, we might suppose that Hegesippus is saying that the name applied to James signified that he was the "Stronghold of the people." But in Ob 1:1 the same Greek word translates the Hebrew צִיר, which means a "person sent on a journey," or a "messenger," and we have in the LXX: περιοχὴν εἰς τὰ ἔθνη ἐξαπέστειλεν, "he sent a messenger to the nations." The similarity of περιοχὴ εἰς τὰ ἔθνη to περιοχὴ τοῦ λαοῦ, the phrase used by Hegesippus, is unmistakable. Therefore Hegesippus may be understood to have stated originally that James was called Obdias, i.e., Obadiah, and therewith to have been the "Messenger of the people" who was pointed to in the book of the same name (Ob 1:1). Since Obadiah means "servant of Yahweh," the designation is the same as that of James in Jas 1:1, "servant of God" (θεοῦ . . . δοῦλος). Eusebius likewise quotes both Clement of Alexandria and Hegesippus in a description of the death of James. He was thrown down from the pinnacle of the Temple, stoned, and clubbed. Josephus (*Ant.*

XX 9, 1 §200) reports the same event briefly. The procurator Festus was dead (A.D. 61), his successor Albinus was still en route, and the high priest, Ananus, taking advantage of the opportunity, "called together the Sanhedrin, and brought before them the brother of Jesus, the so-called Christ, James by name, together with some others, and accused them of violating the law, and condemned them to be stoned." From the references to the procurators the death of James the Just must have been in A.D. 61/62.

§42. Quoting the *Memoirs* of Hegesippus, Eusebius (*Ch. Hist.* IV 22, 4) describes the choice of a successor to James: "And after James the Just had suffered martyrdom, as the Lord had also on the same account, Symeon, the son of the Lord's uncle, Clopas, was appointed the next bishop. All proposed him as second bishop because he was a cousin of the Lord." In another passage (*Ch. Hist.* III 11) Eusebius identifies this Clopas as the one mentioned in the Gospel (Jn 19:25), and cites Hegesippus to the effect that Clopas was a brother of Joseph so that Symeon was, in that way, a cousin of the Savior. Hegesippus also (according to Eusebius in the first of the two passages just cited) puts the beginning of heresies in the church at the time of the election of Symeon. There were seven sects among the Jewish people, Hegesippus says: Essenes, Galileans, Hemerobaptists, Masbothei, Samaritans, Sadducees, and Pharisees (an enumeration which agrees with that in Justin's *Dialogue with Trypho* [80] in number but not in all the names). From these sects came Thebouthis who, disappointed at not being made bishop instead of Symeon, began to corrupt the church, and Simon (Ac 8:9ff.; Eusebius, *Ch. Hist.* II 13) and other leaders from whom, in turn, came the heretical groups which Hegesippus lists: Simonians, Cleobians, Dosithians, Goratheni, Masbothei, Menandrianists, Marcianists, Carpocratians, Valentinians, Basilidians, Saturnilians (Σιμωνιανοί, Κλεοβιηνοί, Δοσιθιανοί, Γοραθηνοί, Μασβωθεοί, Μενανδριανισταί, Μαρκιανισταί, Καρποκρατιανοί, Οὐαλεντινιανοί, Βασιλειδιανοί, Σατορνιλιανοί).

§43. In A.D. 66 the Jewish War began (Josephus, *War* II 14, 4 §284). Eusebius (*Ch. Hist.* III, 5, 3) says that "the people of the church in Jerusalem had been commanded by a revelation, vouchsafed to approved men there before the war (πρὸ τοῦ πολέμου), to leave the city and to dwell in a certain town of Perea called Pella (Πέλλαν)." Epiphanius (*Pan. haer.* 29, 7, 8 GCS 25, 330) records the same migration of the disciples to live in Pella (ἐν Πέλλῃ), and attributes it to a command of Christ because Jerusalem was going to suffer siege. Pella was a well-known city of the Decapolis, "rich with its waters,"

as Pliny (*Natural History* V 16) says. It is mentioned in the Amarna
Letters (No. 256) under the Canaanite form of its name, *Piḥilu*,[1]
appears in the Talmud as פחל,[2] and is identified today with Khirbet
Fahil, across the Jordan southeast from Scythopolis, near good
springs in Wadi Jurm, eighteen miles south of the Sea of Galilee. If the
Christian church departed from Jerusalem before the war (A.D. 66)
it must have been not long after the martyrdom of James (§41), and
the persecution may have been a reason too for the removal. In Pella
the Christians may have suffered soon again for, at the outbreak of
the Jewish War, parties of Jews sacked a number of Hellenistic cities
including Pella (Josephus, *War* II 18, 1 §458). Of the seven sects of
the Jews just mentioned (§42) the Essenes were probably the people
who had the important center at Qumran near the Dead Sea, which
is now so well known, and other of the groups, particularly other
"baptist" groups (note the Hemerobaptists ['Ημεροβαπτισταί] =
"daily immersers" in the list of Hegesippus), were probably also
located in the Dead Sea—Jordan Valley—Transjordan region. Later
Epiphanius deals in his "Medicine Chest" (*Pan. haer.* XIV–XX)
with seven sects or heresies (αἱρέσεις) among the Jews before Christ
(giving names only partly in agreement with those in the list of
Hegesippus), and mentions after the Hemerobaptists the Nasaraeans
(ἡ αἵρεσις τῶν Νασαραίων) who were found in Galaaditis and Basanitis,
i.e., the regions of Gilead and Bashan extending eastward to the
mountains of Hauran; and the Ossaeans or Sampsaeans (ἡ αἵρεσις τῶν
'Οσσαίων . . . νυνὶ Σαμψαίων καλεῖται) who lived in Nabataea and
Peraea (Περαία = πέραν τοῦ 'Ιορδάνου, "beyond the Jordan") as far
as the land of Moab. When the Jerusalem Christians moved to Pella,
and perhaps to other places in Transjordan, they presumably came
into closer contact with such groups, and the possibility of mutual
influence was increased. Perhaps remnants of the Essenes and of
other Jewish sects, specially the baptismal sects, were in due time
absorbed into Jewish Christianity.[3]

§44. After the destruction of Jerusalem (A.D. 70), as Epiphanius
(*On Weights and Measures* 14–15 [54d–55a] ed. Dean 30–31) states,
the Christians, though perhaps not all of them, returned from their
sojourn in Pella to Jerusalem. In one of his passages (*Ch. Hist.* III
11) on the election of Symeon son of Clopas (Συμεὼν ὁ τοῦ Κλωπᾶ)
as second bishop of Jerusalem, Eusebius puts this event "after the

---

[1] W. F. Albright in BASOR 89 (Feb. 1943), 11 n. 20.
[2] F.-M. Abel, *Géographie de la Palestine*. 1933–38, II 405.
[3] Schoeps, *Theologie und Geschichte des Judenchristentums*, 277.

martyrdom of James and the conquest of Jerusalem which immediately followed," which would appear to place the election somewhat after A.D. 70. The other passage already quoted (§42), however, sounds as if the election transpired more closely upon the martyrdom of James and, in that case, Symeon may have led the group to Pella and then, at the time now being mentioned, back again to Jerusalem. At all events, when Trajan persecuted the Christians in the tenth year of his reign (A.D. 107), Symeon, bishop of Jerusalem, was a martyr by crucifixion, as Eusebius states (*Ch. Hist.* III 32; *Chronicle* GCS Eusebius VII 194: *Simon, filius Cleopae, qui in Hierosolymis episcopatum tenebat, cruci figitur*). He was succeeded by Justus, "one of the many thousands of the circumcision who at that time believed in Christ" (*Ch. Hist.* III 35). Altogether, according to Eusebius (*Ch. Hist.* IV 5), there were fifteen bishops in Jerusalem in the period up to the siege of the city by Hadrian (A.D. 135), but the number seems large and perhaps the names of elders, or names from other cities, have come into the list. All were said to have been of Hebrew descent, and to have been judged worthy of the episcopate because they had truly received the knowledge of Christ (τὴν γνῶσιν τοῦ Χριστοῦ).

§45. In A.D. 130, on an inspection trip in the East, Hadrian visited Jerusalem.[4] In the portion of Zion which had escaped destruction in A.D. 70 he found, according to Epiphanius (*On Weights and Measures* 14 [54c] ed. Dean 30),[5] "the church of God, which was small, where the disciples, when they had returned after the Savior had ascended from the Mount of Olives, went to the upper room." On the southwestern hill (Zion), least damaged by the previous war, a house had evidently been identified as that where the upper room (ὑπερῷον) of Ac 1:13 was (and at least later was also identified as the place of the upper room [ἀνάγαιον, Mk 14:15 Lk 22:12] of the Last Supper),[6] and this became the "small church" (later replaced by a basilica) where the Jerusalem Christian community met. At this time (A.D. 130) Hadrian determined to rebuild Jerusalem as the pagan city of Aelia; and according to Epiphanius, in the passage just cited, he brought as overseer of the work a relative of his and a Greek interpreter from Sinope in Pontus by the name of Aquila. Aquila was greatly impressed when he saw the disciples of the apostles working miracles, and asked to be baptized. When he continued to practice astrology, however, he was expelled from the church. At

[4] Stewart Perowne, *Hadrian.* 1960, 134f., 146ff.
[5] Epiphanius seems to think the visit took place in A.D. 117.
[6] Clemens Kopp, *Die heiligen Stätten der Evangelien.* 1959, 378ff.

that point he became a proselyte to Judaism (cf. Irenaeus, *Against Heresies* III 21) and made his translation of the OT (§10) in order, Epiphanius says, "so to distort certain of the words occurring in the translation of the Seventy-two that he might proclaim the things testified to about Christ in the divine Scriptures to be fulfilled in some other way." While no other writer prior to Epiphanius states that Aquila was at one time a Christian, the picture of an active Christian community in Jerusalem at this time is confirmed by Eusebius who, in addition to listing the many bishops (§44), also speaks of the large church of Christ (ἐκκλησία Χριστοῦ), made up of Jews, which was in Jerusalem until the time of Hadrian's siege (*Demonstr. evang.* III 5, 108 GCS Eusebius VI 131).

§46. The announced intention of Hadrian to rebuild Jerusalem as a pagan city provoked the rebellion of Bar Kokhba (A.D. 132), which was crushed with the siege and taking of Bethar (Bettir, five miles southwest of Jerusalem) in the eighteenth year of the emperor (134/135). Since Hadrian now forbade all Jews to go into Aelia or the country around it, the Jewish Christian community of Jerusalem came to its end. The "bishops of the circumcision" ceased, the church of Jerusalem (for the Christians soon reverted to the biblical name) was composed of Gentiles, and a new line of bishops, of whom Marcus was the first, assumed the leadership of it (Eusebius, *Ch. Hist.* IV 6; *Chronicle* GCS Eusebius VII 201).

§47. With the exclusion of Jewish Christians from Jerusalem (§46) it may be assumed that many of them went back to Pella, where the Jewish Christian community had already established and perhaps continued to mantain a center (§§43f.), and to other places in the land "beyond the Jordan" (πέραν τοῦ 'Ιορδάνου) where, perhaps ever since the days of his own ministry, the influence of Jesus had been a light-bringing fulfillment of the prophecy of Isaiah (Is 9:1-2; Mt 4:15-16). In giving his account of Hadrian's siege and subsequent exclusion of Jews from Aelia (§46), Eusebius cites as his source Ariston of Pella ('Αρίστων ὁ Πελλαῖος). From a number of ancient references it is known that Ariston was the author of a *Dialogue between Jason and Papiscus concerning Christ* ('Ιάσονος καὶ Παπίσκου ἀντιλογία περὶ Χριστοῦ; *Altercatio Jasonis et Papisci*), which was written probably about 140, was still available to Maximus Confessor in the seventh century, but was afterward lost.[7] The prologue to a

---

[7] MPG V 1277-86; M. J. Routh, *Reliquiae Sacrae.* I (1846), 95-109; ANF VIII 750; Adolf Harnack, *Geschichte der altchristlichen Literatur.* 2d ed. I 1 (1958), 92-95; A. Lukyn Williams, *Adversus Judaeos.* 1935, 28-30.

Latin translation of the *Dialogue*, incorrectly included in the works of Cyprian under the title *Ad Vigilium episcopum de judaica incredulitate*, makes it plain that in this work Jason was a Jewish Christian and Papiscus an Alexandrian Jew.[8] Origen (*Against Celsus* IV 52 ANF IV 521) says that Celsus attacked the book bitterly, but Origen himself speaks of it favorably as "a work in which a Christian is described as conversing with a Jew on the subject of the Jewish Scriptures, and proving that the predictions regarding Christ fitly apply to Jesus; although the other disputant maintains the discussion in no ignoble style, and in a manner not unbecoming the character of a Jew." From the nature of his book it seems most likely that Ariston of Pella was himself a Jewish Christian. Thus from the background of the Jewish Christian community at Pella we have the first known written defence of Christianity against Judaism. Beyond this we must seek for information about the Jewish Christians in the writings of authors of the main Western church, to many of whom Jewish Christianity was obviously a relatively distant and little known entity.

§48. In the *Dialogue* of Ariston (I 1),[9] the Jewish Christian, Jason, is called a Nazaraean (*Nazaraeus*). Since Jesus came from Nazareth (Mk 1:9) he was "the one from Nazareth" (ὁ ἀπὸ Ναζαρέθ) (Mt 21:11; Jn 1:45; Ac 10:38), or "the Nazarene" (ὁ Ναζαρηνός) (Mk 1:24 = Lk 4:34; Mk 10:47; 14:67; 16:6; Lk 24:19). In other passages he is called ὁ Ναζωραῖος (Mt 2:23; 26:71; Lk 18:37; Jn 18:5, 7; 19:19; Ac 2:22; 3:6; 4:10; 6:14; 22:8; 26:9). Both forms, "Nazarene" and "Nazoraean," derive linguistically from Nazareth and mean "inhabitant of Nazareth."[10] Mt 2:23 speaks of the residence of Jesus at Nazareth as fulfilling that which was spoken by the prophets, "He shall be called a Nazarene (Ναζωραῖος)." Prior to this point Mt has given three OT quotations, each introduced as spoken or written by "the prophet" (singular), in the last case Jeremiah being mentioned by name (Mt 1:22; 2:5; 2:17). Now (Mt 2:23) the quotation is introduced as something that was spoken by "the prophets" (plural). The quotation does not correspond with any express statement in the OT. One suggestion to explain it is that it is an allusion to the word Nazirite (נזיר) in Jg 13:7, this book being one of the "Former Prophets" (§5), and the birth of Samson having a number of parallels with the birth

[8] G. Hartel, *S. Thasci Caecili Cypriani opera omnia.* CSEL III 3, 128.
[9] Schoeps, *Theologie und Geschichte des Judenchristentums,* 9.
[10] George F. Moore in *Beginnings of Christianity.* I 1 (1920), 426–32; W. F. Albright in JBL 65 (1946), 397–401.

of Jesus.[11] Another suggestion refers to Is 11:1 where the "branch" that will grow from the roots of Jesse is in Hebrew the *nezer* (נזר). The expectation of the "branch" is also expressed in Is. 4:2; Jer 23:5; 33:15; and Zec 3:8. Here then in "the prophets" (plural), as Mt says, is a word which could well seem in its sound as well as its significance to embody a witness to "the Nazarene." As applied to the Christians the name Nazarenes, Nazoraeans, is found particularly where there is some connection with Judaism. In Ac 24:5 the heresy or sect of the Nazoraeans (Ναζωραίων) is mentioned by Tertullus, spokesman for the high priest. In *Ta'anith* 27b (GBT III 514; SBT II 7, 145) it is stated that fasting is not practiced on Sunday, "because of the Nazaraeans (נוצרים)," that is, because the Christians would take offence.[12] Tertullian (*Against Marcion* IV 8) says that the Jews designate "us," i.e., the Christians, *Nazaraeos*. Therefore we may accept the representation in the *Dialogue* of Ariston of the Jewish Christian as a Nazaraean as entirely historical, and understand that in particular the Jewish Christians preserved from the earliest church the designation for themselves of Nazarenes, Nazoraeans, or Nazaraeans.

§49. Irenaeus (*Against Heresies* I 26, 2; III 21, 1; V 1, 3) is also plainly referring to Jewish Christians when he speaks of the Ebionites. He says that the Ebionites use the Gospel according to Matthew only, and repudiate the apostle Paul. They practice circumcision, observe the customs enjoined by the law, and face toward Jerusalem when they pray. They do not choose to understand that the Holy Spirit came upon Mary (Lk 1:35) but assert, instead, that Jesus was begotten by Joseph. Such is the critical report of Irenaeus concerning the Ebionites. In the piety of the OT, specially in the Psalms, there is frequent mention of the poor and needy, and of the favor which they have in the sight of God. One Hebrew word which is used to designate such persons is אביון as in Ps 49:2 (3), and אביונים (plural) as in Ps 69:33 (34), the latter passage reading (KJV): "For the Lord heareth the poor." In the passages just cited the LXX (Ps 48:3; 68:34) translates "poor" with πένης; in other passages (e.g., Ps 132:15 = LXX 131:15) it uses the synonym πτωχός. In Is 61:1 where it is written, ". . . the Lord has anointed me to bring good tidings to the poor" (RSV margin), a different Hebrew word is used for the "poor" but the LXX translates εὐαγγελίσασθαι πτωχοῖς. This is the passage

---

[11] Eduard Schweizer, *Neotestamentica*. 1963, 51–55; J. A. Sanders in JBL 84 (1965), 169–72.

[12] R. Travers Herford, *Christianity in Talmud and Midrash*. 1903, 171f.

which, according to Lk 4:18, Jesus chose to read in the synagogue at Nazareth: ". . . he has anointed me to preach good news to the poor" (εὐαγγελίσασθαι πτωχοῖς). Jesus also blessed the poor (μακάριοι οἱ πτωχοί, Lk 6:20; Mt 5:3), and in summary of his ministry could say (Mt 11:5), in part, "the poor have good news preached to them" (πτωχοὶ εὐαγγελίζονται). It was natural, therefore, for the earliest church to think of itself as the community in which the divine promises to "the poor" were fulfilled, and to designate itself by this name. That this was actually done is indicated by several NT passages. Speaking clearly to the Christian community, Jas 2:5 writes: "Listen, my beloved brethren. Has not God chosen those who are poor in the world . . . ?" After the conference in Jerusalem, Paul and Barnabas are to go to the Gentiles, but to "remember the poor" (Gal 2:10), and "the poor" are clearly the non-Gentiles, i.e., the Jewish Christians in Jerusalem. In Rom 15:26 Paul writes of the contribution which Gentile churches are sending "for the poor of the saints (εἰς τοὺς πτωχοὺς τῶν ἁγίων) at Jerusalem." The explanation in the following verse of the reason for the contribution shows that the gift is intended for the entire church at Jerusalem; therefore Paul does not mean "the poor among the saints" (RSV) as if "the poor" were only one part among the entire group; but rather he means "the poor" who are also "the saints," and thus he uses in immediate succession and with a euphemistic turn in his grammar the two commonly used expressions for the earliest Christians.[13] It is evident, therefore, that the Ebionites have simply preserved in their own self-designation the commonly used name of the earliest Jewish Christians, only here it is found not in Greek translation (οἱ πτωχοί), but in transliteration directly from the Hebrew: אביונים = Ἐβιωναῖοι = Ebionites.

§50. In contrast with the entirely understandable origin of the name of the Ebionites just indicated (§49), the supposition of Tertullian (*On Prescription against Heretics* XXXIII 5 and 11; SC 46, 133–34; ANF III 259) and other early Christian writers that the sect derived from a personal founder, Ebion (*Hebion*), is obviously a product of the imagination. After establishing his residence at Caesarea, Origen must have passed through the territory of the Jewish Christians on at least two occasions when he made trips to Bostra in the Arabian desert east of Pella (Eusebius, *Ch. Hist.* VI 33 and 37). Origen (*On the Principles* IV 3, 8 [22] GCS Origenes V 334; ANF IV 371) states correctly that "Ebion" means "poor" in Hebrew

---

[13] Hans Lietzmann, *An die Römer.* HZNT 8 3d ed. 123.

(ἐβίων γὰρ ὁ πτωχὸς παρ' Ἑβραίοις ὀνομάζεται), but when he explains that the word applies to the Ebionites because they are poor in understanding (οἱ πτωχοὶ τῇ διανοίᾳ Ἐβιωναῖοι) it is obviously prejudice against the sect that is animating the interpretation. Elsewhere (*Commentary on John* I 1, 7 GCS Origenes IV 4) he remarks that the one hundred and forty-four thousand in Rev 7:4 could not be Jews according to the flesh who were believers in Christ because there were probably not that many of them altogether, and thereby he gives at least a rough idea of how many Jewish Christians there were in the first half of the third century.

§51. Eusebius (*Ch. Hist.* III 27) follows Origen in the disparaging interpretation of the same name (§50), carrying the idea further by explaining that these people were suitably called Ebionites, "because they held poor and mean opinions concerning Christ" (πτωχῶς καὶ ταπεινῶς τὰ περὶ τοῦ Χριστοῦ δοξάζοντας). "They held him to be a plain and ordinary man who had achieved righteousness merely by the progress of his character and had been born naturally from Mary and her husband" (λιτὸν μὲν γὰρ αὐτὸν καὶ κοινὸν ἡγοῦντο, κατὰ προκοπὴν ἤθους αὐτὸ μόνον ἄνθρωπον δεδικαιωμένον ἐξ ἀνδρός τε κοινωνίας καὶ τῆς Μαρίας γεγεννημένον). There were others, however, of the same name, i.e., other Ebionites, who "did not deny that the Lord was born of a Virgin and the Holy Spirit" (ἐκ παρθένου καὶ ἁγίου πνεύματος μὴ ἀρνούμενοι γεγονέναι τὸν κύριον), although they too agreed in not confessing his pre-existence as God and Logos. As to accepted writings, the Ebionites used only the so-called Gospel according to the Hebrews (εὐαγγελίῳ δὲ μόνῳ τῷ καθ' Ἑβραίους λεγομένῳ χρώμενοι). Eusebius also says (*Ch. Hist.* VI 17) that Symmachus, the OT translator (§10), was an Ebionite and in the name of this heresy attacked the Gospel according to Matthew. Whether the identification of Symmachus as an Ebionite is correct is difficult to say, since Epiphanius (*On Weights and Measures* 16 [55c] ed. Dean 32) later declares that Symmachus was a Samaritan who became a Jewish proselyte.

§52. In his "Medicine Chest" for the cure of heresies, Epiphanius gives an extended discussion (*Pan. haer.* XXIX–XXX GCS 25, 321–82) of both the Nazoraeans (Ναζωραῖοι) and the Ebionites (Ἐβιωναῖοι). He specifically mentions the existence of Ebionites on Cyprus (*Pan. haer.* XXX 18, 1 GCS 25, 357), where he was bishop, and this is not unlikely since Jews, and presumably also Jewish Christians, lived on the island, in spite of occasional suppressions and interdictions, for a long time.[14] Although Epiphanius could thus

---

[14] George Hill, *A History of Cyprus.* 1940, 241–43, 247f.

have had firsthand knowledge of the Ebionites, his writing is, as usual, confused and confusing. So, while he seems to treat the Nazoraeans and the Ebionites as two separate sects, it is difficult to know to what extent they comprised two distinct communities, designated respectively by the two names.[15] There were undoubtedly differences, however, among the Jewish Christians, and we have already noted (§51) the observation of Eusebius that some of the Ebionites denied the virgin birth, but others of the same name did not. Epiphanius (*Pan. haer.* XXX 14, 6 GCS 25, 352) also reflects the varieties in the Ebionite movement in another way when he says that Ebion (§50) showed himself in many forms (ὁ ʼΕβίων διὰ πολλῶν μορφῶν ὑποφαίνει ἑαυτόν). Although Epiphanius separates the Nazoraeans and Ebionites, he describes both of them as dwelling in the same great area of Transjordan, and indeed as widely spread in that region (*Pan. haer.* XXIX 7, 7 GCS 25, 330). The Nazoraeans exist in Beroea in Coele-Syria, in the Decapolis in the district of Pella, and in Kochaba (Κωκάβα or Χωχάβα) in Basanitis. Basanitis extends eastward to the Hauran (§43), Kochaba is not certainly identified. Gen 14:15 puts Hobah north of Damascus (LXX: Χωβά, ἥ ἐστιν ἐν ἀριστερᾷ ["on the left," when facing eastward, means to the north] Δαμασκοῦ), perhaps not correctly,[16] and Eusebius, in the *Onomasticon* (GCS Eusebius III 1, 172), accepts this and says that there is also in the same region a village Χωβά, "in which are Hebrews who believe in Christ, called Ebionites." Interestingly enough, Julius Africanus, quoted by Eusebius (*Ch. Hist.* I 7, 14), says that Kochaba was the residence, along with Nazareth, of the δεσπόσυνοι ("ones belonging to the master"), i.e., the relatives of Jesus according to the flesh (οἱ κατὰ σάρκα συγγενεῖς, I 7, 11). Turning to the Ebionites, Epiphanius puts them in much the same region as the Nazoraeans. He writes (*Pan. haer.* XXX 2, 7–9 GCS 25, 335), not without confusion, as often: ". . . at Pella, a town belonging to the Decapolis mentioned in the Gospel, near Batanea and the district of Basanitis, Ebion got his excuse and opportunity. At first their abode was at Kochaba, a village in the district of Karnaim (Carnaim), and Astaroth, in the region of Basanitis, according to the information we have received. . . . But I am now told from other sources, also, of his connection with the locality of Kochaba and Arabia far and wide."

---

[15] Hort, *Judaistic Christianity*, 199.
[16] J. Simons, *The Geographical and Topographical Texts of the Old Testament.* 1959, 215 §362.

Epiphanius says that the Nazoraeans speak Hebrew and read the OT Scriptures in Hebrew (*Pan. haer.* XXIX 7, 4 GCS 25, 329). They also have the Gospel according to Matthew (τὸ κατὰ Ματθαῖον εὐαγγέλιον), written in Hebrew ('Εβραϊστί) in Hebrew characters, as it was originally (καθὼς ἐξ ἀρχῆς ἐγράφη, 'Εβραϊκοῖς γράμμασιν) (*Pan. haer.* XXIX 9, 4 GCS 25, 332). Discussing the Ebionites, Epiphanius likewise speaks of what is in their so-called Gospel according to Matthew, which is not in all regards fully complete (ἐν τῷ παρ' αὐτοῖς εὐαγγελίῳ κατὰ Ματθαῖον ὀνομαζομένῳ, οὐχ ὅλῳ δὲ πληρεστάτῳ), which they call the Hebrew [Gospel] ('Εβραϊκόν) (*Pan. haer.* XXX 13, 2 GCS 25, 349). From this Gospel, Epiphanius gives various quotations (§§197ff.). He also reports (*Pan. haer.* XXX 16, 6f. GCS 25, 354f.) that the Ebionites have certain books which they call Acts of Apostles, and that one book in particular, the Stairways of James ('Αναβαθμοὶ 'Ιακώβου, probably meaning the apostle [cf. *Pan. haer.* XXX 23, 1 GCS 25, 364], but presumably with allusion to Jacob's stairway or ladder in Gen 28:12 [LXX: κλίμαξ 'Ιακώβ]), expresses their opposition to sacrifices and burnt offerings, and also their strong antagonism to Paul.

§53. Jerome also makes confusing statements about the Ebionites and Nazaraeans. In about A.D. 374 he went into the East Syrian desert and stayed for four or five years (*Letters* 5, 17 NPNFSS VI 7f., 20f.). It was presumably at that time that he visited the Nazaraeans (*Nasaraei*) in the Syrian city of Beroea (Ḥalabu in the Mari tablets, and today Ḥalab [Arabic] or Aleppo[17]), as he relates in *Lives of Illustrious Men* (3 NPNFSS III 362), a work written in Bethlehem in 392. There they described to him, he says, a volume containing the Gospel according to Matthew in the Hebrew language in which the apostle and sometime publican originally published it in Judea. The Hebrew text is also preserved, he says, "until the present day in the library at Caesarea which Pamphilus so diligently gathered." In the immediately preceding section (2) of the *Lives of Illustrious Men* Jerome mentions "the Gospel according to the Hebrews . . . which I have recently translated into Greek and Latin and which also Origen often makes use of." Again in *Against the Pelagians* (III 2 NPNFSS VI 472), a work written in 415, Jerome cites "the Gospel according to the Hebrews, which is written in the Chaldee and Syrian language, but in Hebrew characters, and is used by the Nazaraeans to this day (I mean the Gospel according

[17] Philip K. Hitti, *History of Syria*. 1951, 68, 253.

to the Apostles or, as is generally maintained, the Gospel according to Matthew, a copy of which is in the library at Caesarea)." According to this sequence of passages, Jerome must have thought that the Gospel according to the Hebrews which Origen often used, and the Gospel according to Matthew which the Nazaraeans in Beroea described to him and which was also in the library at Caesarea, were one and the same work. We will see (§156) reason to think, however, that Jerome was not correct in all of these statements. In a letter to Augustine written in 404 Jerome speaks of the Ebionites as well as the Nazaraeans, and seems to use both names for one and the same group. Here he also uses the term Min (מין = "heretic"), plural Minim, by which the Jewish Christians were commonly designated in Rabbinical literature.[18] Jerome writes (*Letter* 112, 13 NPNF I 338; NPNFSS VI 214):

> What am I to say about the Ebionites (*de Hebionitis*) who pretend to be Christians? To this day the sect (*heresis*) exists in all the synagogues of the East among the Jews under the name of Minim (*Minaeorum*), and is condemned by the Pharisees, while its adherents are commonly called Nazaraeans (*Nazaraeos*). They believe in Christ the Son of God, born of the Virgin Mary; and they say that he who suffered under Pontius Pilate and rose again, is the same as the one in whom we believe. But while they desire to be both Jews and Christians, they are neither the one nor the other.

§54. Augustine (*Reply to Faustus the Manichaean* XIX 17 NPNF IV 246) also mentions the name of the Nazaraeans (*Nazaraeorum*). He says, however, that "their number is now very small, but the sect still continues." In scattered groups, as on Cyprus (§52), the Jewish Christian sects may have yet for a while maintained an existence, but in their Syrian homeland, isolated from the main church (§40) and condemned by both Jews and the Christians of the main church (§53), they came to their end. Theodoret, bishop of Cyrus east of Antioch, writing (*History of Heresies* II 11 MPG 83, 397) about 453 in the very midst of their former territory, names the Ebionites among the sects of which not even a small remnant remains (οὐδὲ γὰρ βραχὺ τούτων διέμεινε λείψανον, οὐ Κηρινθιανῶν, οὐκ Ἐβιωναίων. . .).

---

[18] Herford, *Christianity in Talmud and Midrash*, 362, 365, 368, 376–79. The term Ebionite is nowhere used in Rabbinical literature.

# 5 / Egyptian Christianity

*Literature:* Alfred J. Butler, *The Ancient Coptic Churches of Egypt.* 2 vols. 1884 (abbreviated BACC); Michael Jullien, "Le culte chrétien dans les temples de l'antique Égypte," in *Études* 92 (1902), 237–53; *History of the Patriarchs of the Coptic Church of Alexandria,* Arabic text edited, translated, and annotated by B. Evetts. 3 vols. 1904 (Patrologia Orientalis, I, V, X); John R. Knipfing, "The Libelli of the Decian Persecution," in HTR 16 (1923), 345–90; H. Idris Bell, *Jews and Christians in Egypt.* 1924; R. Stothmann, *Die koptische Kirche in der Neuzeit.* 1932; J. M. Creed, "Egypt and the Christian Church," and De Lacy O'Leary, "The Coptic Church and Egyptian Monasticism," in *The Legacy of Egypt,* ed. S. R. K. Glanville. 1942, 300–316, 317–31; L. Th. Lefort, *Les Vies coptes de Saint Pachôme et de ses premiers successeurs* (Bibliothèque du *Muséon,* 16). 1943; A. S. Atiya, Y. 'Abd al-Masih, and O. H. E. Burmester, *History of the Patriarchs of the Egyptian Church, Known as the History of the Holy Church, by Sawīrus ibn al-Mukaffa'.* 1943ff.; H. Idris Bell, "Evidences of Christianity in Egypt During the Roman Period," in HTR 37 (1944), 185–208; William H. Worrell, *A Short Account of the Copts.* 1945; Élisabeth Loukianoff, "La forteresse Romaine du Vieux-Caire," in *Bulletin de l'Institut d'Égypte* 33 (1950–51), 285–93; H. Idris Bell, *Cults and Creeds in Graeco-Roman Egypt.* 1953; Alfred Adam, "Grundbegriffe des Mönchtums in sprachlicher Sicht," in ZKG 65 (1953/1954), 209–39; C. H. Roberts, "Early Christianity in Egypt: Three Notes," in JEA 40 (1954), 92–96; Oswald H. E. Burmester, *The Ancient Coptic Churches of Cairo.* 1955; J. M. Plumley, "Early Christianity in Egypt," in PEQ 89 (1957), 70–81; Victor A. Tcherikover and Alexander Fuks, eds., *Corpus Papyrorum Judaicarum.* 1957ff.; Shenouda Hanna, *Who Are the Copts.* 1958; Maria Cramer, *Das christlich-koptische Ägypten einst und Heute, Eine Orientierung.* 1959 (abbreviated CCKÄ); E. M. Forster, *Alexandria.* 1961; Otto F. A. Meinardus, *Monks and Monasteries of the Egyptian Deserts.* 1961; *Atlas of Christian Sites in Egypt.* 1962; *In the Steps of the Holy Family from Bethlehem to Upper Egypt.* 1963; *Christian Egypt, Ancient and Modern.* 1965; cf. *Bulletin de la Société d'Archéologie Copte* 17 (1963–64), pp. 242–43; 18 (1965–66), pp. 293–94.

§55. Like Jewish Christianity (§§40ff.), Egyptian Christianity is relatively little known. It is also important in relation to the NT Apocrypha, because most of the earliest manuscripts containing apocryphal material have been discovered in Egypt (§§118ff.). Therefore a brief notice of Christianity in Egypt must also be given. Alexander the Great took Egypt in 332 B.C. When his generals divided his empire after his death (323 B.C.), Ptolemy, son of Lagus (Λαγός), obtained Egypt. Assuming the title of king after the death of Alexander II, son of Alexander the Great, Ptolemy founded the dynasty of the Ptolemies or Lagidae which ruled Egypt until, with the death of Cleopatra VI Philopater in 30 B.C., it became part of the Roman Empire. The Arab conquest was in A.D. 641 (§88).

§56. In ancient times the westernmost branch of the Nile entered the Mediterranean Sea near the town of Canopus at the headland of Aboukir. Offshore somewhat to the west was an island which is mentioned already by Homer (*Odyssey* IV 355) under the name of Pharos (Φάρος), derived perhaps from "Pharaoh." On shore on a small eminence was the early settlement of Rhakotis. Behind this was Lake Mareotis, then much larger than now, and connected with the Nile by canal. Since there was also a canal from the Nile near the capital city of Memphis to the Red Sea (§87), this place was in a position of importance comparable to that of Port Said today. Here, around Rhakotis as a nucleus, Alexander ordered the building of the new city of Alexandria which, under the Ptolemies, became the capital of Egypt. Planned by the famous architect, Deinocrates of Rhodes, Alexandria formed a great rectangle between the sea and the lake. Running almost straight through the city from east to west was the wide thoroughfare, Canopic Street, and crossing it from north to south was the Street of the Soma. The Soma at the intersection was the burial place of Alexander. Other streets ran parallel to these major arteries, forming rectangular blocks, and the entire city was divided into five quarters numbered by the first five letters of the Greek alphabet. From the mainland a dike—the Heptastadion, "seven stades long"—connected the city with the Pharos island and created a major harbor on either side. On the island rose the famous lighthouse, built by the architect Sostratus, contemporary of Eratosthenes and Euclid, and probably dedicated in 279 B.C. under Ptolemy II Philadelphus. Here, too, under the same Ptolemy, the translators of the LXX are supposed to have worked (§9). Somewhere in the vicinity of the Soma, probably, was the Mouseion, the great intellectual center of the city, with its famous "Mother" Library (§59).

On the hill at the ancient village of Rhakotis was the Temple of Serapis (§§58f.).

§57. Even before Alexander, Greeks, Jews, Persians, and other foreigners settled in Egypt. After the foundation of Alexandria, that city became a great world metropolis. Around A.D. 100 Dio Chrysostom said in his *Thirty-Second Discourse to the People of Alexandria* (36):

> Not only have you a monopoly of the shipping of the entire Mediterranean by reason of the beauty of your harbors, the magnitude of your fleet, and the abundance and the marketing of the products of every land, but also the outer waters that lie beyond are in your grasp, both the Red Sea and the Indian Ocean. . . . For Alexandria is situated, as it were, at the crossroads of the whole world, of even the most remote nations thereof, as if it were a market serving a single city, a market which brings together into one place all manner of men, displaying them to one another and, as far as possible, making them a kindred people (ὁμοφύλους).

Farther on (40) he spoke of those who might be found mingling in the same audience in the Alexandrian theater:

> . . . not merely Greeks and Italians and people from neighboring Syria, Libya, Cilicia, nor yet Ethiopians and Arabs from more distant regions, but even Bactrians and Scythians and Persians and a few Indians.

§58. In this cosmopolitanism of "kindred people" (§57) there was a strong tendency toward religious unity. The Jews were traditionally monotheists, and doubtless attracted some of the Gentiles by this teaching. The Persians also traditionally disliked idolatry and tended toward monotheism. In paganism itself there was a strong movement toward syncretism. The chief Egyptian deities received Greek names as when, for example, Amun became Zeus, Horus Apollo, and Hathor Aphrodite. Asian deities were introduced and accepted as Egyptian gods as when, for example, Astarte (identified by the Greeks with Aphrodite) was made the daughter of Ptah. So the polytheistic paganism of antiquity became itself in the end almost a monotheism in which all the gods were but particular manifestations of one universal divine reality. Beyond that, religious unity was aimed at in two further ways, by the introduction of the new deity Serapis (§59), and by the development of a dynastic cult (§60).

§59. Osiris, the dying and living god of vegetation, was known in Egypt from early times. So, too, was the Apis bull of Memphis, whose cult presumably goes back to a primitive worship of cattle. Already in the New Kingdom, Osiris and Apis—and other deities, too—were compounded, and texts read, for example: "Osiris-Apis-Atum-Horus in one, the great god." [1] In particular the Apis bull after his death (probably not just a single dead bull, but the whole series from the earliest to the latest) was identified with Osiris and known as Osiris-Apis. In Greek this name became Osorapis or Oserapis, and then Sarapis (Σάραπις) or Serapis (Σέραπις). Serapis was worshiped not only at Memphis but also at Rhakotis where, Tacitus (*Histories* IV 83–84) says, there was an ancient shrine dedicated to Serapis and Isis. When Ptolemy I "was giving the new city of Alexandria walls, temples, and religious rites," he built at the ancient site a new and large temple of Serapis. That Tacitus gives various reports of the introduction of the god from Sinope in Pontus, and from Seleucia in Syria, as well as from Memphis in Egypt, may be understood as attesting the equation of Serapis with various foreign deities including, as Tacitus also explains, Aesculapius because he cures the sick, and Jupiter as the supreme lord of all things. A place of worship of Serapis was called a Serapeum (Σεραπεῖον). The Serapeum at Memphis had long been famous (Strabo, *Geography* XVII 1, 32); now this one at Alexandria became a great institution. When the "Mother" Library at the Mouseion (§56) was burned in the war with Julius Caesar, Cleopatra began a new collection and placed this "Daughter" Library, which became greater than its predecessor, at the Serapeum. The "Daughter" Library, too, was destroyed, perhaps in A.D. 391 when the Patriarch Theophilus led a mob against the Serapeum, and surely finally in the time of the Arab invasion (§55). In the Serapeum, cult meals were held. This invitation, for example, has been preserved on a papyrus of the second century of the Christian era (OP 110): "Chaeremon requests your company to dinner at the table of the lord Sarapis in the Serapeum tomorrow, the fifteenth, at nine o'clock." From this great center and world port, the cult of Serapis spread throughout the whole Greco-Roman world. In the second century of the Christian era, a young man from Philadelphia in the Fayum entered the Roman navy and sailed to Misenum near Naples. Experiencing storm on the way, he wrote back to his father: "I thank the lord Serapis

---

[1] Henri Frankfort, *Kingship and the Gods*. 1948, 146, 196.

(ἐυχαριστῶ τῶ κυρίω Σεράπιδι) that, when I was in peril in the sea, he saved me immediately." [2]

§60. The development of a dynastic cult was natural enough in Egypt where, by long tradition, the ruler of Egypt was a god. Among the Greeks, however, it was more usually only after death that divine honors were paid to an outstanding man. In the case of Ptolemy I, divine honors were accorded him as Soter, the Savior, by some during his lifetime; after death both he and Berenice, his wife, were deified. In the case of Ptolemy II, when his sister and wife, Arsinoe, died (270 B.C.), he deified her as Arsinoe Philadelphus ("the brother-loving") and, after that, both of them were worshiped as θεοί ἀδελφοί ("fraternal gods"). From then on, all the reigning Ptolemies, with their wives, were considered divine. Such (§§58–60) was the "pagan amalgam" [3] in Egypt in the Greco-Roman period.

§61. Unabsorbed in this setting but not unaffected by it were the Jews and the Jewish religion. Jews had lived in Egypt from relatively early times. The well-known Elephantine papyri, of the Persian period and the end of the fifth century, give information concerning a Jewish colony on the island of Elephantine which was probably established about the time Nebuchadrezzar took Jerusalem. These Jews worship Yahweh, who is called Yahu, but three other divine names occur and it is not certain if this means polytheism or if the names stand for aspects of Yahweh. After Alexander, many more Jews came to Egypt, some as refugees from persecution, some as captives in war, some as enlistees in armies, some for commercial and other reasons. The papyri attest their presence in the region of Thebes, in the Fayum, and in the Delta; in other words, throughout Egypt. Philo (*Flaccus* VI 43), in the middle of the first century of the Christian era, says that there were not less than a million Jews resident in Alexandria and Egypt.

§62. At one place there was actually a Jewish temple. As Josephus relates (*War* I 1, 1 §33; VII 10, 2f. §§422ff.; *Ant.* XII 9, 7 §§387f.; XIII 3, 1ff. §§62ff.), Onias, son of the high priest at Jerusalem, fled from the oppression of Antiochus IV Epiphanes and was favorably received by Ptolemy VI Philometor (181–146 B.C.). Ptolemy gave him a tract one hundred and eighty stades from Memphis in the nome of Heliopolis and here, inspired, Josephus says (*War* VII §432; *Ant.* XIII §64), by Is 19:19, Onias built a town on the model of

---

[2] FLP 408.
[3] Bell, *Cults and Creeds in Graeco-Roman Egypt*, 1ff.

Jerusalem and a temple. In one place (*War* I §33) Josephus says
the temple was like that in Jerusalem; in another (*War* VII §427)
he says it was not like that in Jerusalem, but resembled a tower,
yet had an altar on the model of that in the home country. The name
of the site was Leontopolis (Λεόντων πόλις), and it is identified with
Tell el-Yehudiyeh ("the Mound of the Jews"), twenty miles north
of Cairo.[4]

§63. Alexandria was the location of by far the largest single Jewish
community. Here Jews were "joint inhabitants" (συγκατοικισθέντας)
with the other Alexandrians from the earliest times (Josephus, *Ant.*
XIX 5, 2 §281). They lived at first in the fourth (δ') quarter of the
city, but in his time Philo (*Flaccus* VIII 55) seems to say that they
comprised the majority in two quarters and were scattered as well in
the rest of the five (§56). Between the native inhabitants of Alexandria and the Jewish settlers there was, however, according to
Josephus (*War* II 18, 7 §487), from the time of Alexander on,
"incessant strife."

§64. As far as the rulers of Egypt were concerned, the Ptolemies
seem, on the whole, to have treated the Jews relatively well, and
Ptolemy II Philadelphus in particular was always favorably remembered for his encouragement of the work on the LXX (§9). According
to 3 Macc (2:25ff.), however, when Ptolemy IV Philopator defeated
Antiochus III at Raphia (217 B.C.) and then was repulsed in an
attempt to enter the holy of holies at Jerusalem, he returned to
Egypt and attacked the Jews. Josephus (*Against Apion* II 5 §§53ff.)
tells a similar story but attributes the event to Ptolemy IX Euergetes
II (Physkon). Worse trouble was experienced under the Romans.
In A.D. 38 Flaccus, the Roman governor in Alexandria under Gaius
(Caligula), allowed the Greeks to mock Herod Agrippa I (who was
passing through Alexandria) and to put statues of the emperor in
the synagogues and demand divine worship of the emperor from
the Jews, and then evidently encouraged the mobs in the anti-Jewish
pogrom which followed. In A.D. 40 Philo led an embassy to Caligula
to request that emperor worship not be required of the Jews, but an
anti-Semitic demagogue named Apion led a rival embassy, and only
at the beginning of the reign of Claudius was an imperial edict
issued which required that the Jews be not deprived of their rights
and privileges. Of these events accounts are given by Philo in *Against
Flaccus* and *Embassy to Gaius*, and by Josephus in *Against Apion*

---

[4] W. M. Flinders Petrie, *Hyksos and Israelite Cities*. 1906, 1f., 19ff.

and *Ant.* XVIII 8, 1 §§257–59; XIX 5, 2 §§278–85. Again, after the Jews of Caesarea were massacred in A.D. 66, the Jews of Alexandria held a public meeting to arrange an embassy to Nero, but were set upon by the Greeks and then attacked by the Roman legions under the Roman governor, Tiberius Alexander (Josephus, *War* II 18, 1 and 7f. §§457, 490ff.). When Masada fell (A.D. 73), some of the Sicarii (σικάριοι) escaped to Egypt and tried to foment insurrection among the Jews there. The leaders of the Jewish council of elders (γερουσία) repudiated them, but when Lupus, Roman governor of Alexandria, reported the disturbance to the emperor, Vespasian ordered demolition of the Jewish temple at Leontopolis (§62). So Lupus and his successor, Paulinus, closed the temple, the only Jewish temple remaining in existence after the destruction of the one at Jerusalem three years before. "The duration of the temple from its erection to its closure," says Josephus (*War* VII §436) as he concludes his account of the matter, "was three hundred and forty-three years," a figure which would be more probable if it were two hundred and forty-three years (i.e., c. 170 B.C.–A.D. 73). According to Dio (*Roman History* LXVIII 32), Eusebius (*Ch. Hist.* IV 2), and other ancient sources, a great revolt of the Jews broke out in the eighteenth year (A.D. 115) of Trajan (the date given by Eusebius), when another Lupus was Roman governor of all Egypt. The revolt took place in Alexandria and the rest of Egypt, in Cyrene, and in Cyprus, and was expected to break out in Mesopotamia too. It was crushed or averted by Roman action in all these places. To Egypt, Trajan sent his famous general, Marcius Turbo, with infantry, cavalry, and navy, and many Jews were slain. Finally, in A.D. 415, in the climax of hostilities between Jews and Christians in Alexandria, the Patriarch Cyril, acting in apparent defiance of the governor Orestes, seized the synagogues, drove the Jews out of the city, and permitted the crowds to plunder their goods. "Thus the Jews who had inhabited the city from the time of Alexander the Macedonian were expelled from it, stripped of all they possessed, and dispersed some in one direction and some in another." This event, thus described by Socrates (*Ch. Hist.* VII 13), may be taken as the end of Hellenistic Judaism in Alexandria, even as the sacking of the Serapeum by the Patriarch Theophilus in A.D. 391 (§59) marked the official end of Alexandrian paganism.

§65. Here in Egypt the Jews used the Greek language and therefore had need for the Greek translation of the Scriptures which is the Septuagint (§9). Here also they encountered Greek philosophy, and Philo of Alexandria (c. 20 B.C.–A.D. 54) gave his notable, allegorical statement of the ideas and beliefs of the Jewish religion in the categories of Greek thought. Likewise, sects arose, of which the best known is that of the Therapeutae, described by Philo in *On the Contemplative Life* (cf. Eusebius, *Ch. Hist.* II 17). With a center on Lake Mareotis, men and women pursued an ascetic life. They devoted themselves to study, meditation, and prayer, assembled on the sabbath, and also met on each fiftieth day for a special common meal of great simplicity.

§66. Into this setting, chiefly compounded religiously in the Greco-Roman period of Egyptian paganism (§§58ff.) and Egyptian Judaism (§§61ff.), came the missionaries of other religions. As we have already noted (§57), people from as far away as India were a not unfamiliar sight in Alexandria and, in fact, already in the third century B.C. the Indian emperor, Aśoka, sent emissaries of the Buddhist religion to Egypt.[5] When Christianity came it was under no such royal patronage. Indeed exactly how it came in the first place is not too easy to make out. In the account of the Day of Pentecost in Ac 2 residents of "Egypt and the parts of Libya belonging to Cyrene" are listed among those present, "both Jews and proselytes," in Jerusalem. Presumably some were converted, and presumably some of these returned to their homes, which would account for the first introduction of Christianity into Egypt. In Ac 18:25 it is said of the native Alexandrian Jew Apollos, who was an eloquent man and well informed in the Scriptures, that "he had been instructed in the way of the Lord" (οὗτος ἦν κατηχημένος τὴν ὁδὸν τοῦ κυρίου). Here the verb κατηχέω, used in the passive, means "to be taught by word of mouth," and implies the catechumen. While the foregoing is the reading in the chief manuscripts, in the fifth or sixth century Codex Bezae (D) the reading is: ὃς ἦν κατηχημένος ἐν τῇ πατρίδι τὸν λόγον τοῦ κυρίου. The word πατρίς means "fatherland, home, native place," hence this says that "he had been instructed in his own native place in the word of the Lord," and means that Apollos must have received Christian instruction in Alexandria already in the middle of the first century.

§67. Early church tradition is more specific, however, and attributes the official founding of the church in Egypt to Mark, who is well known in the NT. There he is called first by his Jewish name, John, and after that by his "other name," i.e., his adopted Roman name, Mark (Ac 12:12, 25). His mother was Mary, in whose house the Jerusalem Christians gathered (Ac 12:12). He was a companion

[5] FAWR 262.

of Paul and Barnabas on part of the "first missionary journey" (Ac 13:5, 13) and, after that, went with Barnabas, his cousin (Col 4:10), to Cyprus (Ac 15:37, 39). He is mentioned not only in the Pauline letters (Col 4:10; Phm 24; 2 Tim 4:11), but also in 1 Pet 5:13. The last reference reads in part: "She who is at Babylon . . . sends you greetings; and so does my son Mark." In Rev (14:8, etc.) "Babylon" is almost certainly a symbolic name for Rome, and the same reference is presumably most likely in 1 Pet 5:13, as Eusebius (*Ch. Hist.* II 15) already explains. It is true, however, that there was also a Babylon in Egypt. The latter Babylon is mentioned by Josephus (*Ant.* II 15, 1 §315), Diodorus of Sicily (I 46, 3), and Strabo (XVII 807), and is represented by impressive Roman ruins in Old Cairo (§§86f.). If this were the Babylon of 1 Pet 5:13 there would be NT evidence for the connection of Mark with Egypt.

§68. After the NT the earliest references to Mark connect him with Peter and with Rome. Papias of Hierapolis (quoted by Eusebius, *Ch. Hist.* III 39, 15) says that Mark wrote down what he had heard from Peter. Irenaeus (*Against Heresies* III 1, 1 ANF I 414) states that after the deaths of Peter and Paul (probably A.D. 64 or 67) Mark handed down in writing the things which Peter had proclaimed. Clement of Alexandria (quoted by Eusebius, *Ch. Hist.* II 15; VI 14, 6–7) says that Mark wrote on the basis of the preaching of Peter at Rome but without either approval or disapproval from the apostle. Origen (quoted by Eusebius, *Ch. Hist.* VI 25, 5) says that Mark composed the Second Gospel according to the instructions of Peter.

§69. The tradition that Mark went to Egypt is at least earlier than Eusebius, for he introduces such a tradition with the word φασίν, "they say." Having just quoted 1 Pet 5:13, Eusebius goes on (*Ch. Hist.* II 16): "And they say that this Mark was the first that was sent to Egypt, and that he proclaimed the Gospel which he had written, and first established churches in Alexandria." Later Eusebius also writes (*Ch. Hist.* II 24): "When Nero was in the eighth year of his reign, Annianus succeeded Mark the evangelist in the administration of the parish of Alexandria." In the *Chronicle* of Eusebius (in the Latin version made by Jerome) there is this notation (GCS Eusebius VII 179) in the third year of Claudius (A.D. 43): "Mark the evangelist, the interpreter of Peter, proclaims Christ in Egypt and Alexandria." There is also this notation (GCS Eusebius VII 183) in the eighth year of Nero (A.D. 61/62): "After Mark the evangelist, Annianus was ordained as the first bishop of the church of Alexandria, and held office for twenty-two years." The tradition handed on by Eusebius, therefore, stated that Mark preached in

Egypt and Alexandria beginning in 43, founded the church in Alexandria, and in 61/62 appointed Annianus as his successor in care of it.

§70. The tradition that Mark preached in Egypt is also recorded by other writers. Epiphanius (*Pan. haer.* LI 6, 10 GCS 31, 256) says that after Mark wrote the Gospel in Rome, Peter sent him to the land of Egypt. Chrysostom (*Homilies on Mt* I 7 NPNF X 3) says that Mark composed his Gospel in Egypt. Jerome (*Lives of Illustrious Men* 8 NPNFSS III 364) says that Mark had written a short gospel at Rome, which obtained the approval of Peter, and brought this with him when he first came to preach at Alexandria. He also says that Mark died in the eighth year of Nero and was buried at Alexandria, being succeeded by Annianus. At least in the date of Mark's death Jerome was probably drawing a false inference from Eusebius who said indeed that Mark was succeeded by Annianus in that year but not that he died at that time (§69). The *Acts of Barnabas* (Περίοδοι καὶ μαρτύριον τοῦ ἁγίου Βαρνάβα τοῦ ἀποστόλου; *Acta Barnabae*), which purport to be written by Mark but are actually a small apocryphal book probably written in Cyprus not earlier than the fifth century, relate the later travels and martyrdom on Cyprus of Barnabas, and the departure thereafter of Mark for Egypt. "We came down to the seashore," writes the author in the name of Mark, "and found an Egyptian ship and, going on board, landed at Alexandria. And there I remained teaching the word of the Lord to the brethren who came. . . ." (26 ed. Bonnet AAA II 2, 301f.). Writing in the fourteenth century, but drawing upon earlier sources, Nicephorus Callistus gives a somewhat more detailed narrative concerning Mark in his *Church History* (II 43 MPG 145, 875–76). Mark was a nephew (ἀδελφιδοῦς) of Peter. In the reign of Tiberius (d. A.D. 37), he preached in Egypt, Libya, and to the barbarians. Then, at the dictation of Peter (ὑπαγορεύοντος Πέτρου), he wrote down the Gospel according to Mark. After that he did great works in Cyrene and its five cities (Πεντάπολις), built churches and appointed clergy and bishops, and returned to Alexandria. In Alexandria he lived in the place called the "Cattle-Pasture" (ἐν τοῖς Βουκέλου ὀνομαζομένοις) with some of the brethren, and preached Christ freely. On a sudden, however, those who served idols (οἱ τῶν εἰδώλων θεραπευταί) came upon him, bound his feet with ropes, and dragged him off. In prison, the Lord appeared to him and promised him future glory. Cruelly dragged again through the public squares, he commended his soul to God and died.

§71. The tradition thus attested (§§69–70) in outside sources is essentially that which is maintained in the Coptic Church (§§80ff.).

The service used from ancient times in the celebration of the Eucharist in the Church of Alexandria is known as the Liturgy of St. Mark. The chief manuscript in which the ancient liturgy is preserved is Codex Rosannensis, found at Rossano in Calabria, Italy, dating probably from the twelfth century.[6] The liturgy may have been revised by Cyril, who became patriarch of Alexandria in 412, and there appears to be clear reminiscence of its language in the correspondence of Cyril.[7] In 1899 a manuscript was discovered in the Laura Monastery at Mount Athos which contains prayers of Sarapion.[8] He was bishop at Thmuis near Lake Menzaleh in the Delta (cf. Herodotus II 166), and was a friend of Athanasius and the hermit Antony, and the prayers were probably written around 350. Again the language manifests a close correspondence with the Liturgy of St. Mark and, accordingly, the liturgy must be at least this old and is presumably yet older. In the liturgy, just after prayer for those who have fallen asleep in Jesus, and after remembrance of patriarchs, prophets, apostles, and martyrs, and just before the deacon reads the tablets (τὰ δίπτυχα) with the names of the dead, come the words:

> Especially remember those whose memory we this day celebrate, and our holy father Mark, the apostle and evangelist, who has shown us the way of salvation.[9]

§72. In the Coptic Church the work which holds somewhat the place of the *Liber Pontificalis* in the Roman Catholic Church is known as *The History of the Patriarchs of Alexandria*.[10] This was written in Arabic toward the end of the tenth century by Severus ibn al-Muqaffaʻ, Monophysite bishop of al-Ashmunain in Upper Egypt, a contemporary and opponent of the well-known Melchite (§84) patriarch of Alexandria, Eutychius, also known by the Arabic name of Saʻid ibn al-Biṭriq (A.D. 933–40). In his own preface to the work, Severus says (ed. Evetts I 115) that he found histories written in Greek and Coptic, and requested the assistance of qualified Christian

---

[6] F. E. Brightman, *Liturgies Eastern and Western*. 1896, 113–43; ANF VII 551–60; DACL 1:1, 1194.

[7] J. H. Srawley, *The Early History of the Liturgy*. 1949, 48.

[8] John Wordsworth, *Bishop Sarapion's Prayer-Book* (translated from the edition of G. Wobbermin). 1899.

[9] Brightman, *Liturgies Eastern and Western*, 128; ANF VII 556.

[10] Ed. Evetts, 1904; Atiya, ʻAbd al-Masih, and Burmester, 1955ff. See the *Literature* above.

brethren in translating these into the Arabic tongue, then current among the Egyptian people. Another preface says (ed. Evetts I 106) that Severus found these sources in various monasteries and in the form of scattered fragments in the hands of the Christians. A copy of part of one of these sources has probably been found in a tenth-century parchment manuscript in the Bibliothèque Nationale, Paris, containing fragments of a Coptic version of the *Church History* of Eusebius, which seems to be the original of parts of the Arabic translation of Severus.[11] Severus carried the *History* to the fifty-fifth patriarch in succession, Sanuthius I (859–67), and later authors then continued the work in later periods.[12] The *History* begins (I–II ed. Evetts I 135–48) with Mark as the first patriarch, and gives a narrative essentially as follows. In a city of the Pentapolis called Cyrene lived two brothers, Aristobulus and Barnabas. They had great possessions, and knew well the OT. When, in the time of Augustus, they were robbed by Berbers and Ethiopians, they moved to Palestine near Jerusalem. The two brothers had a cousin who was the wife of Simon Peter. The son of Aristobulus was John Mark. He used to visit Peter, and learned the Christian doctrines from him. Mark became one of the seventy disciples, and it was he who carried the water jar into the house of Simon the Cyrenian at the time of the Last Supper. It was also in his house that the disciples were present when Christ, after the resurrection, came to them while the doors were shut. Later Mark went to Rome with Peter and then, in the fifteenth year after the ascension (presumably meaning about 44), Peter sent him to Alexandria. Mark was the first to preach in Egypt, Africa, and Pentapolis. In Alexandria his first convert was a cobbler named Annianus. After two years in Pentapolis, Mark came back to Alexandria and built a church in the place called the Cattle-Pasture, near the sea and near a rock-quarry. Then the idolaters came upon him in the sanctuary, fastened a rope around his throat, and dragged him through the streets. After imprisonment, in which Christ appeared to him, he was dragged again to his death. His body was to be burned in a place called Angelion ($τὸ$ ’$Aγγέλιον$), but was obtained by the brethren and buried in the eastern part of the church. The day of his martyrdom was the last day of "Barmudah" (= Pharmuthi 30 = April 25). After Mark, as the next chapter in

[11] W. E. Crum in *Proceedings of the Society of Biblical Archaeology* 24 (1902), 62–84.
[12] Strothmann, *Die Koptische Kirche in der Neuzeit*, 106.

the *History* (ed. Evetts I 149) continues, Annianus was enthroned as patriarch. Since Annianus served twenty-two years and died in the second year of the reign of Domitian (the second full calendar year of Domitian in the Egyptian calendar was August 29, 83—August 28, 84), his patriarchate began in 62/63.[13] Such is the account in *The History of the Patriarchs of Alexandria*.

§73. It is obvious that many obscurities surround the earliest history of Christianity in Egypt (§§66ff.) and in the adjacent territory of Cyrene and its Pentapolis which figured prominently in the foregoing narratives (§§70, 72). But other evidence in Egypt also shows that Christianity must certainly have been there from an early time. The earliest known papyrus and parchment fragments and manuscripts of the Greek text of the NT come from Egypt.[14] Rylands Papyrus Gk. 457 ($P^{52}$), a tiny fragment of the Fourth Gospel from the first half of the second century, is followed by many other papyri with portions of the NT. The Leland C. Wyman parchment (0220), a fragment of Rom from the latter part of the third century, is followed by the great Codices Vaticanus, Sinaiticus, and Alexandrinus (§§13ff., 33ff.), all of which may have come from Egypt. Apocryphal and Gnostic manuscripts from Egypt, representing Christianity in their own way, will be dealt with later (§§118ff.).

§74. Secular writings also contain incidental allusions to Christianity in Egypt. In the case of private letters which may be from Christian authors the evidence is often uncertain.[15] An unmistakable example, however, is found in the Amherst Papyrus (I 3a) which was written in the third century by an Egyptian Christian at Rome to Christians in the Arsinoite nome.[16] It gives instruction to deliver certain money to "Maximus the Papas" (Μαξίμω τῶ πάπ[α). The Greek word πάπας or πάππας, originally a child's word for father (πατήρ), as in the *Odyssey* (VI 57) where Nausicaa had something to tell her "father dear" (πατρὶ φίλῳ), and begins, "Papa dear" (Πάππα φίλε), becomes in due time, through Latin *papa*, the designation for "bishop" and "pope." In the present letter the reference is undoubtedly to the "pope," i.e., the bishop, Maximus, who was patriarch of

---

[13] For the accepted list of patriarchs of the Coptic Church from 1. Mark I (55–62), and 2. Annianus (62–84), through 112. Cyril V (1874–1927) see Strothmann, *Die Koptische Kirche in der Neuzeit*, 157f.

[14] FLP 417ff.

[15] H. Idris Bell in HTR 37 (1944), 185–208; C. H. Roberts in JEA 40 (1954), 92–96.

[16] Adolf Deissmann, *Licht vom Osten*. 4th ed. 1923, 172–79.

Alexandria A.D. 264–82. Miscellaneous documents also contain occasional references which have something to do with Christianity in Egypt. An example is found in Oxyrhynchus Papyrus 43. The *recto* contains a list of military supplies, and is dated in the eleventh year of Diocletian, the tenth year of Maximian, and the third year of Constantius, this being (in terms of a full calendar year of reign in the Egyptian calendar) the year from August 29, 295 through August 28, 296. The document on the *verso*, probably written not long afterward, is a list of night watchmen at Oxyrhynchus, with the distribution of their posts in relation to the chief streets and public buildings of the city. The public buildings include temples of Sarapis and of Isis. Two streets are named from two churches in the north and the south of the town respectively. The word for "street" ($\dot{\rho}\dot{\upsilon}\mu\eta$) is abbreviated $\rho$, and watchmen are mentioned as in $\dot{\rho}(\dot{\upsilon}\mu\eta)$ $\tau\tilde{\eta}$ $\beta o\rho\iota\nu[\tilde{\eta}]$ $\dot{\epsilon}\varkappa\varkappa\lambda\eta\sigma\dot{\iota}\alpha$, "northern church street" (I 10), and in $\dot{\rho}(\dot{\upsilon}\mu\eta)$ $\tau\tilde{\eta}$ $\nu o\tau\iota\nu\tilde{\eta}$ $\dot{\epsilon}\varkappa\varkappa\lambda\eta\sigma\dot{\iota}\alpha$, "southern church street" (III 19).

§75. Meanwhile Christianity in Egypt had come into full prominence with the flourishing of the famous Catechetical School at Alexandria. Eusebius (*Ch. Hist.* V 10) calls it a "school of sacred learning" ($\delta\iota\delta\alpha\sigma\varkappa\alpha\lambda\epsilon\tilde{\iota}o\nu$ $\tau\tilde{\omega}\nu$ $\dot{\iota}\epsilon\rho\tilde{\omega}\nu$ $\lambda\dot{o}\gamma\omega\nu$) and names Pantaenus ($\Pi\dot{\alpha}\nu$-$\tau\alpha\iota\nu o\varsigma$), a learned man and educated in Stoicism, as in charge of it in the time of Commodus (180–92). Pantaenus also went on a mission to preach in India. There, among persons who knew of Christ, he found the Gospel according to Matthew ($\tau\dot{o}$ $\varkappa\alpha\tau\dot{\alpha}$ $M\alpha\tau\theta\alpha\tilde{\iota}o\nu$ $\epsilon\dot{\upsilon}\alpha\gamma\gamma\dot{\epsilon}\lambda\iota o\nu$) written in Hebrew letters ('$E\beta\rho\alpha\dot{\iota}\omega\nu$ $\gamma\rho\dot{\alpha}\mu\mu\alpha\sigma\iota$).[17] Jerome adds the details (*Lives of Illustrious Men* 36 NPNFSS III 370) that Pantaenus went at the invitation of legates from India (which is not unlikely in view of the world fame of Alexandria and the well-attested presence upon occasion of Indians in the city [§§57, 66]); that he was sent by Demetrius, bishop of Alexandria (189–231); that he brought back with him to Alexandria the Gospel according to Matthew in Hebrew characters; and (in *Letter* 74) that he preached in India to the Brahmans. Associated with Pantaenus or succeeding him in the school was Clement, and after him the head was Origen, both Clement and Origen being famous and well-known Christian theologians many of

---

[17] Eusebius says that this Gospel was left in India by Bartholomew. Otherwise Bartholomew was supposed to have labored in the region of the Bosporus (R. A. Lipsius in SWDCB I 22). But for the relations of Egyptian Christianity to Christianity in India see Albrecht Dihle, "Neues zur Thomas-Tradition," in *Jahrbuch für Antike und Christentum* 6 (1963) 54–70.

whose voluminous Greek writings have come down to us. The school was still continuing in the time of Eusebius, but it disappears from view by the end of the fourth century, and in Alexandria today its site is completely unknown.

§76. At least three of the persecutions well-known in the history of the early church fell heavily upon the church in Egypt. The persecution of Septimius Severus (202) was felt specially in Egypt. In it Clement withdrew from Alexandria and Leonides, the father of Origen, was martyred (Eusebius, *Ch. Hist.* VI 1–3). Under Decius (250), Dionysius, head of the catechetical school and patriarch of Alexandria (247–64), was forcibly carried away by friends to safety in the Libyan desert, while many other Alexandrian and Egyptian Christians perished, and Origen, then at Caesarea, was tortured and died a few years later at Tyre (*Ch. Hist.* VI 39ff.). At this time Decius required of all adults certificates attesting the making of sacrifices to the pagan gods, and many of these, known as *libelli*, have been found in Egypt.[18] In some cases in Egypt, North Africa, and elsewhere, Christians capitulated and this precipitated the problem of how to deal with the lapsed, which Cyprian discusses in his treatise *On the Lapsed* (ANF V 437–47), written in 251. Diocletian was named emperor on September 17, 284; in 286 entrusted the West to his friend, Maximian, while he retained the East; and in 292 associated Galerius with himself in the East. Galerius, in turn, made his nephew Maximinus (305–13) governor of Syria and Egypt with the rank of Caesar and, after the death of Galerius (311), the title of Augustus. Early in 303 Diocletian issued the first of the edicts which launched the terrible persecutions which raged until Galerius in 311, on his deathbed, issued an edict of toleration; and Constantine, in 313, declared freedom of religion and brought peace to the church. In Egypt the calendar year beginning on Thoth 1 (August 29), 284, was taken as the first year of the Era of Diocletian and, in view of the events just referred to, as the first year of the Era of the Martyrs.[19] According to a widespread conception, the day of a saint's martyrdom was his "birthday" and, in a similar way of thought, this beginning of suffering was deemed the birthday of the church. Accordingly, the Coptic Church has continued to reckon years in this era, and to designate a date as in a certain "year of the martyrs" (*anno martyrum*).

[18] Knipfing in HTR 16 (1923), 345–90.
[19] FHBC 131f. §217.

§77. In the time of the persecutions (§76), Christians fled to the deserts and adopted a way of life which became deeply characteristic of Egyptian Christianity. Discussing the monks (the Latin *monachus* is the equivalent of the Greek μοναχός, meaning "solitary," from μόνος, "alone") of Egypt, Jerome (*Letter* 22, A.D. 384) speaks of "anchorites" (from ἀναχωρεῖν, "to withdraw") who dwell in solitude, and of "coenobites" or "cenobites" (from κοινὸς βίος, "a common life") who live in a community (*in commune viventes*). The way of the anchorites was introduced by Paul and made famous by Antony, says Jerome, and could even claim John the Baptist as a first example. While he himself was in the desert of Syria (374 or 375), Jerome wrote a *Life* (NPNFSS VI 299–303) of this Paul, who is known as Paul of Thebes, or Paul the Hermit. As a young man, Paul was highly skilled in both Greek and Egyptian learning. In the Decian persecution (250), he escaped to the desert, found a mountain cave for a dwelling, with palm and spring for food and drink, and settled there permanently. Antony, Jerome says (*Life of Paulus* 7 ff.), was more than twenty years younger and, on one occasion paid a visit, in admiration, to Paul. Sozomen (*Ch. Hist.* I 13) says that Antony developed the monastic way of life "to the summit of exactness and perfection." He came from an illustrious family at Coma on the borders of Upper Egypt, but gave away his possessions and went into solitude, where he subsisted on bread and water, and continued much in fasting and prayer. Athanasius wrote a *Life of Antony* (NPNFSS IV 188–221) between 356 and 362, and said (Prologue) that for monks his life provided "a sufficient pattern of discipline." At the time, according to Athanasius (*Life* 3), the monks (μοναχοί) did not know the distant desert, but conducted their practices near their own villages. Antony, too, at first devoted himself to discipline (ἄσκησις) outside his house. Then (12f.) he found a ruined fort by the Nile and dwelt there in what he called (39) his cell (μοναστήριον) for twenty years. In the persecution under Diocletian and Maximinus (303–11) he went to Alexandria, desirous of martyrdom, and ministered to the confessors in the mines and prisons (46f.). Then (49ff.) he went to a mountain (Mount Kolzim) in the inner desert, near the Red Sea, where he spent the rest of a long life, dying at the age of nearly one hundred and five years (89ff.).

§78. Pachomius also, according to the record of Sozomen (*Ch. Hist.* III 14), began to "practice philosophy" (as the living of this kind of life was often called) alone in a cave, but soon called together some young monks for training. They lived together in many cells, and took their meals at a common refectory in silence. Thus Pachomius became the founder of cenobitic monasticism. His community, Sozomen says, was established at Tabenna in the Theban district, whence the members were called Tabennesians, but they became numerous and were found elsewhere in Egypt. Some half-dozen biographies of Pachomius have been more or less completely preserved in Coptic papyri and parchments dating from the sixth to the twelfth centuries, and also in Greek, Latin, Syriac, and Arabic versions. The earliest may have been written originally within fifteen or twenty years of the death of Pachomius (A.D. 346). Of the various manuscripts the Coptic are considered by Lefort, their editor and translator, the most important. According to these sources,[20] Pachomius was the son of pagan parents and a native of Esneh (Latopolis) in Upper Egypt. Early in the reign of Constantine he was taken into military service and then released. Thereupon he went to the village of Sheneset in the region of Diospolis. Diospolis (or Diospolis Parva as the Greeks called it in distinction from Diospolis Magna or Thebes) was on the left or west bank of the Nile near the end of the great curve which the river makes below Thebes, and had been the ancient Egyptian city of Hou, capital of the seventh nome in Upper Egypt. Three miles farther down the river on the same side, at the point of the present railroad bridge, is the village of Nag Hammadi. Across the Nile on the east side is a large and precipitous desert mountain, Jebel et-Tarif. At the foot of this mountain, five miles before the railroad crosses to Nag Hammadi, the village of Qaṣr es-Sayad marks the site of Sheneset. The ancient Egyptian town at this place, whose name was preserved in Coptic as Sheneset, was known in Greek as Χηνοβόσκιον, meaning Goose-Pasture. Here, in what the *Life* calls a "desert village, scorched by the intensity of the heat," Pachomius settled and here he was baptized. Here also he placed himself under the guidance of a highly regarded anchorite by the name of Palamon, who lived in the desert not far from the village. Today the Deir Anba Palamon or Monastery of Father Palamon stands near Qaṣr es-Sayad and not far from the Nile. Beyond it there is a small stretch of desert (known locally as Kula el-Gaza), with Jebel et-Tarif rising above it, and this is probably the very desert of Palamon.[21]

§79. After seven years with Palamon, Pachomius went on up the Nile about ten miles to an abandoned village on the river bank, named Tabennesi.[22] Here, probably around 322, he established the

---

[20] Lefort, *Les Vies coptes de Saint Pachôme*, 80ff.

[21] L. Th. Lefort in *Le Muséon* 52 (1939), 383–87.

[22] Lefort, *Les Vies coptes de Saint Pachôme*, 91.

monastic community to which Sozomen also referred (§78). The fact that Sozomen says in his account that this was "in the island of Tabenna," can be explained as the error of a copyist who wrote ἐν Ταβέννῃ νήσῳ instead of ἐν Ταβεννήσῳ. In fact the last part of the Greek name, Ταβεννῆσος, is probably not derived from the Greek word νῆσος ("island") at all, but may represent the name of the Egyptian goddess Isis while, according to one theory, the whole name may mean the Palms of Isis. Later the numbers of the monks increased so that Pachomius established another monastery somewhat to the north at an abandoned village called Pbow (*pbou*).[23] This place is to be identified with the present-day Faw (which is actually two villages, Faw el-Bahri or "Faw of the North," and Faw el-Kebli or "Faw of the South"), eight miles up the river from Deir Anba Palamon. The identification is established by the fact that Faw is actually a transliteration in Arabic of the Coptic name, Pbow, without the article (π). Also a basilica was built here in the fifth century in honor of Pachomius, of which the ruins are yet to be seen.[24] Since by this identification Pbow was eight miles up the river from Sheneset-Chenoboskion, and since Pachomius went up about ten miles from Sheneset to Tabennesi, the latter place must have been about two miles upstream from Faw. Thus all the sites were on the right bank and within about ten miles of each other. From Tabennesi and Pbow other monasteries also were established, one at Sheneset-Chenoboskion, where Pachomius had first become a Christian and lived under the guidance of Palamon, and at yet other places.[25] The Rule which Pachomius drew up for the government of the monasteries is extant in fragments of the original Coptic, in excerpts from a shorter Greek version, and in a Latin translation made by Jerome about 404 from the entire Greek text.[26] Jerome also says (*Letter* 127, 5 NPNFSS VI 254f.) that it was from priests of Alexandria and from Athanasius himself that his friend Marcella learned "of the life of the blessed Antony, then still alive, and of the monasteries in the Thebaid founded by Pachomius," and thus was attracted, with Paula and Eustochium, to the monastic life. So the Egyptian influence spread widely.

§80. Earliest Christianity in Egypt evidently made its headway chiefly among the Greek population of Egypt. The early Greek

[23] *Ibid.*, 115f.
[24] Lefort in *Le Muséon* 52 (1939), 387–93.
[25] *Ibid.*, 379f.
[26] A. Boon and L. Th. Lefort, *Pachomiana Latina*. Bibliothèque de la Revue d'Histoire Ecclésiastique, 7. 1932.

manuscripts of the NT (§73), the Greek letters written by Egyptian Christians (§74), and the Greek writings of Clement and Origen (§75), all show the prevailing use of this language among the Egyptian Christians as well as among the Egyptian Jews (§65). Alongside the imported Greek language, the native Egyptian tongue, of course, always persisted also. On the famous Rosetta Stone an inscription of 196 B.C. in honor of Ptolemy V Epiphanes is written in hieroglyphic script or "sacred carvings," the ancient picture writing probably by then understood only by the learned priests; in *demotic* or "common" script, as the Greeks called it, a more cursive writing of the hieroglyphic as it developed in the Persian, Greek, and Roman periods; and in Greek, the widespread use of which we have just emphasized. Finally, as the last stage in the long development of the Egyptian language, the Demotic was transformed into Coptic. In this stage it was still the ancient Egyptian language, and it was written as it sounded, but now in Greek characters. Since the twenty-four letters of the Greek alphabet were insufficient to reproduce all the sounds of the Egyptian language, in due time seven additional characters were adopted from the Demotic, making thirty-one in all. In contrast with the Demotic which provided only consonants, the new Coptic script had vowels too. To this language the Greek adjective, αἰγύπτιος, meaning "Egyptian," was naturally applied. The stem of this word, γυπτ, became *gypt* or *kypt*, and it was thus that the terms "Copt" and "Coptic" arose. The first example presently known of an Egyptian text written in Greek letters, with some additional Demotic characters, is a magical text found among the Oxyrhynchus papyri, datable around A.D. 150.[27]

§81. When Christianity began to make progress among the indigenous population of Egypt it was undoubtedly, except in the case of the more highly educated people, among those who spoke the Egyptian language. Interest in the indigenous Egyptians, and participation on their part in Christianity, is attested from the middle of the third century. When the patriarch Dionysius (247–64) was carried away to safety in the Decian persecution (§76), it was by the action of "country people" (Eusebius, *Ch. Hist.* VI 40, 5), and such peasants were undoubtedly native Egyptians who took the part of their leader against the soldiers who were threatening him. Also the life and work of the anchorite Antony (c. 270) (§77) and the cenobite Pachomius (d. 346) (§§78f.) were undoubtedly very influential

[27] W. E. Crum in JEA 28 (1942), 20–31.

among the masses of the people. In fact Athanasius says that Antony himself "had not learned letters," and he pictures him as speaking to certain monks "in the Egyptian tongue" (*Life of Antony* 16, 73 NPNFSS IV 200, 215). Also we learn that already as a boy of eighteen or twenty (say around 250–55) Antony heard the Gospel read in church (*Life of Antony* 2 NPNFSS IV 196) and, since he did not know Greek, this must have been in the Egyptian language and presumably in Coptic. As for Pachomius (d. 346), we have already noted (§79) that he probably wrote his famous *Rule* in its original form in Coptic. The first native Egyptian Christian of whom it is explicitly stated that he wrote both in Greek and in Coptic (συνεγρά-ψατο δὲ Ἑλληνικῶς τε καὶ Αἰγυπτιακῶς) is Hieracas (Ἱερακᾶς), of whom Epiphanius (*Pan. haer.* LXVII, 1, 1f., 3, 7f. GCS 37, 132f, 136) also relates that he was born (c. 270) in Leontopolis in the nome of Heliopolis in Lower Egypt, that he wrote many books including commentaries on the OT and NT, and lived to be over ninety years of age.[28] At present the oldest known biblical manuscript in Coptic is a copy of the Gospel according to John, which is dated paleographically around 300. This was found in 1923 in a buried jar in the neighborhood of Roman or early Coptic graves near the village of Hamamieh, twenty-seven miles south of Asyut. The manuscript was a papyrus codex, of which forty-three leaves, or fragments thereof, have survived, with the text of Jn extending from 2:12 to 20:20.[29] Another copy of the Gospel according to John, written in Fayumic Coptic (§83), owned by the University of Michigan (P. Mich. Inv. 3521), and preserving text from Jn 6:11 to 15:11, is probably to be dated in the early part of the fourth century.[30]

§82. Of all those who spoke and wrote in Coptic the most famous was Shenoute. On the west side of the Nile midway between Nag Hammadi and Asyut, near the ancient Athribis (now Medinet Atrib, seven miles northeast of Sohag and across the river from Akhmim), the White Monastery (Deir el-Abiad) was founded about 350 by a certain Pgol and taken over about 385 by his nephew, Shenoute.

---

[28] Cf. C. Schmidt in ZNW 24 (1925), 221.

[29] Herbert Thompson, *The Gospel of St. John according to the Earliest Coptic Manuscript*. British School of Archaeology in Egypt Publications, 36. 1924; Viktor Stegemann, *Koptische Paläographie*. Quellen und Studien zur Geschichte und Kultur des Altertums und des Mittelalters, C, 1. 1936, 11–12 and Pl. 1 Fig. 2.

[30] Elinor M. Husselman, *The Gospel of John in Fayumic Coptic*. 1962.

During his long administration Shenoute (d. 466) attracted a wide
following, and his numerous writings, including sermons, letters,
and other works, have ever since been regarded as comprising the
most classical Coptic literature.[31]

§83. The Coptic language existed in a number of dialects. Research
in the relatively large number of early Coptic manuscripts now
available, indicates at least the following[32]: (1) Sahidic was the main
dialect. It may have been the official language of the better educated
indigenous Egyptians even before the coming of Christianity; it
probably originated in the Delta and was the official dialect of Alexandria during most of the Coptic period, and from there it spread
into the Fayum and Upper Egypt. It was the dialect used by Shenoute
(§82). (2) Akhmimic (A) is represented in texts found near Akhmim,
but also in other texts, and may have originated at Thebes and
spread northward from there. (3) Subakhmimic (A²) designates a
dialect represented in the Gospel according to John found near Asyut
(§81), and in some of the Gnostic manuscripts found at Chenoboskion
(§§125f.). (4) Middle Egyptian is the dialect of a number of fragmentary manuscripts, including a parchment with Rom 4:15-24 which
Grenfell and Hunt found at Oxyrhynchus.[33] (5) Fayumic designates
the dialect of numerous texts found in the Fayum. It is represented
in the Coptic annotations in the margin of the Chester Beatty Papyrus of Isaiah, a Greek codex of the first half of the third century,[34]
and in the early fourth-century Michigan papyrus of the Fourth
Gospel (§81). (6) Bohairic may have been the spoken dialect of
Memphis, and become the principal dialect in the Delta, even as
Sahidic became the principal dialect of the whole of Upper Egypt.

§84. In 431 Shenoute (§82) accompanied the Patriarch Cyril I
(412-44) to the Council of Ephesus. There, as is well known in the
history of dogma, Cyril was supported in his doctrine, according to
which in Jesus Christ the human nature was virtually absorbed into
the divine, and it was proper to speak quite literally of Mary as the
Mother of God (Θεοτόκος); and Nestorius, monk of Antioch and
patriarch of Constantinople, was condemned for his doctrine that

---

[31] Johannes Leipoldt, *Schenute von Atripe und die Entstehung des national-
ägyptischen Christentums*. TU 25, 1. 1903; and in *Geschichte der christlichen
Litteraturen des Orients*. 2d ed. 1909, 147-52.
[32] Paul E. Kahle, *Bala'izah*. 1954, I, 193-278.
[33] W. E. Crum in JEA 13 (1927), 21, 25-26.
[34] Frederic G. Kenyon, *The Chester Beatty Biblical Papyri*. Fasciculus VI,
Text 1937, Plates 1958.

Christ had both a divine and a human nature.[35] Again in 451 Shenoute was invited by the Patriarch Dioscurus (444–54) to take part in the Council of Chalcedon, but was prevented by illness and died some years later. At Chalcedon, as is also well known, Dioscurus was deposed and a creed was adopted in which, although Mary was still the Mother of God (Theotokos), Jesus Christ was one Person in whom a completely divine and a completely human nature were inseparably but also unconfusedly united, the property of each of the two natures being fully preserved.[36] Most of the churches in Egypt and, in the long run, in Syria and Nubia and Ethiopia, refused to accept the decision of Chalcedon and, in the spirit of Cyril, maintained that Jesus Christ had only a divine, and not a divine-human nature. This is the Monophysite or "one nature" doctrine and, on the basis of it, these churches separated themselves from Rome and Constantinople. Probably the most influential later leader of the Monophysite movement was Jacob Baradai, who was born near Edessa, wandered for nearly forty years from the Euphrates to Egypt, and died (578) in the monastery of Cassianus on the border of Egypt. In these lands over which Islam was soon to sweep, however, some of the churches adhered to the "orthodox" faith of Chalcedon and maintained communion with Constantinople. From their adherence to emperor and pope they were thought of as belonging to the "king's church" and, from the word for "king" (*melek*), were called Melchites or Malkites. It was most distinctively in the fifth century, then, that a national Christian Church emerged in Egypt, characterized by Monophysite doctrine and Coptic speech. Although many persecutions were yet to be endured, and although Coptic was to give way before Arabic which was well established as the official language of Egypt by the tenth or eleventh century, this church has endured until today and in its services the liturgical language is still the Coptic.

§85. Few tangible evidences survive of the meeting places of the Egyptian Christians in the first three centuries of the Christian era. The situation was of course changed when in 313 Constantine issued his edict of toleration for Christianity, and when in 392 Theodosius I (379–95) forbade the practice of pagan worship. The Burial Church of St. Menas, excavated by Carl M. Kaufmann in the Mareotic Desert southwest of Alexandria, provides a remarkable example of

---

[35] Adolph Harnack, *History of Dogma*, tr. from 3d German edition c. 1900, reprinted 1961. IV, 165ff.

[36] *Ibid.*, 215ff.

what was done. Building work over the grave of the martyr was perhaps begun under Constantine; under Theodosius a large basilica was erected; under Arcadius (395–408) a yet larger basilica was added.[37] With the closing of the Egyptian temples to pagan worship, in accordance with the edict of Theodosius, the Christians were also able in many cases to move into them as, for example, at Dendera, Edfu, Luxor, and elsewhere. They often selected the vestibule or the hypostyle hall, between the court and the sanctuary, as the place for the church, or they built adjacent to the temple. Remaining evidences of their presence are columns, crosses, paintings, inscriptions, and graffiti.[38] In the temples, as elsewhere in Egypt, they of course saw the *ankh*, the hieroglyphic sign for "life," and sooner or later this passed into a form of the Christian cross, a tau cross with a loop at the top (♀), known as the *crux ansata*, the cross furnished with a handle.[39] Socrates (*Ch. Hist.* IV 17) and Sozomen (*Ch. Hist.* VII 15) relate that when, in 391, with the permission of Theodosius, the patriarch Theophilus destroyed the Serapeum in Alexandria (§59), hieroglyphic characters were found which had the form of crosses, and pagan converts to Christianity explained that they signified "life to come" (ζωὴν ἐπερχομένην), a meaning the adaptability of which to the Christian faith is evident.

§86. Of Coptic church buildings existing today, some of the oldest are found in Old Cairo. Opposite the pyramids, on the east bank of the Nile, between Memphis and Heliopolis (On), was a place where Horus and Seth were said to have contended. Babylonians or Persians settled here, and when the Romans conquered Egypt in 30 B.C. they made it a military center. In 25/24 B.C. the geographer Strabo sailed up the Nile with the Roman prefect of Egypt, Aelius Gallus. Strabo mentions Heliopolis, then writes (*Geography* XVII 1, 30):

> And, having sailed farther up the river, one comes to Babylon, a stronghold, where some Babylonians had withdrawn in revolt and then successfully negotiated for permission from the kings to build a settlement; but now it is an encampment of one of the three legions that guard Egypt.

The role of the Babylonians is elucidated by Diodorus (I 56, 3) in this way:

---

[37] FLP 546f.
[38] Jullien in *Études* 92 (1902), 237–53.
[39] DACL 3:2, 3120–23.

And it is said that the captives brought from Babylonia revolted from the king, being unable to endure the hardships entailed by his works; and they, seizing a strong position on the banks of the river, maintained a warfare against the Egyptians and ravaged the neighboring territory, but finally, on being granted an amnesty, they established a colony on the spot, which they also named Babylon after their native land.

Josephus, however, speaks (*Ant.* II 15, 1 §315) of "the site of Babylon, founded by Cambyses when he subjugated Egypt" (i.e., in 525 B.C.). Another explanation for the name of Babylon has also been proposed. In this vicinity there is an island in the Nile, now called Roda. With reference to nearby Heliopolis (On), it was known as Per-hapi-n-On, "House of the Nile of On," and this, it is suggested, sounded to the Greeks like "Babylon."[40]

§87. In whatever way the name originated, Strabo is witness (§86) that there was a Roman encampment in his time at "Babylon" on the Nile. As he describes the place Strabo says that a ridge extended from the encampment to the Nile, and that water was conducted up from the Nile by wheels and screws operated by one hundred and fifty prisoners. This fits well with a ridge which runs from a detached rock of the Moqattam range toward the Nile. Two hundred yards to the north (and opposite the St. Georges Station on the railway which runs up the Nile to Helwan) is the area now called Qaṣr esh-Shama, the Castle of the Candle. Here a Roman wall, still traceable in much of its extent, surrounded a roughly quadrilateral area nearly one thousand feet in length and from three hundred to six hundred feet in width. The wall was built of successive layers of brick and stone, five courses of stone alternating with three courses of brick. The wall still exhibits a thickness of eight feet at the base, and may have reached a height of eighty feet. On the west side, and at that time probably on the edge of the river, were two huge round towers which are still relatively well preserved. On the south side, which was probably also on the water, were three rounded bastions and a gateway. On the east and north sides at least portions of yet more of the rounded bastions have been identified.[41] In the study of these ruins Grégoire Loukianoff found the name of Apollodorus.[42] This

---

[40] C. H. Becker in EI I 550; Karl Baedeker, *Ägypten.* 8th ed. 1928, 42.
[41] BACC I, 155–81.
[42] É. Loukianoff in *Bulletin de l'Institut d'Égypte* 33 (1950–51), 287.

was the famous architect from Damascus who is mentioned by Procopius (*Buildings* IV 6, 13) as the "master-builder" of Trajan. In Rome he built the Forum of Trajan and Trajan's Column. Trajan came to Egypt in 98 and it was presumably at this time that the same architect built for him this strong fortress near the site of the original Roman encampment. Deriving information from the geographer Artemidorus of Ephesus (104 B.C.), Strabo mentions (*Geography* XVII 1, 25) the ancient Egyptian canal which ran through the Bitter Lakes to the Red Sea and the Arabian Gulf, having been cut by Sesostris, presumably Senusert I of the Twelfth Dynasty, and worked on also by Necho and Darius I (cf. Aristotle, *Meteorologica* I 14, 352b; Diodorus I 33; Herodotus II 158). Since the geographer, Claudius Ptolemy (A.D. 100–178), mentions (*Geography* IV 5, ed. Edward L. Stevenson, 1932, 103) "the stream Traianus" as on the border of Arabia and Aphroditopolis, and as flowing through "the city Babylon" (καὶ ἐν μεθορίοις 'Αραβίας καὶ 'Αφροδιτοπόλεως δὶ ἧς καὶ Βαβυλῶνος πόλεως ὁ Τραϊάνος ποταμὸς ῥεῖ), and on his "Third Map of Africa" shows the *Traianus fluvius* as coming into the Nile at Babylon, it is probable that Trajan also worked on this canal and that it opened into the Nile at the point guarded by the same fortress of Babylon.

§88. That Babylon became the center of an important Christian community is attested by the presence at the Second Council of Ephesus in 449 of Cyrus, bishop of Babylon (Κύρος ἐπίσκοπος Βαβυλῶνος).[43] When the Arab conqueror, 'Amr ibn-al-'Asi, took Egypt in 641, Babylon was defended through a long siege by the Jacobite Copts and the Melchite Greeks together, but the former finally betrayed the latter and the fortress was taken. The fortress and its surroundings were left as a Christian city, however, while the place to the north where the conqueror had pitched his tent became the new capital of the country, known as al-Fustat (from φόσσατον, *fossatum*, "surrounded by trenches," "camp"). Here 'Amr built a mosque, and ibn-Tulun built a new one in 879. As capital of Egypt the city grew rapidly. Like the country the city also was called Miṣr, and reference was made to both Miṣr al-Fustat and Miṣr al-Bablun. Later the Fatimid conqueror Jawhar laid out a new quarter yet farther north, and built a new mosque, al-Azhar (972). After the planet Mars, known as Qahir, "the triumphant," this city was called al-Qahirah, from which comes the name Cairo.[44]

---

[43] H. Munier, *Recueil des listes épiscopales de l'Église Copte.* 1943, 19.
[44] FAWR 509f., 524f.

§89. Old Cairo is still an important Coptic center, and Qaṣr esh-Shama (§87) is inhabited largely by Copts. Approximately in the center of the ancient fortress area is the Coptic church called Abu Sarga. At this place, twenty feet below the modern ground level of Old Cairo, and often inundated, is a small crypt. The room, twenty feet long and fifteen feet wide, is divided by slender columns into nave and north and south side aisles, and the roof is vaulted. Entrance is by steps at either end of the west wall. There is a semicircular recess in each of the other three walls, that in the east wall providing an apse and place for an altar. In front thereof, a circular marble slab in the nave floor marks the supposed location of an ancient well. At the end of the south aisle there is a baptistery in the form of a cylindrical stone vessel into which, according to Coptic ritual, the child to be baptized is dipped three times.[45] Traditionally this is where the Holy Family rested when they came to Egypt (Mt 2:14f.), and this is probably one of the oldest sacred sites in the history of Christianity in Egypt. As for the present form of the crypt, it is believed by some to date from the sixth century. As for the main church above, nearly ninety feet long and fifty feet wide, the nave floor is itself a dozen feet below the average ground level of Old Cairo, and the main altar is directly over the marble slab in the floor of the crypt below. The church bears the name of St. Sergius (probably a soldier-martyr under Maximian in 309), and is mentioned for the first time toward the end of the seventh century in connection with the choice of Isaac (689–92) as Coptic patriarch. In spite of various alterations in the course of time, the church is essentially basilical in plan and typical of many Coptic churches. At the western end a narthex gives access to nave and north and south side aisles, which are marked off by marble columns evidently taken from ancient Roman buildings. At the eastern end is the choir where the priests officiate and steps descend to the crypt; and the sanctuary (*heikal*) with the main altar, and two side chapels. These areas are shut off by high, carved, adorned wooden screens.[46]

§90. The name of the church called al-Muallaqa means the "Hanging" Church. It is suspended over the Roman gateway between two of the Roman bastions on the south side of Qaṣr esh-Shama (§87). A sycamore panel carved with a representation of the entry of Jesus into Jerusalem on Palm Sunday, found over a doorway of the church and placed in the Coptic Museum (§91) (No. 1885),

[45] *Bulletin de la Société d'Archéologie Copte* 11 (1945, published in 1947), 75.
[46] BACC I, 181–205; CCKÄ 18–20.

bears a date in Greek characters equivalent to A.D. 349 and evidently indicates an origin in the fourth century for this church.[47] The church is mentioned in the time of the Patriarch Joseph (831–49), when it was destroyed in the great persecution which took place under the Umayyads. It was rebuilt in the tenth century, and in the eleventh century, when the Patriarch Christodulos (1047–78) transferred the patriarchate from Alexandria to Cairo, it was for a time the patriarchal church. Through the years many restorations have been made, and the present façade is quite modern.[48] Another church in the area was dedicated to St. Michael. This, according to ancient references, was the last church held by the Melchites, about 725, when for a time all the other Egyptian churches passed into the hands of the Jacobites; and in the next century this church was sold by the Patriarch Michael III (867–95) to the Jews.[49] In form it is a small Coptic basilica, standing opposite one of the bastions in the east wall of Qasr esh-Shama, and it is still in use as a Jewish synagogue. There is also still a Melchite church in the Qasr esh-Shama. This is the Greek Orthodox Church of St. George, which is under the rule of the Orthodox patriarch of Alexandria. It is built directly on top of the northernmost of the two great Roman towers on the west side of the enclosure.[50]

§91. Within Qasr esh-Shama, between the southern Roman tower and the al-Muallaqa church, is the Coptic Museum. It was founded in 1908 by Markus Simaika Pascha, under the Coptic patriarch Cyril V (1874–1927), and was directed from 1949 to 1965 by Pahor Labib. As the official repository for Christian antiquities in Egypt, it is the place where certain of the manuscripts we will describe later (§§124ff.) are kept.

[47] Hanna, *Who Are the Copts*, 99.
[48] BACC I, 206–35; CCKÄ 20–23.
[49] BACC I, 169f.
[50] BACC I, 163.

# 6 / Gnosticism

*Literature:* Wilhelm Bousset, *Hauptprobleme der Gnosis.* 1907; Ernesto Buonaiuti, *Gnostic Fragments.* 1924; Eugène de Faye, *Gnostiques et gnosticisme, étude critique des documents du gnosticisme chrétien aux IIe et IIIe siècles.* 2d ed. 1925; R. Reitzenstein, *Die hellenistischen Mysterienreligionen.* 3d ed. 1927; Werner Foerster, *Von Valentin zu Herakleon, Untersuchungen über die Quellen und die Entwicklung der valentinianischen Gnosis.* 1928; F. C. Burkitt, *Church and Gnosis.* 1932; Walther Völker, ed., *Quellen zur Geschichte der christlichen Gnosis.* 1932; Gilles Quispel, *Gnosis als Weltreligion.* 1951; Rudolf Bultmann, *Gnosis.* Bible Key Words from Gerhard Kittel's *Theologisches Wörterbuch zum Neuen Testament,* V. 1952; Hans Leisegang, *Die Gnosis.* 4th ed. 1955; Hans-Joachim Schoeps, *Urgemeinde, Judenchristentum, Gnosis.* 1956; Hans Jonas, *The Gnostic Religion.* 1958, 2d ed. 1963; R. McL. Wilson, *The Gnostic Problem.* 1958; Robert M. Grant, *Gnosticism and Early Christianity.* 1959; Jacques Dupont, *Gnosis, La connaissance religieuse dans les épitres de Saint Paul.* 1960; Robert M. Grant, *Gnosticism, A Source Book of Heretical Writings from the Early Christian Period.* 1961 (abbreviated GGSB).

§92. It is also necessary to give a brief explanation concerning Gnosticism, because some of the manuscripts with which we shall have to deal are commonly recognized as Gnostic in character. The Greek verb γινώσκω or γιγνώσκω means "to know," or "to come to know," and the related noun, γνῶσις, *gnosis,* means "knowledge." The word may refer to quite ordinary, everyday knowledge as when Josephus (*Ant.* VIII 6, 5 §171), for example, speaks of "all the things . . . that come to our knowledge through hearsay" (πάντα . . . τὰ δι' ἀκοῆς εἰς γνῶσιν ἐρχόμενα). It may refer to the knowledge of God and, in particular, to that supernatural, mystical kind of knowledge which was offered in the mystery religions of the Hellenistic world. An example of these religions is provided by the cult of Osiris (§59), which spread from Egypt into Greece at least as early as the fourth century B.C., and was widespread throughout the

Roman Empire. Herodotus (II 170f.) gives a brief description of the cult as it was practiced at Saïs, the supposed burial place of Osiris in the Delta in Egypt. He says that the Egyptians called the ceremonies "the mysteries" (τὰ μυστήρια), and himself refrains from giving extended details or even naming the god, out of respect for the secret nature of what was done. He writes:

> There is also at Saïs the burial-place of him whose name I deem it forbidden to utter in speaking of such a matter. . . . Great stone obelisks stand in the precinct; and there is a lake hard by. . . . On this lake they enact by night the story of the god's sufferings, a rite which the Egyptians call the Mysteries. I could speak more exactly of these matters, for I know the truth, but I will hold my peace.

§93. Although he elsewhere (*Moralia* 417C) professed the intention to be as reticent as Herodotus (§92) about the Mysteries, Plutarch (A.D. c. 46–c. 120) wrote an entire treatise, addressed to Clea, a priestess at Delphi, on the cult of Isis and Osiris. In a paragraph near the beginning (*Moralia* 351–52 = *Isis and Osiris* 2), he gives a plain statement of the way in which the search for truth was understood and carried on in the mystery religions; makes an interesting if incorrect attempt to connect the name of the Egyptian goddess Isis with the Greek word οἶδα, "know"; connects, probably correctly, the name of Typhon (as the Greeks called Seth, the enemy of Osiris) with τύφω, "raise a smoke, puff up," and uses this etymology to suggest the conceited character of this god; speaks of knowledge (*gnosis*) of "the Lord of All" (the title designates Osiris, at whose birth, according to a later passage [355], a voice cried, "The Lord of All advances to the light") as the aim of participation in the mystery; and sees the very name of the shrine of Isis (taking Iseion as if derived from οἶδα, "know," and ὄν, "being") as implying a promise of the comprehension of reality. The entire paragraph conveys very well the idea of *gnosis* as understood in the Mysteries, and reads as follows:

> Therefore the effort to arrive at the Truth, and especially the truth about the gods, is a longing for the divine. For the search for truth requires for its study and investigation the consideration of sacred subjects, and it is a work more hallowed than any form of holy living or temple service; and, not least of all, it is well-pleasing to that goddess whom you worship, a goddess exceptionally wise and a lover of wisdom (σοφὴν καὶ φιλόσοφον), to whom, as her name at least seems to indicate, knowledge and understanding are in the highest degree appropriate. For Isis is

a Greek word, and so also is Typhon, her enemy, who is conceited, as his name implies, because of his ignorance and self-deception. He tears to pieces and scatters to the winds the sacred writings, which the goddess collects and puts together and gives into the keeping of those that are initiated into the holy rites, since this consecration, by a strict regimen and by abstinence from many kinds of food and from the lusts of the flesh, curtails licentiousness and the love of pleasure and induces a habit of patient submission to the stern and rigorous services in shrines, the end and aim of which is the knowledge of him who is the First, the Lord of All, the Ideal One (ὧν τέλος ἐστὶν ἡ τοῦ πρώτου καὶ κυρίου καὶ νοητοῦ γνῶσις). Him does the goddess urge us to seek, since he is near her and with her and in close communion. The name of her shrine also clearly promises knowledge and comprehension of reality (γνῶσιν καὶ εἴδησιν τοῦ ὄντος); for it is named Iseion, to indicate that we shall comprehend reality if in a reasonable and devout frame of mind we pass within the portals of her shrines.

§94. In the OT דֵּעָה, דַּעַת, and cognate words mean "knowledge," and are regularly translated in the LXX by γνῶσις or ἐπίγνωσις (the ἐπί in the latter form suggesting mental direction toward and, therefore, discernment and thorough knowledge). Knowledge (דֵּעָה) is an attribute of God in 1 S 2:3, "the Lord is a God of knowledge" (LXX, 1 S 2:3, θεὸς γνώσεων κύριος); and it is he who bestows it (דַּעַת) upon men, as in Ps 94:10, "He who teaches men knowledge" (LXX, Ps 93:10, ὁ διδάσκων ἄνθρωπον γνῶσιν). As for knowledge of God on the part of man, it is equivalent to experience of the reality of God, and only the righteous man can be said to know God. Thus Hos 4:6 finds the people destroyed for lack of knowledge (דַּעַת = ἐπίγνωσις), and Hos 6:6 sets the desired knowledge of God in parallel with steadfast love; while Pr 2:5, using the same words, puts the knowledge of God in parallelism with the fear of the Lord. In such a framework of thought, even the tree of the knowledge of good and evil (τὸ ξύλον τοῦ γινώσκειν καλὸν καὶ πονηρόν) in Gen 2:17 is hardly a magical source of theoretical knowledge, but rather simply a forbidden object where the transgression of the divine command will result in the knowledge (דַּעַת) through experience of what wrong is like.[1]

§95. The essential NT conception of knowledge is in line with that of the OT. Here, too, knowledge is an attribute of God, as in Rom

---

[1] O. A. Piper in IDB III 43.

11:33 where Paul speaks wonderingly of "the depth of the . . . knowledge of God" (ὦ βάθος . . . γνώσεως θεοῦ). And here, too, knowledge of God on the part of man, now made possible in a new way through Jesus Christ, is an all-important end, but clearly involves obedience and not just the acquisition of theoretical information. For example, in 2 Cor 10:5, Paul writes of casting down every "height" (ὕψωμα) that is raised up against the knowledge of God (κατὰ τῆς γνώσεως τοῦ θεοῦ), and speaks in the same sentence of bringing captive every thought into obedience to Christ. Likewise in Col 1:9f., being filled with "the knowledge of his will" (τὴν ἐπίγνωσιν τοῦ θελήματος αὐτοῦ), is put in parallelism with leading a life worthy of the Lord. But in 1 Cor 13:2, Paul mentions knowledge (γνῶσιν) along with the mysteries (τὰ μυστήρια); and in 1 Cor 14:6 lists knowledge between revelation (ἀποκάλυψις) and prophecy (προφητεία). In these two passages, therefore, gnosis seems to have something of the connotation of the supernatural and the mystical, as in the mystery religions (§§92f.). Again, in 1 Tim 6:20, there is warning against the "contradictions of what is falsely called knowledge" (ἀντιθέσεις τῆς ψευδωνύμου γνώσεως). These "antitheses of pseudonymous gnosis" (as we may literally translate the Greek) are evidently the tenets of a movement for "knowledge" which has become a cult in and of itself. To religion of this sort the name Gnosticism may properly be given.

§96. The search for gnosis could be conducted solely within paganism, as the example of the cult of Isis and Osiris (§93) has already shown. Within paganism there was, of course, widespread syncretism (§58), and in his account of Isis and Osiris Plutarch explains that Osiris was identified with Dionysus (356B), Seth with Typhon (367D), and Isis with Athena (376A). As a phenomenon of pagan syncretism, Gnosticism could combine the most varied elements. After a visit to the Greek colony of Borysthenes in Pontus, Dio Chrysostom returned to his native city of Prusa in Bithynia and delivered, probably in A.D. 101, an address (his Thirty-sixth or Borysthenitic Discourse). In it he reported "a myth (μῦθος) which arouses admiration as sung in secret rites by the Magi." The myth, which Dio Chrysostom gives in detail (XXXVI 39–61), had to do with "the perfect chariot of Zeus," and had been learned by the Magi, they said, from Zoroaster. According to the myth, the universe is constantly driven along a single path as if by a very skillful and powerful charioteer. The charioteer drives four horses. The outermost horse is flame-colored and marked with the sun and moon (Helios and Selene). The next horse is black, but bright when in the sunshine. The next is sacred to Poseidon. The innermost horse is also harnessed to the chariot, but remains always in its place, immovable. The four horses normally run their course in harmony but, upon one occasion, the outermost caused the whole universe to be burned with fire. On another occasion, the horse sacred to Poseidon caused the world to be deluged with a mighty flood. Again, the four horses merge into one, as if they were wax figures molded together, and therewith the existent universe is transformed and made new, appearing once again as a thing of brilliant beauty and inconceivable loveliness. Since the Magi learned their myth from Zoroaster it must be of Persian origin. The divine forces, however, bear the names of Greek gods, and the doctrine is like that of the Stoics, who taught that the universe consists of four concentric spheres, earth, water, air, and fiery ether where the stars have their place. In the myth, the innermost immovable horse is the earth; the one sacred to Poseidon is the water; the one bright in the sunlight but dark in the shadow is the air; and the outermost fiery one, marked with sun and moon, is the ether. The Stoics also taught that the universe is destroyed in periodic conflagrations, and made new again afterward; and there were flood stories among the Greeks, connected with the names of Ogygos and Deucalion. The myth communicated by the Magi in secret rites was, therefore, an amalgam of pagan ideas, Persian, Greek, and Stoic.

§97. The Gnostic synthesis could include Jewish elements along with pagan. A Greek magical papyrus in Leiden, written about A.D. 350, is entitled the "Eighth Book of Moses." It provides crude formulas for the practice of magic, but also contains a cult prayer. The prayer is addressed to the most high God, who has created all, but is himself self-created, who sees all things but is himself unseen (τὸν πάντα κτίσαντα, σὲ τὸν αὐτογέννητον, τὸν πάντα ὁρῶντα καὶ μὴ ὁρώ-μενον). "Thou art the invisible Aeon of the Aeons" (ἀόρατος εἶ Αἰὼν Αἰῶνος), says the suppliant, and proceeds to call upon God with magical words which he says are Hieroglyphic, Hebrew, and Egyptian. In a second version of the prayer, to be used after certain additional preparations have been made, the suppliant praises God as once was done by Helios and by the angel in charge of punishments, the latter being Osiris in his role as judge of the dead. In the description at this point one sees the sun-boat sailing across the sky, while the companions of Helios who are in the boat with him, the ninefold deity, the falcon, and the dog-headed ape, also join in the praise. The last one says to God, "Thou art the number of the year, Abrasax" (Ἀβρασάξ, $a = 1 + \beta = 2 + \rho = 100 + a = 1 + \sigma = 200 + a = 1 + \xi = 60 = 365$). Then a cosmological myth unfolds. The most high

God laughed seven times, and seven gods came into being who encompass the cosmos (οἵτινες τὸν κόσμον περιέχουσιν). These were Light (φῶς); Water (ὕδωρ), which was divided into the three oceans above, upon, and under the earth; Mind (νοῦς), which was named Hermes; Genna (γέννα), or propagation; Fate (μοῖρα); Time (καιρός); and Soul (ψυχή). Mind disputed with Fate for supremacy, but God gave to Fate the rule of the cosmos. When Soul appeared, God whistled, and the earth gave birth to the Pythian serpent, who knew all things ahead of time. When God saw the serpent, he clicked with his tongue, and it looked as if the earth cast up a god. Then God said, "Iao" ('Ιαώ), and a god was born from the sound, who is lord of all (ὅς πάντων ἐστιν κύριος). After only a little more, the myth breaks off and the magical recipes are resumed. But it is already evident that the Gnostic system represented here was compounded of both pagan and Jewish elements. The gods who ride on the sun-boat are Egyptian; Greek deities and philosophical principles appear; but the last god, the lord of all, is Yahweh (יהוה) under a Greek form of his name. Likewise the whole document goes under the name of Moses.[2]

§98. It is obvious that movements of such pronouncedly syncretistic character as the Gnostic cults, would readily tend also to absorb into their systems elements of Christian origin when these became available. Or, as would lead to substantially the same result, some Christians in a syncretistic environment might tend to develop Christianity in the direction of a Gnostic amalgam. As we have seen (§44), Eusebius (*Ch. Hist.* IV 5) says that the fifteen Jewish Christian bishops of Jerusalem in the period prior to Hadrian (A.D. 135) were accounted worthy of the position because they had truly received the knowledge of Christ (τὴν γνῶσιν τοῦ Χριστοῦ). In saying that they had received this knowledge "truly," he uses the word γνησίως. This is the adverbial form of the adjective γνήσιος, a shortened form of γενέσιος, which means literally "belonging to the true race" and, hence, "genuine" or "true." The *gnosis* of Christ which the Jerusalem bishops had was, therefore, in the judgment of Eusebius, evidently not of any heretical sort but must rather have been in line with the "knowledge" of which the NT essentially speaks (§95).

§99. But Eusebius (*Ch. Hist.* IV 22, 4f.; cf. III 32, 8) also says (and here, as we have seen [§42], he quotes Hegesippus) that already from the time when Symeon was chosen head of the Jerusalem church

---

[2] Karl Preisendanz, *Papyri Graecae magicae.* 1928–31, II, 90–97.

in succession to James the Just (A.D. 61/62), the unity of the church, previously uncorrupted by vain discourses, was divided by corrupt doctrines and pseudonymous gnosis (1 Tim 6:20). He then gives the names of a number of heresies and heretical leaders. Since at this point Eusebius is evidently still quoting Hegesippus, whose *Memoirs* were written about 180, the heresies named must all have originated within one hundred or one hundred and twenty years after the death of James. Of the several groups mentioned, we will notice the Simonians (§§100f.), the Basilidians (§§102ff.), and the Valentinians (§§107ff.).

§100. The Simonians (Σιμωνιανοί) derived their name from Simon (Σίμων). Simon is named in Ac 8:9ff. as a magician in Samaria who was converted by Philip (cf. Ac 6:5) and afterward tried to purchase the power to confer the Holy Spirit but was rebuked by Peter. His practice of magic is described (Ac 8:9) with a participial form of the verb μαγεύω, which literally means "to be a Magus (μάγος)." As mentioned frequently by Herodotus, the Magi (μάγοι) were a Median tribe (I 101), who explained dreams (I 107), offered sacrifices (I 132), interpreted celestial phenomena (VII 37; cf. Mt 2:1f.), and used wizards' spells (VII 191). In Ac 13:6f., the Magus, Elymas Bar-Jesus, was associated with the proconsul, Sergius Paulus, at Paphos on Cyprus. Philo (*Special Laws* III 101) speaks highly of the true "magic" (μαγική) of the Magi, namely, "the scientific vision by which the facts of nature were presented in a clearer light"; but also says that there were others who perverted the art, being nothing but charlatans and mendicants. Of Simon it was said by the people of Samaria (Ac 8:10) that he was the power (δύναμις) of God which is called Great.

§101. Justin Martyr (*Apology* I 26) says that Simon was from the village of Gitto (near Flavia Neapolis [Nablus]), and was in Rome in the time of Claudius (41–54). Also a woman, named Helena, was associated with him of whom it was said that she was "the first thought generated by him" (τὴν ὑπ' αὐτοῦ ἔννοιαν πρώτην γενομένην). In his Ἔλεγχος καὶ ἀνατροπὴ τῆς ψευδωνύμου γνώσεως ("Refutation and Overthrow of Pseudonymous Gnosis"), more briefly called *Adversus haereses*, Irenaeus says (*Against Heresies* I 23, 1–4) that Simon claimed to have appeared among the Jews as the Son, to have descended in Samaria as the Father, to have come to other nations in the character of the Holy Spirit, and to be himself the loftiest of all powers. Also Irenaeus reports the teaching that, even as Simon (δύναμις) generated Helena (ἔννοια), so also she descended to the lower regions of space and generated angels and powers by whom the world was formed. In the process she herself became a captive of the lower powers, and was what was meant by the lost sheep (Mt 18:12 = Lk 15:4). So he, the Great Power, appeared among men as a man, although he was not a man, in order to free Helena, and those others who are his too, from the rule of those who made the world. Simon and the Simonians, Irenaeus concludes, were those from whom "what is falsely called knowledge" (1 Tim 6:20) took its beginning. He also names Menander as the successor of Simon. Eusebius (*Ch. Hist.* II 13), bases his account of Simon largely upon Justin and Irenaeus, agrees with Irenaeus in making Simon "the first author of all heresy" (πάσης ἀρχηγὸν αἱρέσεως πρῶτον), and adds an account (II 14) of how Peter contended against him in Rome.

§102. The Basilidians (Βασιλειδιανοί) were the followers of Basilides (Βασιλείδης). As already noted (§29), Basilides is mentioned in the Muratorian Fragment not long after the middle of the second century. Clement of Alexandria (*Stromata* VII 17) says more precisely that Basilides, like Valentinus (§107), arose under Hadrian (117–38) and continued under Antoninus Pius (138–61). Irenaeus (*Against Heresies* I 24, 1) and Eusebius (*Ch. Hist.* IV 7, 3) place his work in Alexandria. Eusebius, in the same passage just cited, gives the name of a certain Agrippa Castor as having written a refutation of the mysteries (τὰ ἀπόρρητα) of Basilides, and quotes him to the effect that Basilides wrote twenty-four books on the Gospel (εἰς τὸ εὐαγγέλιον βιβλία). Clement (*Stromata* IV 12) quotes from the twenty-third book of the *Exegetica* of Basilides, which is presumably the same work referred to by Agrippa Castor. The material quoted has to do with the question of sin and suffering in the light of divine Providence. According to Clement, the hypothesis advanced by Basilides was that the soul which has sinned in a previous existence is punished by suffering in this life, with this difference, however, that the elect soul has the honor of martyrdom, while the other soul is purged by punishment appropriate to its misdeeds.

§103. Irenaeus (*Against Heresies* I 24) gives a relatively brief summary of the doctrines of Basilides. According to this presentation, Basilides taught that there is an unborn and nameless Father, from whom proceeded by emanation a whole series of principalities and angels, who occupy three hundred and sixty-five heavens. The angels who dwell in the lowest heaven, namely, that which is visible to us, formed all the things that are in the world, and made allotments among themselves of the nations which are on earth. The chief of them is thought to be the God of the Jews. This God desired to make the other nations subject to his own people; hence the other nations resisted him, and the other nations were at enmity with his nation. The Father, therefore, sent his first-begotten Nous (νοῦς = Mind)— who is called Christ—to bestow on those who believe in him deliverance from the power of those who made the world. He appeared on earth as a man, and wrought miracles. He did not suffer death. Simon of Cyrene, who bore his cross, was transformed to look like him, and was crucified. Jesus received the form of Simon and, standing by, laughed at them. Then he ascended, invisibly, to him who sent him. Those who know these things are freed from the power of the principalities who formed the world. The result of this doctrine could be a sense of emancipation not only from the principalities but also from ordinary moral standards. Presumably because it was possible, in the light of the doctrine, to look upon all material things with a certain contempt, it was also possible to hold that whatever was done in the realm of the material was of little consequence. Thus some who followed upon Basilides and also upon Carpocrates (Καρποκράτης; for Carpocrates see Irenaeus, *Against Heresies* I 25; and for the Carpocratians cf. §42), says Irenaeus (*Against Heresies* I 28), "have introduced promiscuous intercourse and a plurality of wives, and are indifferent about eating meats sacrificed to idols, maintaining that God does not greatly regard such matters." On the other hand the view that everything material is very far removed from the nameless Father and essentially very evil could lead to the position that everything material should be denied and avoided as far as possible. Thus Irenaeus (*Against Heresies* I 24, 1) mentions Saturninus (Σατορνῖνος), "who was of that Antioch which is near Daphne," along with Basilides, and later (*Against Heresies* I 28, 1) explains that Saturninus was one of those from whom sprang the movement of the Encratites ('Εγκρατεῖς). In Greek ἐγκράτεια (from ἐν, "in" + κράτος, "strength"), like Latin *continentia*, means "self-control," hence the Encratites were the self-controlled ones. This was meant, however, in the sense of a radical abstinence and continence, based on a conviction of the intrinsic impurity of the things renounced. So the Encratites who sprang from Saturninus, and also from Marcion, as Irenaeus says (*Against Heresies* I 28, 1), "preached against marriage, thus setting aside the original creation of God, and indirectly blaming him who made the male and female for the propagation of the human race." Some of them also "introduced abstinence from animal food, thus proving themselves ungrateful to God, who formed all things."

Tatian also, Irenaeus adds, who taught a system of Aeons like the Valentinians, joined Marcion and Saturninus in declaring "that marriage was nothing else than corruption and fornication."

§104. Hippolytus (*Refutation of All Heresies* VII 8–15) gives a relatively extensive account of the teachings of Basilides and his followers, from which we learn the following: Basilides claimed to have received secret discourses from Matthias (Ματθίας), which the latter in turn had heard in the form of special instructions from the Savior. Basilides taught that there was a time when there was nothing. Since there was nothing, God himself was "nonexistent." Then the nonexistent God made a nonexistent universe out of what was nonexistent (οὐκ ὢν θεὸς ἐποίησε κόσμον οὐκ ὄντα ἐξ οὐκ ὄντων). He "hypostatized," or caused to subsist, a certain single seed which contained in itself the entire mixture of all the seeds of the universe (ὑποστήσας σπέρμα τι ἓν ἔχον πᾶσαν ἐν ἑαυτῷ τὴν τοῦ κόσμου πανσπερμίαν). In the seed was a threefold Sonship, in every respect of the same substance with the non-existent God (υἱότης τριμερής, κατὰ πάντα τῷ οὐκ ὄντι θεῷ ὁμοούσιος). Of this threefold Sonship, one portion was composed of fine particles (λεπτομερές), one of coarse particles (παχυμερές), and one was in need of cleansing (ἀποκαθάρσεως δεόμενον). The fine portion ascended forthwith to the nonexistent One, being drawn, as is each being in its own way, by his exceedingly great beauty and loveliness. The coarse portion was not able to hurry upward, therefore equipped itself with the Holy Spirit like a wing. But the Holy Spirit was not of the same substance as the Sonship, therefore was eventually left behind by this second ascending portion of Sonship. Thereupon the Holy Spirit became a firmament between the hypercosmic and the cosmos, i.e., between the supermundane realm and the universe (στερέωμα [Gen. 1:6 LXX] τῶν ὑπερκοσμίων καὶ τοῦ κόσμου μεταξύ). The third portion of the Sonship, which needed cleansing, remained meanwhile in the great heap of the mixture of seeds of the universe, where it both conferred and received benefits.

§105. At this point there was begotten from the cosmic seed-mixture, the Great Archon, the Head of the universe (ὁ μέγας ἄρχων, ἡ κεφαλὴ τοῦ κόσμου), who is of inexpressible beauty, magnitude, and power. He rose to the firmament, did not suppose that there was anything beyond, and did not know that the Sonship remaining in the seed-mixture was wiser than he; therefore he considered himself the wise architect (σοφὸς ἀρχιτέκτων) and proceeded to create every part of the universe. He begot a Son, wiser than himself, and seated him at his right hand. The Archon may also be called the Demiurge (ὁ δημιουργός = craftsman, maker, creator), and the place of his throne is called the Ogdoad (ὀγδοάς), or the Eight. Another Archon then arose out of the seed-mixture. His place is called the Hebdomad (ἑβδομάς), or the Seven. He also made a Son who was wiser than himself. The whole universe was now finished, as well as the hypercosmic things, but the third Sonship which had been left in the seed-mixture still needed to be reinstated above. So the Gospel came into the universe. It came from the Sonship, and it came to the Archon in the Ogdoad through the Son who sat beside him. The Son, known also as the Christ, instructed the Archon, and the Archon learned what the Nonexistent is, what the Sonship is, what the Holy Spirit is, what the arrangement of all things is, and how these things will be restored. This is the wisdom spoken in a mystery (ἡ σοφία ἡ ἐν μυστηρίῳ λεγομένη). The Archon was now afraid, and confessed the sin he had committed in magnifying himself. Then the Gospel came, in similar fashion and with similar result, to the Archon of the Hebdomad. This Archon was the one who spoke to Moses in Ex 6:2-3, and the statement in that passage that the name of the Lord was not made known means that the Archon of the Hebdomad did not reveal the name of the Archon of the Ogdoad. In the Hebdomad are innumerable principalities and powers and authorities (ἀρχαὶ καὶ δυνάμεις καὶ ἐξουσίαι), as well as three hundred and sixty-five heavens whose Archon is Abrasax (§97) because his name comprises the calculated number 365 (ψῆφον τξε'), which corresponds also with the number of days in the year.

§106. At this point it must be remembered that, even though the Gospel had illuminated the Ogdoad and the Hebdomad, the third Sonship was still in the seed-mixture (§104). It had been left there, in fact, in order to benefit the souls which were in a state of formlessness (τὰς ψυχὰς ἐν ἀμορφίᾳ), and also to receive benefit. Now the light (τὸ φῶς) came on down from the Ogdoad and the Hebdomad, and illuminated Jesus the son of Mary. Thereupon, the third Sonship which had been left below, followed Jesus and ascended and came above after being cleansed. When the entire Sonship comes to be above the boundary which is marked by the Spirit, i.e., the boundary between the cosmos and the hypercosmic realm (§104), then the creation will receive mercy (τότε ἐλεηθήσεται ἡ κτίσις). From the Archon of the Ogdoad on down, a great ignorance (ἄγνοια) will come upon the whole universe, so that nothing may desire anything contrary to nature. Concerning things above there will be neither tidings nor knowledge (γνῶσις) among things below, in order that the souls below may not be tormented by longing after impossibilities, as if a fish were to desire to graze on the mountains with sheep. And thus the restoration (ἀποκατάστασις) of all things will take place. As for Jesus, through whom the third Sonship was cleansed, it was his bodily (σωματικόν) part which suffered, which came from formlessness (ἀμορφίας) and reverted into formlessness. The psychic (ψυχικόν) part of his being rose again (ἀνέστη); it belonged to the Hebdomad, and reverted to the same. The part of his being which belonged to the elevated dwelling-place of the Great Archon, he raised, and it remained with the Great Archon. And the part which belonged to the dividing Spirit, he carried upward, and it remained in the dividing Spirit. In creation the different orders of created things had been confused together. Jesus became the first fruits (ἀπαρχή) of the differentiation of the various orders of created things, and his passion (πάθος) took place for no other reason than to accomplish the differentiation of what had been confused.

§107. The Valentinians (Ο ὑαλεντινιανοί) were the followers of Valentinus (Ο ὑαλεντῖνος). Like Basilides (§102), he too is mentioned in the Muratorian Fragment not long after the middle of the second century (§29). Clement of Alexandria (Stromata VII 17, 106 GCS Clemens Alexandrinus III 75; ANF II 555) places Valentinus, like Basilides (§102), under Hadrian (117–38) and Antonius Pius (138–61). Irenaeus (Against Heresies III 4, 3) refers to popes (whose dates are only approximate in this period) rather than emperors, and says that Valentinus came to Rome in the time of Hyginus (137–41), flourished under Pius (I) (141–54), and remained until Anicetus (154–66). He was active in Rome, we may conclude, approximately A.D. 138–60. Epiphanius (Pan. haer. XXXI 2, 3 GCS 25, 384) states that Valentinus was born on the coast of Egypt, and was instructed in Greek education in Alexandria. Tertullian (On Prescription Against Heretics 30) describes him as a disciple of Platonism. In Rome, according to Irenaeus (Against Heresies III 4, 3), he took public part in the church but also taught in secret and was, at last, excommunicated. Irenaeus (Against Heresies I 11) says that Valentinus shaped the principles of the Gnostic heresy (γνωστικὴ αἵρεσις) into a distinctive character in his own school. Tertullian (On Prescription Against Heretics 38) contrasts him with the well-known Marcion, in regard to treatment of the Scriptures. Marcion openly used the knife, not the pen, to make such excision of the Scriptures as suited him. Valentinus proceeded with more cunning mind and skill. He adapted his matter to the Scriptures, yet actually took away more, and added more, by removing the proper meaning of each word and adding fantastic arrangements of nonexistent things. In Tertlulian's time the Valentinians were a very large body of heretics, as this author says in his treatise *Against the Valentinians* (1).

§108. In the *Stromata*, Clement of Alexandria quotes several passages from letters and homilies by Valentinus (GGSB 143–45). In these he speaks of the Father who alone is good, of the divine nature of Jesus, and of the living Aeon to which the world is as much inferior as an image is to a living person. In creation, the One put into man the seed of substance from above. Man, however, uttered such great things that he terrified the angels, and they speedily marred the work. The heart of man is the abode of many demons. Only by the presence of the Good, in manifestation through the Son, can the heart become pure.

§109. The fragments quoted by Clement (§108) are not extensive enough to give any full idea of the system of thought set forth by Valentinus. As far as they go, they do not suggest as complex a system as Irenaeus ascribes to him. Irenaeus may, therefore, be reporting some later developments as well as the original teaching of Valentinus. Irenaeus says (*Against Heresies* I 11) that Valentinus taught: There is an inexpressible Dyad, whose two parts may be called Arretus (ἄρρητος = Unspeakable) and Sige (σιγή = Silence). From this Dyad emanated (προβεβλῆσθαι) a second Dyad, namely, Pater (πατήρ = Father) and Aletheia (ἀλήθεια = Truth). From the Tetrad arose another Tetrad, namely, Logos (λόγος = Word) and Zoe (ζωή = Life), Anthropos (ἄνθρωπος = Man) and Ecclesia (ἐκκλησία = Church), thus constituting in all the primary Ogdoad. From Logos and Zoe ten powers (δυνάμεις) were produced, from Anthropos and Ecclesia came twelve. All that has been described thus far constitutes the Pleroma (πλήρωμα = Fullness), i.e., "the fully explicated manifold of divine characteristics . . . forming a hierarchy and together constituting the divine realm." [3] In the Pleroma a being named Horos (ὅρος = Limit) separates the Bythus (βυθός = Depth), where the uncreated Father is, from the rest of the Pleroma where the created Aeons (αἰῶνες) are. One of the twelve beings who emanated from Anthropos and Ecclesia, fell from its original condition, i.e., fell quite out of the Pleroma, and produced the remainder of the universe (τὴν λοιπὴν πραγματείαν). Another being named Horos (Limit) separates the Pleroma from that which is outside it. The being who fell out of the Pleroma became the mother of

[3] Jonas, *The Gnostic Religion*, 181.

Christ, who was able to return to the Pleroma. The mother was unable to return, however, and brought forth another son, the Demiurge (δημιουργός), who is the supreme ruler (παντοκράτωρ) of everything under him. Jesus emanated from Christ who returned to the Pleroma (although other ideas of his origin were advanced too), and the Holy Spirit emanated from Ecclesia. Many more details of the system of Valentinus (and perhaps of its amplification by his followers) are given by Hippolytus (*The Refutation of All Heresies* VI 24–32); while Epiphanius (*Pan. haer.* XXXI GCS 25, 382–438) draws upon both Irenaeus and Hippolytus for his account and also adds additional material.

§110. Among the followers of Valentinus, the most prominent was Ptolemaeus (Πτολεμαῖος), or Ptolemy. Irenaeus (*Against Heresies* Preface 2) calls the school of Ptolemaeus a flower picked (ἀπάνθισμα) from that of Valentinus and, in the first eight chapters of *Against Heresies*, gives an extended summary of Valentinian doctrines which are probably essentially those of Ptolemaeus. "They say," Irenaeus begins, "that in the invisible and ineffable heights above there exists a certain perfect, pre-existent Aeon (τέλειον Αἰῶνα προόντα)." This Aeon (Αἰών) they call Proarche (προαρχή = Fore-Beginning), Propator (προπάτωρ = Fore-Father), and Bythus (βυθός = Depth). Eternal and unbegotten (ἀίδιόν τε καὶ ἀγέννητον), he remained through countless ages (ἐν ἀπείροις αἰῶσι) in profound serenity and quiescence. With him was Ennoia (ἔννοια = Thought), also called Charis (χάρις = Grace) and Sige (σιγή = Silence). When Bythus determined to put forth or cause to emanate (προβαλέσθαι) from himself the beginning of all things, he put this project (προβολήν) into Sige, like seed into the womb, and she brought forth Nous (νοῦς = Mind). Nous is like and equal to him who produced him, and alone comprehends the greatness of his Father. Nous is also called Monogenes (μονογενής = Only-Begotten), and Pater (πατήρ = Father), and Arche (ἀρχή = Beginning) of all things. Along with him was produced the feminine Aletheia (ἀλήθεια = Truth). Thus was constituted the first Tetrad, namely, Bythus and Sige, then Nous and Aletheia. Nous or Monogenes also sent forth Logos (λόγος = Word) and Zoe (ζωή = Life), and from them came Anthropos (ἄνθρωπος = Man) and Ecclesia (ἐκκλησία = Church). This made the original Ogdoad, four masculine-feminine pairs, each joined in union (κατὰ συζυγίαν) with the other. It is obvious that this account is much the same, only somewhat more detailed, than that with which we have already become familiar with respect to Valentinus (§109). Here, too, the process of emanation goes on until there are in all also $8 + 10 + 12 = 30$ Aeons, who constitute the invisible and spiritual Pleroma. It was to set forth the mystery of these Aeons (τὸ μυστήριον τούτων τῶν Αἰώνων) that the Savior did no public work for thirty years (cf. Lk 3:23); while the first, third, sixth, ninth, and eleventh hours mentioned in the parable of the laborers in the vineyard (Mt 20:1–16) point to the same mystery, for 1 + 3 + 6 + 9 + 11 = 30. The Aeon who was derived from Anthropos and Ecclesia and fell out of the Pleroma (§109) was the youngest of that group of twelve, and was named Sophia (σοφία = Wisdom). Her experiences are now narrated at some length, and it is held that she was ultimately restored to her place in the Pleroma. Then, lest any of the Aeons should fall into a calamity similar to that of Sophia, Christ and the Holy Spirit were emitted by Monogenes, in accordance with the foreknowledge of the Father. Christ proclaimed among the Aeons the knowledge of the Father (τὴν τοῦ Πατρὸς ἐπίγνωσιν), namely, that he cannot be comprehended, seen, or heard, but can only be known through Monogenes (cf. Jn 1:18). The Holy Spirit taught the Aeons what the true rest (ἀνάπαυσις; cf. κατάπαυσις in Heb 4:1–10; and cf. §§110, 241, 313, 325, 331, 334, 341, 357, 374) is, and everything was established and brought into a state of perfect repose. Then, acting in perfect harmony, the Aeons emitted an emanation to the honor and glory of Bythus, a being of the most perfect beauty, the very star and perfect fruit of the Pleroma, namely Jesus. He is called Savior, and Christ, and Logos, and All because he is from all (κατὰ πάντα, διὰ τὸ ἀπὸ πάντων εἶναι).

§111. Continuing the account, what transpired outside the Pleroma is told in detail. While the First Sophia Aeon returned to the Pleroma, her Desire (ἐνθύμησις), which was also called Achamoth ('Αχαμώθ, evidently derived from חכמה, "wisdom"), remained of necessity outside the Light and the Pleroma, in an intermediate place of Shadow and Void called the Middle (μεσότης). She sought for the Light, but Horos hindered her. As he did so, he exclaimed "Iao" ('Ιαώ, probably from יהוה [§97]), and this was the origin of that name. The Second or Lower Sophia was the Mother who made the Demiurge and he, in turn, made heaven, earth, and man. While man received his psychic nature (τὴν ψυχήν) from the Demiurge, he has his body (τὸ σῶμα) from the earth (ἀπὸ τοῦ χοός), his flesh (τὸ σαρκικόν) from matter (ἀπὸ τῆς ὕλης), and his spiritual man (τὸν πνευματικὸν ἄνθρωπον) from the Mother Achamoth. Evidently reckoning body and flesh together in one category, it was also said that there are three elements in man, the material (τὸ ὑλικόν), the psychic (τὸ ψυχικόν), and the spiritual (τὸ πνευματικόν). The material must of necessity perish. The psychic, which is between the material and the spiritual, can go to either side according to its inclination. The spiritual is supposed to be united with the psychic in order to assume shape, and then the two elements can be instructed together in conduct. The Demiurge also, according to at least one version of the doctrine, emitted Christ as his own Son. At the baptism the Savior from the Pleroma descended upon Christ but, since the Savior could not experience suffering, was taken away from him when he was led before Pilate. The passion of the Lord really pointed to what happened to the last of the Aeons, and his cry on the cross, "My God, my God, why hast thou forsaken me?" (Mt 27:46), simply indicated that Sophia was abandoned by the Light and restrained by Horos from going forward. Although Achamoth was wandering outside the Pleroma, she was sought after by the Savior, as he indicated when he said that he came for the lost sheep (Mt 18:12 = Lk 15:4; cf. §101). The consummation (συντέλεια) will take place when all that is spiritual (πνευματικόν) has been shaped and perfected in knowledge (γνώσει). This refers to the spiritual men who have perfect knowledge concerning God, and have been initiated into the mysteries of Achamoth. Everything that is of a material nature must end in decay. That which is of a psychic nature may choose what is worse and end in destruction, or choose what is better and find rest in the place of the Middle. Psychic men do not have perfect knowledge (τελείαν γνῶσιν). They get strength through works and "mere" faith (δι' ἔργων καὶ πίστεως ψιλῆς βεβαιούμενοι). They must practice continence and good conduct (ἐγκράτειαν καὶ ἀγαθὴν πρᾶξιν) if they are to be saved and attain at last to the place of the Middle. For those who are spiritual and perfect (πνευματικοῖς τε καὶ τελείοις), however, such a course of conduct is not at all necessary. They will be entirely and undoubtedly saved, not by means of conduct, but just because they are spiritual by nature. It is not conduct which leads one into the Pleroma, but simply the seed (σπέρμα) which is sent from there like an infant child (νήπιον), and goes back thither when it is perfected (τελειούμενον). When all the seed shall have come to perfection, then their Mother Achamoth will leave the Middle and enter the Pleroma. There she and the Savior will be united as bride and bridegroom. The spirituals (οἱ πνευματικοί) also, putting off their psychic natures (τὰς ψυχάς) and becoming intelligent spirits (πνεύματα νοερά), will enter the Pleroma, there to be given as brides to the angels who attend the Savior. The Demiurge will move into the place of the Mother Sophia, in the Middle, and there the psychic natures of the righteous will find rest (τὰς τῶν δικαίων ψυχὰς ἀναπαύσεσθαι). Then the fire which is hidden in the universe will blaze forth and burn.

It will destroy all matter, and itself as well, and then have no more existence. "Such," says Irenaeus at the end of the eighth chapter of *Against Heresies* (at least according to a note preserved at that point in Latin), "are the views of Ptolemaeus."

§112. A letter of Ptolemaeus addressed to a certain Flora is preserved by Epiphanius (*Pan. haer.* XXXIII 3–7 GCS 25, 450–57). In it Ptolemaeus distinguishes three parts in the OT Law: (1) the ethical precepts which Jesus came not to destroy but to fulfill (Mt 5:17); (2) the ordinances which were interwoven with injustice, and were abrogated by Jesus; (3) the symbolical part, such as sacrifices, etc., which were done away with in literal application, but kept as images of transcendent things. As for the source of such a Law as this, it cannot have come from the perfect God (as its imperfect nature shows); nor can it have come from the devil (as we may suppose that Marcion, for example, might have taught), since that would be an unlawful thought to utter; but it must have come from the Demiurge, who dwells in the Middle, and is inferior to the perfect God but superior to the adversary.

§113. Marcus (Μάρκος) was another Valentinian leader, the teachings and practices of whom, and of whose followers, Irenaeus describes (*Against Heresies* I 13–22). The Marcosians evidently observed the Eucharist in some form, and Marcus was reputed to be able to do certain magical tricks with the wine. Some of the group had a rite in which a bridal chamber (νυμφών) was constructed, and a mystical initiation was performed with the pronunciation of certain secret expressions. They affirmed that this was a spiritual marriage (πνευματικὸν γάμον), celebrated after the likeness of the unions above (τῶν ἄνω συζυγιῶν) (cf. §§110, 356). Others led candidates to water and baptized them, "into the name of the unknown Father of the universe, into Truth the mother of all, into him who came down into Jesus, into unity and redemption and fellowship with the Powers." Others repeated numerous mysterious words. After baptism, the initiated person was anointed with balsam. Others said that it was superfluous to bring persons to the water. Instead, they mixed oil and water together, and poured the mixture on the heads of those being initiated, using formulas such as already mentioned. "And this," says Irenaeus, "they want to be the redemption (τὴν ἀπολύτρωσιν)" (cf. §354). Yet other sects which sprang like a Hydra-headed monster, as Irenaeus (*Against Heresies* I 30, 15) says, from the school of Valentinus, were the Barbelo group and the Sethians. The Barbelo group (*Against Heresies* I 29) gave a prominent place to Barbelo, who seems to have been a feminine power who emanated from the unnamed Father, and

who played much the same role as Sophia did in some of the systems
(§110). The Sethians (*Against Heresies* I 30) emphasized the role of
Ialdabaoth. He was the son of Sophia, and himself had a son named
Nous, who was also the Serpent (from the Greek ὄφις, "serpent," this
group was also known as the Ophites). It was Ialdabaoth who made
man in his own image, and breathed his own light-spirit into him, then
tried to get this luminous power back again. Adam and Eve became
the parents not only of Cain and Abel, but also of Seth and Norea
(whereby a wife was provided for Seth). Seth was *"another* seed
instead of Abel," as Eve said (Gen 4:25), therefore (it was concluded)
of a different generation, superior to Cain and Abel, and he was
deemed the ancestor of the true children of God (although in some
systems he may also have been confused with the Egyptian Seth, the
enemy of Osiris[4]). Finally the consummation of all things will take
place when all the light that is scattered here below is gathered
together on high, in an incorruptible Aeon.

§114. It is obvious that the proliferation of speculations in Valen-
tinianism, as in Gnosticism in general, could go on almost endlessly.
Indeed Irenaeus (*Against Heresies* I 18, 1) says of the Valentinians:
"Every day each one of them, as he is able, invents something new;
for no one is considered perfect unless he produces great untruths
among them." They evidently wrote many books. We have already
seen that the followers of both Valentinus and Basilides wrote books
which the Muratorian canon repudiates (§29), and that Irenaeus
(*Against Heresies* I 20, 1) speaks of the inexpressible number of
apocryphal and spurious writings which the Marcosians fabricated
(§4). The title of one Valentinian book is specifically mentioned by
Irenaeus (*Against Heresies* III 11, 9). He says it was a "comparatively
recent writing." Since *Against Heresies* was written under Pope
Eleutherus (174–89), say about 180, the Valentinian book must have
appeared not long before that date. The title of the book, Irenaeus
says, is *The Gospel of Truth,* but, he adds, it is totally unlike the
Gospels which have been handed down from the apostles. Among the
Coptic manuscripts from Nag Hammadi there is a treatise which
begins, "The Gospel of Truth. . . ." (§§336ff.). These opening words
at once suggest that we have here, in Coptic translation, the very
book to which Irenaeus referred. This is supported by the fact that
the doctrines presented, while not as elaborate as those of Ptolemaeus
(§§110f.), and perhaps not even as elaborate as those attributed to

---

[4] Doresse, *The Secret Books of the Egyptian Gnostics,* 104f., 274.

Valentinus by Irenaeus (§109), are unmistakably Valentinian in character. Therefore we have here a Valentinian treatise of an early period (before A.D. 180), probably the book named by Irenaeus, and possibly, in the opinion of some, a book written by Valentinus himself.

§115. Two other forms of religious syncretism, both of which have decided Gnostic affinities, need be mentioned here only most briefly. The so-called Hermetic literature comprises a number of treatises usually dated in the second and third centuries of the Christian era. As Lactantius (*Divine Institutes* I 6), among others, tells us, the Greek Hermes was identified with the Egyptian Thoth (Tat), scribe of the gods, was known as Hermes Trismegistus (Thrice-greatest Hermes), and was supposed to have written many books relating to the knowledge of God. The first treatise of the extant *Corpus Hermeticum* is called *Poimandres*. Here Poimandres, the "Shepherd of Men," identifies himself with the Nous of the godhead, and reveals to Hermes the mysteries of the creation of the universe and of the fall of man, whereby the latter became a mixed being of both mortal and immortal character. Except for evident acquaintance with the biblical story of creation, the Hermetic system seems to be entirely pagan. The other system to be mentioned is that of Manicheism. Mani was probably of Persian origin, and was born (A.D. 216) and educated at Ctesiphon (near Baghdad) where, in 242, he began to preach a new religion. He traveled widely in Persia, China, and India, and was influenced by the Iranian, Buddhist, and Christian religions. In fact he called himself the Paraclete and, as such, the successor of Zoroaster, the Buddha, and Jesus. Finally in 277 under the Sasanian king, Bahram I, he suffered a terrible martyrdom. Manichean manuscripts were found at Turfan in Central Asia in the late nineteenth century; and in the form of Coptic papyri in Egypt in 1931. According to these and other sources, Mani taught that the primal principles were Light and Darkness, that it was as a consequence of their intermingling that this world was made, and that eventually heaven and earth will pass away and the Light be separated again from the Darkness.

§116. As far as specific doctrines are concerned, it is evident that the name of Gnosticism comprehends a variety of teachings. It is also evident, however, that in the entire movement there are several unmistakable underlying principles. Along with the term Gnosticism itself, the terms of dualism, polydynamism, and docetism may be used to designate these principles. Dualism appears everywhere in the great difference which is presupposed between the distant spiritual world and the present, material, and evil world. Polydynamism supposes a large number of more or less spiritual forces in the cosmos and in the hypercosmic realm. Of these forces it could only be the inferior ones among which the creator of the present imperfect world could be found. Docetism describes the earthly life of the Savior, who descends from the realm above into this present evil realm, as only seeming to be a real human life. And Gnosticism, in the essential meaning of the term, emphasizes that only through the obtaining of knowledge, particularly knowledge about the powers and events which figure in the cosmic and hypercosmic drama, can the spiritual nature of man be so illuminated as to make its way, at last, back to the higher realm to which it properly belongs. As far as man's conduct of his own life is concerned, he who has "knowledge" of the evil nature of the present world may view it with such abhorrence as to undertake the radical renunciation found among the "self-controlled" with their ideal of eunuchry or, at the other extreme, may view the material world with such contempt as to consider any mode of conduct in it, even the most libertine, quite irrelevant to the state and fate of the soul (§103).

# 7 / Modern Discovery of
New Testament Apocrypha

*Literature:* James Baikie, *Egyptian Papyri and Papyrus-Hunting.*
no date; U. Bouriant, *Mémoires publiés par les membres de la
Mission Archéologique Française au Caire.* IX 1 (1892), 3
(1893); Ulrich Wilcken, *Griechische Ostraka aus Aegypten und
Nubien.* 1899; Bernard P. Grenfell, Arthur S. Hunt, and David
G. Hogarth, *Fayum Towns and Their Papyri.* 1900; Victor R.
Gold, "The Gnostic Library of Chenoboskion," in BA 15 (1952),
70–88; Pahor Labib, *Coptic Gnostic Papyri in the Coptic Museum
at Old Cairo.* I, 1956 (abbreviated LCGP); Jean Doresse, *The
Secret Books of the Egyptian Gnostics.* 1960; W. C. van Unnik,
*Newly Discovered Gnostic Writings.* 1960; W. C. van Unnik,
*Evangelien aus dem Nilsand.* 1960; Søren Giversen, "Nag
Hammadi Bibliography 1948–1963," in ST 17 (1963), 139–87;
James M. Robinson, "The Coptic Gnostic Library Today," in
NTS 14 (1968), 356–401; and see §121 for *The Oxyrhynchus
Papyri,* Vols. I–XXXII, 1898–1967; §122 for Berlin Papyrus
8502; §123 for Egerton Papyrus 2; and §127 for the Nag
Hammadi manuscripts.

§117. Interest in the NT Apocrypha has been sustained and
increased by the striking and unexpected manuscript discoveries
which have been made from time to time and even recently. Ancient
manuscripts were written most often either on papyrus or on parchment, and either in roll or in codex form.[1] In Greek they were written
in the relatively separate upstanding characters of a literary hand
ultimately known as the uncial script, or in the relatively round and
more or less connected characters of a cursive hand ultimately known
as the minuscule script, and the establishment from datable manuscripts that certain styles of handwriting were in use at certain times
gives a clue for the paleographical dating of newly discovered manu-

[1] FLP 386ff.

scripts.[2] Also it is interesting to note that already in the earliest Christian manuscripts known, divine names and theological terms are abbreviated by writing perhaps two or three letters of the word and drawing a line above, e.g., $\overline{KC}$ = κύριος = "Lord"; $\overline{\Theta C}$ = θεός = "God"; and $\overline{IH}$ = 'Ιησοῦς = "Jesus," all of which abbreviations occur in the Egerton Papyrus 2 (§123) of not later than A.D. 150.[3]

§118. Egypt, with its very dry climate, was an area where such manuscripts (§117), buried in the sand, endured for a long time, and it is from Egypt that the largest number of manuscripts, both on papyrus and on parchment, from the early Christian period have come. The first modern discovery of ancient Egyptian papyri of this period was made by Egyptians digging in the Fayum district, which corresponds with the ancient Arsinoite nome. They are said to have come upon a pottery jar containing some fifty papyrus rolls, and to have burned all but one. The one manuscript, a list of persons who worked on the embankments of Ptolemais Harbor (on the canal from Arsinoë to Oxyrhynchus) in A.D. 191/192, came into the hands of Cardinal Stefano Borgia and was published in 1778.[4] Known as the *Charta Borgiana*, this first Greek papyrus to reach Europe from Egypt aroused interest in such materials and, in following years, many more papyri became known.

§119. In Upper Egypt on the east bank of the Nile some sixty miles south of Asyut is the town of Akhmim (§§82f.), which the Egyptians called Khen-min, and the Greeks Chemmis or Panopolis (Πανὸς πόλις), since the Egyptian god Min was identified with the Greek Pan. It was a "great city" according to Herodotus (II 91), and the capital of the Chemmite nome. In a hill at Akhmim are Egyptian tombs of the Eighteenth to Twentieth Dynasties. Extending nearly half a mile to the north and west of this hill is a Christian cemetery. It was in use from the fifth to the fifteenth centuries, and the oldest part is that nearest the foot of the hill. In the winter of 1886/1887 the French Archeological Mission at Cairo was excavating in this cemetery. Some six hundred and fifty feet northeast of the hill they found the tomb of a monk, and in it two Greek manuscripts. One was a mathematical text written on papyrus; the other was a parchment manuscript containing portions of apocryphal books. The latter manuscript, with which we are here concerned, was a codex

---

[2] C. H. Roberts, *Greek Literary Hands 350 B.C.–A.D. 400*. 1956.
[3] H. Idris Bell and T. C. Skeat, *Fragments of an Unknown Gospel*. 1935, 2–4.
[4] Wilcken, *Griechische Ostraka aus Aegypten und Nubien*, I, 339.

containing thirty-three leaves approximately six inches high and four and one-half inches wide. The script indicates a date probably in the eighth or ninth century. The pages are not numbered, but may be spoken of as if they were. Page 1 is adorned with an irregular but somewhat ornate cross. On each end of the crossbar is another small cross. Beneath the crossbar, on either side of the vertical member, are the Greek letters Alpha and Omega. Pages 2–10 contain a portion of the Gospel according to Peter (§§264ff.). Page 2 is headed by a small cross, and Page 10 concludes with three crosses and an ornamental design. Pages 11–12 are blank. Pages 13–19 (bound in the codex in the wrong order) contain a fragment of the Apocalypse of Peter. Page 20 is blank. Pages 21–66 contain two fragments of the Greek text of the Book of Enoch.

§120. In the winter of 1895/1896, Bernard P. Grenfell, Arthur S. Hunt, and David G. Hogarth, working on behalf of the Graeco-Roman Branch of the Egypt Exploration Fund in London, began a systematic search in Egypt specifically aimed at the recovery of ancient papyri. They started their explorations in the Fayum, then turned the next year to Behnesa, just to the south. The present Behnesa represents the ancient Oxyrhynchus, which was the capital of the Oxyrhynchite nome, as Arsinoë (the present Medinet el-Fayum) was the capital of the Arsinoite nome. Here at Oxyrhynchus in their second season of work (1896/1897) in Egypt, and on their second day at Behnesa (January 11, 1897), they unearthed a fragmentary leaf of papyrus, nearly six by four inches in size, written on both sides. Examining the fragment later in the week, Hunt recognized the Greek word κάρφος, which means "speck" or "mote," and was at once reminded of the saying of Jesus recorded in Mt 7:3-5 = Lk 6:41f. In fact the leaf contained a series of sayings of Jesus, some known from the canonical Gospels, others previously unknown and extracanonical. The style of handwriting indicated a date probably in the third century of the Christian era. A day or two afterward another leaf was found, with a portion of the first chapter of Mt, which appeared to be somewhat later in style but still probably within the third century. Grenfell suggested that both documents might be the remains of the library of some Oxyrhynchite Christian who perished in the persecution of Diocletian (A.D. 303), whose books were thereafter thrown away.

§121. In all, Grenfell and Hunt worked at Behnesa for six seasons, concluding with the winter of 1906/1907, and Grenfell also purchased documents at the site in 1919/1920. Publication of the great amount of material obtained was begun promptly and is still continuing in a series of volumes entitled *The Oxyrhynchus Papyri* (abbreviated OP; Vol. I by Grenfell and Hunt, 1898, to Vol. XXXII by E. Lobel, 1967), in which the published papyri are numbered sequentially, the numbers reaching, in the volumes just mentioned, from 1 to 2653. The papyrus with the sayings of Jesus, discovered as just described (§120), constitutes OP 1. In February 1903, in a second season at Behnesa, Grenfell and Hunt found a second set of extracanonical sayings of Jesus. On one side of a fragmentary piece of papyrus about nine by three inches in size was a survey-list of various pieces of land, on the other side, written later, were sayings of Jesus, some familiar from the canonical Gospels, others found here for the first time. This manuscript, with the sayings of Jesus, constitutes OP 654. In the same second season at Behnesa, eight badly damaged pieces of a papyrus roll were found, with both canonical and extracanonical words of Jesus. This is OP 655. In December 1905 Grenfell and Hunt found at Behnesa a small parchment leaf with Gospel materials (OP 840), in 1911 Hunt published a small Gospel-type fragment (OP 1081), and in 1914 Grenfell and Hunt published two papyrus fragments also with Gospel materials (OP 1224). All of these will be described more fully later (§§216ff.).

§122. In 1896 a Coptic papyrus was obtained in Cairo by C. Reinhardt and placed in the Egyptian section of the Berlin Museum, where it was designated as Berlin Papyrus (Papyrus Berolinensis) 8502. Since the manuscript came through the hands of a dealer in antiquities in Akhmim, it was probably discovered somewhere in the vicinity of that city (§119). In its original form the manuscript was a codex of seventy-two leaves. The first two pages, and the last page, were left blank and unnumbered. The other pages were numbered from 1 to 141. Today the unnumbered pages and also Pages 1–6, 11–24, and 133–34 are missing. The pages average approximately five and one-half inches high and four and one-half inches wide. The text is in Sahidic (§83), and the script is believed to belong in the fifth century, perhaps in the early part of the century. Altogether the codex contains four works: (1) from the beginning of the manuscript to Page 19, Line 5, the Gospel according to Mariam (§§322–25); from Page 19, Line 6 to Page 77, Line 7, the Apocryphon of John (§§328–35); from Page 77, Line 8 through Page 127, the Sophia of Jesus Christ (§§326–27); and on Pages 128–41 the Acts of Peter. In the year of its acquisition Carl Schmidt reported on the manuscript in a *Sitzungsbericht der preussischen Akademie der Wissenschaften* (1896, 839–47). In 1903 Schmidt published the fourth work (Acta Petri) in the manuscript in a volume called *Die alten Petrusakten im Zusammenhang mit der apokryphen Apostelliteratur nebst einem neu entdeckten Fragment untersucht* (TU 24, 1). Due, however, to the vicissitudes of two World Wars, it was only in 1955 that the balance of the manuscript was published by Walter C. Till, *Die gnostischen Schriften des koptischen Papyrus Berolinensis 8502* (TU 60 V, 5).

§123. In 1934 a collection of Egyptian papyri, the exact provenance of which was unknown, was purchased from a dealer by the British Museum and placed in the Egerton Collection of that institution. Upon examination it was found that one group of fragments, designated as Egerton Papyrus 2 (cf. §117), contained materials about Jesus both similar to and different from canonical Gospel materials. These texts were published forthwith by H. Idris Bell and T. C. Skeat, *Fragments of an Unknown Gospel* (1935). There are three fragments in the group, small in size, and written on both sides. The handwriting points to the second century, probably around A.D. 150 or earlier. Both incidents and conversations connected with Jesus are recorded (§§207–15).

§124. Without undertaking to mention all the finds which have been made, we may come now to the remarkable and relatively recent discovery of the manuscripts which are best known in connection with the name Nag Hammadi. It will be recalled (§78) that Nag Hammadi is a village on the west bank of the Nile where the river makes its great curve below Luxor (ancient Thebes), and that across the river at the foot of Jebel et-Tarif is the village of Qasr es-Sayad, marking the site of ancient Sheneset-Chenoboskion. This is where, about A.D. 315, Pachomius settled and studied with Palamon, and where, before his death (346) he founded one of his monasteries. It was probably in one of the tombs or caves at the eastern foot of Jebel et-Tarif that the find was made, but since it became known through Nag Hammadi the latter name has continued to attach to the manuscripts. The date was in 1946, as far as can be determined, and the discovery was made by Egyptian workers. They are said to have come upon a large pottery jar—such as is called a *zir*—containing papyrus manuscripts, which they sold for three Egyptian pounds. Thirteen codices were found, containing about a thousand large leaves of which four-fifths were in relatively good condition. Through various channels and by virtue of various maneuvers these came at last into the secure possession of scholarly institutions. One codex, not quite complete, was purchased in 1952 for the Jung Institute in Zurich and presented to Carl G. Jung. By 1956 all the other codices and a few leaves belonging to the manuscript which went to Zurich were in the possession of the Coptic Museum (§91) in Old Cairo. It is said to be the intention also that finally the Jung Codex, as the manuscript in Zurich is called, shall be placed in the Coptic Museum, so that the entire find will be together in one place.

§125. While all of the manuscripts are written on papyrus, nine of the codices were found still bound in leather. The writing is all in Coptic, most of it in Sahidic, some showing Akhmimic influence, and some in Subakhmimic (§83). On the basis of language and paleography the manuscripts are probably to be dated in the first half of the fourth century[5] or, as some think, in the second half of the fourth century and the beginning of the fifth.[6] In many cases, however, the Coptic manuscripts are quite certainly translations from Greek originals, and the latter can be shown, at least in some cases, to have been as early as the second century. As for the general character of the materials preserved here, it is clearly Gnostic. It has been suggested that the hiding away of this group of books took place at the latest at the beginning of the fifth century, when the Pachomian monasteries were winning their struggle against Gnostics in this region.[7]

§126. The thirteen Nag Hammadi codices have commonly been said to contain a total of forty-nine separate parts, including in some cases more than one copy of one and the same work. The numbering of the codices and their component parts has been done differently, however, by different writers. The classification by Jean Doresse may be seen in his *The Secret Books of the Egyptian Gnostics*, 142–45. The classification by Henri-Charles Puech and W. C. van Unnik may be seen in van Unnik's *Newly Discovered Gnostic Writings*, 16–17, and *Evangelien aus dem Nilsand*, 26–28. The classification adopted at the Coptic Museum in Old Cairo is given for Codices I–VI by Martin Krause and Pahor Labib in *Die drei Versionen des Apokryphon des Johannes im Koptischen Museum zu Alt-Kairo* (Abhandlungen des Deutschen Archäologischen Instituts Kairo, Koptische Reihe, 1), 1962. In the second volume of the same series the classification will be given for Codices VII–XIII, and in the meantime this classification has been kindly supplied to me personally by Dr. Pahor Labib. In Codices I–VI Dr. Labib numbers thirty-two treatises rather than the thirty-one recognized by Doresse, and in Codices VII–XIII he counts nineteen writings rather than eighteen

---

[5] LCGP I, 1.
[6] Van Unnik, *Newly Discovered Gnostic Writings*, 18.
[7] Doresse, *The Secret Books of the Egyptian Gnostics*, 135.

as given by Doresse. In the thirteen codices, therefore, following the analysis by Labib, there are fifty-one tractates. In some cases, as already stated, there is more than one copy of one and the same work. In some cases, also, titles are lacking, or have been supplied provisionally by the editor. Table 11 shows the three systems of classification of the thirteen codices, indicated by the names of Doresse, Puech, and Labib, respectively, and itself follows the classification of codices and tractates by Labib, which may now be accepted as definitive. Labib's Page and Line numbers for the several works are also given in the same Table. For example, the first work in the first codex is A Letter of James, and it extends from Page 1, Line 1, to Page 16, Line 30. Notations are also included as to the dialects of Coptic (§83) in which the works are written.

§127. Of the foregoing works (§126) only a few have, as yet, been published, but these include some of the evidently most important. In the Jung Codex (Codex I in Table 11), Pages 16–43 contain *The Gospel of Truth*. Pages 16–32 and 37–43, which are in Zurich, were published by Michel Malinine, Henri-Charles Puech, and Gilles Quispel, *Evangelium Veritatis* (1956); and Pages 33–36, which are in Old Cairo (§124), were published by the same scholars and Walter Till, *Evangelium Veritatis (Supplementum)* (1961). The foregoing contain French, German, and English translations. Another English translation is given by Kendrick Grobel, *The Gospel of Truth* (1960). In *Coptic Gnostic Papyri in the Coptic Museum at Old Cairo*, I (1956) (abbreviated LCGP), Pahor Labib gives a photographic reproduction of Codex I, Plates 1–46, and Codex II, Part a, Plates 47–158. In this photographic reproduction of Codex I, Plates 9, 10, 6, and 5 represent the Old Cairo pages of the Jung Codex. In the photographic reproduction of Codex II, Plate 47, Line 1, to Plate 80, Line 9, is *The Apocryphon of John*; Plate 80, Line 10, to Plate 99, Line 28, is *The Gospel according to Thomas*; Plate 99, Line 29, to Plate 134, Line 19, is *The Gospel according to Philip*; Plate 134, Line 20, to Plate 145, Line 23, is *The Hypostasis of the Archons*; and Plate 145, Line 24, to the end of Plate 158, is the first part of *A Work without a Title* (as it is called in Table 11). The three copies of *The Apocryphon of John* (Table 11: Codex II, No. 1; Codex III, No. 1; and Codex IV, No. 1) have been edited, with German translation, by Martin Krause and Pahor Labib, *Die drei Versionen des Apokryphon des Johannes im Koptischen Museum zu Alt-Kairo* (1962). *The Gospel according to Thomas* has been published, with an English translation, by A. Guillaumont, H.-Ch. Puech, G. Quispel, W. Till, and Yassah 'Abd al Masīḥ (1959); and another English translation has been given by

TABLE 11

*The Contents of the Nag Hammadi Manuscripts*

---

Codex I Labib = II Puech = XIII Doresse (the larger part of this is the Jung Codex) (The tractates in this Codex are written in Subakhmimic.)
1. A Letter of James, 1, 1—16, 30
2. The Gospel of Truth, 16, 31—43, 24
3. A Tractate concerning the Resurrection, 43, 25—50, 18
4. A Tractate concerning the Three Natures, 51, 1—134, at the end
5. A Prayer of the Apostle, 135, 1—136, at the end

Codex II Labib = III Puech = X Doresse (The tractates in this Codex are written for the most part in Sahidic, with some influence of Akhmimic and Subakhmimic.)
1. The Apocryphon of John, 1, 1—32, 9
2. The Gospel according to Thomas, 32, 10—51, 28
3. The Gospel according to Philip, 51, 29—86, 19
4. The Hypostasis of the Archons, 86, 20—97, 23
5. A Work without a Title, 97, 24—127, 17
6. The Exegesis concerning the Soul, 127, 18—137, 27
7. The Book of Thomas the Athlete, 138, 1—145, 19

Codex III Labib = I Puech = I Doresse (The tractates in this Codex are written in Sahidic.)
1. The Apocryphon of John, 1, 1—40, 11 (a second copy of this work, see Codex II, No. 1, above)
2. The Sacred Book of the Great Invisible Spirit, 40, 12—69, 20
3. The Letter of the Blessed Eugnostus, 70, 1—90, 13
4. The Sophia of Jesus Christ, 90, 14—119, 18
5. The Dialogue of the Savior, 120, 1—149, 17

Codex IV Labib = VIII Puech = II Doresse (The tractates in this Codex are written in Sahidic.)
1. The Apocryphon of John, 1, 1—49, 28 (a third copy of this work, see Codex II, No. 1, and Codex III, No. 1, above)
2. The Sacred Book of the Great Invisible Spirit, 50, 1—83, at the end (a second copy of this work, see Codex III, No. 2, above)

Codex V Labib = VII Puech = III Doresse (The tractates in this Codex are written in Sahidic.)

1. The Letter of the Blessed Eugnostus, 1, 1—17, at a point which cannot be determined because of the bad condition of the sheet (a second copy of this work, see Codex III, No. 3, above)
2. The Apocalypse of Paul, 17, at an indeterminate point—24, 9
3. The Apocalypse of James, 24, 10—44, approximately the middle of the page
4. The Apocalypse of James, 44, approximately the middle of the page—63, 32 (a second work with the same title as No. 3)
5. The Apocalypse of Adam, 64, 1—85, 32

Codex VI Labib = XI Puech = VI Doresse (Most of the tractates in this Codex are written in Sahidic, but in the fourth tractate there is some influence of Akhmimic and Subakhmimic.)

1. The Acts of Peter and the Twelve Apostles, 1, 1—12, 22
2. The Thunder; Perfect Mind, 13, 1—21, 32
3. Authentic Word, 22, 1—35, 24
4. The Thought of Our Great Power, 36, 1—48, 15
5. A Work without a Title, 48, 16—51, 23
6. A Work whose Title is Not Preserved, 52, 1—63, 32
7. The Prayer which They Spoke, 63, 33—65, 7
8. A Work whose Title Has Been Erased, 65, 8—78, at the end

Codex VII Labib = V Puech = VII Doresse (Sahidic)

1. The Paraphrase of Shem, 1, 1—49, 9
2. The Second Logos of the Great Seth, 49, 10—70, 12
3. The Apocalypse of Peter, 70, 13—84, 14
4. The Teachings of Silvanus, 84, 15—118, 7
5. The Apocalypse of Dositheos, or The Three Stelae of Seth, 118, 10—127, 27
   (a) The First Stela of Seth, 118, 24—121, 17
   (b) The Second Stela of Seth, 121, 18—124, 15
   (c) The Third Stela of Seth, 124, 16—127, 27
   (d) A Remark of the Scribe, 127, 28–32

Codex VIII Labib = IX Puech = IV Doresse (Sahidic)

1. The Discourse of Truth by Zostrian (title in cryptogram), 1, 1—132, 9
2. The Letter of Peter to Philip, 132, 10—140, 26

Codex IX Labib = X Puech = V Doresse (Sahidic)
1. An Apocalypse whose Title is Not Preserved, 1, 1—27, 10
2. A Treatise without a Title, 27, 11—29, 5
3. A Treatise whose Title is Not Preserved, 29, 6, to the end of the codex

Codex X Labib = XII Puech = VII Doresse (Sahidic, with Akhmimic influence) (This codex is very badly preserved.)
1. A Treatise whose Title is Preserved only Fragmentarily
2. A Treatise whose Title is Not Preserved

Codex XI Labib = VI Puech = VIII Doresse (The work of two scribes can be discerned in this codex. The first scribe wrote the first two tractates in Subakhmimic. The second scribe wrote the second two tractates in Sahidic. The pages are preserved only fragmentarily.)
1. The Interpretation of the Gnosis
2. A Treatise without a Title
3. The Allogenes
4. The Supremes

Codex XII Labib = XIII Puech = XI Doresse (Sahidic) (The codex is badly preserved.)
1. A Part of a Moral Treatise

Codex XIII Labib = IV Puech = IX Doresse (Sahidic) (The codex is not well preserved.)
1. The Triple Discourse of the Triple Protennoia
    (a) The First Logos of Protennoia
    (b) The Second Logos of Protennoia (?)
    (c) The Third Logos of Epiphania
2. A Treatise without a Title

---

Robert M. Grant with David N. Freedman under the title, *The Secret Sayings of Jesus* (1960). *The Gospel according to Philip* has been translated into German by Hans-Martin Schenke in TL 84 (1959), 1–26; into English by C. J. de Catanzaro in JTS 13 (1962), 35–71; and by R. McL. Wilson, *The Gospel of Philip* (1962); and into German by Walter C. Till, *Das Evangelium nach Philippos* (Patristische Texte und Studien, ed. by K. Aland and W. Schneemelcher, 2, 1963). The fifth tractate in Codex II, *A Work without a Title*, as it is called in Table 11, has been edited and translated into

German by Alexander Böhlig and Pahor Labib, *Die koptisch-gnostische Schrift ohne Titel aus Codex II von Nag Hammadi* (Deutsche Akademie der Wissenschaften zu Berlin, Institut für Orientforschung, Publication No. 58, 1962).

# 8 / Gospel Materials in
## New Testament Apocrypha

*Literature:* See §129.

§128. By NT Apocrypha we mean writings which raise some claim, in title, form, or content, to be like the books of the canonical NT, but which are not in that canon (§38). The chief kinds of writings found in the canonical NT are known as Gospels, Acts, Letters (or Epistles), and Revelation (or Apocalypse). In all four categories, extracanonical or apocryphal materials are to be found. In the present book the Prolegomena (§§1ff.) are intended to be relevant—as far as they go in their discussion of what the Apocrypha are, of the areas of Jewish, Egyptian, and Gnostic Christianity through which they have been transmitted, and of how they have been found—to all the NT Apocrypha. From this point on, however, it is intended to deal only with materials which are in some wise—in title, form, or content—like the materials which are found in the Gospels of the canonical NT.

§129. In §39 the chief published collections of the NT Apocrypha as a whole were listed. It is obvious that these contain the specifically Gospel-type materials of which we are now speaking. In addition to Hennecke-Schneemelcher, *Neutestamentliche Apokryphen*, I, *Evangelien* (3d ed. 1959) (abbreviated HSNTAE), listed already there (§39), we also have two other volumes devoted exclusively to the apocryphal Gospels. These are: P. Giuseppe Bonaccorsi, *Vangeli Apocrifi* (1948) (abbreviated BVA); and Aurelio de Santos Otero, *Los Evangelios Apocrifos* (1956) (abbreviated SEA). Additional literature on particular topics will be cited as we proceed.

§130. It is our intention, therefore, to look now for Gospel-type materials which are outside the canonical NT. Within this area we wish also, for the purposes of the present book, to establish further limitations. The total mass of material included by our definition—namely, material in some degree like canonical Gospel material in name, form, or content—is very extensive. A great deal of it would be recognized by most readers as being legendary, in the sense of being spun out and embellished imaginatively, or as being mythological in character, in the sense of the Gnostic type of speculation with which we have become familiar (§§92ff.). Such material is not without its own importance, and may in fact be of prime importance for the study of certain phases of thought in the history of the church, and we shall necessarily consider no little amount of it. But in turning to material which is, in any way, designated Gospel material, the ordinary reader will presumably, in the first place, be thinking of material which conveys information about Jesus. Therefore our primary concern, in looking through the extracanonical Gospel materials, is to ask whether there is any of it which should actually be considered along with the canonical Gospel materials in the attempt to gather information about the actual life and teachings of Jesus. The canonical Gospels are all available to us in their earliest accessible form, as Greek manuscripts. Beneath the Greek forms *may* lie earlier Aramaic and/or Hebrew forms of the present Gospels, or Hebrew and/or Aramaic sources upon which they depended but, even if so, such forms or sources are not now available to us. Since our oldest actually available sources, i.e., the canonical Gospels, are available in the form of Greek manuscripts and since they have, in turn, been translated into many different languages at later dates, it is a natural supposition that generally the earliest of the noncanonical materials will also be preserved first of all in Greek. Beyond that, materials found in other languages, e.g., in Latin or in Coptic, will presumably at best be translations of earlier Greek sources, and in some cases (e.g., §§288ff.) it can be plainly demonstrated that that is what they are. There are, indeed, references to Hebrew and/or Aramaic sources, but such sources have not yet been found and, if manuscripts purporting to be such were actually found, it would still be necessary to study them to ascertain, if possible, whether they were written originally in a Semitic language, or whether they were themselves translations from Greek sources. Therefore, since our primary interest in looking at the apocryphal Gospel-type materials is to see if there are any which should be considered along with the canonical Gospels in the effort to obtain information about the life of Jesus, and since the canonical Gospels as the oldest otherwise available sources in that regard are themselves in Greek, it will provide a method of delimiting some material as of primary concern, in what is a vast total mass of material, if we focus our attention chiefly upon that which is available in Greek. Exceptions may exist in cases where church fathers, themselves writing in another language than Greek, quote in their language (e.g., in Latin, as in §146) a saying of Jesus of which they know; and in cases where a Greek original is only partly available upon which a more extensive translation in another language can, at that point, be demonstrated to rest, so that the balance of the translation may also be supposed to reproduce the lost balance of the Greek original, and may therefore be considered as of special importance (as, e.g., in §§288ff.).

Accordingly, as a method of limiting the focus of the present book to that which we consider, and that which we suppose the ordinary reader would consider, as the most important material in the field of our investigation, we will look primarily at texts available in Greek and, in addition thereto, at texts of the exceptional sorts described in the preceding sentence. In line with this principle, it will be texts in Greek, together with some in Latin, which will be printed in their original language and numbered as Texts 1–86. As for the Coptic manuscripts, not a few of which can be shown to rest probably upon Greek sources, where the Greek sources are lacking we will not attempt to print the texts in the original language, but will follow the best available translations of the Coptic in modern languages and, on that basis, give quotations only in English. With respect to all the Coptic materials and translations in the present book I wish to acknowledge with thanks the kind assistance of Dr. Pahor Labib, Director of the Coptic Museum in Old Cairo (§91). He has read all the Coptic sections (§§117–27, 282–389), has personally supplied me prior to his own publication with the details of his classification of Codices VII–XIII of the Nag Hammadi manuscripts (§126), and with respect otherwise to all that I have done with the Coptic has certified that "everything is correct." In the printing of original texts in Greek and Latin we will follow the practice of many editors (e.g., Klostermann, KT 8, etc.) and omit initial capitalization at the beginning of sentences, but in translations will follow normal English usage. Still at the point of limiting the scope of our survey, it will be obvious from what has been said that we will be interested in the oldest evidence that we can obtain, and therefore we shall plan to look chiefly at witnesses and manuscripts in the first four centuries after Christ, that is, approximately from A.D. 30 to 430. The dates of the witnesses cited, falling almost all within the period just mentioned, may be seen in the List of Ancient Sources; and the dates of manuscripts are indicated as they are discussed.

# II. Texts

# A. Quotations

## 1 / Quotations of Isolated Sayings

*Literature:* Alfred Resch, *Agrapha*. 1889, rev. ed. 1906 (abbreviated RA); Erich Klostermann, *Apocrypha*, III, *Agrapha, Slavische Josephusstücke, Oxyrhynchos-Fragment 1911.* KT 11, 2d ed. 1911; Leon E. Wright, *Alterations of the Words of Jesus as Quoted in the Literature of the Second Century.* 1952; Helmut Köster, *Synoptische Überlieferung bei den apostolischen Vätern* (TU 65). 1957; JUSJ 54ff.; SEA 115–30; HSNTAE 52–55.

### 1 / The Nature of the Quotations

§131. Many sayings of Jesus are quoted, more or less exactly, or alluded to, more or less plainly, by writers of the early church. In the case where a saying of this sort is similar to a saying of Jesus found in the canonical Gospels the question arises whether the saying is derived by the early church writer from the canonical Gospel or from a tradition, oral or written, similar to that upon which the canonical Gospel also drew. Likelihood of direct derivation from a canonical Gospel would appear to be greatest where there is identity or very great similarity in wording and where there is express reference to a written source. Yet even when these indications are present the matter is not always beyond doubt. Consider, for example, a quotation found in the Letter of Barnabas, a book which dates perhaps around A.D. 130 and is now usually accounted a part of the Apostolic Fathers (§37). Barn 4:14 reads:

ὡς γέγραπται, πολλοὶ κλητοί, ὀλίγοι δὲ ἐκλεκτοί
as it is written, Many [are] called, but few chosen

Except for the omission of dispensable words, the quotation is in exact agreement with Mt 22:14, which reads:

πολλοὶ γάρ εἰσιν κλητοί, ὀλίγοι δὲ ἐκλεκτοί
For many are called, but few chosen.

The formula of citation, "as it is written," seems to guarantee a written source, and the exact agreement with Mt 22:14 seems to make it probable that the quotation was taken directly from the canonical Gospel. If so, this is the first time in the church fathers that a NT citation is introduced by the authoritative formula long used (Mk 7:6, etc.) with reference to the "scriptures" (αἱ γραφαί) (Mk 12:24, etc.) of the OT. It may be argued, of course, that it is unlikely that material from one of the four Gospels would be cited by this formula at as early a date as it is customary to give to Barn, and then it becomes necessary to suppose that this saying was "written" in some other place which cannot now be identified. Or it may be thought that the saying more probably came to Barnabas through oral tradition, and Barnabas was simply in error in citing it as if he had derived it from a documentary source. Yet the express reference to the fact that it was "written," and the close agreement with Mt 22:14 makes it still well possible that the canonical Gospel was the source upon which Barnabas drew. Many other examples of such quotations, and of the complexities in which the analysis of them is often involved may be seen in the study by a Committee of the Oxford Society of Historical Theology of *The New Testament in the Apostolic Fathers* (1905), and in Köster, *Synoptische Überlieferung bei den apostolischen Vätern* (1957). All together the material exhibits very varying degrees of similarity to the canonical sayings, and is also introduced in various ways. Where the criteria of identity or very close similarity to a canonical saying, and of introduction by reference to a written source, are not present, the likelihood appears greater that we must suppose derivation from oral tradition or from a written source other than the canonical Gospels. Recurring to the example in Barnabas (4:14) just cited, if the saying is derived from the canonical Gospels it is only Mt 22:14 which can be that source, since at this point Mt 22:14 is not paralleled in the other canonical Gospels. In other cases the matter is complicated further by the fact that the canonical passage itself stands, in the same form or in variant forms, at more than one place in the canonical Gospels. In such cases, where a canonical passage is adduced for comparison with a passage from another writer, it is of course necessary to cite the several relevant references in the canonical Gospels. In modern theory on the interrelationships of the Synoptic Gospels, Mk is usually considered a source of Mt and Lk, and the citation of parallel passages often gives priority to Mk, e.g., Mk 1:2f. = Mt 3:3 = Lk 3:4. But in the early centuries Mk was less used than Mt and Lk (see the evidence in the volume by the Oxford Society of Historical Theology, and the comment by Köster, *Synoptische Überlieferung bei den apostolischen Vätern*, 61; and cf. §§312, 360, 371). In any particular case the evidence must, of course, be assessed for itself, but in general the probability is that Mt or Lk will be the source rather than Mk in cases where the passage in question is found in either or both of those Gospels as well as in Mk. Therefore it will be appropriate in all that follows to cite such evidence normally in the canonical order of Mt, Mk, Lk, and where the Fourth Gospel comes in too, Jn.

§132. There are also not a few sayings of Jesus quoted by early church writers which are different enough from anything in the canonical Gospels that the question must be raised as to whether they do not indeed come from tradition apart from that which is known in the canonical sources. Yet here too the analysis is often beset with all kinds of complexities. It is not always beyond doubt whether the church writer positively intends to cite a given saying as a saying of Jesus. In the formula of citation the name of Jesus, or one of his titles, or both, are sometimes given explicitly, as, e.g., Lord (Text 1 in §135), Savior (Text 6 in §140), or Lord Jesus Christ (Text 5 in §139). But again (e.g., Text 2 in §136), only the word φησί is used. This third person singular present indicative form of the verb φημί, "to say," is used entirely normally and frequently in Greek to introduce direct discourse, either preceding the statement quoted, or inserted after the first word or words of it, or even coming at the close of a direct quotation (Lk 7:40). The present tense imparts a vivid quality to the quotation, but may also be translated as a past. Used personally, the word introduces someone's utterance as, e.g., in Mt 13:29, ὁ δέ φησιν, "But he says" (cf. ASV), or "But he said" (RSV); in Mt 14:8, φησίν, "she says," or "she said"; and in Heb 8:5, of God, γάρ φησιν, "for he says." The word may also be used impersonally, and here may take a plural subject as well as a singular. Used impersonally, the translation "it is said," may be appropriate; or, with the supposition of a plural subject as in 2 Cor 10:10, "they say." In this way the word is also used with Scripture quotations. In 1 Cor 6:16, e.g., Gen 2:24 is introduced with φησίν, which may be translated, "it says"; or, thinking of the Author of Scripture, "He says" (cf. KJV, ASV, Berkeley Version); or "Scripture says" (New English Bible, cf. Goodspeed); or, in analogy to ὡς γέγραπται (§131), "as it is written" (RSV). It is obvious, therefore, that when φησί is the only word by which a saying is introduced, as is often the case in the early church writers, there may be ambiguity as to the source from which the saying is supposed to come. There may be clues, however, in the context or in the nature of the saying, and in the texts given below we believe there is reason to think that the writers intend to introduce them as sayings of Jesus.

§133. Even when it is plain that the church writer is giving a saying which he intends to present as coming from Jesus, there are still abundant possibilities for confusion. Materials derived from other parts of the Scriptures may be remembered and mistakenly attributed to Jesus. Text 2 in §136 and Text 5 in §139 are examples where this possibility may at least be raised. Materials from the canonical tradition may be reproduced with so much freedom and rephrased so completely—whether intentionally or unconsciously—that they have the appearance of a new and different saying. Text 1 in §135 is an example where this possibility may at least be considered. Again, material may be presented in such a way that it is difficult to tell how much of it the writer intends to be taken as a saying of Jesus. There is an example of this situation in the case of Text 3 in §137 where a recognizably canonical saying of Jesus is followed immediately by an additional statement which could be a further noncanonical saying of Jesus, or could be a comment by the writer. In our own opinion, however, Texts 1, 2, and 3 are all examples of sayings which are intentionally attributed to Jesus and which have been transmitted through extracanonical channels.

§134. Whether noncanonical sayings of Jesus found in the works of early church writers came to those authors through oral channels or in written documents, is another question which it is often very difficult to answer. In the case of the saying in §131, which we think came from a canonical source, the formula of citation, "as it is written," makes it probable that the author of Barn derived it from a written source, presumably from Mt. In the case of many other sayings, which are not introduced with so specific a formula, it may be questioned whether the author who writes down the saying has himself derived it from a written document or from oral tradition. In general we may perhaps suppose that the earlier the writer is the more chance there is that he derived the saying from oral tradition, the later he is the more likely it is that he derived the saying from some written source. Many such questions remain open. In what follows (§§135–51) we give the sayings attributed to Jesus, which seem most likely to be independent sayings transmitted through channels outside of the documents which became the canonical NT. These sayings are quoted in the Letter of Barnabas, and by Justin, Clement, Tertullian, Origen, Hippolytus, and Epiphanius, and we present them according to this chronological order of these authorities. In some cases the saying, or a similar one, is quoted by more than one writer, but we usually cite only the oldest authority. When such sayings have been found and listed, the question still remains whether they come from Jesus himself or not. The present compilation does not answer that question, but it does assemble material which seems to have some claim to consideration along with canonical material in the never-ending endeavor to assess the available records and to discern in them that which most probably comes from the life and teachings of Jesus himself. Comments along with the texts generally bear on the congruity, or lack of congruity, of the noncanonical material with the material already known in the canonical records. This may be taken as implying the opinion of the present writer that within the canonical NT there is preserved an authentic tradition concerning Jesus, and that those extracanonical materials which are congruent therewith are witnesses not without value to the same tradition.

## 2 / Barnabas

§135. The Letter of Barnabas was cited above (§131) for an early example of a quotation of a saying of Jesus from, probably, a canonical source. In the same work are sayings, the possibility of whose derivation from noncanonical sources must at least be considered seriously. Barn 6:13 reads:

TEXT 1

λέγει δὲ κύριος· ᾽Ιδοὺ ποιῶ τὰ ἔσχατα
ὡς τὰ πρῶτα.

But the Lord says: Behold, I make the last things
like the first.

This saying is somewhat similar to, but also somewhat different from, the sayings found in Mt 19:30 (and parallels), "But many that are first (πρῶτοι) will be last (ἔσχατοι), and the last first"; and in Mt 20:16, "So the last (ἔσχατοι) will be first (πρῶτοι), and the first last." In view of the similarity, it is possible that Barn is making a loose quotation of the canonical sayings in a concentrated form. In view of the difference, it is possible, and we will judge probable, that Barn is drawing an independently transmitted saying from some noncanonical source. The canonical saying evidently implies a reversal of conditions in the age to come. The saying in Barn 6:13 may convey the same meaning, or may imply a restoration in the coming age to the state of a former time. In either case an eschatological expectation is expressed.

§136. Barn 7:11 reads:

TEXT 2

> οὕτω, φησίν, οἱ θέλοντές με ἰδεῖν καὶ
> ἅψασθαί μου τῆς βασιλείας ὀφείλουσιν θλιβέντες
> καὶ παθόντες λαβεῖν με.

Thus, he says, Those who wish to see me and
to take hold of my kingdom, must through tribulation
and suffering obtain me.

This saying is somewhat reminiscent of Ac 14:22, which reads:

> καὶ ὅτι διὰ πολλῶν θλίψεων δεῖ ἡμᾶς
> εἰσελθεῖν εἰς τὴν βασιλείαν τοῦ θεοῦ

and [saying] that through many tribulations we must
enter the kingdom of God

The possibility should, therefore, perhaps be reckoned with, that the author of Barn had the latter saying in mind, but remembered it incorrectly as having been a saying of Jesus, and then reproduced it freely in his own language. But the Book of Acts otherwise includes a saying of Jesus which is not in the Gospels (Ac 20:35), and the language of Paul often contains reminiscences of words of Jesus, so it could be that some otherwise unattested saying of Jesus underlies both the words in Ac 14:22 and the quotation in Barn 7:11. Yet again it is possible that there is no connection between Barn 7:11 and Ac 14:22, and that Barn 7:11 is indeed quoting directly some saying that came to the author in some noncanonical source as a saying of Jesus. Tribulation (θλίψις) is, of course, part of the expectation of Jesus for the world, and for the disciples in the world, according to the canonical Gospels (Mt 13:21; Mk 13:19; Jn 16:21, etc.); and so too is suffering (πάσχω, πάθημα) both for himself and for those who follow him (Mt 16:21, etc.). The figurative use of the verb ἅπτω, in the sense of "take hold of" (ἅψασθαί μου τῆς βασιλείας), is peculiar to Barn 7:11 and does not occur in the canonical Gospels. The second aorist active infinitive of λαμβάνω is found, however, in Lk 19:12 with the meaning, "to receive . . . a kingdom" (λαβεῖν . . . βασι-λείαν), and in other forms the same verb occurs in Mk 4:16 with the sense of receiving the word (τὸν λόγον . . . λαμβάνουσιν), in Jn 1:12

with the meaning, "received him" (ἔλαβον αὐτόν), and in Jn 13:20 with the meaning, "receives me" (ἐμὲ λαμβάνει). The language of the saying, therefore, is not irreconcilable with that of the canonical tradition.

## 3 / Justin

§137. Justin Martyr, *Apology* I 15, 8, quotes the words of Jesus in Mt 9:13 = Mk 2:17 = Lk 5:32, "I came not to call the righteous, but sinners to repentance," and then goes on immediately with the further statement:

TEXT 3

> θέλει γὰρ ὁ πατὴρ ὁ οὐράνιος τὴν μετάνοιαν
> τοῦ ἁμαρτωλοῦ ἢ τὴν κόλασιν αὐτοῦ.
>
> For the heavenly Father desires the repentance
> of the sinner rather than his punishment.

In the absence of quotation marks in the Greek, it is possible that this statement is the comment of Justin, following upon the preceding quotation. But in what follows, Justin continues to make brief introductory statements and then to follow them with several sentences of what Jesus said, and it seems probable that in the above example he is still intending to be quoting the saying of Jesus, not interjecting an affirmation of his own. The additional statement is in harmony with the canonical statement which it follows, and elsewhere in the canonical records Jesus certainly speaks not only of repentance (μετάνοια, Lk 5:32, etc.) but also of punishment (κόλασις, Mt 25:46), and of the will (θέλημα) of the heavenly Father (Mt 18:14).

§138. Justin Martyr, *Dialogue with Trypho* 35, 3, quotes Mt 7:15 in slightly altered form, "For he said, Many will come in my name, clothed outwardly in sheepskins, but inwardly they are ravenous wolves," and then adds immediately another saying which he unmistakably intends as another saying of Jesus:

TEXT 4

> καί· ἔσονται σχίσματα καὶ αἱρέσεις.
> and: There will be divisions and heresies.

The prediction is appropriate in the context of a warning against false prophets (Mt 7:15). In the canonical Gospels, σχίσμα designates a rent or tear in a garment (Mt 9:16 = Mk 2:21) and a division among people (Jn 7:43, etc.); and, at least in the Book of Acts, αἵρεσις is the word for the party or sect of the Sadducees (Ac 5:17) and of the Pharisees (Ac 15:5; 26:5). Paul uses both words in 1 Cor 11:18-19, and this passage, or even the later situation in the church with regard to "heresies," could have given rise to the saying. It is still by no means impossible, however, that Jesus himself could have anticipated such divisions.

§139. Justin Martyr, *Dialogue with Trypho* 47:

TEXT 5

> διὸ καὶ ὁ ἡμέτερος κύριος ᾿Ιησοῦς Χριστὸς
> εἶπεν· ἐν οἷς ἂν ὑμᾶς καταλάβω,
> ἐν τούτοις καὶ κρινῶ.

Wherefore also our Lord Jesus Christ
said: In whatever things I shall take you,
in these I shall judge you.

It is possible that the saying is a variation of Ezk 33:20, which reads in the LXX:

> ἕκαστον ἐν ταῖς ὁδοῖς αὐτοῦ κρινῶ ὑμᾶς.
> I will judge each of you according to his ways.

The similarity is hardly sufficient, however, to support the theory of such a derivation of the saying. If there is a connection it could be that Jesus made a statement which was to some extent based upon the prophetic utterance, but even that scarcely seems likely. Actually the thought in the saying as attributed to Jesus has some similarity to what is said in Mt 24:40-42 = Lk 17:34f., 39, and could be an independently transmitted saying of Jesus.

## 4 / Clement of Alexandria

§140. In an appendix to his *Stromata*, Clement of Alexandria gives a number of extracts from the writings of Theodotus, who was a

Valentinian Gnostic.[1] According to this source (*Excerpts from Theodotus 2*, 2 GCS 17, 106), Theodotus quoted a saying of Jesus as follows:

TEXT 6

> διὰ τοῦτο λέγει ὁ Σωτήρ·
> σώζου σὺ καὶ ἡ ψυχή σου.

> Because of this the Savior says:
> Be saved, you and your soul.

There may be a reminiscence here of Gen 19:17, which reads in the LXX:

> σώζων σῶζε τὴν σεαυτοῦ ψυχήν.
> Surely save your own soul.

Likewise in Lk 17:28–33 the remembrance of the experience of Lot is brought into connection with an urgent warning, so the saying could come from Jesus.

§141. Between a quotation from Paul (1 Cor 13:12) and others from Proverbs (11:21, 24 LXX), Clement of Alexandria, *Stromata* I 19, 94, 5 (GCS 52, 60), gives this saying:

TEXT 7

> εἶδες γάρ, φησί, τὸν ἀδελφόν σου,
> εἶδες τὸν θεόν σου.

> For, he says, you have seen your brother,
> you have seen your God.

Later, in *Stromata* II 15, 70, 5 (GCS 52, 150), between quotation of the famous Greek saying, "Know yourself" (γνῶθι σαυτόν) and the injunction of Jesus to love God with all your heart, and your neighbor as yourself (Mt 22:37, 39 and parallels), Clement gives the identical quotation. Also Tertullian, *On Prayer* 26, gives the same in the form, "He says, You have seen your brother, you have seen your Lord." The spirit of the saying seems entirely in harmony not only with Mt 22:37, 39, and parallels, which Clement cites along with it in his second passage, but also with Mt 25:40.

---

[1] Cf. Harnack, *Geschichte der altchristlichen Literatur bis Eusebius*, 2d ed. 1:1, 181.

§142. Clement of Alexandria, *Stromata* I 24, 158, 2 (GCS 52, 100):

TEXT 8

αἰτεῖσθε, γάρ φησι, τὰ μεγάλα
καὶ τὰ μικρὰ ὑμῖν προστεθήσεται.

For it is said, Ask for the great things,
and the small things shall be added unto you.

Origen, *On Prayer* 14, 1, gives the same saying, and adds:

καὶ αἰτεῖτε τὰ ἐπουράνια
καὶ τὰ ἐπίγεια ὑμῖν προστεθήσεται.

and ask for the heavenly things,
and the earthly things shall be added unto you.

The saying is a parallel to Mt 6:33 = Lk 12:31 (and cf. Mt 7:7 = Lk 11:9 for αἰτεῖτε), and the question is whether it is a later paraphrase of the canonical saying, or an independently transmitted saying of Jesus having equally good claim to authenticity. The additional words given by Origen may presumably be taken as a later expansion.

§143. Clement of Alexandria, *Stromata* I 28, 177, 2 (GCS 52, 109), says that the Scripture (ἡ γραφή), in its desire to make us true dialecticians (διαλεκτικούς), exhorts:

TEXT 9

γίνεσθε δὲ δόκιμοι τραπεζῖται,
τὰ μὲν ἀποδοκιμάζοντες, τὸ δὲ καλὸν κατέχοντες.

Be approved money-changers,
rejecting some things, but holding fast what is good.

This statement actually contains two sayings, and the latter is a quotation, only slightly changed, of 1 Th 5:21:

πάντα δὲ δοκιμάζετε, τὸ καλὸν κατέχετε
but test everything, hold fast what is good

Origen, *Commentary on John* 19, 2 (RA 119), quotes both sayings, explicitly attributing the first ("Be approved money-changers") to Jesus, and the latter to Paul. Epiphanius (*Pan. haer.* XLIV 2, 6 GCS 31, 192) quotes Apelles, Gnostic disciple of Marcion, as stating that the saying, γίνεσθε δόκιμοι τραπεζῖται, is found "in the Gospel" (ἐν τῷ εὐαγγελίῳ). In Mt 21:12 = Mk 11:15 the tables (τραπέζας) of the money-changers are mentioned, but these officials are called by the name κολλυβιστής, derived from a small coin (κόλλυβος). In Mt 25:27, however, the name τραπεζίτης, derived from τράπεζα, is found. This name is translated either money-changer, or banker (RSV). Since figurative comparisons of the life of discipleship with the activities of various workers are familiar in the canonical teachings of Jesus, and since the money-changer, as the object of comparison in this saying, was perfectly familiar in the surroundings of Jesus, the possibility exists that the saying actually came from Jesus. The interpretation of it by the church writers cited above in terms of Paul's words in 1 Th 5:21 is presumably correct. The further possibility then exists that Paul knew this as a saying of Jesus and based his own statement on it.

§144. In an extended discussion of marriage and the single life, Clement of Alexandria cites verbally a number of passages from 1 Cor 7 and then (*Stromata* III 15, 97, 4 GCS 52, 241) quotes, in the same regard, a saying of the Lord:

TEXT 10

> πάλιν ὁ κύριός φησιν· ὁ γήμας
> μὴ ἐκβαλλέτω καὶ ὁ μὴ γαμήσας
> μὴ γαμείτω.

> Again the Lord says: Whoever has married,
> let him not cast out, and whoever has not married,
> let him not marry.

The thought is in substantial agreement with 1 Cor 7:10f., 27, 32ff., but since, in the same context, Clement quotes explicitly from 1 Cor 7, yet attributes the saying presently under discussion directly to the Lord, it is hardly likely that Clement himself combined Pauline thoughts in this short formulation and ascribed it incorrectly to Jesus. In fact Paul says in 1 Cor 7:10 that the charge he gives originates not with himself but with the Lord. The teaching is also generally in harmony with Mt 19:3ff. and 19:10ff. Therefore it may be a saying which was attributed to Jesus and preserved outside the canonical Gospels, and even a saying which Paul knew (cf. §143) and was applying in his own way in his statements in 1 Cor 7.

§145. In another passage Clement of Alexandria cites Barn 6:8-10 where our Lord is praised for placing in us wisdom and understanding of his secrets (σοφίαν καὶ νοῦν τῶν κρυφίων αὐτοῦ), and then remarks

(*Stromata* V 10, 63, 7 GCS 52, 368) that this agrees with what the Lord has said "in a certain Gospel":

TEXT 11

> οὐ γὰρ φθονῶν, φησί,
> παρήγγειλεν ὁ κύριος ἔν τινι εὐαγγελίῳ·
> μυστήριον ἐμὸν ἐμοὶ καὶ τοῖς υἱοῖς
> τοῦ οἴκου μου.

> For it was not grudgingly, it is said,
> that the Lord announced in a certain Gospel:
> My mystery is for me and for the sons
> of my house.

In Mk 4:10 and parallels, Jesus speaks of the mystery or secret (μυστήριον) of the kingdom of God, which is given to the disciples but not to those outside; and Jn 8:35 speaks of the son who, in contrast with the slave, continues in the house for ever. Thus, although the present saying is characterized by a certain exclusiveness, that is not unparalleled in the canonical Gospels.

## 5 / Tertullian

§146. In his work *On Baptism* XX (CCSL I 294; ANF III 679), Tertullian cites the saying of Jesus in Mt 26:41 = Mk 14:38, cf. Lk 22:46, "Watch and pray that you may not enter into temptation." Then he states (XX 2) that another saying had preceded this one, namely:

TEXT 12

> *neminem intemptatum regna caelestia consecuturum.*
> No one untempted can obtain the celestial kingdoms.

Since the canonical saying was uttered in Gethsemane, Tertullian evidently means that the noncanonical saying which he gives as having preceded it, was expressed by Jesus at a shortly prior time, perhaps at the Last Supper or on the way to Gethsemane. It is in fact somewhat akin in thought to what Jesus said at the Last Supper in

Lk 22:28-29, and is appropriate enough as the passion history moves
toward its climax.

## 6 / Origen

§147. Origen, *Homily on Jeremiah* XIV 5 (GCS Origenes III 110)
cites this saying as written "in the Gospel":

TEXT 13

> καὶ ἐν τῷ εὐαγγελίῳ ἀναγέγραπται·
> καὶ ἀποστέλλει ἡ σοφία τὰ τέκνα αὐτῆs.

> And it is written in the Gospel:
> And wisdom sends forth her children.

Lk 7:35 (cf. Mt 11:19) mentions the "children" of wisdom. Lk 11:49
quotes the "Wisdom of God" in a statement about sending prophets
and apostles. The language of the statement quoted by Origen is,
therefore, paralleled by language in the canonical Gospels. At the
same time the possibility is raised that Origen's quotation is based
freely on the canonical Gospel passages, but the difference of formulation militates against that supposition.

§148. Origen, *Commentary on Matthew* XIII 2 (GCS 40, 183):

TEXT 14

> καὶ 'Ιησοῦς γοῦν φησίν·
> διὰ τοὺς ἀσθενοῦντας ἠσθενοῦν
> καὶ διὰ τοὺς πεινῶντας ἐπεινῶν
> καὶ διὰ τοὺς δειψῶντας ἐδιψῶν.

> And Jesus in truth says:
> Because of the sick they were sick,
> and because of the hungry they were hungry,
> and because of the thirsty they were thirsty.

The quotation is strongly reminiscent of Mt 25:35-36. It could be a
free rendering of the canonical passage, but again the distinctiveness
of phrasing suggests the possibility of an independent saying.

## 7 / Hippolytus

§149. Hippolytus, *Commentary on Daniel* IV 60 (BHP 6, 110), says that the Lord was telling the disciples about the coming of the holy kingdom, and how glorious and marvelous it would be, and Judas asked him who, then, would see these things.

TEXT 15

> ὁ δὲ κύριος ἔφη·
> ταῦτα ὄψονται οἱ ἄξιοι γενόμενοι.

But the Lord said:
Those who become worthy will see these things.

The setting of this saying sounds like the scenes which are familiar in the apocryphal Gospels (e.g., §§323, 327, 330, 338, 375, 378, 388–89) where Jesus discourses with the disciples either after the pattern of Mt 24 and parallels, or after the pattern of Ac 1:6ff., and the saying may be surmised to have had a place in some such Gospel. In and of itself, however, the saying contains concepts that are familiar in the canonical Gospels. The verb ὁράω occurs frequently, e.g., "to see a sign" (σημεῖον ἰδεῖν) in Mt 12:38, and "you will see me" (ὄψεσθέ με) in Jn 16:16. Likewise the idea of being "worthy" is often emphasized, as in Mt 10:37f., "worthy of me" (μου ἄξιος).

## 8 / Epiphanius

§150. Shortly following a quotation of Jn 1:12, and just prior to a quotation of Jn 5:46, Epiphanius, *Pan. haer.* LXVI 42, 8 (GCS 37:1, 79), also quotes Jesus as follows:

TEXT 16

> καὶ διὰ τοῦτο λέγει· ὁ λαλῶν
> ἐν τοῖς προφήταις, ἰδοὺ πάρειμι.

And therefore he says: He who speaks
in the prophets, behold, I am here.

The saying, although noncanonical, would fit well with other
Johannine sayings, and it is interesting that it is included along with
such.

§151. Mt 10:10 reads, "for the laborer deserves his food" (ἄξιος
γὰρ ὁ ἐργάτης τῆς τροφῆς αὐτοῦ), and 1 Tim 5:18 repeats the saying in
the form, "The laborer deserves his wages" (ἄξιος ὁ ἐργάτης τοῦ μισθοῦ
[Codex Sinaiticus reads τῆς τροφῆς] αὐτοῦ). Epiphanius, *Pan. haer.*
LXXX 5, 4 (GCS 37:2, 490), quotes this saying, presumably intending it as a saying of Jesus, but giving it in a form like that found in
1 Tim 5:18, ἄξιος γὰρ ὁ ἐργάτης τοῦ μισθοῦ αὐτοῦ. Then, with only the
connecting word "and" (καί), he adds a noncanonical saying of related import:

TEXT 17

ἀρκετὸν τῷ ἐργαζομένῳ ἡ τροφὴ αὐτοῦ.
Sufficient for the laborer is his food.

This presumably means that the laborer is to be satisfied with his
recompense, and may be compared with the statement in 1 Tim 6:8
("but if we have food and clothing, with these we shall be content")
in which the future passive of the related verb, ἀρκέω, is used. Together the two sayings call for a worthy reward for the worker, but
also for satisfaction with a worthy reward, and the one seems as
likely as the other to have been uttered by Jesus.

## 9 / *The Importance of the Quotations*

§152. The foregoing Texts (1–17) are not the only sayings scattered
throughout the works of the early church writers which have, upon
occasion, been taken as sayings of Jesus. They are, however, the ones
out of the larger number which seem to us to have the best claim,
through the relative antiquity and standing of the authors who cite
them, and through their own intrinsic character, to be at least considered in the search for any materials which may stand alongside the
canonical materials of the same sort. There are not many altogether

and, as we have observed in comments made above, in some or many of these there may be reasons for thinking that they could have originated in ways other than as sayings really deriving from Jesus and transmitted through channels outside the canon. Yet in their character all of these sayings have points of contact with the canonical tradition and appear deserving of notice along with the sayings which are in the canon.

# 2 / Quotations from Indicated Books

*Literature:* Erwin Preuschen, *Antilegomena.* 2d ed. 1905; Erich Klostermann, *Apocrypha,* II, *Evangelien.* KT 8, 3d ed. 1929; Martin Dibelius, *A Fresh Approach to the New Testament and Early Christian Literature.* 1936; BVA 2–15; SEA 32–61; HSNTAE 75–117.

## 1 / The Nature of the Quotations

§153. In the citation of isolated sayings of Jesus by the early church writers (§§131ff.), it was occasionally remarked that a given saying was found "in a certain Gospel" (Text 11 §145), or "in the Gospel" (Text 9 §143 Epiphanius; Text 13 §147). In at least some of these cases it was presumably what we would call an apocryphal Gospel that was meant but, in the lack of more specific identification, it is not possible to say which one. In other cases, however, the church writers give quotations which they identify as coming from books or Gospels which they name (not necessarily always correctly) or otherwise allude to, which are other than the four canonical Gospels. We turn now to the earliest and most important of these quotations and, through them, seek to get some idea of the books from which they are said to come. As before (§134), we cite the materials in the chronological order of the sources upon which we are dependent in respect to them.

## 2 / The Teaching of Peter

§154. In his Letter to the Smyrnaeans Ignatius argues (II) against Docetists (§116) who say that Christ only seemed to suffer (λέγουσιν τὸ δοκεῖν αὐτὸν πεπονθέναι), and affirms (III 1) his own knowledge and belief that even after the resurrection Christ was in the flesh (ἐγὼ γὰρ καὶ μετὰ τὴν ἀνάστασιν ἐν σαρκὶ αὐτὸν οἶδα καὶ πιστεύω ὄντα). Then he tells (III 2) how the risen Christ came to those with Peter and said to them:

TEXT 18

λάβετε, ψηλαφήσατέ με καὶ ἴδετε,
ὅτι οὐκ εἰμι δαιμόνιον ἀσώματον.

Take, handle me, and see
that I am not a bodiless demon.

Ignatius states no source from which he has derived this saying. The situation is obviously much the same as is described in Lk 24:36ff., where also (v. 39) the phrase ψηλαφήσατέ με ("handle me") occurs. But in Lk the word πνεῦμα ("spirit") is used, and not δαιμόνιον. In Greek, however, the latter term is used not only for "demons" in the sense of evil spirits as in Lk 8:30 and elsewhere, but also for "divinities" as in Ac 17:18. In Smyr III 2 the question at issue is whether the disciples are seeing a δαιμόνιον which is without a tangible body, hence the translation "ghost" or "phantom" would also be acceptable. In Lk 24:39 Christ says that "a spirit has not flesh and bones" (πνεῦμα σάρκα καὶ ὀστέα οὐκ ἔχει); here he says that he is, in literal translation of the words, "not a bodiless demon" or, as alternative translations run, "not an incorporeal spirit" (Lightfoot, *The Apostolic Fathers*, II ii 296), or "not a phantom without a body" (Lake, *The Apostolic Fathers*, LCL I 255). In this statement Ignatius could simply be giving the gist of Lk 24:36ff. in his own language. He has already declared (Smyr II) that those who say that Christ only seemed to suffer, themselves only seem to exist (αὐτοὶ τὸ δοκεῖν ὄντες), and that in the end their experience will be like their opinions, that is, they themselves will be bodiless and ghostlike (ἀσωμάτοις καὶ δαιμονικοῖς). If this is Ignatius' own language, then he could also have rephrased Lk 24:39, using the words δαιμόνιον ἀσώματον. The reverse argument seems more convincing, however, namely, that both adjectives are applied to the Docetists in Smyr II because of the striking saying about to be quoted in Smyr III 2. In that case Ignatius would have derived the saying from some source in which it stood already, but which he does not himself name.

§155. The same saying that is given in Smyr III 2 (Text 18 §154) is also quoted by Origen in the Preface (8) to his work *On the Principal Doctrines*, where the text reads in the Latin translation of Rufinus, *non sum daemonium incorporeum,* "I am not a bodiless demon" (GCS Origenes V 15; ANF IV 241). Here Origen says that this saying is quoted out of a little treatise entitled *Petri Doctrina,* the "Teaching of Peter." In the *Ch. Hist.* III 3, 1–2 Eusebius enumerates the writings under the name of Peter with which he is acquainted. 1 Pet is acknowledged as genuine. 2 Pet does not belong to the canon. Other writings which have not been universally accepted are the so-called Acts of Peter, the Gospel which bears his name, and the Preaching, and the Apocalypse. The "Preaching of Peter" (Κήρυγμα Πέτρου, *Praedicatio Petri*) could perhaps be the same work as that which Origen calls the "Teaching of Peter" but it is not necessarily the same since the name is actually different. In his own summary of the writings of Ignatius, Eusebius (*Ch. Hist.* III 36, 11) quotes the same saying in the Letter to the Smyrnaeans which we are discussing and says that he does not know from what source Ignatius took it. Therefore the saying was probably not in the "Preaching of Peter," a book which was known to Eusebius. Accordingly it becomes more probable that the "Teaching of Peter" was a separate work, unknown to Eusebius, and a work from which Ignatius could have derived the saying about the "bodiless demon."

§156. Jerome, however, complicates the matter by attributing the same saying (Text 18 §154) to a different source. In his *Lives of Illustrious Men* 16 (NPNFSS III 366) he says:

> Ignatius . . . wrote . . . *To the Smyrnaeans* and especially *To Polycarp.* . . . In this last he bore witness to the Gospel which I have recently translated, in respect of the person of Christ saying, "I indeed saw him in the flesh after the resurrection and I believe that he is," and when he came to Peter and those who were with Peter, he said to them, "Behold! handle me and see that I am not a bodiless demon. And straightway they touched him and believed."

Later in the Preface to his *Commentary on Isaiah* XVIII (CCSL 73A) Jerome again attributes the same saying to the same source:

> For when the apostles thought him a spirit (*spiritum*) or, according to the Gospel of the Hebrews which the Nazaraeans (*Nazaraei*) read, a bodiless demon (*incorporale daemonium*), he said to them. . . .

In spite of these unhesitating statements, the witness of Jerome is not beyond question. The statement that Ignatius made the quotation under consideration in his Letter to Polycarp is of course incorrect, since the quotation is actually in his Letter to the Smyrnaeans. The statement that the quotation bore witness to the Gospel which Jerome himself had recently translated, also requires scrutiny. Earlier in *Lives of Illustrious Men* (2) (cf. above §53) Jerome spoke of the Gospel according to the Hebrews, said that he had recently translated it into Greek and Latin, and that Origen often used it. It is true, as we shall see (§167), that Origen quoted from the Gospel according to the Hebrews, but he did so while he was still in Alexandria and he gave the quotation in Greek, both of which facts make it probable that he was using a Greek book. Clement of Alexandria also quoted from the Gospel according to the Hebrews in Greek (§166), and Hegesippus referred to it in apparent contrast with an Aramaic Gospel (§165). If, as seems probable, this evidence means that the Gospel according to the Hebrews was originally in Greek, then Jerome would have had no need to translate it into Greek.

In *Lives of Illustrious Men* (3) (cf. above §53) Jerome also said that in Beroea the Nazaraeans described to him a book containing the Gospel according to Matthew in its original Hebrew language; in *Against the Pelagians* (III 2) (cf. above §53) he said that the Gospel according to the Hebrews was written in the Aramaic language but in Hebrew characters, and was the same as the Gospel according to Matthew or the Gospel according to the Apostles; and in both of these last two passages he said that there was also a copy of the text in the library at Caesarea. Jerome may well be correct that there was an Aramaic Gospel in use among the Nazaraeans in Beroea, a copy of which was also in the library at Caesarea. If it bore some resemblance to the canonical Gospel according to Matthew it could have been taken for the Semitic original of that work. Jerome could also have intended to translate this Aramaic Gospel into Greek and Latin and, with that intention in mind, have spoken of it as if he had already done so. But it does not seem likely that he had actually translated the work from which Ignatius took the quotation in Smyr III 2, for he gives as if it were included in the quotation which Ignatius allegedly took from this source not only the saying proper but also Ignatius' own affirmation of belief that the risen Christ was "in the flesh" (§154). Therefore Jerome was quoting directly neither from Ignatius nor from his alleged source, but more probably from some secondhand source, perhaps from Eusebius (§155). Eusebius himself, however, would presumably have known the Aramaic Gospel which was still in the library at Caesarea in the time of Jerome, and he also knows the Gospel according to the Hebrews (§169). Since he says (§155) that he does not know from whence Ignatius derived the quotation we are discussing, it is not likely that the saying came from either the Aramaic Gospel in the library at Caesarea or the Gospel according to the Hebrews. Jerome must have been mistaken, then, as to the original source of the saying, even as he was also confused as to which letter of Ignatius it was in and as to exactly what the text of the saying was. Accordingly, the older witness of Origen (§155) may be preferred to the later and confused affirmations of Jerome, and it may be judged probable that Ignatius derived the saying, which he himself quotes without giving the source, from an otherwise unidentified work called the "Teaching of Peter" (*Petri Doctrina*).

## 3 / The Gospel According to the Egyptians

§157. In the foregoing case (§§154–56) a quotation was given by an early writer (Ignatius) without a statement of the source, and then the same quotation was repeated by a later writer (Origen) with a statement of the source ("The Teaching of Peter"), although a yet later writer (Jerome) complicates the matter by indicating a still different source ("The Gospel according to the Hebrews"). In respect to the next work now to be considered, the same situation prevails to the extent that a quotation is given first without identification of source and then, later, is given again with indication of the work in question. In the so-called Second Letter of Clement, which probably dates before 150 and surely not later than 170 (see the List of Ancient Sources) is found (2 Clem 12, 2) the following quotation. It is introduced as a statement made by the Lord himself (αὐτὸς ὁ κύριος) in answer to an interrogation by someone as to when his kingdom (αὐτοῦ ἡ βασιλεία) would come. He said:

TEXT 19A

> ὅταν ἔσται τὰ δύο ἕν,
> καὶ τὸ ἔξω ὡς τὸ ἔσω,
> καὶ τὸ ἄρσεν μετὰ τῆς θηλείας
> οὔτε ἄρσεν οὔτε θῆλυ.

> When the two shall be one,
> and the outside as the inside,
> and the male with the female
> neither male nor female.

§158. Recognizably the same quotation is given by Clement of Alexandria and ascribed to a specific source. In his *Stromata* III 13, 91ff. (GCS Clemens Alexandrinus II 238f.; ANF II 398) Clement deals with and controverts the teachings of Julius Cassianus ('Ιούλιος Κασσιανός). This teacher, Clement says (III 13, 92), came out of the school of Valentinus (ὁ δ' ἐκ τῆς Οὐαλεντίνου ἐξεφοίτησε σχολῆς), and was (III 13, 91) the originator of Docetism (ὁ τῆς δοκήσεως ἐξάρχων) (§116). From the date of Valentinus (§107) we may suppose that Cassianus, his follower, was active about A.D. 170, and from the concern with him of Clement of Alexandria may also suppose that he taught in Egypt. Among the writings of Cassianus was a treatise entitled (III 13, 91) *On Continence*, or *On Eunuchry* (Περὶ ἐγκρατείας ἢ περὶ εὐνουχίας), from which Clement quotes. Two of the quotations (III 13, 91–92) reject all sexual intercourse and constitute a teaching similar, as Clement points out, to that of Tatian (§103). The third quotation, which is that with which we are here concerned, is introduced by Clement (III 13, 92) with these words: "Accordingly Cassianus says: When Salome inquired when the things she had asked about would be known, the Lord said." Then follows the quotation (III 13, 92, 2):

TEXT 19B

> ὅταν τὸ τῆς αἰσχύνης ἔνδυμα πατήσητε
> καὶ ὅταν γένηται τὰ δύο ἕν
> καὶ τὸ ἄρρεν μετὰ τῆς θηλείας
> οὔτε ἄρρεν οὔτε θῆλυ.

When you have trampled on the garment of shame
and when the two become one
and the male with the female
neither male nor female.

As compared with the quotation in 2 Clem (§157), there is here added the statement about trampling on the garment of shame, while that about the outside being as the inside is omitted. Otherwise the wording is almost the same, ἄρσεν (ἄρσην) being replaced with the later ἄρρεν (ἄρρην). Then Clement adds: "Now in the first place we do not have this word in the four Gospels which have been transmitted to us, but in the Gospel according to the Egyptians (ἀλλ' ἐν τῷ κατ' Αἰγυπτίους)." Thus Clement of Alexandria tells us the source of the quotation which stands without source ascription in 2 Clem; at the same time 2 Clem remains as the earlier witness to show that the Gospel from which the quotation came must have been in existence in the early part of the second century. In his attitude toward this Gospel according to the Egyptians, Clement speaks as if he did not place it on a level with the canonical Gospels but still did not repudiate it entirely. While in its teaching the text in question might be considered to rest back upon Gal 3:28, Cassianus evidently found in it a strong Gnostic Encratite (§§103, 116) implication, and Clement attempted to deny this by explaining that Cassianus was ignorant of the fact that the male impulse really signifies wrath, and the female, lust.

§159. Whether certain other quotations in 2 Clem, the source of which is not given, should also be ascribed to the Gospel according to the Egyptians, is not certain.[1] Some of them can be explained plausibly as free quotations or expansions of canonical material, and none is as radically different from the canonical tradition as is the saying above (Text 19), so as to make it truly probable that it too comes from the Gospel according to the Egyptians.

§160. In Clement's *Stromata* III 6, 45, 3 (GCS Clemens Alexandrinus II 217) this conversation between Salome and the Lord is recorded. Salome asked:

TEXT 20A

> μέχρι πότε θάνατος ἰσχύσει;
> How long will death have power?

The Lord said:

> μέχρις ἂν ὑμεῖς αἱ γυναῖκες τίκτητε.
> As long as you women bear children.

Clement again (cf. §158) combats the obvious Encratite implication of the saying by explaining that the Lord said this, not as if life were bad and the creation evil, but simply as teaching the normal sequence of birth and death which is evident in nature (οὐχ ὡς κακοῦ τοῦ βίου ὄντος καὶ τῆς κτίσεως πονηρᾶς . . . ἀλλ' ὡς τὴν ἀκολουθίαν τὴν φυσικὴν διδάσκων).

§161. In sequence with the foregoing passage (Text 20 §160) Clement cites in *Stromata* III 9, 63 (GCS Clemens Alexandrinus II 225) another saying addressed to Salome. This is quoted, he says, by those who array themselves against the creation of God because of what is euphemistically called continence (διὰ τῆς εὐφήμου ἐγκρα-

---

[1] HSNTAE 112–14.

τείας), i.e., it is quoted by the Encratites, and the saying is carried, Clement believes, in the Gospel according to the Egyptians. The Savior said (III 9, 63, 2):

TEXT 21

> ἦλθον καταλῦσαι τὰ ἔργα τῆς θηλείας.
> I came to destroy the works of the female.

§162. Very shortly hereafter Clement (*Stromata* III 9, 64, 1) quotes again the question of Salome much as before (§160):

TEXT 20B

> μέχρι τίνος οἱ ἄνθρωποι ἀποθανοῦνται;
> How long will men die?

and the answer of the Lord in almost identical fashion:

> μέχρις ἂν τίκτωσιν αἱ γυναῖκες.
> As long as women bear children.

§163. In *Stromata* III 9, 66, 2 (GCS Clemens Alexandrinus II 226) Clement speaks about people who do everything except walk in the evangelical rule according to truth (οἱ πάντα μᾶλλον ἢ τῷ κατὰ τὴν ἀλήθειαν εὐαγγελικῷ στοιχήσαντες κανόνι). As if it were not fitting to participate in procreation, they cite this saying of Salome:

TEXT 22

> καλῶς οὖν ἐποίησα μὴ τεκοῦσα.
> I have done well, then, in not bearing children.

Clement himself asks why these people do not also cite the answer of the Lord, which he evidently understands in other than an Encratite sense, namely, the words:

> πᾶσαν φάγε βοτάνην,
> τὴν δὲ πικρίαν ἔχουσαν μὴ φάγῃς.
> Eat every plant,
> but do not eat the one which has bitterness.

§164. Here, then, in Clement is a series of passages (Texts 19–22 §§158–63) in which a dialogue or dialogues between Salome and Jesus are recorded. Although Clement endeavors to argue against the interpretation, all the passages are evidently intended in the first place to convey an Encratite doctrine. Two passages (Texts 19 and 21) are ascribed by Clement to the Gospel according to the Egyptians. All, because of the similarity of setting and teaching, probably come from the same work. In the lack of any indication to the contrary, we may assume that this work was written in the language in which it is quoted by 2 Clem and Clement of Alexandria, namely, Greek. Cited mainly by an Alexandrian authority, and bearing the name it does, the Gospel according to the Egyptians was no doubt an Egyptian work. As we have seen (§158), it must be dated as early as the early part of the second century. It may be taken, therefore, as representing the Gnostic-Encratite movement as it existed in Egypt in the early second century.

## 4 / The Gospel According to the Hebrews

§165. As far as our records go, Hegesippus is the first witness to the existence of the Gospel according to the Hebrews. In the *Ch. Hist.* IV 22 Eusebius refers to and quotes from, evidently with high regard, the writings of Hegesippus "in the five books of Memoirs which have come down to us" (ἐν πέντε τοῖς εἰς ἡμᾶς ἐλθοῦσιν ὑπομνήμασιν). In one of the quotations which Eusebius gives (IV 22, 3), Hegesippus tells of visiting Rome and mentions Anicetus (154–66), Soter (166–74), and Eleutherus (174–89), hence was probably there in their time but had his home somewhere else. The statement of Eusebius about Hegesippus with which we are now concerned is this (IV 22, 8):

ἔκ τε τοῦ καθ' 'Εβραίους εὐαγγελίου καὶ τοῦ Συριακοῦ καὶ ἰδίως ἐκ τῆς 'Εβραΐδος διαλέκτου τινὰ τίθησιν.

And from the Gospel according to the Hebrews, and from the Syriac and particularly from the Hebrew language he makes some extracts.

According to this statement Hegesippus made some extracts, i.e., quoted some passages, from two works. One is the Gospel according to the Hebrews. The other is "the Syriac," presumably another Gospel written in Syriac. In fact Hegesippus took special interest in quotations from "the Hebrew language," and Eusebius adds that this shows that he was a convert from among the Hebrews. By the Hebrew language or dialect Eusebius normally means Aramaic,[1] and Syriac is a form of Aramaic.[2] Therefore the quotations from the Aramaic ("Hebrew dialect") were from the Aramaic ("Syriac") Gospel. Accordingly it may be presumed that the other work was not in Aramaic, which would leave it most likely that it was in Greek. If a Gospel written in Greek was known as the Gospel according to the Hebrews it must mean that it was in use among Greek-speaking, Jewish Christians. That the work of this name is cited already by Hegesippus shows that it must have been in existence at least by the middle of the second century. These conclusions about the probable language and date of the Gospel according to the Hebrews are supported by the fact that the first explicit quotations which we have from this work are made by Clement of Alexandria and Origen (§§166–67), Greek Christian writers of the end of the second and beginning of the third centuries. The fact that the first quotations are made by these Alexandrian writers suggests further that the Gospel according to the Hebrews may have originated in Egypt, although the acquaintance with it of Hegesippus, himself a convert from among the Hebrews, makes it probable that it was also in circulation in the area of Palestine and Syria. Perhaps it was called the Gospel according to the Hebrews to differentiate it as the Gospel used by the Jewish Christians in Egypt from the Gospel according to the Egyptians, the latter in that case being the Gospel which was in use among the Egyptian Christians (§164) who had come out of a pagan background.

§166. The quotation by Clement is found in his *Stromata* II 9, 45, 5 (GCS Clemens Alexandrinus II 137; ANF II 358), where he gives the following saying as written (γέγραπται) in the Gospel according to the Hebrews (τῷ καθ' 'Εβραίους εὐαγγελίῳ):

TEXT 23A

ὁ θαυμάσας βασιλεύσει,
καὶ ὁ βασιλεύσας ἀναπαήσεται.

He who wonders shall reign,
and he who reigns shall rest.

What is evidently the same text in a somewhat fuller citation is given in *Stromata* V 14, 96, 3 (GCS Clemens Alexandrinus II 389; ANF II

---

[1] HSNTAE 78.
[2] A. Jeffery in IDB I 189.

467), but without mention at this point of the source from which it is taken.

TEXT 23B

> οὐ παύσεται ὁ ζητῶν, ἕως ἂν εὕρῃ·
> εὑρὼν δὲ θαμβηθήσεται,
> θαμβηθεὶς δὲ βασιλεύσει,
> βασιλεύσας δὲ ἐπαναπαήσεται.

He who seeks will not cease until he find;
and having found he will be astounded,
and being astounded he will reign,
and reigning he will rest.

This saying in its fuller form is found in almost the same words, although only fragmentarily preserved, in a saying in Oxyrhynchus Papyrus 654 (§218) and also in the Coptic Gospel according to Thomas (§289). Since OP 654 and the Gospel according to Thomas do not otherwise coincide with the fragments we are able to recover of the Gospel according to the Hebrews, it is not probable that the papyrus is a part of a copy of this Gospel. Rather it is simply indicated that this particular saying was current where the Gospel and the papyrus both originated, which also agrees with placing the Gospel according to the Hebrews in Egypt (§165). The conception of "rest" as the highest goal is typical of Gnostic thought (§110) but, since this is an otherwise current saying which has been taken up into the Gospel it is not necessary to conclude that the Gospel according to the Hebrews itself is essentially Gnostic, indeed in other sayings it seems not to be.

§167. Origen quotes from the Gospel according to the Hebrews in his *Commentary on John*, the first four volumes of which were probably written at Alexandria between 226 and 229.[3] Here in II 12 (6) (GCS Origenes IV 67; ANF IX 329) he remarks that if any one accepts the Gospel according to the Hebrews (ἐὰν δὲ προσιῆταί τις τὸ καθ᾽ Ἑβραίους εὐαγγέλιον), there the Savior himself says:

TEXT 24

> ἄρτι ἔλαβέ με ἡ μήτηρ μου, τὸ ἅγιον πνεῦμα,
> ἐν μιᾷ τῶν τριχῶν μου καὶ ἀπήνεγκέ με
> εἰς τὸ ὄρος τὸ μέγα Θαβώρ.

---

[3] Johannes Quasten, *Patrology* II (1953), 49.

> Then my mother, the Holy Spirit, took me
> by one of my hairs and carried me off
> to the great mount Tabor.

Also in his *Homilies on Jeremiah* XV 4 (GCS Origenes III 128) Origen begins, "But if any one accepts the (saying)" (εἰ δέ τις παραδέχεται τό), and then continues with the same quotation in only slightly abbreviated form:

> Then my mother, the Holy Spirit, took me
> and carried me off
> to the great mount Tabor.

It is usually assumed that this is a variant to Mt 4:8 in the account of the temptation of Jesus and, if this is correct, Jesus is evidently represented as narrating that event to the disciples himself. Such a representation was presumably intended to answer the natural question as to how the disciples knew about an event which happened to Jesus in his solitude. The facts that the Spirit took Ezekiel by a lock of his head from the land of the Chaldeans to Jerusalem (Ezk 8:3), and that an angel lifted Habakkuk by his hair from Judea to Babylon (Bel 36), may have suggested the manner of transport. For the conception of the Holy Spirit as the mother of Jesus, comparison may be made with the Coptic Letter of James found in the Jung Codex (§§124, 126) in which Jesus calls himself the "son of the Holy Spirit."[4] Since the comparison is with a Coptic work, support is again given to the idea that the Gospel according to the Hebrews comes from Egypt (§165). Basically, no doubt, the idea of the Holy Spirit as the "mother" rests back upon the fact that the word spirit, although it is neuter in Greek (τὸ πνεῦμα), is feminine in Hebrew (רוח, Gen 1:2, etc.). The present saying obviously represents a quite different tradition of the temptation from that in the Synoptic Gospels. Also the evidences of thought development, including the possible use of ideas from Ezk 8:3 and Bel 36, suggest a relatively late stage in tradition.

§168. In the extant writings of Origen there is one other quotation, of some length, which is said to be from the Gospel according to the Hebrews. This is found, however, not in the Greek text of Origen but only in an expanded Latin version and may, therefore, come only from a reviser of his work. In character this passage is closely related to an account in the Synoptic Gospels, therefore may be only erroneously attributed to the Gospel according to the Hebrews, since that

[4] H.-Ch. Puech and G. Quispel in *Vigiliae Christianae* 8 (1954), 12.

Gospel appears, from the preceding quotation by Origen (§167), to be of a quite different type from the Synoptics. The quotation in the Latin version will, therefore, be left for consideration at a later point (§176).

§169. In addition to his mention of the use of the Gospel according to the Hebrews by Hegesippus (§165), Eusebius makes certain other references to the same work. As we have seen (§31 Table 9), in relation to the canon he puts it in the sequence of writings which he labels "spurious," remarking that some have placed it there, but saying also that in it "those of the Hebrews who have accepted Christ take a special pleasure" (*Ch. Hist.* III 25, 5). It was, accordingly, a favorite book of Jewish Christians. In telling about the Ebionites (§51) he says that they used only the Gospel according to the Hebrews and made little account of the rest (*Ch. Hist.* III 27, 4). As to the content of this Gospel, Eusebius gives us one item of information. Mentioning that Papias relates a "story about a woman who was accused before the Lord of many sins," Eusebius states that this story is contained in the Gospel according to the Hebrews (*Ch. Hist.* III 39, 17). Whether Papias derived the story from this Gospel, and could thereby be cited as an early witness to the existence of the Gospel according to the Hebrews, or whether he obtained it from some other source, perhaps from oral tradition, is not said. Eusebius himself, however, knows the story as one that was in the Gospel according to the Hebrews. From the brief description of the nature of the story it cannot be identified positively, but is usually thought to be that which has found its way into the Fourth Gospel in an addition in the Koine text (Jn 7:53–8:11) which is not in the Egyptian text.

§170. It has already been established (§§53, 156) that the statements of Jerome about the Gospel according to the Hebrews are not only confusing but probably actually confused, particularly in consequence of what appears to be his erroneous identification of this Gospel with a different Aramaic Gospel in use among the Nazaraeans at Beroea and extant in his day in a copy in the library at Caesarea. It has also been established (§§165ff.) that the Gospel according to the Hebrews was probably a Greek work originating in Egypt and quite different from the Synoptic Gospels, and (§156) that the Gospel used by the Nazaraeans was probably an Aramaic work and perhaps somewhat similar to the canonical Gospel according to Matthew. If our analysis of the confusion in Jerome is correct, he may easily attribute to the Gospel according to the Hebrews quotations which actually come from the Gospel used by the Nazaraeans, and vice versa. Jerome does, in fact, attribute a considerable number of quotations to the Gospel according to the Hebrews (which he refers to in varied phraseology), but of these we may ourselves prefer to list as probably coming from that source only those which appear to be quite different in character from the Synoptic tradition, and to suppose that those of greater kinship with the Synoptic tradition and particularly with the Gospel according to Matthew may actually come from the Gospel used by the Nazaraeans (§§175ff.).

§171. In his *Commentary on Isaiah* IV 11, 2 (CCSL LXXIII 148), Jerome refers to the Gospel written in the Hebrew language which the Nazaraeans read (*euangelium quod Hebraeo sermone conscriptum legunt Nazaraei*) and says that the following passage is found written (*scripta*) in it:

TEXT 25

> *factum est autem cum ascendisset dominus*
> *de aqua, descendit fons omnis spiritus sancti,*
> *et requieuit super eum, et dixit illi: fili mi,*
> *in omnibus prophetis exspectabam te, ut uenires,*
> *et recquiescerem in te. tu es enim requies mea,*
> *tu es filius meus primogenitus, qui regnas*
> *in sempiternum.*

> And it came to pass when the Lord came up
> out of the water, the whole fount of the Holy Spirit descended,
> and rested upon him, and said to him: My Son,
> in all the prophets I was waiting for you, that you might come,
> and that I might rest in you. For you are my rest;
> you are my firstborn Son, who reigns
> forever.

The designation of the source of this saying as the Gospel which the Nazaraeans read, and the parallelism of the phrase, "when the Lord came up out of the water," with Mt 3:16 = Mk 1:10, might suggest that this saying comes from the Nazaraean Gospel rather than the Gospel according to the Hebrews (§170). For the most part, however, the account is quite different from the account of the baptism in Mt and the Synoptics, and the manner in which the Holy Spirit addresses Jesus as "My Son" agrees with the conception in Text 24 and with the mention of Jesus as the "son of the Holy Spirit" in the Coptic source cited in connection therewith (§167). Therefore attribution of the saying to the Gospel according to the Hebrews is probable.

§172. Two more sayings quoted by Jerome (Texts 26 and 27) are much in harmony with the spirit of the teachings of Jesus as known in the canonical Gospels, but lack specific parallels there and may, accordingly, be considered to come from the Gospel according to the Hebrews rather than from the Nazaraean Gospel (§170). In his *Commentary on Ezekiel* 18, 7 (KT 8, 11 No. 24), Jerome says that in the Gospel according to the Hebrews which the Nazaraeans read, there is put among the greatest sins:

TEXT 26

> *qui fratris sui spiritum contristaurit.*
> Who has grieved the spirit of his brother.

§173. In his *Commentary on Ephesians* 5, 4 (KT 8, 11 No. 25), Jerome says that "we read in the Hebrew Gospel" (*in Hebraico euangelio*) that the Lord spoke to the disciples:

TEXT 27

> *et numquam (inquit) laeti sitis, nisi*
> *cum fratrem uestrum uideritis in caritate.*
> And never (he said) be joyful except
> when you look on your brother with love.

§174. The longest quotation which we have from the Gospel according to the Hebrews is given by Jerome in the second chapter of his *Lives of Illustrious Men* (NPNFSS III 362) where he tells about James, the brother of the Lord and the head of the church at Jerusalem after the apostles (§§40f.). Here he cites the Gospel according to the Hebrews, and mentions the frequent use of it by Origen. Since Jerome is not too clear about this Gospel (§156), and since Origen quoted from it directly (§167), Jerome may have taken the quotation at secondhand from Origen which would, in this case, give better attestation for it than if we depended upon Jerome alone. Jerome cites the Gospel as saying, "after the account of the resurrection of the Savior" (*post resurrectionem saluatoris refert*):

TEXT 28

> *dominus autem, cum dedisset sindonem*
> *seruo sacerdotis iuit ad Iacobum et apparuit ei.*
> *eurauerat enim Iacobus se non comesurum panem*
> *ab illa hora qua biberat calicem domini,*
> *donec uideret eum resurgentem a dormientibus.*

But the Lord, when he had given the linen cloth to the servant of the priest, went to James and appeared to him. For James had sworn that he would not eat bread from that hour in which he had drunk the cup of the Lord until he should see him rising again from among them that sleep.

Then a little farther on (*rursusque post paululum*), continues Jerome, it says:

> *adferte (ait dominus) mensam et panem.*
> Bring (said the Lord) a table and bread.

And immediately, says Jerome, as he completes the quotation, it is added:

> *tulit panem et benedixit et fregit*
> *et dedit Iacobo iusto et dixit ei:*
> *frater mi, comede panem tuum, quia*
> *resurrexit filius hominis a dormientibus.*
>
> He took bread and blessed and broke
> and gave it to James the Just and said to him:
> My brother, eat your bread, for
> the Son of man is risen from among them that sleep.

This narrative is certainly different from that of the canonical Gospels. It presupposes that James, the brother of the Lord, was present at the Last Supper. It relates that the risen Christ gave "the linen cloth" (cf. Mt 27:59; Mk 15:46; Lk 23:53; Jn 19:40) to the servant of the priest, and thereby makes him the first witness to the resurrection. It describes the first appearance of the risen Christ to a known leader of the early church as being vouchsafed to James. The prominence of James the Just, brother of the Lord and, by the testimony of Josephus as well as of Christian writers (§41), leader of the Jewish Christians, is appropriate in a Jewish Christian document, and the entire passage may be taken as our most characteristic excerpt from the Gospel according to the Hebrews.[5] At the same time the account will not be devoid of historical foundation for Paul, too, certifies that there was a known appearance of the risen Christ to James (1 Cor 15:7).

[5] Dibelius, *A Fresh Approach to the New Testament and Early Christian Literature*, 81f.

## 5 / The Gospel of the Nazaraeans

§175. We have seen (§165) that Hegesippus, who is our earliest witness to the Gospel according to the Hebrews, mentions, in apparently clear distinction from it, a Syriac Gospel, i.e., one existing presumably in Aramaic.

§176. As also already noted, Origen gives one quotation from the Gospel according to the Hebrews (Text 24 §167) which embodies a quite different concept (the Holy Spirit as the mother of Jesus) from that in any parallel passage in the canonical Gospels, and another quotation attributed to the same source, consideration of which was deferred (§168) until now. The latter passage is found in Origen's *Commentary on Matthew* XV 14 (GCS Origenes X 389–90), but is only in the Latin translation and not in the Greek text, therefore may come from a reviser of the work and not from Origen himself. The quotation given, which is of some length, is said to be written in the Gospel according to the Hebrews (*scriptum est in evangelio quodam, quod dicitur secundum Hebraeos*). In this case, however, in contrast with the other quotation (Text 24), the tradition is very similar to Synoptic tradition. As might be expected in an account adduced in a *Commentary on Matthew*, the material is closely parallel to an account in Mt, namely Mt 19:16-24, with parallels in Mk 10:17-25 and Lk 18:18-25. The text reads:

TEXT 29

> *dixit (inquit) ad eum alter divitum:*
> *magister quid bonum faciens vivam? dixit*
> *ei: homo, legem et prophetas fac.*
> *respondit ad eum: feci. dixit ei:*
> *vade, vende omnia quae possides et*
> *divide pauperibus, et veni, sequere me.*
> *coepit autem dives scalpere caput suum*
> *et non placuit ei. et dixit ad eum dominus:*
> *quomodo dicis: feci legem et prophetas?*
> *quoniam scriptum est in lege: diliges*
> *proximum tuum sicut teipsum, et ecce*
> *multi fratres tui filii Abrahae*

*amicti sunt stercore, morientes prae fame,*
*et domus tua plena est multis bonis,*
*et non egreditur omnino aliquid ex ea*
*ad eos. et conversus dixit Simoni*
*discipulo suo sedenti apud se: Simon,*
*fili Ionae, facilius est camelum intrare*
*per foramen acus quam divitem*
*in regnum caelorum.*

The other one of the two rich men (it says) said to him:
Teacher, what good thing can I do and live? He said
to him: Man, do what is in the Law and the Prophets.
He answered him: I have done it. He said to him:
Go, sell all that you possess, and
distribute to the poor, and come, follow me.
But the rich man began to scratch his head,
and it did not please him. And the Lord said to him:
How can you say, I have done what is in the Law and the
Prophets?
When it is written in the law: You shall love
your neighbor as yourself, and behold,
many of your brothers, sons of Abraham,
are clothed in filth, dying of hunger,
and your house is full of many good things,
and not anything at all of it goes out
to them. And he turned and said to Simon,
his disciple, who was sitting by him: Simon,
son of Jonah, it is easier for a camel to enter in
through the eye of a needle than for a rich man
to enter into the kingdom of heaven.

As compared with Mt and the Synoptic tradition, changes found here
appear intended to make a livelier story, as, e.g., the facts that
there are two rich men and that, upon hearing the saying of Jesus,
the one begins to scratch his head in puzzlement. In addition to the
direct parallel with Mt 19:16-24, there is a similarity of attitude in
the description of the rich man's house full of good things, none of
which goes forth to those dying of hunger, with that in the parable
of the rich man and Lazarus in Lk 16:19-31. Also Semitic, biblical,
and Palestinian flavor is preserved, e.g., in the phrase "sons of
Abraham." The present passage, quotation of which in Origen's
works we may owe to a reviser, is different, therefore, from the
quotation (Text 24) which Origen himself makes from the Gospel

according to the Hebrews and may be judged more probably to come from some other work and only incorrectly to be attributed to the Gospel according to the Hebrews. The other work, whatever it may be, is, to judge from this example, relatively similar to Mt, yet different from it.

§177. Eusebius makes specific mention of the Gospel according to the Hebrews (§169), and in apparently clear distinction from it (§179) speaks of another Gospel which was in circulation among the Jews. In the Syriac version of his *Theophany*, he discusses the statement of Jesus about division in households which is found in Mt 10:34-36 (with a parallel in Lk 12:51-53), and then says that the basic cause of the division of souls which takes place in such households is given in another teaching of Jesus. The latter saying, Eusebius declares (*Theophany* IV 12, 140 GCS Eusebius III 2, 183), "we have found somewhere in the Gospel which is (circulated) among the Jews in the Hebrew language." It says:

TEXT 30

> I choose for myself the most worthy,
> whom my Father in heaven gives me.

From this, Eusebius adds, one can learn that in all households in which the word of Jesus triumphs, the better are separated from the worse.

§178. There is also a Greek fragment, which probably belongs to the *Theophany* of Eusebius, which outlines a variant version of the parable of the talents in Mt 25:14-30 and says that this other version is found in "the Gospel (written) in Hebrew characters." The passage (KT 8, 9 No. 15) reads:

TEXT 31

ἐπεὶ δὲ τὸ εἰς ἡμᾶς ἧκον Ἐβραϊκοῖς
χαρακτῆρσιν εὐαγγέλιον τὴν ἀπειλὴν
οὐ κατὰ τοῦ ἀποκρύψαντος ἐπῆγεν, ἀλλὰ κατὰ
τοῦ ἀσώτως ἐζηκότος—τρεῖς γὰρ δούλους περιεῖχε,
τὸν μὲν καταφαγόντα τὴν ὕπαρξιν τοῦ δεσπότου
μετὰ πορνῶν καὶ αὐλητρίδων, τὸν δὲ πολλαπλασιάσαντα
τὴν ἐργασίαν, τὸν δὲ κατακρύψαντα τὸ τάλαντον.
εἶτα τὸν μὲν ἀποδεχθῆναι, τὸν δὲ μεμφθῆναι μόνον,
τὸν δὲ συγκλεισθῆναι δεσμωτηρίῳ—ἐφίστημι, μήποτε
κατὰ τὸν Ματθαῖον μετὰ τὴν συμπλήρωσιν τοῦ λόγου

τοῦ κατὰ τοῦ μηδὲν ἐργασαμένου
ἡ ἐξῆς ἐπιλεγομένη ἀπειλὴ οὐ περὶ αὐτοῦ,
ἀλλὰ περὶ τοῦ προτέρου κατ᾽ ἐπανάληψιν λέλεκται,
τοῦ ἐσθίοντος καὶ πίνοντος μετὰ τῶν μεθυόντων.

But since the Gospel (written) in Hebrew
characters which has come to us turns the threat
not against the man who hid (the talent), but against
the man who lived riotously—for (the master) had three
servants,
one who wasted his master's substance
with harlots and flute-girls, one who multiplied
the earnings, and one who hid the talent;
accordingly one was accepted, but one was only rebuked,
and one was shut up in prison—I wonder whether
in Matthew after the saying
against the man who did nothing,
the threat which is then uttered is not concerning him
but, resumptively, concerning the first man,
who ate and drank with the drunken.

§179. The Gospel from which Eusebius makes these two citations
(Texts 30 and 31) is not the Gospel according to the Hebrews, for
elsewhere he uses that title plainly (§169), but does not do so here.
The Gospel cited here is one which circulates among the Jews and is
written in the Hebrew language or in Hebrew characters, which
could be in Aramaic. It could be the same Aramaic Gospel to which
Hegesippus refers (§175). It was similar to the canonical Gospel
according to Matthew, for the passages cited by Eusebius are related
to passages in Mt, but it was different from Mt, for Eusebius institutes comparison between the two (§178), and uses the one to illumi-
nate the other (§177).

§180. Jerome, we have already noted (§§156, 170), probably con-
fuses the Gospel according to the Hebrews which he mentions
repeatedly, and a Gospel in Hebrew or Aramaic which the Nazaraeans
at Beroea (Aleppo) described to him, of which there was also a copy
in the library at Caesarea. This Jerome also sometimes identifies
with the Gospel according to Matthew. Since the copy at Caesarea
would have been accessible to Eusebius of Caesarea, and since the
Gospel in Hebrew characters which Eusebius cites was similar to but
not identical with Mt (which similarity could account for Jerome's
thinking that such a work was the Hebrew original of Mt), the
Gospel cited by Eusebius (and perhaps also referred to by Hegesippus

[§175] and quoted from in the Latin text of Origen [§176]) could be this latter Gospel of the Nazaraeans of which Jerome has imprecise knowledge and concerning which he makes confusing statements. The confusion in Jerome extends to his quotations which probably come indiscriminately from both the Gospel according to the Hebrews and the Gospel of the Nazaraeans, perhaps by way of secondary sources (which could account for the confusion), under various source references such as to the Gospel according to the Hebrews, the Hebrew Gospel, the Gospel which the Nazaraeans read, etc. In the endeavor to classify these quotations as found in Jerome, it has been suggested (§170) that materials quite different from those of the canonical tradition may have stood in the Gospel according to the Hebrews, materials more like those of the Synoptic tradition in general and like what is in Mt in particular may have been in the Gospel which was used by the Nazaraeans. Following these criteria, certain sayings quoted by Jerome have already been listed under the Gospel according to the Hebrews (§§171–74); others will now (§§181–88) be listed as deriving perhaps from the Gospel of the Nazaraeans.

§181. In *Lives of Illustrious Men* (KT 8, 6 No. 2; NPNFSS III 362) Jerome speaks of Matthew and the Gospel which he wrote, the Hebrew original of which Jerome says is preserved in the library at Caesarea and was also described to him by the Nazaraeans of Beroea (§156). He goes on to say that where Matthew quotes the OT he does not follow the Septuagint but the Hebrew. As two examples of this practice he cites (*Lives of Illustrious Men* 3) two sayings, as follows:

TEXT 32

> *ex Aegypto vocaui filium meum.*
> Out of Egypt have I called my son.

TEXT 33

> *quoniam Nazaraeus vocabitur.*
> For he shall be called a Nazaraean.

These correspond to the quotations in Mt 2:15 and 2:23 but, in the light of Jerome's reference to the Gospel of the Nazaraeans, may have stood in that source too.

§182. In *Against the Pelagians* III 2 (KT 8, 6 No. 3; NPNFSS VI 472) Jerome speaks of the Gospel according to the Hebrews which is used by the Nazaraeans, is also the Gospel according to the Apostles

or the Gospel according to Matthew, and is, in one copy, in the
library at Caesarea. From this so-described source he cites the
following passage:

TEXT 34

> *ecce mater domini et fratres eius dicebant ei:*
> *Joannes baptista baptizat in remissionem peccatorum,*
> *eamus et baptizemur ab eo. dixit autem eis:*
> *quid peccaui, ut uadam et baptizer ab eo?*
> *nisi forte hoc ipsum quod dixi ignorantia est.*

> Behold, the mother of the Lord and his brothers said to him:
> John the Baptist baptizes for the forgiveness of sins,
> let us go and be baptized by him. But he said to them:
> In what have I sinned that I should go and be baptized by him?
> Unless, perhaps, what I have said is (a sin of) ignorance.

This text seems to embody later thought about why it was necessary
for Jesus to be baptized, even as the same problem is dealt with from
another approach in Mt 3:13-15.

§183. Immediately following his quotation of the preceding passage (§182) Jerome gives another quotation (*Against the Pelagians*
III 2 KT 8, 8 No. 10) which he says is in the same volume (*in eodem
volumine*). It is a parallel and variant account of the conversation
between Jesus and Peter in Mt 18:21-22 with the added features
that a teaching of Jesus occasions the question by Simon, and that
an additional statement occurs in the answer of Jesus. The passage
reads:

TEXT 35

> *si peccauerit (inquit) frater tuus in uerbo*
> *et satis tibi fecerit, septies in die suscipe eum.*
> *dixit illi Simon discipulus eius: septies in die?*
> *respondit dominus et dixit ei: etiam ego dico tibi,*
> *usque septuagies septies. etenim in prophetis quoque*
> *postquam uncti sunt spiritu sancto,*
> *inuentus est sermo peccati.*

> If (he says) your brother has sinned with a word
> and has made reparation to you, receive him seven times in a day.
> Simon, his disciple, said to him: Seven times in a day?
> The Lord answered and said to him: Yes, I say to you,
> up to seventy times seven times. For in the prophets also,

after they were anointed with the Holy Spirit,
a word of sin was found.

§184. The remaining quotations to be cited from Jerome (§§184–88) are all in his *Commentary on Matthew*. In this work, in comment on Mt 6:11 (KT 8, 7 No. 7) he states that in the Gospel which is called according to the Hebrews, in place of "bread necessary to support life" (*supersubstantiali pane*), he found

TEXT 36

> *mahar*
> which means, he explains,
> *crastinum*
> "of tomorrow."

So the sense of the saying, in Jerome's interpretation of what he finds in this Gospel, is: "Our bread of tomorrow, i.e., of the future, give us this day" (*panem nostrum crastinum, id est futurum, da nobis hodie*).

§185. On Mt 12:13 (KT 8, 8 No. 8) Jerome comments that in the Gospel which is used by the Nazarenes and the Ebionites, which he had translated from Hebrew into Greek, and which was called by most people the authentic Matthew (*Matthaei authenticum*) (§156), the man with the withered hand appealed to Jesus with these words:

TEXT 37

> *caementarius eram, manibus uictum quaeritans;*
> *precor te, Iesu, ut mihi restituas sanitatem,*
> *ne turpiter mendicem cibos.*
> I was a mason, seeking a living with my hands;
> I beseech you, Jesus, to restore health to me,
> so that I may not have to beg food in ignominy.

§186. Mt 23:35 mentions Zechariah the son of Barachiah, as having been murdered between the sanctuary (ναός) and the altar. Zechariah the son of Berechiah is the name of the well-known OT prophet (Zec 1:1), but there is no information otherwise that he met this sort of violent death. In 2 Ch 24:20-22, however, it is recorded that Zechariah the son of Jehoiada the priest was stoned in the court of the house of the Lord. In the Hebrew Scriptures Abel was the first righteous man wickedly murdered (Gen 4:8) and, since Chronicles was the last book in the canon (§5), Zechariah the son of Jehoiada was the last. The mention in Mt 23:35 of "all the righteous blood shed

on earth, from the blood of innocent Abel to the blood of Zechariah
. . . whom you murdered between the sanctuary and the altar"
could, therefore, be a summary of all such scriptural tragedy, if it
is Zechariah the son of Jehoiada who is meant. Actually the words
"the son of Barachiah" are not in the original text of Codex Sinaiticus
at this point, and probably represent an incorrect addition to the
text in the other manuscripts. At this point (Mt 23:35) in his *Commentary on Matthew* Jerome says that he finds in the Gospel which
the Nazarenes use, in place of son of Barachiah (*Barachiae*), son of

TEXT 38

*Ioiadae*
Joiada.

This is presumably a correction of the incorrect text, or a provision
of identification where such was lacking.

§187. In the *Commentary on Matthew* at Mt 27:16 (KT 8, 10 No.
18), Jerome says that in the Gospel which is written according to the
Hebrews Barabbas is interpreted as

TEXT 39

*filius magistri eorum*
son of their teacher.

Barabbas (בר־אבא) means "son of (the) father." Jerome's Latin
presumably corresponds to בר־רבן, "son of (the) rabbi, *or* teacher."
Since a rabbi or teacher might well be called "father" (cf. Mt
23:9), both names may have essentially the same meaning.

§188. Again on Mt 27:51 (KT 8, 10 No. 20), which speaks of how
the curtain of the temple was torn in two, Jerome comments that the
following reading was found in the Gospel which he frequently
mentions:

TEXT 40

*superliminare templi infinitae*
*magnitudinis fractum esse atque diuisum*
the lintel of the temple of boundless
size was broken and even forced asunder.

§189. The sayings which have thus been collected (§§176–88)
from the writings of Origen, Eusebius, and Jerome, as perhaps
belonging to an Aramaic Gospel which was in use among the Nazarae-

ans, are characterized for the most part by a rather close relationship to the Gospel according to Matthew. In spite of the supposition of Jerome (§156) to that effect, these sayings cannot be considered as representing the Semitic original of Mt, because most often they seem to be an elaboration (e.g., Text 29) or correction (e.g., Text 38), and hence a secondary version, of much the same tradition found in Mt. Since Mt is itself the most Jewish-Christian of the canonical Gospels, this Gospel which seems to stand in the same general stream of tradition is no doubt correctly recognized as a Jewish-Christian work. Beroea (Aleppo) and the wider area of the Nazaraeans (§52) would indeed be likely as the place of its circulation. If it is the Aramaic Gospel mentioned by Hegesippus (§175) it must have been in existence at least as early as the middle of the second century.

# 6 / The Gospel of the Naassenes

§190. Among the Gnostics described by Irenaeus were those who gave special prominence to the figure of the serpent (§113). Some identified the serpent with Nous, the son of Ialdabaoth (*Against Heresies* I 30, 5); others asserted that Sophia, the mother of Ialdabaoth, herself became the serpent (*Against Heresies* I 30, 15). From ὄφις, the Greek word for "serpent," these Gnostics were known as Ophites. In his *Refutation of All Heresies*, Hippolytus begins with those who have made bold to descant upon the serpent (ὄφιν ὑμνεῖν), and explains that they are called Naassenes (Ναασσηνοί) from the Hebrew language, in which the serpent is called *naas* (νάας [= נחש] δὲ ὁ ὄφις καλεῖται). Hippolytus also speaks of some of the sources used by the Naassenes/Ophites. They evidently ascribe their system to James, the head of the Jerusalem church (§§40f.), through Mariamme, presumably one of the Mary's of the Gospel tradition, probably Mary Magdalene (cf. §§241, 243, 271, 309, 322, 327, 379). They refer, says Hippolytus (*The Refutation of All Heresies* V 7, 1), to the heads of very numerous discourses (πολλῶν πάνυ λόγων τὰ κεφάλαια) which they assert James the brother of the Lord handed down to Mariamme (ἅ φησι παραδεδωκέναι Μαριάμμῃ τὸν Ἰάκωβον τοῦ κυρίου τὸν ἀδελφόν). They teach that the soul is very difficult to discover and hard to understand, and does not remain always in the same form, and these changes of the soul, Hippolytus says (V 7, 9), they have as they are set down in the Gospel entitled according to the Egyptians (ἐν τῷ ἐπιγραφομένῳ κατ' Αἰγυπτίους εὐαγγελίῳ). They also hand down, says Hippolytus (V 7, 20), a passage which occurs in the Gospel entitled according to Thomas (ἐν τῷ κατὰ Θωμᾶν ἐπιγραφομένῳ εὐαγγελίῳ), and this passage he quotes explicitly (§282 Text 85).

§191. In his further exposition (*The Refutation of All Heresies* V 7 and 8) of the heresy of the Naassenes, Hippolytus quotes the following sayings (Texts 41–43). Concerning the substance of the seed which is a cause of all existent things (περὶ τῆς τοῦ σπέρματος οὐσίας, ἥτις ἐστὶ πάντων τῶν γινομένων αἰτία) (cf. §104), the Naassenes affirm that it produces and forms all things that are made but is itself none of them, and it puts all things in motion but is itself unmoved (ἀκίνητον εἶναι τὸ πάντα κινοῦν). This one alone is good (τοῦτον εἶναί φησιν ἀγαθὸν μόνον), and it was concerning this one that the Savior spoke when he said (V 7, 26):

TEXT 41

> τί με λέγεις ἀγαθόν; εἷς ἐστὶν ἀγαθός,
> ὁ πατήρ μου ὁ ἐν τοῖς οὐρανοῖς, ὃς ἀνατέλλει
> τὸν ἥλιον αὐτοῦ ἐπὶ δικαίους καὶ ἀδίκους
> καὶ βρέχει ἐπὶ ὁσίους καὶ ἁμαρτωλούς.

> Why do you call me good? One is good,
> my Father who is in heaven, who makes
> his sun rise on the just and on the unjust,
> and sends rain on the pious and on the sinners.

It is obvious that the saying combines and slightly alters material which is otherwise found in Mt 19:17 = Mk 10:18 = Lk 18:19 and Mt 5:45.

§192. According to *The Refutation of All Heresies* V 8, 11 the Naassenes quote and make their own application of this saying of the Savior:

TEXT 42

> ἐὰν μὴ πίνητέ μου τὸ αἷμα καὶ φάγητέ
> μου τὴν σάρκα, οὐ μὴ εἰσέλθητε εἰς τὴν
> βασιλείαν τῶν οὐρανῶν· ἀλλὰ κἂν πίητε,
> φησί, τὸ ποτήριον ὃ ἐγὼ πίνω, ὅπου ἐγὼ
> ὑπάγω, ἐκεῖ ὑμεῖς εἰσελθεῖν οὐ δύνασθε.

> Unless you drink my blood and eat
> my flesh, you will not enter into the
> kingdom of heaven; but even if you drink,

he says, the cup which I drink, where I
go, there you cannot come in.

Again there is a combination of material which is known in Jn 6:53,
Mt 20:22 = Mk 10:38, and Jn 8:21; 13:33.

§193. According to *The Refutation of All Heresies* V 8, 23 the
Naassenes make this quotation:

TEXT 43

> τάφοι ἐστὲ κεκονιαμένοι, γέμοντες,
> φησίν, ἔσωθεν ὀστέων νεκρῶν, ὅτι
> οὐκ ἔστιν ἐν ὑμῖν ἄνθρωπος ὁ ζῶν.

You are whitewashed tombs, full,
he says, within of dead men's bones, because
there is not in you the living man.

Here the first part of the statement is almost the same as Mt 23:27;
as for the last part it is not certain whether it is intended to be part
of the saying or simply a report of how the Naassenes interpret the
saying, but it appears to be part of the saying itself and therewith
it provides an extracanonical version of the same.

§194. It is evident that the material in these three sayings (Texts
41–43) is largely the same as corresponding material in the four
canonical Gospels. As compared with the canonical Gospels, there
is in the sayings some rearrangement, and possibly some addition
of other material. Free quotation from the canonical Gospels may
account for these phenomena, yet it is also possible that the material
was incorporated in, and is here taken from, a Gospel which circulated
among the Naassenes/Ophites. We have seen (§190) that they were
credited with use of the Gospel according to the Egyptians and the
Gospel according to Thomas. As far as we are acquainted with those
two Gospels (§§157–64, 282–321), they do not seem to have contained
these sayings.

## 7 / The Gospel of the Ebionites

§195. As we have seen (§49), Irenaeus says (*Against Heresies* I 26,
2) that the Ebionites use only the Gospel according to Matthew, and
also (*Against Heresies* III 21) that they assert that Jesus was begotten

by Joseph. This assertion collides not only with Lk 1:35, as Irenaeus points out (*Against Heresies* V 1, 3), but also with Mt 1:16 in most texts. In the major codices (Sinaiticus, Vaticanus, etc.) Mt 1:16 reads:

> Ἰακὼβ δὲ ἐγέννησεν τὸν Ἰωσὴφ
> τὸν ἄνδρα Μαρίας,
> ἐξ ἧς ἐγεννήθη Ἰησοῦς ὁ λεγόμενος χριστός.

> and Jacob the father of Joseph
> the husband of Mary,
> of whom Jesus was born, who is called Christ.

The Koridethi Codex (Θ or 038), written between the seventh and ninth centuries, and the Ferrar Group (φ or Family 13) of minuscules (13, 69, 124, 346, etc.), written between the eleventh and fifteenth centuries, give this reading:

> Ἰακὼβ δὲ ἐγέννησε τὸν Ἰωσὴφ
> ᾧ μνηστευθεῖσα παρθένος Μαριὰμ
> ἐγέννησεν Ἰησοῦν τὸν λεγόμενον χριστόν.

> and Jacob the father of Joseph,
> to whom having been betrothed the virgin Mary
> bore Jesus who is called Christ.

The Curetonian Syriac (sy<sup>c</sup>), written probably in the middle of the fifth century, reads:

> and Jacob the father of Joseph,
> to whom was betrothed the virgin Mary,
> who (*fem.*) bore Jesus the Christ.

The feminine gender used as indicated in this version shows unmistakably that the intended statement is that Mary bore Jesus, not that Joseph was the father of Jesus, and this supports the understanding of the Koridethi-Ferrar reading as saying that Mary (who had been betrothed to Joseph) bore Jesus. The Sinaitic Syriac (syr<sup>s</sup>), probably written in the early fifth century, however, has this reading:

> and Jacob the father of Joseph;
> Joseph, to whom was betrothed the virgin Mary,
> was the father of Jesus who is called Christ.

Here it is not unlikely that we have simply the error of a Syriac translator who was working with a Greek text like that preserved in the Koridethi and Ferrar manuscripts,[1] and the fact that he, like the translator of syr^c, repeats the word "virgin" ($\pi \alpha \rho \theta \acute{\epsilon} \nu o \varsigma$) which is in the Koridethi-Ferrar text but not in the Sinaiticus-Vaticanus text, supports that supposition. From this evidence, therefore, it seems probable that the only text of Mt 1:16 which was available in the time of Irenaeus, and of the Ebionites before him, declared, not that Joseph was the father of Jesus, but simply that Mary was the mother of Jesus, a statement which does not collide with either Lk 1:35 or Mt 1:25. But the assertion of the Ebionites that Jesus was begotten by Joseph would collide with Mt 1:16–25 and it seems unlikely that our canonical Gospel according to Matthew was *the* Gospel of the Ebionites, as Irenaeus says. More probably they had a different Gospel, here erroneously called the Gospel according to Matthew.

§196. Eusebius also (§51) says (*Ch. Hist.* III 27, 2–3) that the Ebionites, except for one group among them, denied the virgin birth, and he says (*Ch. Hist.* III 27, 4) that they used only the so-called Gospel according to the Hebrews. Likewise Jerome says (*Commentary on Matthew* 12:13 KT 8, 8 No. 8) (§185) that the Ebionites as well as the Nazaraeans (§§180ff.) use the Gospel which he had translated from Hebrew into Greek, i.e., the Gospel according to the Hebrews (§156), which most people called the authentic Matthew. From the best-authenticated quotations from the Gospel according to the Hebrews (§§165ff.), however, we have considered that one of the most characteristic conceptions in that work was that of the Holy Spirit as the mother of Jesus (Text 24 §167), and of Jesus as the Son of the Holy Spirit (Text 25 §171). This conception is hardly in line with the belief of the main body of the Ebionites that Jesus was "a plain and ordinary man who . . . had been born naturally from Mary and her husband" (Eusebius, *Ch. Hist.* III 27, 2; cf. above §51). Therefore it is not probable that they used the Gospel according to the Hebrews any more than the Gospel according to Matthew (§195). Since the Gospel of the Nazaraeans seems also to have been similar to Mt (§189), it is not likely that the Gospel used by the Ebionites is to be equated with that Gospel either. If the Gospel used by the Ebionites cannot be identified with the canonical Gospel according to Matthew, nor with the Gospel according to the Hebrews (in spite of the affirmations of Eusebius and Jerome), nor with the Gospel of the Nazaraeans, we may look farther for any evidence as to the existence of yet another Gospel which was used distinctively by the Ebionites,

---

[1] Bruce M. Metzger in JBL 77 (1958), 362.

and for any quotations which could come from such a Gospel, quotations which would present distinctive ideas of the Ebionites.

§197. In his undeniably confused and confusing account of the Ebionites (§52), Epiphanius (*Pan. haer.* XXX 13, 2 GCS 25, 349) says that they have a so-called Gospel according to Matthew, which is not in all regards complete, which they call the Hebrew Gospel. Here he may be under the same misapprehension as Jerome (§196) to the effect that the Gospel used by the Ebionites was the Gospel according to the Hebrews, which itself went back to the Hebrew Gospel according to Matthew. But Epiphanius proceeds to give a number of quotations from the Gospel which he has just mentioned, and these quotations form a series in which distinctive ideas occur, thus justifying the assumption that we have here, in fact, excerpts from a Gospel different from any hitherto considered, a work which we may designate as the Gospel of the Ebionites. In the Hebrew Gospel, says Epiphanius (*Pan. haer.* XXX 13, 2–3 GCS 25, 349–50), it is reported that:

TEXT 44

ἐγένετό τις ἀνὴρ ὀνόματι ᾽Ιησοῦς, καὶ αὐτὸς
ὡς ἐτῶν τριάκοντα, ὃς ἐξελέξατο ἡμᾶς. καὶ ἐλθὼν
εἰς Καφαρναοὺμ εἰσῆλθεν εἰς τὴν οἰκίαν Σίμωνος
τοῦ ἐπικληθέντος Πέτρου καὶ ἀνοίξας τὸ στόμα αὐτοῦ
εἶπεν· παρερχόμενος παρὰ τὴν λίμνην Τιβεριάδος
ἐξελεξάμην ᾽Ιωάννην καὶ ᾽Ιάκωβον, υἱοὺς Ζεβεδαίου,
καὶ Σίμωνα καὶ ᾽Ανδρέαν καὶ Θαδδαῖον καὶ Σίμωνα
τὸν ζηλωτὴν καὶ ᾽Ιούδαν τὸν ᾽Ισκαριώτην, καὶ σὲ
τὸν Ματθαῖον καθεζόμενον ἐπὶ τοῦ τελωνίου ἐκάλεσα
καὶ ἠκολούθησάς μοι. ὑμᾶς οὖν βούλομαι εἶναι
δεκαδύο ἀποστόλους εἰς μαρτύριον τοῦ ᾽Ισραήλ.

There was a certain man named Jesus, and he was
about thirty years of age, who chose us. And when he came
to Capernaum he entered into the house of Simon
who is called Peter, and he opened his mouth
and said: As I passed along by the lake of Tiberias,
I chose John and James, sons of Zebedee,
and Simon and Andrew and Thaddaeus and Simon
the Zealot and Judas Iscariot, and you,
Matthew, sitting at the tax office, I called

and you followed me. You, therefore, I desire to be
twelve apostles for a witness to Israel.

In this passage it is notable that the apostles are speaking as a group
("who chose us"), i.e., their authority is back of this Gospel, and
Matthew, in particular, is singled out ("and you, Matthew"), thus
is probably thought of as the author. Furthermore, Jesus himself
narrates the call of the disciples, giving an account which appears
to rest upon Synoptic parallels, particularly including Lk 3:23.

§198. Using only the connecting word "and," Epiphanius continues
with the next quotation (*Pan. haer.* XXX 13, 4 GCS 25, 350):

TEXT 45

ἐγένετο ᾿Ιωάννης βαπτίζων, καὶ ἐξῆλθον
πρὸς αὐτὸν Φαρισαῖοι καὶ ἐβαπτίσθησαν καὶ πᾶσα
῾Ιεροσόλυμα. καὶ εἶχεν ὁ ᾿Ιωάννης ἔνδυμα ἀπὸ
τριχῶν καμήλου καὶ ζώνην δερματίνην περὶ τὴν
ὀσφὺν αὐτοῦ. καὶ τὸ βρῶμα αὐτοῦ, φησί, μέλι ἄγριον,
οἷ ἡ γεῦσις ἡ τοῦ μάννα, ὡς ἐγκρὶς ἐν ἐλαίῳ.

It came to pass that John was baptizing, and there went out
to him Pharisees and were baptized, and all
Jerusalem. And John had a garment of
camel's hair, and a leather girdle around
his waist. And his food, it says, was wild honey,
the taste of which was that of the manna, like a cake in olive oil.

In contrast with Mt 3:4 = Mk 1:6, the locusts are omitted from the
diet of John, and the description of the honey is elaborated with a
comparison of its taste to the taste of the OT manna. In Greek the
word locust is ἀκρίς, and "cake" or "pancake" is ἐγκρίς. In Num
11:8 LXX the taste of the manna is described as like the taste of a
cake made with oil (ἡ ἡδονὴ αὐτοῦ ὡσεὶ γεῦμα ἐγκρὶς ἐξ ἐλαίου). The
author has obviously derived his description of the taste of the wild
honey from this OT description, and was no doubt led to think of the
latter by the similarity of the words ἀκρίς and ἐγκρίς. Therefore he
was thinking and writing in Greek.

§199. A little later Epiphanius gives another quotation (*Pan. haer.*
XXX 13, 6 GCS 25, 350) and this, he says, is the beginning of the
Gospel of the Ebionites (ἡ δὲ ἀρχὴ τοῦ παρ᾿ αὐτοῖς εὐαγγελίου). In our
transcription which follows, a few words are enclosed in angled

brackets to show that they are omitted in the text of Epiphanius at this point, but can be supplied from where he repeats part of the quotation a little later (*Pan. haer.* XXX 14, 3 GCS 25, 351). The passage reads:

TEXT 46

> ἐγένετο ἐν ταῖς ἡμέραις Ἡρῴδου βασιλέως
> τῆς Ἰουδαίας ⟨ἐπὶ ἀρχιερέως Καϊάφα⟩,
> ἦλθέν ⟨τις⟩ Ἰωάννης ⟨ὀνόματι⟩ βαπτίζων
> βάπτισμα μετανοίας ἐν τῷ Ἰορδάνῃ ποταμῷ,
> ὃς ἐλέγετο εἶναι ἐκ γένους Ἀαρὼν τοῦ ἱερέως,
> παῖς Ζαχαρίου καὶ Ἐλισάβετ,
> καὶ ἐξήρχοντο πρὸς αὐτὸν πάντες.

> It came to pass in the days of Herod, king
> of Judea, when Caiaphas was high priest,
> that a certain man named John came baptizing
> with a baptism of repentance in the Jordan river,
> who was said to be of the family of Aaron the priest,
> son of Zechariah and Elizabeth,
> and all went out to him.

Since this is declared to be the beginning of the Gospel, it is evident that this Gospel contained no narrative of the birth of Jesus, which is in keeping with the Ebionite position, denying the virgin birth (§196).

§200. After indicating that the Gospel records much more at this point, Epiphanius continues with this further quotation (*Pan. haer.* XXX 13, 7–8 GCS 25, 350–51):

TEXT 47

> τοῦ λαοῦ βαπτισθέντος ἦλθεν καὶ Ἰησοῦς
> καὶ ἐβαπτίσθη ὑπὸ τοῦ Ἰωάννου. καὶ ὡς ἀνῆλθεν
> ἀπὸ τοῦ ὕδατος, ἠνοίγησαν οἱ οὐρανοὶ καὶ
> εἶδεν τὸ πνεῦμα τὸ ἅγιον ἐν εἴδει περιστερᾶς,
> κατελθούσης καὶ εἰσελθούσης εἰς αὐτόν. καὶ φωνὴ
> ἐκ τοῦ οὐρανοῦ λέγουσα· σύ μου εἶ ὁ υἱὸς ὁ ἀγαπητός,
> ἐν σοὶ ηὐδόκησα, καὶ πάλιν· ἐγὼ σήμερον γεγέννηκά
> σε. καὶ εὐθὺς περιέλαμψε τὸν τόπον φῶς μέγα.
> ὃ ἰδών, φησίν, ὁ Ἰωάννης λέγει αὐτῷ·
> σὺ τίς εἶ, κύριε; καὶ πάλιν φωνὴ ἐξ οὐρανοῦ

πρὸς αὐτόν· οὗτός ἐστιν ὁ υἱός μου ὁ ἀγαπητός,
ἐφ᾿ ὃν ηὐδόκησα. καὶ τότε, φησίν, ὁ ᾿Ιωάννης
προσπεσὼν αὐτῷ ἔλεγεν· δέομαί σου, κύριε,
σύ με βάπτισον. ὁ δὲ ἐκώλυσεν αὐτὸν λέγων·
ἄφες, ὅτι οὕτως ἐστὶ πρέπον πληρωθῆναι πάντα.

When the people were baptized, Jesus also came
and was baptized by John. And as he came up
from the water, the heavens were opened, and
he saw the Holy Spirit in the form of a dove
descending and entering into him. And a voice
from heaven said: Thou art my beloved Son,
in thee I am well pleased. And again: Today I have begotten
thee. And immediately a great light shone around the place.
When John saw this, it says, he said to him:
Who are you, Lord? And again a voice from heaven
(said) to him: This is my beloved Son,
in whom I am well pleased. And then, it says, John
fell down before him and said: I beseech you, Lord,
baptize me. But he prevented him, saying:
Let it be, for thus it is fitting to fulfill all things.

It is evident that this account of John the Baptist and Jesus (Texts
46–47) is built upon the Synoptic record, and in particular that it
gives the voice from heaven three times, first according to Mk 1:11,
then according to Lk 3:22 in the text found in Codex Bezae (D) and
the Old Latin version, and finally according to Mt 3:17. It may also
be significant of the importance here attached to the baptismal event
in relation to Jesus that the Holy Spirit is described not just as
"descending upon him" (καταβαῖνον εἰς αὐτόν) as in Mk 1:10, but as
"entering into him" (εἰσελθούσης εἰς αὐτόν).

§201. Although the Ebionites denied the virgin birth of Christ
and omitted any narrative thereof from their Gospel (§199), they
also denied, Epiphanius says (*Pan. haer.* XXX 14, 5 GCS 25, 351),
that he was a man (ἀρνοῦνται εἶναι αὐτὸν ἄνθρωπον). The basis of this
denial, Epiphanius explains, was

TEXT 48

δῆθεν ἀπὸ τοῦ λόγου οὗ εἴρηκεν ὁ σωτὴρ
ἐν τῷ ἀναγγελῆναι αὐτῷ ὅτι ἰδοὺ ἡ μήτηρ σου
καὶ οἱ ἀδελφοί σου ἔξω ἑστήκασιν, ὅτι τίς
μού ἐστι μήτηρ καὶ ἀδελφοί; καὶ ἐκτείνας

τὴν χεῖρα ἐπὶ τοὺς μαθητὰς ἔφη· οὗτοί εἰσιν
οἱ ἀδελφοί μου καὶ ἡ μήτηρ καὶ ἀδελφαὶ οἱ
ποιοῦντες τὰ θελήματα τοῦ πατρός μου.

evidently from the word which the Savior spoke
when it was announced to him: Behold, your mother
and your brothers stand without, namely, Who
are my mother and brothers? And stretching out
his hand toward the disciples, he said: These are
my brothers and mother and sisters, who
do the will of my Father.

Again the Synoptic Gospels (Mt 12:46-50 = Mk 3:31-35 = Lk
8:19-21) provide the basis of the material.

§202. In a later passage where Epiphanius is explaining that the
Ebionites say that Christ was not begotten of God but created as one
of the archangels, he quotes him as saying, in the Gospel used by the
Ebionites (*Pan. haer.* XXX 16, 5 GCS 25, 354):

TEXT 49

ἦλθον καταλῦσαι τὰς θυσίας, καὶ ἐὰν μὴ
παύσησθε τοῦ θύειν, οὐ παύσεται ἀφ' ὑμῶν ἡ ὀργή.

I came to destroy the sacrifices, and if you do not
cease from sacrificing, the wrath will not cease from you.

Here a radical repudiation of sacrificial cult expresses itself.

§203. Once again, in relation to the observance of the passover
by Jesus, Epiphanius (*Pan. haer.* XXX 22, 4 GCS 25, 363) quotes
from the record which the Ebionites use, and says here that they do
away with the sequence and alter the saying. Epiphanius writes:

TEXT 50

καὶ ἐποίησαν τοὺς μαθητὰς μὲν λέγοντας·
ποῦ θέλεις ἑτοιμάσωμέν σοι τὸ πάσχα φαγεῖν;
καὶ αὐτὸν δῆθεν λέγοντα· μὴ ἐπιθυμίᾳ ἐπεθύμησα
κρέας τοῦτο τὸ πάσχα φαγεῖν μεθ' ὑμῶν;

And they made the disciples, on the one hand, say:
Where will you have us prepare for you to eat the Passover?
and him, forsooth, to say: It is not with desire that I have desired to eat the flesh of this Passover with you, is it?

Here the Ebionite Gospel has turned the affirmation of Lk 22:15,
"With desire I have desired to eat this Passover with you" (ἐπιθυμίᾳ

ἐπεθύμησα τοῦτο τὸ πάσχα φαγεῖν μεθ' ὑμῶν), into an interrogation which expects a negative answer (introduced by μή) and therewith into the direct opposite of the original. Also by the introduction of the word κρέας, "flesh," or "meat," it has emphasized the main dish of the passover meal, namely, the roast lamb (Ex 12:8). The repudiation of the eating of this dish of flesh probably reflects not only a negative attitude toward the sacrificial cult (Text 49 §202), but also a positive vegetarianism. Seen in this light, the deletion of the locusts from the diet of John the Baptist (Text 45 §198) is probably also an expression of vegetarianism.

§204. Thus the Gospel used by the Ebionites, as known from the quotations from it given by Epiphanius (Texts 44–50), was the document of a Jewish-Christian group which repudiated the sacrificial cult of their ancestors, espoused vegetarianism, and regarded Jesus as a man, not born of a virgin but, from his baptism on, uniquely inhabited by the Holy Spirit and thus made the Son of God. The Gospel was evidently written in Greek (§198) and, if Irenaeus knew of it at least vaguely (§195), it was in existence in the second century.

## 8 / Other Books

§205. The foregoing (Texts 18–50 §§154–204) appear to be the earliest and most important quotations from named noncanonical Gospels or similar sources. There are some more quotations of somewhat similar material which can be found, but in general they seem to be presented too ambiguously or to stand too far from the canonical tradition to require detailed presentation within the framework of our inquiry (§130). For example, Clement of Alexandria gives three quotations from the "Traditions of Matthias." In *Stromata* II 9, 45, 4 (GCS Clemens Alexandrinus II 137; ANF II 358), just before quoting, "He who wonders shall reign . . ." from the Gospel according to the Hebrews (§166), Clement says that Matthias in the Traditions (Ματθίας ἐν ταῖς Παραδόσεσι) recommends, "Wonder at what is present" (θαύμασον τὰ παρόντα). In *Stromata* III 4, 26, 3 (GCS Clemens Alexandrinus II 208; ANF II 385) Clement says that it is said that Matthias taught: "To fight with and abuse the flesh (σαρκὶ . . . μάχεσθαι καὶ παραχρῆσθαι), not at all giving in to it for unbridled pleasure, but to make the soul grow through faith and knowledge." Again in *Stromata* VII 13, 82, 1 (GCS Clemens Alex-

andrinus III 58; ANF II 547) Clement quotes what is said to have
been said by "Matthias the Apostle" in the Traditions: "If the
neighbor (γείτων) of an elect man (ἐκλεκτοῦ) sin, the elect man has
sinned; for if he had conducted himself as the Word (λόγος) pre-
scribes, his neighbor also would have felt such respect for his way of
life that he would not have sinned." Although named an apostle in
the last quotation, the identity of Matthias is not altogether certain.
In *Stromata* IV 6, 35, 2 (GCS Clemens Alexandrinus II 263f.; ANF
II 415) Clement quotes Lk 19:8 as a statement of Zacchaeus or,
according to some, of Matthias, a chief tax collector (Lk 19:2). Since
Matthew was also a tax collector (Mt 9:9 = Lk 5:27), Matthias
(Ματθίας or Μαθθίας) may be intended to be the same as Matthew
(Μαθθαῖος or Ματθαῖος). But in Ac 1:23-26 Matthias (Μαθθίας) was
chosen to take the place in the apostleship which Judas Iscariot left
vacant, and it may be this Matthias who is intended in our passages.
In view of the way in which the quotations from Matthias are intro-
duced by Clement it is also not too certain whether they are intended
to be quotations of sayings of Jesus or simply of teachings of Matthias.
In sequence with mention of the Gospel according to Thomas both
Origen (*Homily on Luke* I GCS Origenes IX 5) and Eusebius (*Ch.
Hist.* III 25, 6) mention the Gospel according to Matthias (τὸ κατὰ
Ματθίαν εὐαγγέλιον, Origen), and Eusebius elsewhere (*Ch. Hist.* III
29, 4) reproduces the entire passage from Clement in which the
second quotation above from Matthias is contained. The Traditions
of Matthias cited by Clement may, therefore, have been the same
work as the Gospel according to Matthias known to Origen and
Eusebius, and in that case the quotations given above were presumably intended to be Gospel-type material. The first saying quoted by
Clement is something like the saying in the Gospel according to the
Hebrews (and in OP 654 [§166]) which Clement adduces immediately
afterward, but Clement himself attributes this particular saying not
only to Matthias but also to Plato in his *Theaetetus* (155D: "Wonder
is the only beginning of philosophy," LCL Plato II 54–55), and some
such utterance was evidently a commonplace of ancient philosophy.
The import of the second saying is, perhaps, ambiguous because the
verb παραχράομαι can mean either (with the dative, as in this text)
"abuse" or "misuse," or (with the accusative) "despise" or "treat
with contempt." Hence the admonition to treat the flesh in terms of
the import of this verb could be interpreted, in one way, as a call to
libertinism or, in another way, as a call to asceticism (§116). Both
here (*Stromata* III 4, 25, 6—26, 3 GCS Clemens Alexandrinus II
207–8) and in another passage (*Stromata* II 20, 118, 3 GCS Clemens

Alexandrinus II 177) Clement indicates that the Nicolaitans (cf. Ac 6:5; Rev 2:6, 15) appealed to this text. Clement himself evidently understands the text as an admonition to self-control (ἐγκράτεια), but tells of those who said that certain libertine action of Nicolaus was in consequence of the injunction, "it is necessary to abuse the flesh" (παραχρήσασθαι τῇ σαρκὶ δεῖ). As for the third saying, here at least we are in the realm of concern for neighbor (although the word is γείτων as in Lk 14:12, etc., rather than πλησίος as in Mt 22:39 = Mk 12:31 = Lk 10:27, etc.), and of responsibility if another is caused to sin (cf. Mt 18:6 = Mk 9:42 = Lk 17:1).

For another example, Epiphanius (*Pan. haer.* XXVI 8, 1–3 GCS 25, 284) says that the Gnostics had various books including "Questions of Mary" (ἐρωτήσεις Μαρίας), available in two forms called the Great Questions (μεγάλαι ἐρωτήσεις), and the Little Questions (μικραὶ ἐρωτήσεις), in which Christ was the revealer of practices of lewd conduct (αἰσχρουργία). Then Epiphanius gives the gist of one passage from the Great Questions, a passage which would agree with the libertine understanding of the second quotation (above) by Clement of Alexandria from the Traditions of Matthias. In view of the prominence of Mary Magdalene in Gnostic literature otherwise (§§190, 241, 271, 309, 322ff.) we may assume that she is the Mary who is involved here.

# B. Manuscripts

## 1 / The Classification and Presentation of the Manuscripts

§206. In the case of the manuscripts of the canonical NT the oldest known fragments are written on papyrus, while somewhat later leather, in the form of parchment or vellum, comes into use too.[1] Also the oldest manuscripts are written in Greek, although translations were soon made into other languages too. Likewise in the case of the noncanonical Gospel materials, the oldest are found written on papyrus and in Greek, while parchment records appear somewhat later and, eventually, many other languages are involved too. As a matter of classification, then, in line with common practice with respect to the canonical manuscripts, we will take notice first of noncanonical Gospel materials found in the papyri, after that of materials on parchment, and throughout will be chiefly interested, as explained already (§130), in texts in Greek. As elsewhere, we will take up the materials as far as possible in chronological order, in this case in the chronological order, as far as ascertainable, of the manuscripts. The oldest Greek manuscripts are shown in actual photographs. The transcription of the text employs the usual conventional signs (cf. the Arbitrary Signs in the Lists of Abbreviations). Square brackets [ ] mark portions missing from a text and, upon occasion, supplied by the editor. Round brackets ( ) mark letters or words supplied to fill out an abbreviation in a text, or to express the sense in a translation. Angled brackets ⟨ ⟩ mark portions supplied in a text from some parallel or as required by the context. Braces { } mark superfluous letters or words. Dots . . . indicate missing letters in a text, or omitted portion in a translation or quotation. Restoration of missing portions of texts is done sparingly, generally only where some reasonably unambiguous clue is contained in the context or elsewhere as to what has been lost. Lines of the texts are numbered (by 5's) in accordance with the arrangement of lines

---

[1] FLP 414ff.

in the originals. Punctuation is shown only as it exists in the original, but separation and accentuation of words are supplied in the Greek. After the text is transcribed in this way in as close a reproduction of the original as possible, the translation in turn reproduces the transcribed text as exactly as possible. As far as feasible the same lines are retained. Gaps are allowed to stand, and the restorations which have been made are assumed, but without the necessity for repeating the special marks by which these features have been indicated in the Greek transcription. Unintelligible portions of the Greek text are simply omitted in the translation. In the translation normal English punctuation is employed.

# 2 / Greek Papyri

## 1 / Egerton Papyrus 2

*Literature:* H. Idris Bell and T. C. Skeat, *Fragments of an Unknown Gospel and Other Early Christian Papyri.* 1935; Goro Mayeda, *Das Leben-Jesu-Fragment Papyrus Egerton 2 und seine Stellung in der urchristlichen Literaturgeschichte.* 1946; BVA 42–48; SEA 101–6; HSNTAE 58–60.

§207. Egerton Papyrus 2, which became known in 1934 (§123), consists of three fragments (Figs. 1–2), all written on both sides. The fragments have been numbered (1, 2, and 3) by the editors but, actually, it is difficult to decide in what order they should come. Fragment 1 (Fig. 1) is nearly four and one-half by three and one-half inches in size; Fragment 2 (Fig. 2) is slightly larger than that; and Fragment 3 (Fig. 1) is only about two inches by one inch in size. At the top of Fragment 2 *recto* (Fig. 2 left) part of an original page number can be recognized, but not enough is preserved to make out the number, and page numbers are not preserved on the other fragments. The handwriting, in upright medium-sized uncials, points to the second century and probably around A.D. 150 or earlier. The use of abbreviations in the text has already been noted (§117).

§208. Counting lines with at least a trace of recognizable writing, there are twenty-one lines on the *verso* of Fragment 1 (Fig. 1), and twenty lines on the *recto*. The text continues from *verso* to *recto*, showing that this is a leaf of a codex. We will number the lines consecutively and transcribe now the first thirty-one lines as comprising the first pericope (Text 51) of the entire text.

TEXT 51

verso ]ι.[

]τοῖς νομικο[ῖς

## FIGURE 1.
*Egerton Papyrus 2*

*Fragments 1 and 3*

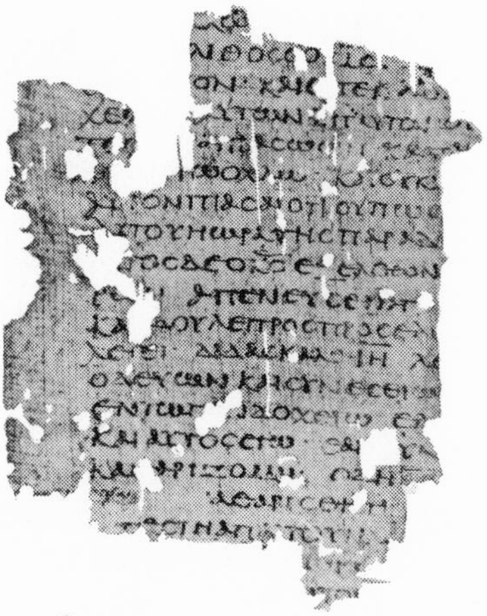

*1 recto*

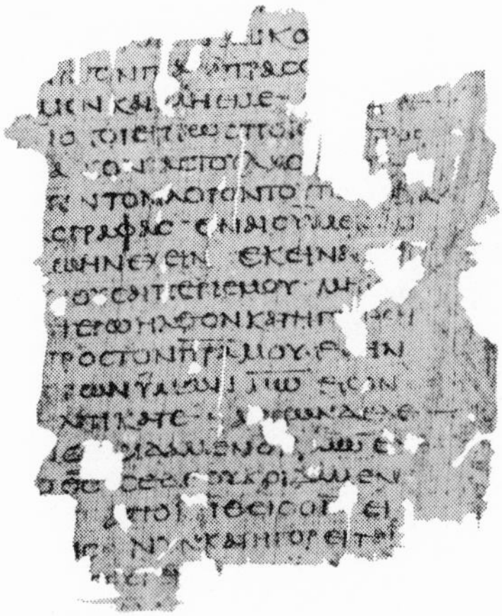

*1 verso*

*3 verso*

*3 recto*

[. . . πά]ντα τὸν παραπράσσ[οντα
[τὸν νό]μον καὶ μὴ ἐμέ
5    ]οποιεῖ πῶς ποιε[ῖ] πρὸς
[δὲ τοὺς] ἄ[ρ]χοντας τοῦ λαοῦ [στ]ρα-
[φεὶς εἶ]πεν τὸν λόγον τοῦτο[ν] ἐραυ-
[νᾶτε τ]ὰς γραφάς· ἐν αἶς ὑμεῖς δο-
[κεῖτε] ζωὴν ἔχειν ἐκεῖναί εἰ[σ]ιν

10    [αἰ μαρτ]υροῦσαι περὶ ἐμοῦ· μὴ δ[ο-]
[κεῖτε ὅ]τι ἐγὼ ἦλθον κατηγο[ρ]ῆσαι
[ὑμῶν] πρὸς τὸν π(ατέ)ρα μοῦ· ἔστιν
[ὁ κατη]γορῶν ὑμῶν Μω(ϋσῆς) εἰς ὃν
[ὑμεῖς] ἠλπίκατε· α[ὐ]τῶν δὲ λε-
15    [γόντω]ν ε[ὖ] οἴδαμεν ὅτι Μω(υσεῖ) ἐλά-
[λησεν] ὁ θ(εό)s· σὲ δὲ οὐκ οἴδαμεν
[πόθεν εἶ]· ἀποκριθεὶς ὁ Ἰη(σοῦs) εἰ-
[πεν αὐτο]ῖs· νῦν κατηγορεῖται
[ὑμῶν ἡ ἀ]πιστεί[α
20                    ]ιλε.[
                    ].[


recto    [. . . τῷ ὄ]χλῳ [. . . .]β[
            ]λίθους ὁμοῦ λι[θάσω-]
        σι[ν αὐ]τόν· καὶ ἐπέβαλον [τὰς]
25    χεῖ[ρας] αὐτῶν ἐπ' αὐτὸν οἱ [ἄρχον-]
        τες [ἵν]α πιάσωσιν καὶ παρ[
            ]τῷ ὄχλῳ· καὶ οὐκ ἐ[δύναντο]
        αὐτὸν πιάσαι ὅτι οὔπω ἐ[ληλύθει]
        αὐτοῦ ἡ ὥρα τῆς παραδό[σεως]
30    αὐτὸς δὲ ὁ κ(ύριο)s ἐξελθὼν [ἐκ τῆς χειρὸς αὐ-]
        τῶν ἀπένευσεν ἀπ' [αὐτῶν]


verso        to the lawyers
        every one who does contrary to
        the law, but not me
5        . . .
        turning to the rulers of the people
        he spoke this saying: You search[1]
        the scriptures, in which you think
        that you have life; it is they
10        that bear witness to me. Think not
        that I came to accuse
        you to my Father. There is
        one who accuses you, even Moses, in whom
        you have hoped. But when they said,

---

[1] Both here and in Jn 5:39 the verb form (ἐραυνᾶτε, ἐρευνᾶτε) can be either indicative, "You search," or imperative, "Search."

15  We know well that God spoke
to Moses; but as for you, we do not know
whence you are, Jesus answered and said
to them: Now your unbelief
is accused.
20  . . .

. . .

recto            to the crowd
stones together to stone
him. And the rulers laid
25  their hands on him
in order that they might arrest him and deliver
him to the crowd. And they were not able
to arrest him, because there was not yet come
the hour of his betrayal.
30  But he himself, the Lord, escaped from their hands
and went away from them.

§209. At the broken beginning of the foregoing pericope (Text 51) it seems evident that, although the name is missing, it is Jesus who is speaking to a group of lawyers. The verb at the beginning of his statement is lost, too, but must have been something like "accuse," "condemn," or "punish." This sentence (Lines 3–4), "[Punish] every one who does contrary to the law, but not me," and the sentence in Lines 18–19, "Now your unbelief is accused," are otherwise unknown sayings of Jesus. The balance of the pericope, however, is evidently derived from a combination of materials which are also available in the Fourth Gospel, as may be seen by comparing the text with Jn 5:39, 45; 9:29; 8:59; 7:30; and 10:39. If this pericope and the Fourth Gospel used a common source, the two otherwise unknown sayings might be derived from that source; if the pericope has been made up out of the materials in Jn then, perhaps, the author is responsible for the two added sayings. At one point in particular the comparison with Jn involves an interesting variation. This is at the point of the sentence found in Lines 8–10, which reads in the Papyrus:

ἐν αἷς ὑμεῖς δο-
[κεῖτε] ζωὴν ἔχειν ἐκεῖναί εἰ[σ]ιν
[αἱ μαρτ]υροῦσαι περὶ ἐμοῦ.

in which you think
that you have life; it is they
that bear witness to me.

At this point the text of the Fourth Gospel (Jn 5:39), in the major codices, reads differently, as follows (the lines being arranged as in the Papyrus):

> ὅτι ὑμεῖς δο-
> κεῖτε ἐν αὐταῖς ζωὴν αἰώνιον ἔχειν· καὶ ἐκεῖναί εἰσιν
> αἱ μαρτυροῦσαι περὶ ἐμοῦ.
>
> because you think
> that in them you have eternal life; and it is they
> that bear witness to me.

In the Curetonian Syriac (syr<sup>c</sup>) and certain Old Latin manuscripts (a b), however, the text is not only given as in the major Greek manuscripts but there is also a "doublet" reading with these words (again arranged here in lines as in the Papyrus):

> *in quibus pu-*
> *tatis vos vitam habere; hae (haec) sunt*
> *quae de me testificantur.*
>
> in which you think
> that you have life; it is they
> that bear witness to me.

Here we have the identical reading with that of the Papyrus. One wonders, therefore, whether the author of the Papyrus used the Fourth Gospel in a different text than that of the major Greek codices, or whether he derived this saying (and perhaps others, such as the two otherwise unknown sayings) from a separate tradition rather than from the Fourth Gospel.

§210. The second pericope is found in Lines 32–41 on the *recto* of Fragment 1 (Fig. 1) of Papyrus Egerton 2. It reads:

TEXT 52

> recto    καὶ [ἰ]δοὺ λεπρὸς προσελθ[ὼν αὐτῷ
> λέγει· διδάσκαλε ᾿Ιη(σοῦ) λε[προῖς συν-]
> οδεύων καὶ συνεσθίω[ν αὐτοῖς]
> 35    ἐν τῷ πανδοχείῳ ἐλ[έπρησα]
> καὶ αὐτὸς ἐγώ· ἐὰν [ο]ὖν [θέλῃς]
> καθαρίζομαι· ὁ δὴ κ(ύριο)s [ἔφη αὐτῷ]
> θέλ[ω] καθαρίσθητι· [καὶ εὐθέως]
> [ἀ]πέστη ἀπ᾿ αὐτοῦ ἡ λέπ[ρα ὁ δὲ κ(ύριο)s]
> 40    [εἶπεν αὐτῷ] πορε[υθεὶς ἐπίδει-]
> [ξον σεαυτὸ]ν τοῖ[s ἱερεῦσι

*recto*   And behold a leper came to him
and said: Teacher Jesus, traveling with lepers
and eating with them
35   in the inn, I became a leper
also myself. If, therefore, you will,
I am made clean. Then the Lord said to him:
I will; be clean. And immediately
the leprosy left him. And the Lord
40   said to him: Go and show
yourself to the priests.

§211. This account (Text 52) seems plainly to depend upon Mt
8:2-4 = Mk 1:40-44 = Lk 5:12-14, while the mention of "the priests"
in the plural in Line 41 may be derived from Lk 17:14. Variations in
language as compared with any single Synoptic account suggest that
the material may be used from memory. Also the story is enlivened
by the statement of how the disease was contracted.

§212. The third pericope is comprised in Lines 43-59 which are
found on the *recto* of Fragment 2 (Fig. 2). The text reads:

TEXT 53

*recto*   νόμενοι πρὸς αὐτὸν ἐξ[ετασ-]
τικῶς ἐπείραζον αὐτὸν λ[έγοντες]
45   διδάσκαλε 'Ιη(σοῦ) οἴδαμεν ὅτι [ἀπὸ θ(εο)ῦ]
ἐλήλυθας ἃ γὰρ ποιεῖς μα[ρτυρεῖ]
ὑπὲρ το[ὑ]ς προφ(ήτ)ας πάντας [λέγε οὖν]
ἡμεῖν· ἐξὸν τοῖς βα(σι)λεῦσ[ιν ἀποδοῦ-]
ναι τὰ ἀν[ή]κοντα τῇ ἀρχῇ ἀπ[οδῶμεν αὐ-]
50   τοῖς ἢ μ[ή] ὁ δὲ 'Ιη(σοῦς) εἰδὼς [τὴν δι-]
άνοιαν [αὐτ]ῶν ἐμβρειμ[ησάμενος]
εἶπεν α[ὐτοῖς]· τί με καλεῖτ[ε τῷ στό-]
ματι ὑμ[ῶν δι ]δάσκαλον· μ[ὴ ἀκού-]
οντες ὃ [λ]έγω· καλῶς 'Η[σ(αΐ)ας περὶ ὑ-]
55   μῶν ἐπ[ρο]φ(ήτευ)σεν εἰπών· ὁ [λαὸς οὗ-]
τος τοῖς [χείλ]εσιν αὐτ[ῶν τιμῶσιν]
με ἡ [δὲ καρδί]α αὐτῶ[ν πόρρω ἀπέ-]
χει ἀπ' ἐ[μοῦ μ]άτη[ν με σέβονται]
ἐντάλ[ματα]

*recto*   coming to him
tested him with a question, saying:

FIGURE 2.

*Egerton Papyrus 2*

recto

verso

45    Teacher Jesus, we know that
      you have come from God, for the things you do testify
      beyond all the prophets. Therefore tell
      us: Is it allowable to render to kings
      the things which pertain to their rule? Shall we render
50    to them, or not? But Jesus, knowing
      their thought, being moved with indignation,
      said to them: Why do you call me with your
      mouth, Teacher, when you do not
      hear what I say? Well did Isaiah

55    prophesy concerning you when he said: This
      people honors me with their lips,
      but their heart is far
      from me. In vain do they worship me,
      precepts

§213. The material found in this account (Text 53) appears to come
chiefly from the Synoptic Gospels, with some items from the Fourth
Gospel, all rather freely quoted and combined. The statement (Lines
45–46) about the Teacher come from God is presumably derived from
Jn 3:2. The conclusion of the same sentence (Lines 46–47, "the things
you do testify beyond all the prophets") is without canonical parallel.
The phrasing of the question about the tribute money (Lines 48–50)
varies the question in the Synoptic record (Mt 22:15-22 = Mk
12:13-17 = Lk 20:26) which is the main basis of the present account.
The indignation of Jesus (Line 51) is a trait found elsewhere in the
Synoptics, and the same verb used to express it here (ἐμβριμάομαι) is
found in Jn 11:33. The question in Lines 52–54 is reminiscent of
Lk 6:46 and 18:19, but differently phrased. The Isaiah (29:13)
quotation in Lines 55ff. is only slightly different in order from the
same quotation in Mt 15:7-9 = Mk 7:6-7, and also slightly different
from the LXX.

§214. The fourth pericope in Egerton Papyrus 2 consists of Lines
60–75 on the *verso* of Fragment 2 (Fig. 2). The text follows:

TEXT 54

*verso*
60        ]τῳ τόπῳ [κ]ατακλεισαν-
          ]ὑποτέτακτα[ι] ἀδήλως
          ]τὸ βάρος αὐτοῦ ἄστατο(ν)
          ]ἀπορηθέντων δὲ ἐκεί-
          [νων ὡς] πρὸς τὸ ξένον ἐπερώτημα
65        [αὐτοῦ π]εριπατῶν ὁ ᾽Ιη(σοῦς) [ἐ]στάθη
          [ἐπὶ τοῦ] χείλους τοῦ ᾽Ιο[ρδ]άνου
          [ποταμ]οῦ καὶ ἐκτείνα[ς τὴν] χεῖ-
          [ρα αὐτο]ῦ τὴν δεξιὰν [. . .]μισεν
          κ]αὶ κατέσπειρ[εν ἐπ]ὶ τὸν
70        ]ον· καὶ τότε [. . . .] κατε-
          ]ενον ὕδωρ· εν[. . .]ν τὴν
          ]· καὶ ἐπ[. . .]θη ἐνώ-
          [πιον αὐτῶν ἐ]ξήγα[γ]εν [δὲ] καρπὸ(ν)

]πολλ[. . . . . .] εἰς χα-
75    ]τα[. . . . . .]υτους·


*verso*
60        in the place shut up
         put under secretly
         its weight uncertain
         But when they were perplexed
         at his strange question
65    Jesus, as he walked, stood
         on the bank of the Jordan
         River and stretched forth
         his right hand
         and sowed on the
70        And then
         water
         and        before
         them brought forth fruit
         . . .
75    . . .

§215. As far as can be made out in this badly preserved account (Text 54), the subject is an event which is not paralleled in the canonical Gospels. The place, at any rate, is plain, for Jesus is said to have stood on the bank of the Jordan (Lines 65–66). The verb κατασπείρω, "to sow (upon)," is also unmistakable in Line 69, while in Lines 72–73 the restoration seems reasonably well assured which gives a statement about the bringing forth of fruit ἐνώ[πιον αὐτῶν], i.e., "before them," or "in the presence of them." Therefore it would appear that Jesus wrought some miracle upon the Jordan bank which involved the sowing of seed and immediate ripening of fruit. In the small remaining portion of Egerton Papyrus 2, namely, Fragment 3 *verso* and *recto* (Fig. 1), only individual words and portions thereof are preserved, and it is not possible to ascertain the sense of what was once written there.

## 2 / Oxyrhynchus Papyrus 654

*Literature:* Bernard P. Grenfell and Arthur S. Hunt, *New Sayings of Jesus and Fragment of a Lost Gospel from Oxyrhynchus.* 1904; OP IV No. 654; KT 8, 20–22; Hugh G. Evelyn White, *The Sayings of Jesus from Oxyrhynchus.* 1920; BVA 48–53; SEA 97–101; HSNTAE 61–66.

§216. Because each document has a relationship to the Gospel according to Thomas (§§282ff.), Oxyrhynchus Papyri 654, 1, and 655, are to be considered together. In the order of their discovery (§§120f.), OP 1 would, of course, be the first to be discussed. In the chronological order of the manuscripts, OP 655 would be the first, since its hand-writing appears to be the oldest (§232). But the materials which the three papyri contain are clearly related to materials which are found in the Gospel according to Thomas in a sequence corresponding to the placement of the papyri in the order, 654, 1, and 655. Accordingly, it is in that order that we take them up. At this point the three papyri will be presented, one after the other. Later (§§288ff.) their common relationship to the Gospel according to Thomas will be considered. Oxyrhynchus Papyrus 654 (Fig. 3) was found by Grenfell and Hunt at Behnesa in 1903 (§121). The text is written on the *verso* of a piece of papyrus about nine by three inches in size. The other side (*recto*) of the document contains a survey-list of various pieces of land, written in a cursive hand attributed to the end of the second or beginning of the third century. It was evidently after that that the text with which we are concerned was inscribed on the back side of the survey document. Here (*verso*) the handwriting is in upright uncials of medium size which are considered to belong to the middle or end of the third century. The text consists of forty-two lines, and may be divided into six sections.

§217. The first section (Lines 1–5), which we will label as our own Text 55, is an introduction and reads, as far as the words are preserved and with reasonably well-assured restorations, as follows:

TEXT 55

οὗτοι οἱ {οἱ} λόγοι οἱ [. . . οὓς ἐλά-]
λησεν 'Ιη(σοῦ)ς ὁ ζῶν κ[

καὶ Θωμᾶ καὶ εἶπεν [
αν τῶν λόγων τούτ[ων . . .]
5   οὐ μὴ γεύσηται [


These are the words . . . which
Jesus the living spoke
and Thomas and he said
of these words
5   will not taste

§218. The foregoing introduction (Text 55) contains a saying
(Lines 3–5) which is presumably a saying of Jesus. Each of the remaining sections of the text consists of, or contains, a saying of Jesus
too. Each saying was probably introduced, when the text was intact,
with the words, λέγει 'Ῑῡ̄ς, "Jesus says," or "Jesus said." Although
these words are missing in the broken-away part of the Papyrus at
the beginning (Line 5) of our next saying (Text 56), they may be
read in Lines 9, 21, 27, and 36. Supposing that "Jesus says" stood
at the end of Line 5, the second section of the text began there and
continued to the beginning of Line 9. From Line 6 to the beginning
of Line 9 this second saying, with probable restorations, reads:

TEXT 56

μὴ παυσάσθω ὁ ζη[τῶν . . .]
εὕρῃ καὶ ὅταν εὕρῃ [. . . θαμ-]
βηθεὶς βασιλεύῃ κα[ὶ . . . ἀναπαήσεται


Let him who seeks not cease
finds, and when he finds . . . a-
mazed he will reign and . . . will
rest.

As already noted (§166), this saying is quoted by Clement of Alexandria from the Gospel according to the Hebrews, but it was probably a
current saying which was incorporated in that work as well as in the
present one, and thus it is not indicated that this papyrus is part of a
copy of the Gospel according to the Hebrews.

§219. The third saying occupies Lines 9–21.

FIGURE 3.

*Oxyrhynchus Papyrus 654*

TEXT 57

λέγει Ἰ[η(σοῦ)ς . . .]
10  οἱ ἕλκοντες ἡμᾶς [
ἡ βασιλεία ἐν οὐρα[νῷ . . .]
τὰ πετεινὰ τοῦ οὐρ[ανοῦ . . .]
τί ὑπὸ τὴν γῆν ἐστ[ιν . . .]
οἱ ἰχθύες τῆς θαλά[σσης . . .]

15    τες ὑμᾶς καὶ ἡ βασ[ιλεία . . .]
     ἐντὸς ὑμῶν [ἐ]στι [
     γνῷ ταύτην εὑρή[σει . . .]
     ἑαυτοὺς γνώσεσθε [
     ἔστε ὑμεῖς τοῦ πατρὸς τοῦ τ[
20    γνῶσθε ἑαυτοὺς ἐν [
     καὶ ὑμεῖς ἔστε ἡ πτο[


     Jesus says
10    who draw us
     the kingdom in heaven
     the birds of the heaven
     what is under the earth
     the fish of the sea
15    . . . you. And the kingdom
     is within you
     knows, will find this
     you will know yourselves
     you are of the Father
20    you know yourselves in
     And you are

Here we have at least one parallel with Synoptic tradition, namely,
the statement in Lines 15–16 that the kingdom is ἐντὸς ὑμῶν, the same
phrase that is in Lk 17:21. Translatable as either "within you," or
"in the midst of you," it seems evident that here in the Papyrus it
must be rendered "within you," since there is also mention almost
immediately (Line 18) of self-knowledge.

§220. The words λέγει 'Ιη(σοῦ)s presumably stood at the end of
Line 21 and introduced the fourth saying which continues through
Line 27.

TEXT 58

     οὐκ ἀποκνήσει ἄνθ[ρωπος . . .]
     ρων ἐπερωτῆσαι πα[
     ρων περὶ τοῦ τόπου τῆ[s . . .]
25    σετε ὅτι πολλοὶ ἔσονται π[ρῶτοι ἔσχατοι καὶ]
     οἱ ἔσχατοι πρῶτοι καὶ [
     σιν

a man will not hesitate

... to ask

... about the place of the

25 ... For many first will be last and

the last first and

. . .

As far as the words are preserved, Lines 25–26 give a text almost identical with Mk 10:31 (cf. Mt 19:30; Lk 13:30), and the restoration in terms of that parallel is undoubtedly valid. Mk 10:31, written in lines corresponding to the lines in OP 654, reads:

$$\pi o\lambda\lambda o i\ \delta \dot{\epsilon}\ \ddot{\epsilon}\sigma o\nu\tau a\iota\ \pi\rho\tilde{\omega}\tau o\iota\ \ddot{\epsilon}\sigma\chi a\tau o\iota\ \varkappa a i$$
$$o i\ \ddot{\epsilon}\sigma\chi a\tau o\iota\ \pi\rho\tilde{\omega}\tau o\iota$$

§221. The fifth saying comprises Lines 27–31.

TEXT 59

$$\lambda \acute{\epsilon}\gamma\epsilon\iota\ \,\text{'}\text{I}\eta(\sigma o\tilde{\nu})s\cdot\ [.\ .\ .\ \ddot{\epsilon}\mu\pi\rho o\sigma\text{-}]$$
$$\theta\epsilon\nu\ \tau\tilde{\eta}s\ \ddot{o}\psi\epsilon\omega s\ \sigma o\nu\ \varkappa a i\ [$$
$$\dot{a}\pi\dot{o}\ \sigma o\tilde{\nu}\ \dot{a}\pi o\varkappa a\lambda\nu\varphi\langle\theta\rangle\acute{\eta}\sigma\epsilon\tau[a i\ \sigma o\iota.\ \ o\dot{\nu}\ \gamma\acute{a}\rho\ \dot{\epsilon}\sigma\text{-}]$$
30    $$\tau\iota\nu\ \varkappa\rho\nu\pi\tau\dot{o}\nu\ \ddot{o}\ o\dot{\nu}\ \varphi a\nu\epsilon[\rho\dot{o}\nu\ \gamma\epsilon\nu\acute{\eta}\sigma\epsilon\tau a\iota]$$
$$\varkappa a i\ \tau\epsilon\theta a\mu\mu\acute{\epsilon}\nu o\nu\ \ddot{o}\ o[\dot{\nu}\varkappa\ .\ .\ .]$$

Jesus says: . . . be-

fore your sight and

from you, will be revealed to you. For nothing

30  is hidden that shall not be made manifest

and buried that shall not

With the very probable restorations indicated, the text in Lines 29–30 is identical with Lk 8:17 (cf. also Mk 4:22; Mt 10:26; Lk 12:2). In lines corresponding with OP 654, Lk 8:17 reads:

$$o\dot{\nu}\ \gamma\acute{a}\rho\ \dot{\epsilon}\sigma\text{-}$$
$$\tau\iota\nu\ \varkappa\rho\nu\pi\tau\dot{o}\nu\ \ddot{o}\ o\dot{\nu}\ \varphi a\nu\epsilon\rho\dot{o}\nu\ \gamma\epsilon\nu\acute{\eta}\sigma\epsilon\tau a\iota$$

§222. The sixth saying is introduced by a question which appears to be asked by the disciples, although actual mention of them is lost in a break in the Papyrus. This section, with the question and the saying, occupies Lines 32–39.

TEXT 60

35

[ἐξ]ετάζουσιν αὐτὸν ο[ἰ μαθηταὶ αὐτοῦ καὶ]
[λέ]γουσιν πῶς νηστεύ[σομεν καὶ πῶς]
[εὐξώμ]εθα καὶ πῶς [
[. . . . κ]αὶ τί παρατηρήσ[ομεν . . .]
]ν λέγει 'Ιη(σοῦ)s [
]ειται μὴ ποιεῖτ[ε . . .]
]ης ἀληθείας ἀν[
]ν ἀ[π]οκεκρ[υμμένη . . .]


His disciples question him and
say: How shall we fast and how
shall we pray and how
35    . . . and what shall we observe
Jesus says
. . . do not do
. . . truth . . .
. . . hidden


Of the seventh and last saying in OP 654 only a word or two are
legibly preserved in Lines 40–42.

TEXT 61

40      [. . . . . . μα]κάρι[os] ἐστιν[
]ω ἐστ[ι . . .]
]ιν[


40          blessed is
is
. .

## 3 / *Oxyrhynchus Papyrus 1*

*Literature:* Bernard P. Grenfell and Arthur S. Hunt, ΛΟΓΙΑ
IHCOY, *Sayings of Our Lord.* 1897; OP I No. 1; KT 8, 19; BVA
52–57; SEA 92–97; HSNTAE 66–70.

§223. Oxyrhynchus Papyrus 1 (Figs. 4–5), discovered by Grenfell
and Hunt at Behnesa in 1897 (§120), is a text written on both the *verso*
and the *recto* of a papyrus leaf about six by four inches in size. The
handwriting is much like that of OP 654 (§216), namely, an uncial
script of medium size and upright character, and this manuscript, like
the other one, doubtless belongs in the third century. At the upper
right-hand corner of the *verso* (Fig. 4) is a page number ($\iota a$ = 11),
which shows that this was a leaf of a codex. Again we have a series of
sayings and, as far as the Papyrus is preserved at the appropriate
place, we find that each is introduced, just as in OP 654 save that the
abbreviation of the name of Jesus is slightly different, with the words,
λέγει 'Ῑs, "Jesus says."

§224. With Line 1 of the *verso* (Fig. 4) we are in the midst of a
saying which is evidently continued from the preceding page. This
saying extends to near the end of Line 4 where the word λέγει, followed by 'Ῑs at the beginning of Line 5, introduces the next saying.
The text reads:

TEXT 62

> καὶ τότε διαβλέψεις
> ἐκβαλεῖν τὸ κάρφος
> τὸ ἐν τῷ ὀφθαλμῷ
> τοῦ ἀδελφοῦ σου
>
> and then you will see clearly
> to cast out the mote
> that is in the eye
> of your brother.

With only a transposition in location of the verb, ἐκβαλεῖν, the saying
is identical with Lk 6:42 which reads, if written in corresponding

FIGURE 4.

*Oxyrhynchus Papyrus 1*

*verso*

lines, as follows:

καὶ τότε διαβλέψεις
τὸ κάρφος
τὸ ἐν τῷ ὀφθαλμῷ
τοῦ ἀδελφοῦ σου ἐκβαλεῖν

§225. Lines 4–11 contain the second saying.

TEXT 63

λέγει
5  'Ι(ησοῦ)ς ἐὰν μὴ νηστεύση-
ται τὸν κόσμον οὐ μὴ
εὕρηται τὴν βασιλεί-
αν τοῦ θ(εο)ῦ καὶ ἐὰν μὴ
σαββατίσητε τὸ σάβ-
10  βατον οὐκ ὄψεσθε τὸ(ν)
π(ατέ)ρα

Jesus
says: If you do not fast
to the world, you will not
find the king-
dom of God; and if you do not
keep the sabbath as sab-
bath, you will not see the
Father.

§226. The third saying is in Lines 11–22.

TEXT 64

λέγει 'Ι(ησοῦ)ς ἔ[σ]την
ἐν μέσῳ τοῦ κόσμου
καὶ ἐν σαρκεὶ ὤφθην
αὐτοῖς καὶ εὗρον πάν-
15  τας μεθύοντας καὶ
οὐδένα εὗρον δειψῶ(ν)-
τα ἐν αὐτοῖς καὶ πο-
νεῖ ἡ ψυχή μου ἐπὶ
τοῖς υἱοῖς τῶν ἀν(θρώπ)ων
20  ὅτι τυφλοί εἰσιν τῇ καρ-
δίᾳ αὐτῶ[ν] καὶ [οὐ] βλέ-
[πουσι . . .]

Jesus says: I stood
in the midst of the world,
and in flesh I appeared

to them, and I found all
15 drunken, and
I found none athirst
among them. And
my soul is pained for
the sons of men,
20 because they are blind in
their heart and do not see
. . .

§227. At the bottom of the *verso* of OP 1, Line 22 (§226) is badly damaged, and what followed in the next line or lines is completely lost. With consecutive numbering of the existing lines, Line 23 is the first line at the top of the *recto* (Fig. 5). This line also, like several which follow it, is badly damaged at the left side, and only a word or two are legible at the right end of the line. Since [λέγ]ει ['Ῑς] is probably to be read at the beginning of Line 24, the words at the end of Line 23 must be the end of a saying, the fourth in the series, and this saying probably began originally at the bottom of the *verso* of this leaf. The words which can be made out in Line 23 at the top of the *recto* are:

TEXT 65

[. . . . . . . . . . . . τ]ὴν πτωχεία(ν)

the poverty

§228. The fifth saying is found in Lines 24–31.

TEXT 66

[λέγ]ει ['Ι(ησοῦ)]s ὅπ]ου ἐὰν ὦσιν
25      ε[ἰσὶ]ν ἄθεοι καὶ
[ὅ]που ε[ἷς] ἐστιν μόνος
[λέ]γω ἐγώ εἰμι μετ᾽ αὐ-
τ[οῦ] ἔγει[ρ]ον τὸν λίθο(ν)
κἀκεῖ εὑρήσεις με
30      σχίσον τὸ ξύλον κἀγὼ
ἐκεῖ εἰμι

**FIGURE 5.**
*Oxyrhynchus Papyrus 1*

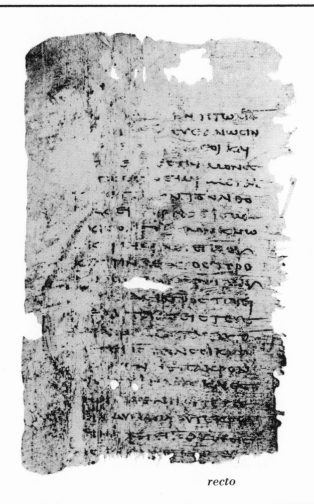

*recto*

Jesus says: Wherever there are
25     they are without gods and
       where one is alone
       I say: I am with him.
       Lift the stone
       and there you will find me;
30     split the wood and I
       am there.

If, as Grenfell and Hunt suggest (OP I 3), Lines 24–25 may be restored and translated to read, "Wherever there are two, they are not without God" ([ὅπ]ου ἐὰν ὦσιν [β', οὐκ] ε[ἰσὶ]ν ἄθεοι), then this statement is a condensed parallel to Mt 18:20, "For where two or three are gathered (οὐ γάρ εἰσιν δύο ἢ τρεῖς συνηγμένοι) in my name, there am I in the midst of them." Likewise the statement in Lines 27–28, "I am with him" (ἐγώ εἰμι μετ' αὐτ[οῦ]), may be compared with Mt 28:20, "I am with you" (ἐγώ μεθ' ὑμῶν εἰμι).

§229. Lines 31–36 contain the sixth saying.

TEXT 67

λέγει 'Ι(ησοῦ)ς οὐ-
κ ἔστιν δεκτὸς προ-
φήτης ἐν τῇ π(ατ)ρίδι αὐ-
τ[ο]ῦ οὐδὲ ἰατρὸς ποιεῖ
35   θεραπείας εἰς τοὺς
γεινώσκοντας αὐτό(ν)


Jesus says:
A prophet is not acceptable
in his country,
nor does a physician perform
35   healings on those
who know him.

It is plain that this saying provides much the same material as Lk 4:23-24, where Jesus quotes the proverb, "Physician, heal yourself" (ἰατρέ, θεράπευσον σεαυτόν), and says, "No prophet is acceptable in his own country" (οὐδεὶς προφήτης δεκτός ἐστιν ἐν τῇ πατρίδι ἑαυτοῦ).

§230. The seventh saying is in Lines 37–42.

TEXT 68

λέγει 'Ι(ησοῦ)ς πόλις οἰκοδο-
μημένη ἐπ' ἄκρον
[ὄ]ρους ὑψηλῦς καὶ ἐσ-
40   τηριγμένη οὔτε πε-
[σ]εῖν δύναται οὔτε κρυ-
[β]ῆναι

Jesus says: A city built
upon the top
of a lofty mountain and firmly
*40* established can neither
fall nor be
hidden.

This is apparently an expansion of what is found in the briefer parallel
in Mt 5:14, "A city set on a hill cannot be hid" (οὐ δύναται πόλις
κρυβῆναι ἐπάνω ὄρους κειμένη).
§231. Lines 42–44 contain the eighth and final saying preserved
in OP 1.

TEXT 69

λέγει 'Ι(ησοῦ)ς ἀκούεις
[ε]ἰς τὸ ἔ[ν ὠ]τίον σου τὸ
. . .
Jesus says: You hear
in your one ear the
. . .

In part the saying is reminiscent of Mt 10:27, "what you hear in the
ear" (ὃ εἰς τὸ οὖς ἀκούετε), but the damaged and broken-off papyrus
makes it impossible to tell how the saying continued.

## 4 / Oxyrhynchus Papyrus 655

*Literature:* OP IV, No. 655; KT 8, 23–24; BVA 34–37; SEA
81–83; HSNTAE 70–72; Robert A. Kraft, "Oxyrhynchus Papyrus 655 Reconsidered," in HTR 54 (1961), 253–62.

§232. Oxyrhynchus Papyrus 655 (Fig. 6) was found by Grenfell
and Hunt at Behnesa in 1903 (§121). Unlike the papyri described
hitherto which were in the form of a codex, OP 655 was in the form
of a roll. Of this scroll, eight badly damaged pieces were recovered.
The major portions appear to relate to each other as arranged in
Fig. 6. The largest fragment is a little over three inches square.

**FIGURE 6.**
*Oxyrhynchus Papyrus 655*

Together they provide a considerable part of one column of writing in the scroll, and the beginning of the lines of the next column adjacent to it on the right. The writing is in fairly small and somewhat sloping uncials. A date probably not later than the middle of the third century, and possibly even earlier, is deemed likely, since at least a few examples of the same style are found already in the second century. Although the fragments as they exist do not preserve any word or formula of introduction such as in OP 654 (§218) and OP 1 (§223), it is evident that again here we have to do with material which is presented as sayings of Jesus. Some of the material has parallels in the canonical Gospels, and at one point (Text 71 Line 18) there is mention of "his disciples," undoubtedly meaning disciples of Jesus.

§233. We begin with the first column which runs down the fragments on the left side (Fig. 6). With relatively small restorations mostly evident from the context, the text reads as follows in Lines 1–17:

TEXT 70

[. . ἀ]πὸ πρωὶ ἔ[ως ὀψὲ]
[μήτ]ε ἀφ' ἐσπ[έρας]
[ἔως π]ρωὶ μήτε [
[τροφῇ ὑ]μῶν τί φά-
5  [γητε μήτε] τῇ στ[ο-]
[λῇ ὑμῶν] τί ἐνδύ-
[ση]σθε [πολ]λῷ κρεί[σ-]
[σον]ές [ἐστε] τῶν [κρί-
νων ἄτι[να α]ὐξά-
10  νει οὐδὲ ν[ήθ]ει [
ἐν ἔχοντ[ες ἔ]νδ[υ-
μα τί ἐν [. . . .] καὶ
ὑμεῖς τίς ἂν προσθ⟨εί⟩η
ἐπὶ τὴν εἱλικίαν
15  ὑμῶν αὐτὸ[ς δ]ώσει
ὑμεῖν τὸ ἔνδυμα ὑ-
μῶν

From early until late,
nor from evening
until early, nor
about your food, what you shall
5  eat, nor about your
clothing, what you shall
put on. Much bet-
ter are you than the lil-
ies which grow
10  but do not spin.

> If you have one gar-
> ment what . . . also
> you. Who can add
> to your stature?
> *15* He himself will give
> you your gar-
> ment.

§234. In this text (Text 70) there are evident correspondences with the discourse on anxiety in Mt 6:25ff. = Lk 12:22ff. In comparison with Lines 4–7 note Mt 6:25, "about your life, what you shall eat, nor about your body, what you shall put on" (τῇ ψυχῇ ὑμῶν τί φάγητε, μηδὲ τῷ σώματι ὑμῶν τί ἐνδύσησθε). In comparison with Lines 8–10 note Mt 6:28, "the lilies . . . how they grow; they neither toil nor spin" (τὰ κρίνα . . . πῶς αὐξάνουσιν· οὐ κοπιῶσιν οὐδὲ νήθουσιν). And in comparison with Lines 13–14 note Mt 6:27, "And which of you . . . can add to his stature (*or* to his span of life) . . . ? (τίς δὲ ἐξ ὑμῶν . . . δύναται προσθεῖναι ἐπὶ τὴν ἡλικίαν αὐτοῦ . . . ;).

§235. Continuing down the first column of OP 655, Lines 17–23 read as follows:

TEXT 71

> λέγουσιν αὐ-
> τῷ οἱ μαθηταὶ αὐτοῦ
> πότε ἡμεῖν ἐμφα-
> *20* νὴς ἔσει καὶ πότε
> σε ὀψόμεθα λέγει
> ὅταν ἐκδύσησθε καὶ
> μὴ αἰσχυνθῆτε

> His disciples
> say to him:
> When will you be mani-
> *20* fest to us, and when
> will we see you? He says:
> When you take off your clothing and
> are not ashamed.

§236. In this text (Text 71) the question of the disciples in its first part (Lines 19–20), "When will you be manifest to us . . . ?" is to some extent reminiscent of the question of Judas (not Iscariot) in Jn 14:22, "How is it that you will manifest yourself to us (ἡμῖν . . . ἐμφανίζειν σεαυτόν) . . . ?" The word ἐμφανής which the disciples use in the Papyrus, is also found in the statement in Ac 10:40 that God "made him manifest . . . to us" (ἔδωκεν αὐτὸν ἐμφανῆ γενέσθαι . . . ἡμῖν). Likewise the question in its second part (Lines 20–21), "and when will we see you?" is reminiscent of the language of Jn 16:16, "Again a little while, and you will see me" (πάλιν μικρὸν καὶ ὄψεσθέ με). The answer which is provided in Lines 22–23, however, has no parallel in the canonical Gospels. Here the key word is the verb ἐκδύω (Line 22), meaning "strip," "undress," or "take off (clothing)." This verb is used in the active voice and with a literal sense in Lk 10:30 where the robbers "stripped" (ἐκδύσαντες) the man who was going down from Jerusalem to Jericho. The same verb is used in the middle voice (signifying that the subject performs an action upon himself) and with a figurative sense in 2 Cor 5:4, "not that we would be un-clothed," or, literally, "we do not want to strip ourselves" (οὐ θέλομεν ἐκδύσασθαι), where the body is thought of as a garment which is taken off in death. In the light of the latter reference the statement in Line 22 could refer to the time "when you strip yourselves" of the earthly body in death, and are not ashamed (cf. also §357). But the words "and are not ashamed" (Lines 22–23) could point back most immediately to the description in Gen 2:25 of Adam and Eve in the Garden of Eden before the fall when they were naked "and were not ashamed" (LXX, καὶ οὐκ ᾐσχύνοντο). In the light of this reference the saying attributed to Jesus could be intended to declare that salvation will be attained when the innocent life of the first man and woman is recovered. With this interpretation the intent of the teaching might be the same as that of the text which Clement of Alexandria quotes from Julius Cassianus and attributes to the Gospel according to the Egyptians (Text 19B §158). The wording of the present text is en-tirely different, however, and it does not follow from the comparison with the text cited by Clement that in OP 655 Lines 22–23 we neces-sarily have an excerpt from the Gospel according to the Egyptians. Rather, the present text will be found, in an expanded form, in the Coptic Gospel according to Thomas (§304), and will be discussed further there (cf. also §§309, 357).

§237. The foregoing texts (Texts 70–71) occupy the major part (Lines 1–23) of the first column of OP 655. On the smaller fragment, shown at the lower left side of Fig. 6, which seems to belong to the same first column, are the remnants of six more lines (Lines 24–29) of text. Here only individual letters or groups of letters are legible, and it is not possible to ascertain the sense. Turning to the right side of the manuscript (Fig. 6) we have only the beginnings of the lines of the second column of writing (§232). Continuing to number the lines consecutively, we have here Lines 30ff. In Lines 30–39, only a letter or two is recognizable in each line. Although the line numbering becomes somewhat uncertain because of the gap which intervenes, the slightly broader part of the Papyrus may be considered to contain Lines 41–50. Below that, on the detached fragment at the lower right side of Fig. 6, only the scantiest remnants of letters can be discerned on a few more lines.

§238. Even Lines 41-50 are very fragmentary, but may perhaps be restored by comparison with canonical parallels. Lines 41–46 recall Lk 11:52 and Mt 23:13. With restorations suggested by these parallels,[1] this text reads:

TEXT 72

> ἐλ[εγε· τὴν κλεῖδα]
> τῆς [γνώσεως ἔ-]
> κρυψ[αν· αὐτοὶ οὐκ]
> εἰσῆ[λθον οὐδὲ τοὺς]
> 45  εἰσερ[χομένους ἀφῆ-]
> καν [εἰσελθεῖν]

> He said: The key
> of knowledge they
> hid; they themselves did not
> enter, nor did they
> 45  allow those who would enter
> to go in.

In explanation of the words supplied in the foregoing, note "the key of knowledge" (τὴν κλεῖδα τῆς γνώσεως), and "you yourselves did not enter" (αὐτοὶ οὐκ εἰσήλθατε), in Lk 11:52; and "nor allow those who would enter to go in" (οὐδὲ τοὺς εἰσερχομένους ἀφίετε εἰσελθεῖν), in Mt 23:13.

---

[1] Cf. KT 8, 23; SEA 83.

§239. In Lines 46–50 the following text may be read, with restorations which seem to be plainly indicated by Mt 10:16.

TEXT 73

[ὑμεῖς]
δὲ γεί[νεσθε φρόνι-]
μοι ὡ[s οἱ ὄφεις καὶ ἀ-]
κέραι[οι ὡs αἱ περιστε-]
50   ρα[ί]


But you,
be wise
as serpents and in-
nocent as
50   doves.

The parallel text in Mt 10:16, written in lines corresponding to these in OP 655, is:

γίνεσθε οὖν φρόνι-
μοι ὡs οἱ ὄφεις καὶ ἀ-
κέραιοι ὡs αἱ περιστε-
ραί.


## 5 / Rylands Papyrus 463

*Literature:* C. H. Roberts, *Catalogue of the Greek and Latin Papyri in the John Rylands Library, Manchester.* III (1938), 18–23; SEA 106–8.


§240. Rylands Papyrus 463 is a fragmentary single leaf, about three and one-quarter by three and one-half inches in size, which was acquired in 1917 and published in 1938 by The John Rylands Library, Manchester. In all probability it came from ancient Oxyrhynchus. The leaf is written on both sides, and bears a page number at the top on each side, κα = 21 on the *recto*, and κβ = 22 on the *verso* (Fig. 7). The script is plain and upright, but irregular and not well proportioned. It is judged to date in the early part of the third century. The *recto* (Page 21) reads as follows:

TEXT 74

τὸ λοιπὸν δρόμου και[ρο]ῦ χρόνου
αἰῶνος ἀνάπαυσιν ἐ[ν] σιγῇ · ταῦ-
τ[α] εἰποῦσα ἡ Μαριάμμη ἐσιώπη-
σε[ν] ὡς τοῦ σωτῆρος μέχρι ὧδε
5    εἰρηκότος ᾽Ανδρέας λέγε[ι ἀ]δελ-
φοὶ τί ὑμεῖν δοκεῖ πε[ρ]ὶ τῶν {πε-
ρὶ τῶν} λαληθέντων ἐγὼ μὲν
γὰρ οὐ πιστεύω ταῦτα [τὸ]ν σ[ω-]
τῆρα εἰρηκέναι · ἐδόκει γ[ὰρ ἐτε-]
10   ρογνωμονεῖν τῇ ἐκ[ε]ίν[ου δια-]
νοίᾳ περὶ τούτ[ω]ν πρα[γμά-]
των ἐξεταζόμενος ὁ σω[τὴρ]
λάθρα γυν[α]ικὶ ἐλάλει καὶ ⟨οὐ⟩ φ[α-]
νερῶς ἵνα πάντες ἀκούσω[μεν]
15   [. . . ἀ]ξιολογοτέραν ἡ[μ]ῶν [
     ]ε[
     ].[

the remainder of the course of the season of the time
of the Aeon rest in silence. When
she had said these things Mariamme was
silent, as thus far the Savior
5    had spoken. Andrew said: Brothers, what do you think of
what has been said? For I, for my
part, do not believe that the Savior
has said these things; for it seems to
10   differ from his thought.
When the Savior was questioned
about these matters,
did he speak secretly to a woman, and not o-
penly in order that we all might hear?
15   . . . more worthy than we
     . . .
     . . .

FIGURE 7.
*Rylands Papyrus 463*

*verso*

§241. The first sentence of this text (Text 74 Lines 1–2) is not fully intelligible because the first part of it is missing, but we recognize the three chief Greek words which have to do with time. καιρός is proper, right, or opportune time; χρόνος is a space or period of time; and an αἰών is an age, an indefinitely or an infinitely long period of time. All of these words are used in the canonical NT, but also lend themselves to Gnostic interpretations where notably the αἰῶνες or Aeons have, as we have seen (§§109f.), a great role as emanations of the divine substance existing within the Pleroma. The words ἀνάπαυσις or "rest" and σιγή or "silence" (Line 2) are also found in the NT (ἀνάπαυσις, e.g., Mt 11:29; cf. κατάπαυσις, Heb 4:1-10; σιγή, e.g., Rev 8:1), and were developed into major concepts in Gnosticism, where Sige ("Silence") is a very lofty entity (§109) and "rest" a very much desired goal (§110). Therefore it seems probable that our fragment opens with the expression of Gnostic ideas, looking toward the attainment in the course of time of "rest" in "silence." In Line 3 we note the appearance of Mariamme (Μαριάμμη). As far as the name goes, Mariamme is a form of the name Mariam (Μαριάμ) and is used, e.g., by Josephus (*Ant.* III 2, 4 §54) as he writes about the sister of Aaron and Moses (RSV, Miriam, but LXX, Μαριάμ, Mariam, in Num 12:1, etc.). Mariam, in turn, is a well-known variant of Mary (Μαρία). For example, in the account of the visit of Mary Magdalene to the empty tomb (Mt 28:1ff. = Mk 16:1ff. = Lk 24:1ff.; Jn 20:1ff.) she is called Mariam in the text of major manuscripts in Mt 28:1 and Jn 20:16, 18. In fact the probability is that the Mariamme of Line 3 is none other than Mary Magdalene, for we know otherwise (§190) that she was considered very important in the handing down of Gnostic traditions. In what follows in Text 74 Andrew takes exception (Lines 5–10) to some report as to what "the Savior" had said. The title "Savior" (σωτήρ) is an infrequent designation of Christ in the canonical Gospels (Lk 2:11; Jn 4:42), but is used characteristically in Oxyrhynchus Papyrus 840 (Text 84 §262), and recurs very frequently in the summary of Valentinian doctrines by Irenaeus (*Against Heresies* I 1-8, cf. above §§109f.). In fact Irenaeus says (*Against Heresies* I 1, 3) that these Gnostics use the term Savior to the exclusion of Lord (κύριος). The further objection that is raised in Lines 11–14, complaining that the Savior had spoken secretly to a woman rather than openly to all the disciples, is introduced without designation of a speaker but from Lines 18–19 on the *verso* we gather that it was Peter who was speaking here.

§242. We turn now to the *verso* (Fig. 7) of Rylands Papyrus 463 and continue to number the lines consecutively from the *recto*.

TEXT 75

> τοῦ σωτῆρος Λευε[ὶ]ς λέγει Πέτρῳ
> Πέτρε ἀ[εὶ] σο[ὶ] τὸ ὀργίλον παράκει-
> 20    ται καὶ ἄρτι οὕτως συνζητεῖ[ς] τῇ
> γυναικὶ ὡς ἀντικείμενος αὐτῇ
> εἰ ὁ σωτὴ[ρ] ἀξίαν αὐτὴν ἡγήσατο

σὺ τὶς εἶ ἐξουθενῶν αὐτὴν πάν-
τως γὰρ ἐκεῖνος εἰδὼς αὐτὴν ἀσ-
25 φ[αλ]ῶ[ς] ἠγάπησεν μᾶλλ[ο]ν αἰσχυ(ν)-
θῶ[με]ν καὶ ἐνδυσάμενο[ι] τὸν
τ[έλειο]ν ἄν(θρωπ)ον ἐκεῖνο τὸ προστα⟨χ-⟩
θ[ὲν ἡ]μεῖν π[ο]ιήσωμεν κηρύσ{ε}-
σ[ειν τὸ] εὐαγγ[έ]λιον μηδὲν ὁ[ρ]ίζον-
30 τ[ες μ]ηδὲ νομοθετ[ο]ῦντες ὡς εἶ-
π[εν ὁ] σωτὴρ [ταῦ]τα εἰπὼν ὁ Λευ-
[εἰς μὲ]ν ἀπ[ελθὼν] ἦρχεν κη[ρύσσειν]
[τὸ εὐαγγέλι]ον [

. . .

the Savior. Levi said to Peter:
Peter, your quick temper is always with
20 you, and even now you argue with the
woman as if you were her adversary.
If the Savior believed her worthy,
who are you to set her at naught?
For he knew her thoroughly and
25 loved her firmly. Rather let us be
ashamed and, putting on the
perfect man, let us do that which was
commanded to us, (namely,) to
preach the gospel, neither marking out
30 limits nor laying down laws (other than) as
the Savior said. When he had said these things, Levi went away and began to preach.
The gospel . . .

. . .

§243. In the foregoing text (Text 75) the word used (Line 19) for
the quick temper of Peter is the same that is in Tit 1:7, where a
bishop, it is said, must not be quick-tempered (μὴ ὀργίλον). The verb
in Line 20, "argue with," is also in the NT, being used with some
frequency by Mk, as in 8:11 where the Pharisees came to Jesus and
began to argue with him (συζητεῖν αὐτῷ). The "perfect man" (Line 27)
is found in Col 1:28 (ἄνθρωπον τέλειον) and Eph 4:13 (ἄνδρα τέλειον),
and the conception of perfection and consummation is also important
in Gnosticism (§111). From these and other points in Rylands Papyrus 463 it would appear that we have here the fragment of a Gnostic

Gospel. From the prominence of Mariamme, i.e., Mary Magdalene, it would appear that we might call this the Gospel according to Mariamme. This will be confirmed when we find (§§322ff.) substantially the present material contained in a longer Coptic manuscript which, at the point corresponding to Lines 33 and following, above, has a text which would represent this in Greek: τὸ εὐαγγέλιον κατὰ Μαριάμ, The Gospel according to Mariam.

## 6 / Rainer Gospel Papyrus

*Literature:* G. Bickell in *Mittheilungen aus der Sammlung der Papyrus Erzherzog Rainer* I (1887), 53–61, "Das nichtkanonische Evangelien-Fragment"; 2–3 (1887), 41–42, "Zum Evangelienfragment Raineri"; 5 (1889), 78–82, "Ein letztes Wort über das Papyrus-Evangelium"; KT 8, 23; BVA 30–33; SEA 89–91; HSNTAE 74.

§244. The Rainer Gospel Papyrus was discovered in 1885 by G. Bickell in the papyrus collection of Archduke Rainer in Vienna. This is only a small fragment (Fig. 8) bearing little more than one hundred characters in Greek. Since it came from the Fayum in Egypt it is sometimes known as the Fayum Fragment. From the handwriting it is judged to belong to the last decades of the third century. The text is plainly parallel to Mt 26:30-35 = Mk 14:26-31, and restorations which seem justified by comparison with the canonical record are included in the transcription of the text which follows. The first line in particular, it may be noted, is very difficult to read, and the transcription and restoration are the most uncertain there.

TEXT 76

[ἐν δὲ τῷ ἐ]ξάγειν ὡς ἐ[ἴ]πε[ν] ὅτι ἅ[παντες]
[ἐν ταύτῃ] τῇ νυκτὶ σκανδαλισ[θήσεσ-]
[θε κατὰ] τὸ γραφὲν πατάξω τὸν [ποιμέ-]
[να καὶ τὰ] πρόβατα διασκορπισθήσ[ονται εἰ-]
5    [πόντος το]ῦ Πέτ(ρου) καὶ εἰ πάντες ο[ὐκ ἐγώ λέ-]
[γει 'Ι(ησοῦ)ς πρὶ]ν ἀλεκτρυὼν δὶς κοκ[κύσει τρὶς]
[σὺ σήμερόν με ἀ]παρν[ήσῃ]

FIGURE 8.
*Rainer Gospel Papyrus*

As he led them out, he said: You will all
this night fall away,
as it is written; I will strike the shepherd, and the sheep will be scattered. When
5    Peter said: Even if all, not I,
Jesus said: Before the cock crows twice, three times
you will today deny me.

§245. For comparison the parallel texts in Mt and Mk may be
written in similar lines. Lines 1–2 correspond with Mt 26:31.

πάντες ὑμεῖς
σκανδαλισθήσεσθε ἐν ἐμοὶ ἐν τῇ νυκτὶ ταύτῃ.

You will all
fall away because of me this night.

Lines 3–4 correspond with Mk 14:27.

ὅτι γέγραπται· πατάξω τὸν ποιμέ-
να, καὶ τὰ πρόβατα διασκορπισθήσονται.

For it is written: I will strike the shepherd, and the sheep will be scattered.

The verb form διασκορπισθήσονται is found here in Mk, as also in Mt 26:31 in the Egyptian text. But in some of the papyri (37 45) and in the Koine text, the form διασκορπισθήσεται is found in Mt 26:31 and could be used, alternatively, in the restoration of Line 4 in the Rainer Papyrus. There is of course no difference in meaning or translation. Again Lines 5–7 in the Rainer Papyrus correspond with Mk 14:29-30.

> ὁ δὲ Πέτρος ἔφη αὐτῷ· εἰ καὶ πάντες
> σκανδαλισθήσονται, ἀλλ' οὐκ ἐγώ.
> καὶ λέγει αὐτῷ ὁ Ἰησοῦς· ἀμὴν
> λέγω σοι ὅτι σὺ σήμερον ταύτῃ τῇ νυκτὶ
> πρὶν ἢ δὶς ἀλέκτορα φωνῆσαι
> τρίς με ἀπαρνήσῃ.

Peter said to him: Even if all
fall away, I will not.
And Jesus said to him: Truly,
I say to you, today, this night,
before the cock crows twice,
you will deny me three times.

As compared with the canonical parallels it is evident that the Rainer fragment presents an abbreviated account but has no independent information to add. It must, therefore, be judged dependent upon Mt and Mk, but whether this was true throughout the larger Gospel, of which the fragment was presumably a part, cannot be ascertained since only so tiny a piece has survived.

## 7 / Oxyrhynchus Papyrus 1081

*Literature:* OP VIII, No. 1081; KT 8, 25; BVA 40–41; SEA 87–89.

§246. Oxyrhynchus Papyrus 1081 was found at Behnesa and published by Arthur S. Hunt in 1911 (§121). This is a leaf from a papyrus codex, broken off at the bottom, and about eight by four inches in size (Figs. 9–10). The handwriting is in plain, slightly inclined uncials, and is considered to belong most probably to the early decades of the fourth century. The text of the *verso* (Fig. 9) is as follows. Since scarcely more than individual words and parts thereof are preserved at the beginning and the end, the translation is limited to Lines 5–23.

TEXT 77

τα γεγονόσι [
το ἐμφανὲς [
λη λυθεῖσα ν[
ρα τε πολλῇ [
5   τῶν ἀφθάρ[τ]ω[ν . . .]
νει ὁ ἔχων ὤ[τ]α τ[
πέραν τῶν [.]κο[.]ν ἀ-
κουέτω κα[ὶ] τοῖς ἀγρη-
γοροῦσιν [ἐγ]ὼ λαλῶ ἔτι
10  προ[σθεὶς ε]ῖπεν πᾶν
τὸ γε[ινόμε]νον ἀπὸ
τῆς [φθορᾶς] ἀπογεί-]
νετ[αι ὡς ἀπ]ὸ φθορᾶς
γεγ[ονὸς τὸ] δὲ γε[ι]νό-
15  μεν[ον ἀπὸ] ἀφ[θ]αρ-
σίας [οὐκ ἀπο]γείν[εται]
ἀλλ[ὰ μ]έν[ει] ἄφ[θαρ-]
τον ὡς ἀπὸ ἀ[φ]θαρσί-]
[α]ς γεγονός [.] τ[
20       ] τῶν ἀν[θρ]ώ[πων]
ἐπλανήθ[ησαν . . .]
μὴ εἰδότ[ες . . .]
φ[θο]ρὰν τα[. . .]
θανον[

5   the things that are incorruptible
    . . . He who has ears
    beyond
    let him hear. Also to those who
    watch, I speak. Besides
10  he added and said: All
    that comes to be from
    corruption perish-
    es, as having come to be
    from corruption; but that which comes
15  to be from incorrup-
    tion does not perish
    but remains incorrupti-
    ble, as having come to be from
    incorruption.

FIGURE 9.
*Oxyrhynchus Papyrus 1081*

*verso*

20   . . . men
have been deceived . . .
not knowing . . .
corruption . . .
. . .

§247. Continuing to number the lines consecutively, we have the following text on the *recto* (Fig. 10). At the beginning the gaps can be restored with considerable plausibility; at the end the text becomes very fragmentary.

**FIGURE 10.**
*Oxyrhynchus Papyrus 1081*

*recto*

TEXT 78

25   ]ι κ(ύρι)ε πῶς οὖν
    ]ισκομεν λέγε[ι]
   [. . . . . . ὁ σ]ωτὴρ διελθο[ῦ-]
   σιν ἐκ τῶν ἀφανῶν κα[ὶ]
   [εἰ]ς τὸ [φῶ]ς τῶν φαινο-
30  [μέ]νων καὶ αὕτη ἡ ἀπό[ρ-]
   ροια τῆ[ς ἐ]ννοίας ἀνα-
   δείξει ὑ[μῖ]ν πῶς ἡ πίστ[ις]

εὑρ[ετ]έ[α] ἡ φαινομέ-
νη τοῦ ἀ[πατρι]κοῦ π(ατ)ρ(ό)s
35  ὁ ἔχων ὦτ[α ἀκού]ειν ἀ-
κουέτω [ὁ τῶν ὅλ]ων δε-
σπότης ο[ὑκ ἔστ]ι π(ατὴ)ρ ἀλλὰ προπά[τωρ ὁ γὰ]ρ π(ατὴ)ρ [ἀρ-]
χή ἐ[σ]τ[ιν τῶν μ]ελλόν-
40  των [. . . . . . . . . . . ἐ]κεινο[
[. . . . . . . . . . . . προ]πάτω[ρ . . .]
]ν ἀπὸ γ[ε]νεᾶς [
]ρω ομ[. .]ε [
]εται αν[
45  ]ω[.]μα αν[
[προπάτ]ωρ θ(εὸ)s π(ατ)ή[ρ . . .]
]πιαντ[.]π[
]ει ἀγέννητ[ος . . .]
]ο μὲν του[
50  ]το[


25     Lord, how then
        The Savior
said . . . : When you pass
from the things that are hidden and
into the light of the things that
30     appear, and this emanation of thought will
show you how the faith
which is to be discovered is that which
appears from the fatherless Father.
35     He who has ears to hear, let
him hear. The Master
of all is not the Father
but the Fore-Father. For the Father
is the beginning of the things to come
40     . . .
              Fore-Father
             from birth

     . . .

     . . .
45     . . .

Fore-Father God Father

. . .

        unbegotten

. . .

*50* . . .

§248. Here again in OP 1081, as in Rylands Papyrus 463 (§§240–43), it is evident that we are in the realm of Gnostic thought. Esoteric and special knowledge seems to be implied in Lines 6–8 and 20–30, although the words, "He who has ears . . . let him hear" (Lines 6–8, 35–36) are, of course, directly out of the canonical Gospels (Mt 13:9 = Mk 4:9 = Lk 8:8, etc.). There are also many words in the text which are characteristic of the Gnostic vocabulary, as may be seen by comparison with our earlier description of Gnostic doctrines (§§100ff.). These include; "Savior" (σωτήρ, Line 27), "emanation" (ἀπόρροια, Lines 30–31), "thought" (ἔννοια, Line 31), "beginning" (ἀρχή, Lines 38–39), and "unbegotten" (ἀγέννητος, Line 48). Most decisive of all for the identification of the background out of which this text comes is the contrast (in Lines 36–38 and probably also in Lines 41 and 46) between the Father (πατήρ) and the Fore-Father (προπάτωρ). It is precisely upon the contrast between the Fore-Father, who is the original, eternal Aeon from whom all existence emanated, and the Father, who belongs only to the second Dyad in the Pleroma, that Irenaeus lays stress (*Against Heresies* I 11 and especially I 1, 1; cf. above §§109–10) as he describes the Valentinian school of Gnosticism. It is also the case with OP 1081, as with Rylands Papyrus 463, that we shall find (§§326ff.) the text recognizably embodied in a later and fuller Coptic manuscript and thereby be enabled to identify the larger work of which it is a part.

## 8 / Oxyrhynchus Papyrus 1224

*Literature:* OP X No. 1224; KT 8, 26; BVA 40–41; HSNTAE 72–73.

§249. Oxyrhynchus Papyrus 1224 was published by Grenfell and Hunt in 1914 (§121). It consists of two fragments (Fig. 11), of which

**FIGURE 11.**
*Oxyrhynchus Papyrus 1224*

*Fragment 1 recto*

*Fragment 2 verso*

the larger is about two and one-half by five and one-half inches, the
smaller about one and one-half by one and three-quarters inches in
size. These are what survive of the tops of leaves of a papyrus codex,
and are written on both sides. Fragment 1 *recto* (the small fragment at
the left in Fig. 11) has a page number ($\rho\lambda\theta$ = 139) at the top of the
column. Fragment 2 *verso* (the large fragment at the right in Fig. 11)
has a page number ($\rho o\delta$ = 174) at the top of the first column. The
number which presumably stood at the top of the second column is
presumably lost with the broken papyrus. On the other side (*recto*)
of the same fragment there are page numbers at the head of each
column, but both numbers are damaged. Two characters remain at
the top of the first column, Omicron (= 70), and Vau (= 6), so

presumably it is a Rho (= 100) which is missing, and the page number here was 176. This was therefore probably a double leaf which was folded in the middle in the quire of the book, and each page contained one column of writing. According to this understanding of the fragment, *recto* column two was page 173, *verso* column one was page 174 (as the preserved number shows), *verso* column two was page 175, and *recto* column one was page 176 (as the reconstructed number indicates). The Papyrus is written in upright uncial characters of medium size, and the date is probably early in the fourth century.

§250. As we have just seen (§249), Fragment 1 *recto* carries at the top the page number 139, therefore the other side (*verso*) must have been either page number 138 or 140. On the *recto* a few words and portions of words are recognizable, but not enough to constitute an intelligible text.

$$]ντι ἐν παντὶ$$
$$]μων ἀμὴν ὑ-$$
$$[μῖν λέγω . . .]εισ[$$
. . . in everything
. . . Truly,
I say to you . . .

On the *verso* even less is to be read, only the word "you" (nominative plural) being complete.

$$σεται ὑμεῖς[$$
$$]ητι[$$

§251. According to our understanding (§249) of the page numbering of Fragment 2, the second column on the *recto* was page 173. The text here may perhaps be read and restored as follows, but is admittedly difficult.

TEXT 79

$$με ἐβάρησεν καὶ [παρεσταμέ-]$$
$$νου ’Ιη(σοῦ) [ἐ]ν ὁράμα[τι λέγει]$$
$$τί ἀθ[υμ]εῖς οὐ γὰρ [$$
$$[σ]ὺ ἀλλὰ ὁ[$$
5   δοὺς ἐπ[

weighed me down. And
Jesus stood by in a vision, and said:

> Why are you disheartened? For not
> you but the
> 5  gave . . .

The verb βαρέω, "weigh down," found here in Line 1, is used by Lk 9:32 in the account of the transfiguration, when it is said that Peter and those with him were "heavy with sleep" (βεβαρημένοι ὕπνῳ). The word ὅραμα, "vision," which is used here in Line 2, occurs in the canonical Gospels only in Mt 17:9 in the account of the transfiguration. For the restoration in Line 1 to make the reading, "Jesus stood by," comparison may be made with Ac 27:23, "there stood by me an angel" (παρέστη . . . μοι . . . ἄγγελος). Whether the verbal correspondences with the account of the transfiguration in Mt and Lk justify the conclusion that the present text is also the fragment of a transfiguration account, is difficult to say because of the slight amount of what has been preserved.

§252. In Fragment 2 the first column of the *verso* was page 174, as shown by the number at the top (§249). Here, too, the text is relatively difficult to restore and understand.

TEXT 80

> [εἶ]πες μὴ ἀποκρεινό-
> [μενος . . . ἀ]πεῖπας π[ο]ίαν σέ
> [φασιν διδα]χὴν καιν[ὴν δι-]
> [δάσκειν . . . ]α[. . .]α καινὸν
> 5        ]θητι καὶ

> you said not making
> answer . . . you have forbidden. What is
> the new teaching that they say you
> teach . . . new
> 5  . . . and

While much of the preceding restoration may be very hypothetical, at least the mention of the "new teaching" in Line 3 seems an assured part of this text, both from the letters actually preserved and also from comparison with Mk 1:27 where there is also mention of the "new teaching" (διδαχὴ καινή) of Jesus.

§253. The second column of the *verso* of Fragment 2 may be recognized as page 175 of the codex, although the page number is missing

(§249). Here the text is more fully preserved and the gaps can be restored with more confidence.

TEXT 81

οἱ δὲ γραμματεῖς κ[αὶ φαρισαῖ-]
οι καὶ ἱερεῖς θεασάμ[ενοι αὐ-]
τὸν ἠγανάκτουν [ὅτι σὺν ἀμαρ-]
τωλοῖς ἀνὰ μέ[σον κεῖται ὁ]
5 δὲ ᾽Ιη(σοῦς) ἀκούσας [εἶπεν οὐ χρείαν]
[ἔχ]ουσιν οἱ ὑ[γιαίνοντες ἰα-]
[τροῦ]

But when the scribes and Pharisees and priests saw him,
they were indignant because
he reclined in the midst with sinners.
5 But when Jesus heard, he said:
Those who are well have no need of a
physician.

The parallelism with Mt 9:11-12 = Mk 2:16-17 = Lk 5:30-31 is plain, and the pronouncement at the end (Lines 5–7) is, as restored, identical with Lk 5:31.

§254. Page 176 of the codex is to be identified with the first column of the *recto* of Fragment 2, where this page number is partially preserved (§249). The restoration of the first three lines of text is highly probable, that of the next two at least plausible.

TEXT 82

[κ]αὶ π[ρ]οσεύχεσθε ὑπὲρ
[τῶν ἐχθ]ρῶν ὑμῶν ὁ γὰρ μὴ ὤν
[κατὰ ὑμ]ῶν ὑπὲρ ὑμῶν ἐστιν
[ὁ σήμερον ὤ]ν μακρὰν αὔριον
5 [ἐγγὺς ὑμῶν γ]ενήσεται καὶ ἐν
]τοῦ ἀντιδί[κου
]ινενων[

And pray for
your enemies. For he who is not

    against you is for you.
    He who today is far off, tomorrow
5   will be near you . . .
        of the opponent
        . . .

The first two sayings (Lines 1–3) are very similar to Mt 5:44 and Lk 9:50; the third (Lines 4–5) is quite in the same spirit, but completely extracanonical.


## 9 / Other Greek Papyri

### (A) BODMER PAPYRUS V

*Literature:* Michel Testuz, ed., *Bodmer Papyrus V.* 1958; HSNTAE 277–90; Emile de Strycker, *La forme la plus ancienne du Protevangile de Jacques.* Subsidia Hagiographica, 33. 1961.


§255. It has been said (§130) that the focus of our inquiry is upon extracanonical materials concerning the life of Jesus, chiefly those which are in Greek and which come from the first four centuries after his lifetime. There are, of course, other papyri which are written in Greek and which contain Gospel-type materials than those dealt with above (§§207–54), but it is the foregoing which fall most clearly within the scope of our undertaking as we have defined its limitations. Other manuscripts fall either partly or altogether outside those limitations. Of such, two examples may be given, but without presentation in full. The first is Bodmer Papyrus V which is, indeed, a relatively early manuscript but which actually has very little to do with the life of Jesus inasmuch as it is mainly interested in Mary, the Mother of Jesus, and in her parents, Joachim and Anna. Therewith it is essentially beyond the limits of our area of concern. The second is Cairo Papyrus 10 735 which has a little more to do with the life of Jesus inasmuch as it includes some mention of the flight to Egypt, but which is relatively late and therewith beyond our limits in time.

§256. Bodmer Papyrus V is a papyrus codex with forty-nine pages, all numbered, of almost perfectly preserved text, written in upright, square, uncial-type script of great regularity and clarity, a script which belongs probably to the third century. The text begins with a title which is repeated in a colophon at the end: γένεσις Μαρίας ἀποκάλυψις Ἰακώβ, "Nativity of Mary, Apocalypse of James." Between the title and the colophon the text may be divided into twenty-five chapters. Chapters 1–16 tell about the rich shepherd, Joachim (Ἰωακείμ), and his wife, Anna (Ἄννα), to whom after long childlessness was born Mary, who became the mother of Jesus. In accordance with Anna's vow (4, 1), when Mary was three years old she was brought to the Temple (7, 2). She lived there until the age of twelve, receiving food from the hand of an angel (8, 1–2). Then Joseph (Ἰωσήφ), being already old and the father of sons, took into his care "the virgin of the Lord" (τὴν παρθένον Κυρίου), but himself went away to build his buildings (οἰκοδομῆσαι τὰς οἰκοδομάς) (9, 1–3). On an occasion when she had gone forth to draw water, Mary received the Annunciation (11, 1–3), and was in her sixth month when Joseph returned from his building work, Mary being now sixteen years old (12, 3; 13, 1). Chapters 17–20 tell about the journey of Joseph and Mary to Bethlehem, and the birth of the child of Mary. The party arrives at the third mile (ἐπὶ μίλιον τρίτον) (17, 2) and soon afterward, when they have come half the way (ἀνὰ μέσον τῆς ὁδοῦ) (17, 3), Joseph finds a cave, leaves Mary in the care of his sons, and goes out to find a midwife in the region of Bethlehem (ἐν χώρᾳ Βηθλεέμ) (18, 1). When the child is born, Salome (Σαλώμη) attests that Mary is indeed a virgin (19, 3—20, 3). In Chapters 21–24 the wise men come to the cave (21), Herod slays the children (22, 1), searches unsuccessfully (22, 3) for John, the son of Elizabeth and Zechariah, and murders Zechariah (23–24). In an epilogue in Chapter 25 the purported author of this work affixes his signature in these words: "But I, James (Ἰάκωβος), who wrote this history in Jerusalem, when a tumult arose upon the death of Herod, withdrew into the desert (ἐν τῇ ἐρήμῳ) until the Jerusalem tumult should cease."

§257. Although the persons are not more precisely identified, the epilogue just quoted (§256) presumably intends to suggest James the brother of the Lord and head of the Jerusalem church (§§40f.) as the author, and to place the writing shortly after the death of Herod the Great, under whom Jesus was born. Actually this Nativity of Mary is dependent upon the infancy narratives of Mt and Lk (e.g., the account of the Annunciation to Mary in 11, 1–3 quotes Lk 1:28, 42; 1:30-31; 1:35, 32; 1:31; Mt 1:21; and Lk 1:38, in that order), and must be later than those Gospels. The tradition of the birth of Jesus in a cave (σπήλαιον) (18, 1) at Bethlehem is attested by Justin (*Dialogue with Trypho* 78 ANF I 237) and, according to references by Jerome (*Letter* 58, 3 NPNFSS VI 120) and Paulinus of Nola (*Letter* 31, 3 CSEL XXIX–XXX 270), can be traced back to before the time of Hadrian, who learned of it and profaned the place with a grove of Tammuz (Adonis). Origen (*Commentary on Matthew* 10, 17 ANF IX 424) explicitly cites the Book of James (βίβλος 'Ιακώβου) as the source of the tradition that the brothers of Jesus mentioned by the evangelist (Mt 13:55, cf. Mk 6:3; Jn 7:5) were the children of Joseph by a former marriage. Origen writes, mentioning also another work in the same connection:

> But some say, basing it on a tradition in the Gospel according to Peter, as it is entitled, or the Book of James, that the brothers of Jesus were sons of Joseph by a former wife, whom he married before Mary.

Since this agrees with the representation in Chapter 9 of the Nativity of Mary it is evidently this same work to which Origen was referring. The work may accordingly be placed in the second century and, in view of congruence with tradition reported by Justin, probably as early as the middle of the second century. Origen also remarks in the same place concerning the tradition found in the Book of James, that "those who say so wish to preserve the honor of Mary in virginity to the end," and this is an accurate statement of what appears to be the purpose of the author of the Nativity of Mary.

§258. The Nativity of Mary, thus preserved in the relatively early Bodmer Papyrus V, is also extant in part or in whole, and with various additions, in many other manuscripts, most of which, however, are not earlier than the tenth century (TEA 1–50). The first editor of the work, Guillaume Postel, in 1552, called it the Protevangelium (meaning the Protogospel) of James, and it has commonly been known by this title (BVA 58–109; SEA 135–88). The Bodmer Papyrus V now gives us access to the work in a relatively early form. Nevertheless the work is much more an account of Joachim and Anna, and of the birth and childhood of Mary, than of anything else, and is obviously written for the enhancement of the honor of Mary (cf. the observation of Origen cited in §257), therefore may be omitted from any more detailed consideration in the framework of our present study which is directed primarily toward records of the life of Jesus (§130). Nevertheless the Protevangelium was widely influential, and many more accounts concerning the motherhood of Mary grew out of it. Needless to say, with those yet later accounts we are also not here concerned.

(B) CAIRO PAPYRUS 10 735

*Literature:* KT 8, 24; BVA 32–35; SEA 91–92; HSNTAE 73–74.


§259. Cairo Papyrus 10 735 preserves a few fragmentary lines on both sides of a small piece of papyrus in which there is mention (*verso*) of Elizabeth and of the coming birth of John, and (*recto*) of Mary and of the flight to Egypt. The manuscript is, however, probably as late as the sixth or seventh century. In addition it has been judged by some to come from a commentary or homily rather than an uncanonical Gospel.[1]

---

[1] Adolf Deissmann, *Licht vom Osten.* 4th ed. 1923, 368–71.

# 3 / Greek Parchments

## 1 / Oxyrhynchus Parchment 840

*Literature:* Bernard P. Grenfell and Arthur S. Hunt, *Fragment of an Uncanonical Gospel from Oxyrhynchus.* 1908; OP V No. 840; KT 31; BVA 36–39; JUSJ 17–18, 36–49, 93–94; SEA 83–87; HSNTAE 57–58.

§260. We turn now from the Greek papyri to the Greek parchments (§206). The manuscript to be mentioned first was found by Grenfell and Hunt at Behnesa in 1905, and published by them in their series, *The Oxyrhynchus Papyri,* as document No. 840. While it is therefore commonly referred to as OP 840, this particular document is a piece of parchment rather than papyrus, and we will call it Oxyrhynchus Parchment 840, thus retaining the series number but giving the correct indication as to material. This piece of parchment, written on both sides, is less than three and one-half by three inches in size, and was once a leaf in a very small codex. The area occupied by the writing is scarcely more than two inches square, but into this small space the scribe, using a very small uncial, compressed on the two sides of the leaf no less than forty-five lines of writing. Viewed on the *verso* side (Fig. 12), the lower right-hand corner of the piece is broken away on the diagonal, otherwise the leaf is quite well preserved. The style of the handwriting is judged to point to a date in the fourth century. In the latter part of the fourth century Chrysostom, preaching at Antioch (*Concerning the Statues,* Homily XIX 14 NPNF IX 470), told "how women and little children suspend Gospels from their necks as a powerful amulet, and carry them about in all places wherever they go." The tiny book from which the present leaf came could have been used in exactly that way. In the course of the account "the Savior" ($o\overline{\sigma\omega}\rho$ = ὁ σωτήρ) converses with a certain Pharisee, and the entire incident and conversation are extracanonical.

FIGURE 12.
*Oxyrhynchus Parchment 840*

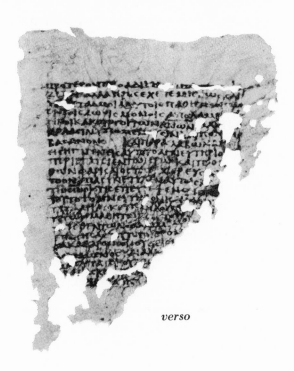

*verso*

§261. At the opening the first seven lines read as follows:

TEXT 83

πρότερον πρὸ ἀδικῆσαι πάντα σοφί-
ζεται ἀλλὰ προσέχετε μή πως καὶ
ὑμεῖς τὰ ὅμοια αὐτοῖς πάθητε οὐ γὰρ
ἐν τοῖς ζωοῖς μόνοις ἀπολαμβάνου-
5  σιν οἱ κακοῦργοι τῶν ἀν(θρώπ)ων ἀλλὰ [κ]αὶ
κόλασιν ὑπομένουσιν καὶ πολ[λ]ὴν
βάσανον

First before he does wrong he treats everything with
sophistry. But take heed lest you
also suffer the same things as they. For not
among the living alone do
5    the evildoers among men receive retribution, but also
they await punishment and much
torment.

In what immediately follows (Lines 7–9) Jesus takes the disciples
into the Temple, so here he is evidently speaking to them somewhere
in Jerusalem and probably on the way to the Temple. He admonishes
the disciples against emulation of sophisticated doers of evil, and
warns of the punishments which follow both in this life and beyond.
This is not out of harmony with the canonical teaching of Jesus,
where (Lk 18:30) he speaks of how men "receive" (ἀπολάβῃ or λάβῃ)
appropriate recompense (cf. Lk 16:25), and where (Lk 16:23) he
speaks of one who is "in torment" (ἐν βασάνοις) in the life beyond.

§262. The text continues in Lines 7–45, where the conversation
with the Pharisee in the Temple is recounted.

TEXT 84

καὶ παραλαβὼν αὐτοὺς
εἰσήγαγεν εἰς αὐτὸ τὸ ἁγνευτήριον καὶ
περιεπάτει ἐν τῷ ἱερῷ καὶ προσε[λ]-
10    θὼν Φαρισαῖός τις ἀρχιερεὺς Λευ[εὶς]
τὸ ὄνομα συνέτυχεν αὐτοῖς καὶ ε[ἶπεν]
τῷ σω(τῆ)ρι τίς ἐπέτρεψέν σοι πατ[εῖν]
τοῦτο τὸ ἁγνευτήριον καὶ ἰδεῖν [ταῦ-]
τα τὰ ἅγια σκεύη μήτε λουσα[μ]έν[ῳ] μ[ή-]
15    τε μὴν τῶν μαθητῶν σου τοὺς π[όδας βα-]
πτισθέντων ἀλλὰ μεμολυ[μμένος]
ἐπάτησας τοῦτο τὸ ἱερὸν τ[όπον ὄν-]
τα καθαρὸν ὃν οὐδεὶς ἄ[λλος εἰ μὴ]
λουσάμενος καὶ ἀλλά[ξας τὰ ἐνδύ-]
20    ματα πατεῖ οὐδὲ ὁ[ρᾶν τολμᾷ ταῦτα]
τὰ ἅγια σκεύη καὶ σ[ταθεὶς εὐθὺς ὁ σω(τὴ)ρ
σ[ὺν τ]οῖς μαθηταῖ[s αὐτοῦ ἀπεκρίθη]
σὺ οὖν ἐνταῦθα ὢν ἐν τῷ ἱερῷ καθα-
ρεύεις λέγει αὐτῷ ἐκεῖνος καθαρεύω ἐλουσά-
25    μην γὰρ ἐν τῇ λίμνῃ τοῦ Δ(αυεὶ)δ καὶ δι' ἑτέρας κλίμακος κατελθὼν δι' ἑτέρας
ἀ[ν]ῆλθον καὶ λευκὰ ἐνδύματα ἐνε-

δυσάμην καὶ καθαρὰ καὶ τότε ἦλθον
καὶ προσέβλεψα τούτοις τοῖς ἁγίοις
30 σκεύεσιν ὁ σω(τὴ)ρ πρὸς αὐτὸν ἀπο-
[κρι]θεὶς εἶπεν οὐαὶ τυφλοὶ μὴ ὁρῶν-
τ[ε]ς σὺ ἐλούσω τούτοις τοῖς χεομένοις
ὕ[δ]ασιν ἐν οἷς κύνες καὶ χοῖροι βέβλην-
[ται] νυκτὸς καὶ ἡμέρας καὶ νιψάμε-
35 [ν]ος τὸ ἐκτὸς δέρμα ἐσμήξω ὅπερ
[κα]ὶ αἱ πόρναι καὶ α[ἱ] αὐλητρίδες μυρί-
[ς]ου[σιν κ]αὶ λούουσιν καὶ σμήχουσι
[καὶ κ]αλλωπίζουσι πρὸς ἐπιθυμί-
[αν τ]ῶν ἀν(θρώπ)ων ἔνδοθεν δὲ ἐκεῖ-
40 [ναι πεπλ]ήρω(ν)ται σκορπίων καὶ
[πάσης ἀδι]κίας ἐγὼ δὲ καὶ οἱ
[μαθηταί μου] οὕς λέγεις μὴ βεβα-
[μμένους βεβά]μμεθα ἐν ὕδασι ζῶ-
[ης . . . τοῖ]ς ἐλθοῦσιν ἀπὸ [
45 [. . . . . . . . . ἀλ]λὰ οὐαὶ [τ]οῖς [

And he took them
and brought them into the place of purification itself, and
walked about in the Temple. And there came
10 up a certain Pharisee, a chief priest, Levi
by name, and met them, and said
to the Savior: Who gave you permission to tread
this place of purification and to look at
these holy vessels, when you have not bathed and
15 when your disciples have not washed their
feet? But being defiled
you have trodden this Temple which is a
clean place, which no other one, except
he has bathed and changed his
20 clothes, walks in or dares to look at these
holy vessels. And the Savior stopped at once
with his disciples and answered:
Are you then, since you are here in the Temple,
clean? That one said to him: I am clean,
25 for I have bathed in the Pool of David,
and I went down into it by one stair and by the other
I came up out, and I have put on white
and clean clothes, and then I came

and looked at these holy
*30*    vessels. The Savior answered him
and said: Woe, you blind, who see
not! You have bathed in these poured-out
waters, in which dogs and swine lie
night and day, and you have washed
*35*    and wiped clean the outer skin, which
also the harlots and the flute-girls a-
noint and wash and wipe clean
and beautify for the de-
sire of men, but within they
*40*    are full of scorpions and
all unrighteousness. But I and
my disciples, of whom you say that we have not immersed ourselves, have been immersed in water of
life . . . coming from
*45*        But woe to the

§263. The designation of the Temple area in which Jesus and the disciples walked with the term τὸ ἱερόν (Lines 9, 17, 23) is in accord with the same usage in the canonical Gospels (Mt 21:12 = Mk 11:11, etc., in distinction from ὁ ναός, the sanctuary, or temple edifice proper, Mt 27:51 = Mk 15:38, etc.). The Pool of David (Line 25) is otherwise unknown in the city of Jerusalem, but that such a pool existed is by no means unlikely. The affirmation that the Pharisee has bathed in water in which dogs and swine lie (Line 33) can possibly be taken figuratively in the sense that unrighteous men, who are as unclean within as dogs and swine, bathe in it and do not, apart from repentance, become clean. Flute-girls (Line 36) are mentioned with an unfavorable connotation in the Gospel of the Nazaraeans (Text 31 §178) too. The contrast of an outward pleasing appearance with inward uncleanness (Lines 37–41) is essentially the same teaching as that found in Mt 23:27-28 where whitewashed tombs are described as outwardly appearing beautiful but within being full of all uncleanness. In general the teaching set forth in the entire incident is not unlike that in the discussion of Jesus with Pharisees recorded in Mt 15:1-20 and Mk 7:1-23. The characteristic designation of Christ as the "Savior" (σωτήρ) (Lines 12, 21, 30) is, however, more like the usage in Gnostic texts than in the canonical Gospels (§241).

## 2 / Other Greek Parchments

### (A) THE AKHMIM FRAGMENT OF THE GOSPEL ACCORDING TO PETER

*Literature: Mémoires publiés par les membres de la mission archéologique française au Caire* IX 1 (1892), 93ff., by U. Bouriant; IX 3 (1893), 217ff., by M. Lods; J. Armitage Robinson and Montague R. James, *The Gospel According to Peter, and the Revelation of Peter.* 2d ed. 1892; H. B. Swete, ΕΥΑΓΓΕΛΙΟΝ ΚΑΤΑ ΠΕΤΡΟΝ, *The Akhmim Fragment of the Apocryphal Gospel of St Peter.* 1893; ANF IX 3–31; Léon Vaganay, *L'évangile de Pierre.* 1930; KT 3, 4–8; BVA 16–29; SEA 68–71, 398–417; HSNTAE 118–24; Othmar Perler, "L'Évangile de Pierre et Méliton de Sardes," in RB 71 (1964), 584–90.

§264. The earliest witness to the existence of a Gospel according to Peter is Serapion. In the *Chronicle* of Eusebius (GCS Eusebius VII 209, 213) Serapion is shown as the eighth bishop of Antioch, taking office in the eleventh year of Commodus (190) and continuing through the reign of Septimius Severus, with his successor, Asclepiades, appointed in the first year of Caracalla (211). In the *Ch. Hist.* VI 12 Eusebius reports that Bishop Serapion wrote a work on the so-called Gospel according to Peter (περὶ τοῦ λεγομένου κατὰ Πέτρον εὐαγγελίου). This Gospel was being read at Rhossus, a city of Syria northwest of Antioch on the Gulf of Issus and, on a visit there, Serapion approved the reading of the book although he had not gone through it himself. Later, however, he was able to obtain the Gospel and read it through. It was used first, he says, "by those whom we call Docetae" (οὓς Δοκητὰς καλοῦμεν), i.e., advocates of the doctrine of Docetism (§116), and as an individual leader of the heresy he names Marcianus (Μαρκιανός). In view of the difference in the spelling of the name, this person is probably not the famous Marcion (Μαρκίων) (§§107, 112) from Pontus, but a local leader of the Docetists at Rhossus. Now, having read the Gospel for himself, Serapion finds that the most part of it is in accordance with the true teaching of the Savior, but that some things have been added to that doctrine.

§265. Origen also mentions the Gospel according to Peter, as we have seen (§257), suggesting it along with the Book of James as a possible source of the teaching that the brothers of Jesus were sons of Joseph by an earlier marriage. Eusebius, as we have also seen (§§31, 155), enumerates six writings under the name of Peter, of which one is the Gospel (*Ch. Hist.* III 3); it is among those works put forward by heretics under the name of the apostles, works which, he says, are not to be placed even among the spurious books (ἐν νόθοις) but are to be cast aside as absurd and impious.

§266. In the parchment codex found at Akhmim in 1886/1887 (§119), Pages 2–10 contain the considerable fragment of a Gospel text written in Greek characters dating probably in the eighth or ninth century. The text is now customarily divided into fourteen chapters and sixty verses. It begins (I 1): τ[ῶν] δὲ 'Ιουδαίων οὐδεὶς ἐνίψατο τὰς χεῖρας, "But of the Jews none washed his hands." The scene is, therefore, that of the handwashing by Pilate (Mt 27:24-25), and the guilt of the Jews is emphasized even more heavily than by Mt. Herod the king also did not wash his hands, and himself gave the command for the Lord to be taken away. In Chapter II Joseph (Mt 27:57ff. = Mk 15:43ff. = Lk 23:50ff.; Jn 19:38ff.) is present as a friend of Pilate and of Jesus and, even ahead of the crucifixion, begs the body for burial. Pilate refers the request to Herod, who replies to "Brother Pilate" that even if no one else had done it they would have taken care of the burial since the sabbath was approaching and the Law required it (Dt 21:22-23). Herod then (II 5) delivered Jesus to the people before the first day of unleavened bread, their feast (καὶ παρέδωκεν αὐτὸν τῷ λαῷ πρὸ μιᾶς τῶν ἀζύμων, τῆς ἑορτῆς αὐτῶν). Thus the crucifixion took place on Friday, the fourteenth day of Nisan, in agreement with the date indicated also by the Fourth Gospel.[1]

§267. In Chapter III the people, rather than the Roman soldiers (Mt 27:27-31 = Mk 15:16-20) mock Jesus with purple garb and crown of thorns. In Chapter IV Jesus is crucified between two malefactors (δύο κακοῦργοι as in Lk 23:32, cf. Mt 27:38 = Mk 15:27; Jn 19:18). He was silent (ἐσιώπα as in Mt 26:63 = Mk 14:61) before the high priest and the author explains (IV 10), with what could be a Docetic interpretation, that this was as if he felt no pain (ὡς μηδένα πόνον ἔχων). The fact that his legs were not broken (Jn 19:33), however, was due to the wish of his enemies that he might have to die in torments. Chapter V tells of the darkness (Mt 27:45 = Mk

[1] FHBC 286ff.

15:33 = Lk 23:44) which covered all Judea, and how many went about with lamps because they supposed that it was already night. The last word of the Lord on the cross (V 19, cf. Mt 27:46 = Mk 15:34) was, "My power, power, thou hast forsaken me" (ἡ δύναμίς μου, ἡ δύναμις, κατέλειψάς με), and when he had said this he was taken up (ἀνελήφθη). According to Eusebius (*Demonstratio evangelica* X 8, 30 GCS Eusebius VI 476), Aquila (§10) translated Ps 22:1 (LXX 21:2) not with ὁ θεός, ὁ θεός μου, "God, my God," but with ἰσχυρέ μου, ἰσχυρέ μου (which Eusebius suggests might more accurately be, ἰσχύς μου, ἰσχύς μου), "My Strength, my Strength." In the same connection (X 8, 33) Eusebius himself remarks that Jesus died because His Strong One, i.e., the heavenly Father, forsook him, being willing that he should go down unto death, even death on a cross (Phl 2:8) (κατελέλοιπεν οὖν αὐτὸν ὁ ἰσχυρὸς αὐτοῦ, θελήσας αὐτὸν μέχρι θανάτου καὶ θανάτου σταυροῦ κατελθεῖν). Likewise in Mt 26:64 = Mk 14:62 (cf. Lk 22:69) there is reference to the Son of man as sitting at the right hand of Power (τῆς δυνάμεως). From these comparisons the alteration of the canonical form of the cry of Jesus into the form found in the present manuscript could be explained as simply a substitution, otherwise familiar in Jewish circles, of the word Power for the word God. But Lk 5:17 says that the power (δύναμις) of the Lord was with Jesus to heal, and Mk 5:30 and Lk 6:19 speak of power going forth from him in miracles of healing, and somewhat along this line Justin Martyr writes (*Dialogue with Trypho* 49, 8): "You can perceive that the concealed power (δύναμις) of God was in Christ the crucified, before whom demons, and all the principalities and powers of the earth, tremble." Again Justin says (*Dialogue with Trypho* 88, 2) that even at birth Jesus was in possession of his power, and in a number of passages (*Dialogue with Trypho* 61, 1–3; 105, 1; 128, 2–3) he equates the power, which was begotten of the Father and sent from the Father, with the Word. Along this latter line of thought the cry of Jesus in the present manuscript could refer to the withdrawal from Jesus of this divine Power which had been in him. In the latter case we have here something which is at least pointing in the direction of Docetic Gnostic thought such as is reported by Irenaeus (§111), where the Savior from the Pleroma came down upon Christ at his baptism but, in order to avoid suffering, was taken away when he was brought before Pilate (*Against Heresies* I 7, 2), and where the cry from the cross is capable of even more esoteric interpretation as showing that Sophia was deserted by the light (*Against Heresies* I 8, 2).

§268. Then (Chapter VI continues) the Jews took down the body of Jesus and Joseph performed the burial. Whereas Jn 19:41 says that in the place of the crucifixion there was a garden (κῆπος) and in the garden a tomb where Jesus was buried, the present text says (VI 24) that Joseph brought the Lord into his own sepulcher which was itself called Joseph's Garden (εἰς ἴδιον τάφον καλούμενον κῆπον Ἰωσήφ). Then (Chapter VII) the Jews lamented their sins, and expressed the anticipation that the end of Jerusalem was at hand. "But I with my companions grieved," writes the purported author (VII 26), "and . . . we hid ourselves, for we were sought for by them as malefactors and as ones who wanted to set the Temple on fire." So they fasted and mourned until the sabbath. Then (Chapter VIII), as in Mt 27:62-66, the Jews asked Pilate for a guard for the sepulcher. In answer to the request, Pilate sent Petronius the centurion with soldiers and they, together with the elders and scribes, rolled a great stone against the entrance to the sepulcher, sealed it with seven seals, pitched a tent, and kept guard.

§269. Early in the morning when the sabbath dawned (πρωίας δὲ ἐπιφώσκοντος τοῦ σαββάτου), Chapter IX continues, a crowd came from Jerusalem and the surrounding country to see the sealed sepulcher. Then in the night in which the Lord's day dawned (τῇ δὲ νυκτὶ ᾗ ἐπέφωσκεν ἡ κυριακή), as the soldiers were keeping watch two by two, there was a loud voice in heaven, and they saw two men come down in much light and enter the tomb, where the stone rolled away of itself. The soldiers (Chapter X) awakened the centurion and the elders and, even while they were telling them what they had seen, they saw three men coming out of the tomb, two supporting the other, and a cross following them. While the heads of the two reached to heaven, the head of the one they led overpassed the heavens. From heaven a voice said (X 41): "You have preached to them that sleep"—thus expressing a doctrine first enunciated canonically in 1 Pet 3:19—and from the cross came the answer (X 42): "Yes."

§270. When (Chapter XI) yet another man descended from heaven and entered the sepulcher, the centurion's company abandoned the place and went to Pilate, even though it was still night, to say to him, "Truly he was Son of God" (ἀληθῶς υἱὸς ἦν θεοῦ) (XI 45, cf. Mt 27:54 = Mk 15:39). Pilate reiterated (XI 46) that he was clean "from the blood of the Son of God." Thereupon, all came and asked him to command the centurion and soldiers to tell no one what they had seen, which Pilate did. "For it is better for us," they said, "to make ourselves guilty of the greatest sin before God, and not to fall into the hands of the people of the Jews and be stoned."

§271. In Chapter XII (cf. Mt 28:1ff. = Mk 16:1ff. = Lk 24:1ff.; Jn 20:1ff.) we read how, "early in the morning of the Lord's day Mary Magdalene, a woman disciple of the Lord" (ὄρθρου δὲ τῆς κυριακῆς Μαριὰμ ἡ Μαγδαληνή, μαθήτρια τοῦ κυρίου), took women friends and came to the sepulcher. As already explained somewhat more fully (§241), the name Μαριάμ, strictly "Mariam," is a well-known variant of Μαρία, "Mary," and is found in major manuscripts in Mt 28:1 and Jn 20:16, 18; while Josephus (*Ant.* III ii 4 §54) also writes (for the sister of Aaron and Moses) the form Μαριάμμη, "Mariamme." Also the term "woman disciple" (μαθήτρια) is found in Ac 9:36. In the sepulcher (Chapter XIII, cf. Mk 16:1-8) the women found a young man (νεανίσκον). He speaks to them, using many of the words of Mk 16:6, and adds at the last, "For he has risen and gone away thither from whence he was sent" (ἀνέστη γὰρ καὶ ἀπῆλθεν ἐκεῖ ὅθεν ἀπεστάλη). Then (XIII 57), as in Mk 16:8, the women "were afraid and fled" (φοβηθεῖσαι ἔφυγον).

§272. In Chapter XIV it is the last day of unleavened bread (τελευταία ἡμέρα τῶν ἀζύμων). With the close of the feast, many went home. "But we the twelve disciples of the Lord" (ἡμεῖς δὲ οἱ δώδεκα μαθηταὶ τοῦ κυρίου), the text continues, "wept . . . and each . . . went to his own home." And then the purported author himself writes (XIV 60): "But I, Simon Peter, and Andrew my brother, took our nets and went away to the sea" (ἐγὼ δὲ Σίμων Πέτρος καὶ 'Ανδρέας ὁ ἀδελφός μου λαβόντες ἡμῶν τὰ λίνα ἀπήλθαμεν εἰς τὴν θάλασσαν). Then he says that "there was with us Levi, the son of Alphaeus, whom the Lord . . ."—and it is at that particular point that the fragment breaks off.

§273. Since the work represented by this manuscript evidently presented itself as a writing of Peter (VII 26; XIV 60), and since the movement of its thought is in the direction of Docetic Gnosticism (IV 10; V 19), it is probable that we have here, in a late copy, a portion of the Gospel according to Peter which was read by Serapion sometime around 200 and referred to by him as if it had been in use by others already for a considerable period of time (§264). As noted above (§§266ff.), the work is obviously dependent at many points upon the four canonical Gospels, therefore is later than they. Therefore a date perhaps in the first half of the second century is indicated as probable for this work. The present manuscript, the Akhmim fragment, however, dating probably in the eighth or ninth century (§266), is so late as to be beyond the time limits within which we focus our major inquiry (§130), therefore the text will not be presented further beyond the excerpts already given in our summary above (§§266-72).

(B) THE GOSPEL OF NICODEMUS

*Literature:* TEA 210–486; SEA 420–500; HSNTAE 330–58.

§274. Tendencies evident in the Gospel according to Peter work further. In that Gospel we have noted (§§266ff.) an interest in Pilate, specially in exonerating him from guilt for the crucifixion and in making him a witness to the divinity of Christ (I 1; XI 46). Justin Martyr (*Apology* I 35, cf. 48) speaks of the crucifixion and says: "And that these things did happen you can ascertain from the Acts of Pontius Pilate" (ἐκ τῶν ἐπὶ Ποντίου Πιλάτου γενομένων ἄκτων). Tertullian (*Apology* 5 and 21) goes further and says that Pilate became a Christian in his own convictions (*pro sua conscientia Christianus*), and sent word about Christ to Tiberius, so that the emperor himself brought the matter before the senate with his own decision in favor of Christ. Eusebius (*Ch. Hist.* II 2) repeats the report of Tertullian, and also tells (*Ch. Hist.* I 9; IX 5, 1) how in the persecution of Daia Maximinus in 311 or 312, forged Acts of Pilate, full of blasphemy against Christ, were circulated to stir up hate against the Christians. Epiphanius (*Pan. haer.* L 1, 5 GCS 31, 245) says that the Quartodecimans thought that they could derive the accurate date of the suffering of the Savior from the Acts of Pilate, and that this date was the eighth day before the Kalends of April, i.e., the twenty-fifth day of March.

§275. The most important Acts of Pilate now extant are contained in the so-called Gospel of Nicodemus. This work is found in various Greek manuscripts, the oldest of which is placed approximately in the twelfth century (TEA LXXIff.), and in translations into Syriac, Armenian, Coptic, Arabic, and Latin. The first part of the work comprises Chapters I–XVI. Here there is an extended and detailed account of the trial, crucifixion, and burial of Jesus. Pilate sends for Jesus, saying (I 2), "Let Jesus be brought with gentleness (ἐπιεικείας)." When Jesus enters, the images of the emperor on the Roman standards bow to him (I 5). But the Jews cry, "We wish him to be crucified" (IV 4), and they have their way, in spite of the fact that (V–VIII) Nicodemus, and the man healed after thirty-eight years of illness (Jn 5:5ff.), and the woman healed from an issue of blood (Mk 5:25ff.), whose name is now given as Bernice or, in the Latin, Veronica, and a multitude of other men and women speak on his behalf. Upon the death of Jesus, Pilate and his wife grieve, and the body is buried by Joseph. After that, however, the Jewish authorities experience various proofs of the resurrection (XII–XVI).

§276. In the Gospel according to Peter there was also (§269) an emphasis (X 41–42) upon the preaching by Christ after the crucifixion to them that sleep, a theme stated first in 1 Pet 3:19. This theme also receives great amplification, and the second part (Chapters XVII–XXIX) of the Gospel of Nicodemus is devoted to it. Here two sons of Simeon, who have themselves returned from Hades, tell in detail of seeing Christ upon his visit there.

§277. Because of their disparate character it may be judged that the two parts just described (§§275–76) were once separate but later combined in the Gospel of Nicodemus. A prologue contained in one Greek manuscript of the entire work (TEA 210ff.) states that a certain Ananias, an officer of the guard and a Christian, searched for the reports which the Jews committed to writing under Pilate, found these, and translated them into Greek in the seventeenth year of Theodosius (II) (424/425). The prologue also gives the date of the passion of the Lord, including the same day, the eighth day before the Kalends of April, to which Epiphanius referred (§274). Therefore this work may be much the same as that which Epiphanius had in mind. While Epiphanius used the title, Acts of Pilate, for the work to which he made reference, the present work is entitled in the same Greek manuscript (TEA 210) referred to above: "Memorials (ὑπομνήματα) of our Lord Jesus Christ Done in the Time of Pontius Pilate." In the prologue in this manuscript the narrative immediately to follow is finally introduced (TEA 213) as what Nicodemus himself drew up as records in the Hebrew language. Therefore in the Latin manuscripts, from the fourteenth century on, the entire work is called the Gospel of Nicodemus (*Evangelium Nicodemi*). If this work is much the same as that to which Epiphanius referred, it goes back at least to the latter part of the fourth century. The extant manuscripts are so late (§275), however, as to exclude the Gospel of Nicodemus from further consideration on our part. Likewise the yet later and even more peripheral apocryphal literature connected with the passion and resurrection of Christ lies beyond our limits (§130).

(c) THE CHILDHOOD GOSPEL OF THOMAS

*Literature:* TEA 140–80; BVA 110–51; SEA 299–324; HSNTAE
290–99.

§278. The extant manuscripts which contain the Childhood Gospel
of Thomas are also so late as to be beyond the limits of our major concern (§130). Two Greek manuscripts of the fifteenth and sixteenth
centuries are the chief witnesses (TEA 140–57), while in addition to
other Greek texts there are also Latin, Syriac, and other versions. The
Greek text is entitled: "Things Told (ῥητά) by Thomas the Israelite
Philosopher concerning the Childhood Works (τὰ παιδικά) of the
Lord." The first story narrated (Chapter II) is about Jesus at the age
of five. On the sabbath he made sparrows of clay, and Joseph rebuked
him. Then he clapped his hands, and they flew away. Other stories
of the wonder-working power of the child fill the book until, in
Chapter XIX the event in the Temple at the age of twelve
(Lk 2:41-52) is narrated. Even the last event is exaggerated, too, in
that the child evidently has limitless wisdom and puts the elders and
teachers of the people to silence as he expounds the sections of the
Law and the sayings of the prophets. In spite of the caricature which
it presented, the Childhood Gospel of Thomas was very influential.
Like the Protevangelium of James, which provided a basis for further
writing about the motherhood of Mary (§258), so too the Childhood
Gospel of Thomas was the source of inspiration for more stories about
the miracles of the marvelous child, Jesus. But obviously those yet
wider ramifications of apocryphal narrative are beyond our present
concern.

# 4 / Summary of the Greek Manuscripts and Introduction of the Coptic Manuscripts

§279. In summary, the following texts have now been presented (§§207ff.): Egerton Papyrus 2 dates in the middle of the second century or earlier (§207); it is dependent upon the Synoptic and Fourth Gospels, and contains some additional extracanonical material, particularly with respect to an apparent miracle. Oxyrhynchus Papyrus 654 is from the middle or end of the third century (§216), Oxyrhynchus Papyrus 1 is from the third century (§223), and Oxyrhynchus Papyrus 655 is from the early or middle third century (§232); all three manuscripts contain sayings of Jesus, some canonical, some extracanonical. Rylands Papyrus 463 dates in the early third century (§240); it is plainly Gnostic in character. The Rainer Gospel Papyrus belongs to the last part of the third century (§244); it is dependent upon Mt and Mk with respect to words of Jesus to Peter. Oxyrhynchus Papyrus 1081 is from the early fourth century (§246); it is also very plainly Gnostic in terminology and thought. Oxyrhynchus Papyrus 1224 is from the early fourth century (§249); it has some sayings of Jesus which are parallel to Synoptic sayings, but one or two sayings which are not canonical. Oxyrhynchus Parchment 840 dates in the fourth century (§260); the extracanonical conversation of Jesus with a Pharisee which it contains has points of contact with Synoptic representations, yet the text calls Jesus "the Savior" as Gnostic texts so characteristically do. If we omit Rylands Papyrus 463 and Oxyrhynchus Papyrus 1081 as openly Gnostic, and the Rainer Gospel Papyrus as little but an abbreviation of material from Mt and Mk, then it is chiefly in Egerton Papyrus 2, OP 654, OP 1, OP 655, OP 1224, and OP 840, that any material exists which might perhaps be considered along with the canonical records as of historical significance with respect to the life of Jesus.

§280. In addition, these manuscripts have also been mentioned, but judged to lie yet farther afield: Bodmer Papyrus V is relatively early since it is attributed to the third century (§256); but the account it gives is chiefly concerned with Mary, the Mother of Jesus, and with her parents, Joachim and Anna; as such it is the first of a large class of literature which deals with such subject matter, but it is not of primary interest with regard to the life of Jesus himself. Cairo Papyrus 10 735 has to do with Elizabeth and John, who became the Baptist, and with Mary and the flight to Egypt, but it is as late as the sixth or seventh century (§259). The Gospel according to Peter is attested as early as the second century (§264) but the Akhmim Fragment whose text is probably from this book is as late as the eighth or ninth century (§266); as known in this Fragment, the work was dependent upon all four canonical Gospels, and in independent features showed the progressive development of secondary interests such as that of the exoneration of Pilate, of late doctrines such as the preaching to them that sleep, and of tendencies looking in the direction of Gnosticism such as an apparent touch of Docetism in the interpretation of the silence on the cross. The Gospel of Nicodemus is available only in manuscripts as late as the twelfth century and onward (§275); late tendencies and doctrines appear in it far more than in the Gospel according to Peter, and it may suffice to have mentioned it as a representative of a large class of such literature concerned with the passion and the resurrection. Finally, the Childhood Gospel of Thomas is available in late manuscripts of the fifteenth and sixteenth centuries (§278); with its narratives about Jesus as a child-worker of crude miracles it will suffice as the representative of the proliferation of stories of this sort.

§281. Since it is the oldest Gospel-type extracanonical material for which we are looking (§130), as far as manuscripts are concerned (§206) it is primarily Greek papyri and parchments in which we are interested. But the oldest manuscripts in other languages are also of interest, particularly where there is demonstrable proof or reasonable likelihood that they rest back upon Greek sources. Due at least in part to the circumstances of climate it is in Egypt that the oldest Greek papyri and parchments thus far known (§§207ff.) in the area of our concern have been preserved. Likewise it is from Egypt that the earliest and most considerable body of such manuscripts in another language has come. Due to the historical circumstances in Egypt, that language is Coptic (§§80ff.), and we have early Coptic texts both on papyrus and on parchment. In some cases it can be shown, since fragments of identical or similar material have actually been found in older Greek texts (§§288ff.), that the Coptic literature rests back upon Greek sources, and this makes it probable that the same is true in other cases too, even though in these cases portions of the hypothetical earlier sources have not actually been found. Therefore, within the limitations set for our inquiry, we have yet to notice some of the oldest Coptic papyri and parchments, containing extracanonical Gospel-type material, and then we shall have completed our attempted task. Again we will consider first the papyri, then the parchments. Among the papyri we will give first place to those where fragments of what are evidently their Greek sources have been found, and these will be taken up in the relative order of the underlying Greek fragments. On this basis we are taking up first the Gospel according to Thomas (underlying which are OP 654 of the middle or end of the third century [§216], OP 1 of the third century [§223], and OP 655 of the third century [§232]), the Gospel according to Mariam (underlying which is Rylands Papyrus 463 of the early third century [§240]), and the Sophia of Jesus Christ (underlying which is OP 1081 of the early fourth century [§246]), and then after that several other of the earliest and most important documents. As already explained (§130), no attempt will be made to reproduce these texts in the original Coptic, but they will be presented in terms of English translations based on the careful translations which are now available in several modern languages. Resting as they often do upon Greek sources, the Coptic texts contain many Greek words. In accordance with the practice of editors of these texts, the Greek word in question will be shown in its basic form in a parenthesis at the relevant point in the English translation or reference.

# 5 / Coptic Papyri

## 1 / The Gospel According to Thomas

*Literature:* cf. above §127; LCGP I, Plates 80, 10—99, 28; A. Guillaumont, H.-Ch. Puech, G. Quispel, W. Till, and Yassah 'Abd al Masīh, *The Gospel According to Thomas.* 1959; Robert M. Grant and David N. Freedman, *The Secret Sayings of Jesus.* 1960; George W. MacRae, "The Gospel of Thomas—LOGIA IESOU?" in CBQ 22 (1960), 56–70; A. J. B. Higgins, "Non-Gnostic Sayings in the Gospel of Thomas," in *Novum Testamentum* 4 (1960), 292–306; Bertil Gärtner, *The Theology of the Gospel According to Thomas.* 1961; Ernst Haenchen, *Die Botschaft des Thomas-Evangeliums.* 1961; A. F. Walls, " 'Stone' and 'Wood' in Oxyrhynchus Papyrus I," in VC 16 (1962), 71–76; H. E. W. Turner and Hugh Montefiore, *Thomas and the Evangelists.* Studies in Biblical Theology, 35. 1962; R. E. Brown, "The Gospel of Thomas and St. John's Gospel," in NTS 9 (1963), 155–77; W. Schrage, *Das Verhältnis des Thomas-Evangeliums zur synoptischen Tradition und zu den Koptischen Evangelienübersetzungen. Zugleich ein Beitrag zur gnostischen Synoptikerdeutung.* ZNW Beiheft 29, 1964; Aelred Baker, "Fasting to the World," in JBL 84 (1965), 291–94.

§282. In *The Refutation of All Heresies* V 7, 20 (cf. above §190) Hippolytus (about 230) says that the Naassenes/Ophites hand down the following passage which occurs in the Gospel entitled according to Thomas (ἐν τῷ κατὰ Θωμᾶν ἐπιγραφομένῳ εὐαγγελίῳ):

TEXT 85

ἐμὲ ὁ ζητῶν εὑρήσει ἐν παιδίοις ἀπὸ
ἐτῶν ἑπτά· ἐκεῖ γὰρ ἐν τῷ τεσσαρεσκαιδεκάτῳ
αἰῶνι κρυβόμενος φανεροῦμαι

He who seeks me will find me in children from
seven years old; for there in the fourteenth
age, having been hidden, I shall be manifest.

§283. In his *Homily on Luke* I (GCS Origenes IX 5), written soon
after 233, Origen mentions two books which do not have a place in his
list of "acknowledged" and "doubted" books of the NT (Table 8 §30),
and which he here speaks of as presumptuous compositions, namely,
the Gospel according to Matthias (§205), and the Gospel according to
Thomas (τὸ κατὰ Θωμᾶν εὐαγγέλιον). Also in his *Homily on Jeremiah*
XX 3, according to the translation by Jerome (MPG XIII 531–32),
Origen quotes a saying attributed to Jesus which will be of interest
in this same connection (§311). Of its source Origen says only that
he has read it somewhere (*legi alicubi*), and he wonders whether
someone just took the role of the Savior, or cited the quotation from
memory, or whether it is indeed a genuine saying. The saying is:

TEXT 86

> qui juxta me est, juxta ignem est;
> qui longe est a me, longe est a regno.
> He who is near me, is near the fire;
> he who is far from me, is far from the kingdom.

§284. Eusebius also mentions the Gospel of Thomas (Θωμᾶ
εὐαγγέλιον) and places it quite outside his lists of "acknowledged,"
"disputed," and "spurious" books, along with several other writings
which he calls "fabrications of heretics" (*Ch. Hist.* III 25, 6–7; cf.
above §31 Table 9).

§285. Cyril of Jerusalem, too, mentions and repudiates the Gospel
according to Thomas. In one place (*Catechetical Lectures* IV 36) he
says that the Manicheans (§115) wrote it (cf. §291); in another place
(*Catechetical Lectures* VI 31) he says that the author was not Thomas,
one of the twelve apostles, but Thomas, one of three wicked disciples
of Mani.

§286. Among the so-called Nag Hammadi papyri discovered, as
will be recalled (§§124–27), about 1946, and dating probably in the
fourth or early fifth century, is a copy of a work entitled, in a colophon
at the end, *peuaggelion pkata thomas*, i.e., The Gospel (εὐαγγέλιον)
according to (κατά) Thomas. In the classification in Table 11 (§126)
it is the second item in Codex II; in the photographic reproduction by
Labib (LCGP I) (§127) it begins on Plate 80, Line 10, and extends to

Plate 99, Line 28. The text is written in Sahidic (§83), and many Greek words are used. Since the text is written continuously it is not always exactly clear as to how many separate units should be recognized in it, but the most customary division is probably that which finds in the entire text a series of one hundred and fourteen sayings. This division, as in the edition by Guillaumont, *et al.* (see the *Literature* above), will be followed here, while references to Plates and Lines as in the same edition (corresponding to the photographic edition by Labib) will also be given. In addition to the translation by Guillaumont, *et al.*, the translations by Grant and Freedman and by Gärtner (also cited in the *Literature* above) will be basic to our understanding of the text.

§287. The text begins: "These are the secret words which Jesus the living spoke, and Didymus Judas Thomas wrote." Then, with only the brief introduction, "And he said," comes the first saying: "Whoever finds the explanation (ἑρμηνεία) of these words will not taste death." After this follows a series of sayings or discourses, the several units usually introduced like the foregoing one, "And he said," or by the words, "Jesus said." In some cases the material is in the form of a conversation introduced by some such statement as, "His disciples (μαθητής) said." Then, in answer to their question or remark, the reply of Jesus is given.

§288. In analysis of the text, the first thing that can be shown is that it incorporates material recognizably and unmistakably similar to that found in Oxyrhynchus Papyri 654, 1, and 655 (cf. §281). At the outset (Plate 80 Lines 10–14) the Coptic text contains an introduction and a first saying which are parallel to Lines 1–5 in OP 654 (Text 55 §217). If we write the translation of the Coptic text in lines corresponding to the lines of the Greek text, the virtual identity of material is unmistakable and the restorations which should be made in the earlier fragmentary text are suggested for the most part with reasonable probability. Here is the translation of the Coptic text, in such lines:

> These are the secret words which
> Jesus the living spoke and Didymus Judas
> Thomas wrote. And he said: Whoever finds the explanation
> of these words
> will not taste death.

And here is the translation of the Greek text, which is the same as in our Text 55 §217 above, but with the additional restorations which appear indicated shown within square brackets:

These are the words, [the secret ones,] which
Jesus the living spoke, [and were written by Didymus Judas,]
even Thomas. And he said: [Whoever finds the explanation]
of these words
will not taste [death.]

In this text, the words "will not taste death," are identical with Jn
8:52 (οὐ μὴ γεύσηται θανάτου), but there the condition is, "If any one
keeps my word," and here it is, "Whoever finds the explanation
(ἑρμηνεία) of these words." Therewith the emphasis has been shifted
to knowledge, and we are pointed to the supposition that we may be
dealing with a Gnostic document.

§289. Altogether OP 654 contains seven sayings of Jesus (Texts
55–61 §§217–22), and the striking fact is not only that these contain
materials similar to materials in the Coptic Gospel according to
Thomas, but that these materials follow in the same sequence in both
documents. In presenting these materials it will suffice now to leave
the translation of the Gospel according to Thomas in lines corresponding as well as may be to the Coptic text, and then to continue
to show the reasonable restorations in the text of the Greek Papyrus.
Saying 2 (Plate 80, 14–19) in the Gospel according to Thomas is:

> Jesus said:
> Let him who seeks not cease seeking until he
> finds, and when (ὅταν) he finds, he will
> be troubled, and when he has been troubled, he will
> marvel and he will
> reign over the All.

Here it is less easily possible to bring Saying 2 in OP 654 (Lines 5–9
Text 56 §218) into complete correspondence with the Coptic text, but
many of the words are the same, as is the general idea of seeking and
finding and marveling or being amazed, with a climax indicated by the
word "reign." This is the saying quoted by Clement of Alexandria as
from the Gospel according to the Hebrews (§166), but if it was in that
work it was also here in the Gospel according to Thomas as well, and
the present evidence shows that OP 654 is to be connected with the
latter work rather than with the Gospel according to the Hebrews.

§290. Saying 3 in OP 654 (Lines 9–21 Text 57 §219) is so fragmentary as to be almost unintelligible in and of itself, but can be understood now as having probably been very close to Saying 3 (Plate 80,
19–81, 5) in the Coptic text. The latter reads:

Jesus said: If
those who lead you say to you:
See, the kingdom is in heaven,
then the birds of the heaven will precede you.
If they say to you: It is in the sea (θάλασσα),
then the fish will precede you.
But (ἀλλά) the kingdom is within you and
it is without you. When (ὅταν) you
know yourselves, then (τότε) you will be known
and you will know that you are
the sons of the living Father. But (δέ) if
you do not know yourselves, then you
are in poverty and you
are poverty.

From the Papyrus alone we gathered that the kingdom talked about was "within" in the sense of self-knowledge, and that understanding is confirmed in the fuller text here.

§291. Saying 4 in OP 654 (Lines 21–27 Text 58 §220) was intelligible in the last part which has canonical parallel, but too fragmentary to be understood in its first part. Now it is seen to be the remnant of an unusual saying which occurs as follows in the Coptic text (Saying 4 Plate 81, 5–10):

Jesus said: The man old in days will not
hesitate to ask
a little child of seven
days about the place (τόπος) of life, and
he will live. For many who are first will be last,
and they will become a single one.

The saying ascribed by Hippolytus (Text 85 §282) to the Gospel according to Thomas, as used by the Naassenes, bears at least some similarity to the present text, and this makes it probable that the work to which Hippolytus referred was the same as that with which we are dealing, although the Naassenes may have had their own revision of it. Likewise the Manicheans may have made use of the Gospel according to Thomas, which would account for Cyril's statements (§285) connecting it with them; but since the Gospel must now be dated well prior to Hippolytus (230) it could not have been written, as Cyril claimed, by a disciple of Mani, since the latter only began to preach in 242 (§115).

§292. Saying 5 (Plate 81, 10–14) in the Coptic text corresponds closely with, and fills in slight gaps in, Saying 5 in OP 654 (Lines

27–31 Text 59 §221). The Coptic text translated in English reads:

Jesus said:
Know what is before your sight,
and what is hidden from you will be revealed
to you. For (γάρ) there is nothing hidden that shall
not be manifest.

§293. In Saying 6 in OP 654 (Lines 32–39 Text 60 §222) we surmised that it was the disciples who asked the initial question, although specific mention of them was lost in a break in the Papyrus, and this surmise is now confirmed by the Coptic text. The latter also fills out the answer of Jesus, which was mostly lost in the fragmentary Papyrus. The translation of the Coptic text (Plate 81, 14–23) runs:

His disciples (μαθητής) asked him
and said to him: Do you want us to fast (νηστεύειν),
and how should we pray and give alms (ἐλεημοσύνη),
and what should we observe (παρατηρεῖν) in diet?
Jesus said: Do not lie;
and what you hate, do not do, for
all things are manifest before heaven.
For (γάρ) there is nothing hidden that shall not
be manifest, and there is nothing covered that
shall remain without being uncovered.

The reply of Jesus in Line 19, "and what you hate, do not do," is evidently derived from Tob 4:15, "And what you hate, do not do to any one," with omission of the words, "to any one," which reduces the saying from a form of the "Golden Rule" to a self-centered saying. Then in Lines 21–22 the saying from Lk 8:17 is repeated as at the end of Saying 5.

§294. In Saying 7 in OP 654 (Lines 40–42 Text 61 §222) scarcely more than the word, "blessed" ([μα]κάρι[ος]) was still to be read, and it could not have been imagined that the following strange saying would be found at the corresponding point in the Coptic text (Plate 81, 23–28):

Jesus said:
Blessed (μακάριος) is the lion which
the man eats and the lion
will become man; and cursed is the man
whom the lion eats and
the lion will become man.

§295. The eight sayings preserved in OP 1 (§§224–31) are found in the Coptic Gospel according to Thomas beginning at Plate 86, Line 12. In the sequential numbering (§286) of the sayings in the Coptic text they are Sayings 26–33. Saying 26 (Plate 86, 12–17), corresponding to Saying 1 in OP 1 (Lines 1–4 Text 62 §224), reads:

> Jesus said: The mote
> that is in your brother's eye you see,
> but (δέ) the beam that is in your own eye, you do not see. When
> (ὅταν) you cast out the beam from your own
> eye, then (τότε) you will see clearly to cast out the mote from your
> brother's eye.

§296. Saying 27 (Plate 86, 17–20), corresponding to Saying 2 of OP 1 (Lines 4–11 Text 63 §225), is as follows, the customary "Jesus said" being lacking at the beginning:

> If you do not fast (νηστεύειν)
> to the world (κόσμος), you will not find the kingdom;
> if you do not keep the sabbath (σάββατον) as sabbath (σάββατον),
> you will not see the Father.

This saying is hardly to be taken as a call for a return to the practices of a strict Judaism in fasting and sabbath observance. Rather, the language of Jewish practice seems to be used with symbolic intent (cf. §112). Fasting to the world is probably an expression for asceticism in general, as it seems to be in Clement of Alexandria, *Stromata* III 15, 99, 4 (GCS Clemens Alexandrinus II 242), when he says, "Blessed are those who fast to the world" (μακάριοι οὗτοί εἰσιν οἱ τοῦ κόσμου νηστεύοντες). Likewise Justin presumably means a spiritual keeping of the sabbath when he writes (*Dialogue with Trypho* XII 3): "The new law requires you to keep perpetual sabbath" (σαββατίζειν ὑμᾶς ὁ καινὸς νόμος διὰ παντὸς ἐθέλει).

§297. Saying 28 (Plate 86, 21–31) corresponds to Saying 3 of OP 1 (Lines 11–22 Text 64 §226), and supplies additional material at the point where the Greek papyrus becomes fragmentary. The Coptic text is translated:

> Jesus said: I stood in the midst of the world (κόσμος),
> and in flesh (σάρξ) I appeared to them;
> I found all of them drunken, I found none
> among them athirst. And my soul (ψυχή) was pained
> for the sons of men, because they are blind
> in their heart and do not see
> that empty they have come into the world (κόσμος),

empty they seek to go out of the world (κόσμος) again.
But (πλήν) now they are drunken.
When (ὅταν) they throw off their wine, then (τότε) they will
repent (μετανοεῖν).

With respect to the statement, "I appeared" (Plate 86, 22; OP 1,
Line 13), the first person singular first aorist indicative passive,
ὤφθην, in the Greek papyrus may be compared with the third person
(ὤφθη) of the same form of the same verb (ὁράω) in Lk 24:34 where
it is said that the risen Lord "appeared" to Simon. But in the present
text Jesus himself speaks and says, evidently with regard to his
earthly life, that he "appeared" and that this was "in flesh." It seems
likely, therefore, that we are to understand this part of the saying in
terms of Docetism (§116).

§298. Saying 29 (Plate 86, 31—87, 2) provides a full text at the
point where only the word poverty is preserved in Saying 4 of OP 1
(Line 23 Text 65 §227). The Coptic text is:

> Jesus said: If the flesh (σάρξ)
> came into existence because of spirit (πνεῦμα) it is a marvel;
> but (δέ) if spirit (πνεῦμα) because of the body (σῶμα),
> it is a marvel of marvels. But (ἀλλά) I marvel
> at how (πῶς) this great wealth
> has made its home in this poverty.

In the context of this saying, the metaphor of wealth making its home
in poverty is presumably a figure of the valuable soul dwelling in the
vile body, a widespread idea in Gnosticism.

§299. Saying 30 (Plate 87, 2-5) appears to have some relationship
to the first part of Saying 5 in OP 1 (Lines 24-31 Text 66 §228), but
the nature of the relationship, and the import of the saying in either
the Greek or the Coptic, are difficult to make out. The Coptic saying
reads:

> Jesus said:
> Where there are three gods,
> they are gods. Where there are two or (ἤ) one, I
> am with him.

The possible restoration and interpretation of the Greek text suggested above (§228) are obviously not supported by the Coptic text,
but the meaning of the Coptic is very obscure in itself unless, as a
remote possibility, it has something to do with the Christian doctrine
of the Trinity. Perhaps the Coptic is itself a result of misunderstand-
ing or mistranslation.

§300. The second part of Saying 5 in OP 1 (Text 66 §228) does not follow at this point in the Coptic text, but is found as Saying 77 (Plate 94, 23–28), this being the only case where a saying in the three Greek papyri (OP 654, 1, and 655) is found in a different order in the Coptic text. Here also, in the Coptic text, the saying as found in OP 1 is introduced by an independent sentence. Saying 77 reads:

> Jesus said: I am the light that is above
> them all, I am the All;
> the All came forth from me and the All
> attained to me. Split wood, I
> am there; lift up the stone, and you will
> find me there.

The first sentence in this saying is doubtless to be recognized as thoroughly Gnostic in character. The theme of light is prominent in Gnostic writings (e.g., §113), and the "All," presumably meaning the totality of being, is also mentioned in such works as the Gospel of Truth (§341). The second sentence, which is the part common to the Coptic and the Greek texts, can be interpreted most simply as promising the invisible presence of Christ to the believer in his daily work, involved with stone and wood, the common materials of human labor. But with the introductory sentence in the Coptic, where Jesus is the "All," the promise seems to be set within the framework of pantheism or, more precisely stated, of panchristism.

§301. Saying 31 (Plate 87, 5–7) is in close agreement with Saying 6 in OP 1 (Lines 31–36 Text 67 §229). This is the first of a series of sayings which are close to the Synoptic tradition. The series extends over the balance of OP 1 and continues yet farther in the Coptic text. At this point (Saying 31) the Coptic text is translated:

> Jesus said: No prophet (προφήτης)
> is acceptable in his village, no physician heals (θεραπεύειν)
> those who know him.

§302. Saying 32 (Plate 87, 7–10) corresponds with Saying 7 in OP 1 (Lines 37–42 Text 68 §230), "firmly established" being changed, perhaps less happily, to "fortified." This is the Coptic:

> Jesus said:
> A city (πόλις) built on a high mountain,
> fortified, cannot fall
> nor (οὐδέ) can it remain hidden.

§303. Saying 33 (Plate 87, 10–17) makes available a full text of which only a small part is preserved in Saying 8 in OP 1 (Lines 42–44

Text 69 §231). The English translation of the Coptic is as follows:

> Jesus said: What you
> hear in your ear (or) in the other ear,
> proclaim upon your housetops.
> For (γάρ) no one lights a lamp and
> puts it under a bushel, nor (οὐδέ) does he put it in a
> hidden place, but (ἀλλά) he sets it on the lampstand (λυχνία),
> so that all who come in
> and go out may see its light.

Here the completion of the saying enables us to see that the entire text combined the materials of Mt 10:27 = Lk 12:3 in the first part, with the materials of Mt 5:15 = Lk 11:33 and Lk 8:16 in the second part, with additional variations of a minor character. Not only are two separate Synoptic sayings, one about hearing and one about lighting a lamp, brought together but the respective versions of Mt and of Lk are interwoven to provide a specially good example of the phenomenon which is frequent enough not only in these texts but also in the church fathers of this period, the phenomenon which has been called that of the "compound text." Whether this means that the materials were quoted from memory, or that there was a deliberate attempt at harmonization of the NT text, is difficult to say.

§304. OP 655 (§§232–39) also contains material which is found in the Coptic Gospel according to Thomas. In Lines 1–17 of OP 655 (Text 70 §233) there is a statement, largely made up out of Synoptic sayings, about freedom from anxiety (§§233–34). In the Coptic text Saying 36 (Plate 87, 24–26) contains only the portion of this material which has to do with not worrying about clothing:

> Jesus said: Do not be anxious from
> morning until evening and from evening
> until morning for what you shall put on.

Then in Saying 37 (Plate 87, 27—88, 1) the Coptic text passes immediately to the question of the disciples and the answer of Jesus that are in OP 655, Lines 17–23 (Text 71 §235). The Coptic text is translated:

> His disciples (μαθητής) said: When
> will you reveal yourself to us, and when
> will we see you? Jesus said: When (ὅταν)
> you take off your clothing and
> are not ashamed, and take your clothes
> and put them under your feet

> like little children, and
> tread on them, then (τότε) (you will be)
> sons of the Living One and you will not be afraid.

With the reference in this passage to being like little children, it seems evident that the intent of the saying is to declare that salvation is a reality when the enlightened man can be so indifferent to the flesh that he is as unashamed of nakedness as an innocent child. Therewith the two sayings (36 and 37) constitute a direct sequence, the former urging freedom from anxiety about clothing, and the latter making it unnecessary anyway. Therewith, also, we are presumably in the realm of a Gnostic depreciation of everything material (§116) and a Gnostic desire to be free of all flesh and everything fleshly (§236). Yet this very freedom from the flesh can also point forward to that final freedom which will come when the flesh is stripped off in death (§357).

§305. In fragmentary Lines 24–50 of OP 655 (§§237–39) it was possible to read an intelligible text only in Lines 41–46 (Text 72 §238) and Lines 46–50 (Text 73 §239). At the point of Lines 24–40, where there is not enough left to read at all, there could have stood the equivalent of Saying 38 (Plate 88, 2–7) in the Coptic text. That saying is translated:

> Jesus said: Many times you have
> desired (ἐπιθυμεῖν) to hear these words
> which I say to you, and you have
> none other from whom to hear them. The days will come
> when you will seek me (and)
> you will not find me.

This appears to be based upon Lk 17:22 and Jn 7:34. Irenaeus (*Against Heresies* I 20, 2) gives a quite similar saying which, he says, the Marcosians (§113) quoted: "I have often desired (ἐπεθύμησα) to hear one of these words, and I had no one who said it." After this, corresponding to Lines 41–50 in OP 655 (Texts 72–73 §§238–39) we have very much the same material as in the Greek papyrus, combined in one passage, in Saying 39 (Plate 88, 7–13) of the Coptic text:

> Jesus said: The Pharisees (Φαρισαῖος)
> and the scribes (γραμματεύς) have received the keys
> of knowledge (γνῶσις), they hid them, and did not (οὔτε) enter,
> and did not allow those who would enter.
> But (δέ) you, be wise (φρόνιμος)
> as serpents and innocent (ἀκέραιος) as
> doves.

§306. Since, as we have now seen (§§288–305), the materials of OP 654, 1, and 655 are incorporated in the Coptic Gospel according to Thomas from Nag Hammadi in substantially the same content and in the same sequence (OP 654 = Coptic Gospel Sayings 1–7; OP 1 = Sayings 26–33; OP 655 = Sayings 36–38), it may be concluded that the Coptic Gospel rests back upon Greek sources related to these papyri and at least as early as they, i.e., reaching back into the second century (§281). Presumably, also, such Greek sources are to be postulated for the Gospel as a whole, and not just for these sections where fortunate circumstance has preserved for us actual related Greek manuscripts.

§307. The next thing that can be shown is that the Coptic Gospel according to Thomas, as we have it, contains many ideas that are congruent with Gnosticism. Already in the portions of the Gospel thus far dealt with, namely, those that are common to the Coptic text and the Greek texts of the three papyri, numerous emphases have been noted that agree with Gnostic doctrines, including the themes of knowledge (§288), self-knowledge (§290), asceticism (§296), Docetism (§297), panchristism (§300), and depreciation of the material (§§298, 304). Also one saying was, according to Irenaeus, quoted by the Marcosian Gnostics (§305). Since most of these apparently Gnostic emphases are found in the Greek texts as well as the Coptic, we may assume that the earlier work to which the Coptic was related was itself already either Gnostic in character, or contained ideas which were readily susceptible of development in the direction of Gnosticism. In the case of Saying 77 (§300), however, it is the first part of the Saying, which is only in the Coptic and not in the Greek, that is most unmistakably Gnostic. Therefore it is possible that the Gnostic interpretation of the underlying material has been heightened in the Coptic version.

§308. Certainly the Gnostic emphasis is also to be found in other parts of the Coptic Gospel where Greek parallels are lacking. For example, in Saying 50 (Plate 89, 31—90, 4), in answer to the question, "From where have you originated?" the answer is indicated, "We have come from the light," which is a thoroughly Gnostic idea of the origin of the light-nature of man in the supernatural light-world (cf., e.g., §113); and in answer to the question, "What is the sign of your Father in you?" the answer is, "It is a movement and a rest," and here the characteristic Gnostic word, ἀνάπαυσις, is used (§110). Again in Saying 62 (Plate 91, 34—92, 2) the typical Gnostic interest in the revelation of mystery (cf. §§92, 95) appears in the saying of Jesus: "I tell my mysteries (μυστήριον). . . . ."

§309. Specially significant is the appearance in the Coptic Gospel of two persons who are otherwise prominent in Gnostic traditions, namely, Salome and Mariham. In Saying 61 (Plate 91, 23–34) Salome enters into dialogue with Jesus. It will be remembered that Salome is prominent in the Gospel according to the Egyptians (§§158ff.), probably an Egyptian Gnostic Encratite work of the second century. In that source also occurs the saying of the Lord to Salome about trampling on the garment of shame (§158), which has already been compared with the saying in OP 655 (§236) and in the Coptic text (§304) about putting one's clothes under one's feet. In Saying 21 (Plate 84, 34—85, 19) Mariham asks Jesus a question and receives a long reply. The first part of this passage is translated from the Coptic as follows:

> Mariham said to Jesus: Whom are your disciples (μαθητής)
> like? He said: They are like
> little children who live in a field
> which is not theirs. When (ὅταν) the owners of the field come,
> they will say: Leave our field to us.
> They take off their clothes before them,
> to leave it to them and to give back
> their field to them.

Here the little children who live in the field are presumably the disciples who live in the world. When they give back the field to its owners they "take off their clothes before them" which, in the present context, must mean that they strip themselves of their bodies in death, an end, to the Gnostic, eminently desirable (cf. §§236, 357). Again in Saying 114 (Plate 99, 18–26) Simon Peter objects to the presence of Mariham, because women are not worthy of life, but Jesus says that he will make her a man so that she too may become a living spirit (πνεῦμα). Then he concludes:

> For every woman who makes herself
> male will enter the kingdom
> of heaven.

In Saying 22 (Plate 85, 20–35) it was said that entrance into the kingdom would be "when you make the two one . . . and when you make the male and the female into a single one." That is comparable to the teaching in the Gospel according to the Egyptians: "When the two shall be one . . . and the male with the female neither male nor female" (Text 19 §§157–58). Here in Saying 114 the woman must become a man in order to enter the kingdom. While this states the matter in a different way, the result aimed at is still really the same, namely, the Gnostic obliteration of the distinction of the sexes. Thus in the two Sayings connected with Mariham we have the enunciation of two preconditions for entering the kingdom, namely, the putting off of the clothing of the flesh (Saying 21), and the making of the female male (Saying 114). According to Hippolytus (*The Refutation of All Heresies* V 8, 44; BHP V 257; ANF V 56), the Naassenes (who derived their doctrine from James the Lord's brother through Mariamme [§190]) taught that precisely these same two things were necessary for all who would enter "the gate of heaven and . . . house of God" (Gen 28:17): "Those who come hither ought to cast off their garments, and all become bridegrooms,[1] having been made male by the virginal spirit." As for Mariham as the name appears in the Coptic text of Sayings 21 and 114, this is undoubtedly the same as Mariam and Mariamme, i.e., none other than Mary Magdalene (§241), under whose name a Gnostic Gospel circulated (§§243, 322ff.). In that Gospel the same idea is found that the woman must become a man (§324).

§310. In its present form, then, the Coptic Gospel according to Thomas is a work with a decided Gnostic cast, and with points of contact with such Gnostic works as the Gospel according to the Egyptians and the Gospel according to Mary Magdalene (§309). There are some points, however, at which the possibility of some relationship with Gospels of quite a different sort may be noted, namely, with Gospels used by the Jewish Christians. It has already been noted (§166) that a saying much like Saying 2 in OP 654 and Saying 2 in the Coptic Gospel according to Thomas, is cited by Clement of Alexandria as found in the Gospel according to the Hebrews. This could be a saying which was taken up both into the Gospel according to the Hebrews and into the Gospel according to Thomas; in which case its ultimate origin is beyond our discerning. In Saying 12 (Plate 82, 25–30) of the Coptic Gospel we have the following text:

> The disciples (μαθητής) said to Jesus:
> We know that you will go away from us. Who is it
> who will be great over us? Jesus said to them:
> Wherever you have come, you will

---

[1] For entering the bridal chamber as synonymous with entering the kingdom, cf. Saying 75 (Plate 94, 11–13): "Jesus said: Many are standing at the door, but the solitary (μοναχός) are the ones who will enter the bridal chamber." For the "solitary," cf. Sayings 16 (Plate 83, 31—84, 4) and 49 (Plate 89, 27–30). For the "bridal chamber" cf. §356.

> go to James the Just (δίκαιος),
> for whose sake heaven and earth came into being.

This James the Just, who is here accorded such a very high place, is undoubtedly the brother of the Lord and the head of the Jerusalem church (§§40f.), who is also featured so prominently in the Gospel according to the Hebrews (§174). Also in Saying 104 (Plate 98, 11–16) Jesus is made to ask, "What, then, is the sin that I have committed?" using almost the same words that are found in our Text 34 (§182), a saying which is credited by Jerome to "the Gospel according to the Hebrews which . . . is used by the Nazaraeans," but which we have listed under the Gospel of the Nazaraeans. Because of these several correspondences it seems probable that the Coptic Gospel according to Thomas draws at least to some extent upon Jewish-Christian traditions or, to state the matter in another way, that some Jewish-Christian traditions were taken up into the Gnosticism which influences the Gospel according to Thomas.

§311. The Coptic Gospel also contains sayings which are otherwise quoted in ancient literature without specific ascription of source. One interesting example is found in Saying 17 (Plate 84, 5–9):

> Jesus said: I will give you what
> eye has not seen and what ear
> has not heard and what hand has not touched
> and what has not come into the heart
> of man.

Ultimately this saying may have been derived from Is 64:4. It is quoted by Paul in 1 Cor 2:9 as "written," but without mention of Jesus or citation of book in which it was written. There is also Saying 82 (Plate 95, 17–19):

> Jesus said: He who is near
> me, is near the fire, and he who is far
> from me, is far from the kingdom.

This is virtually identical with a saying quoted by Origen (Text 86 §283). Whether Origen derived the saying from the Gospel according to Thomas, or from some other work in which it also stood, cannot be determined for Origen says only that he read it "somewhere."

§312. In relation to ascertainable sources, however, by far the largest amount of material in the Coptic Gospel is parallel to texts in the canonical Gospels. Such parallels are found in almost eighty sayings out of the one hundred and fourteen into which the entire text is divided (§286), namely, in the following: 3–6, 8–17, 19–22, 24,

26, 30–36, 38–41, 43–51, 54–57, 61–66, 68–69, 71, 73, 75–79, 86, 89–92, 96, 99, 101–9, 111, 113–14. This material to which there are parallels in the canonical Gospels is almost entirely discourse material, i.e., sayings and also some parables, with very little that is of a narrative sort. The largest number of parallels are found in Mt and Lk. There seem to be no parallels which are found in Mk alone although Mk is, of course, sometimes parallel to Mt and Lk in passages involved (cf. §131). There are also quite a few parallels in Jn. There are also many "compound" (§303) texts which combine materials similar to those in Mt, Lk, and Jn in varying ways. Saying 32 (§302) is an example of a saying comparable to Mt (5:14) alone. Saying 10 (Plate 82, 14–16), "I have cast fire upon the world . . . ," is an example related to Lk (12:49) alone. In Saying 108 (Plate 98, 28–30) the words, "Whoever drinks from my mouth . . . ," are presumably related to Jn 4:14 and 7:37. Saying 33 (§303) is an example of the interweaving of material like that in Mt and Lk. Saying 38 (Plate 88, 2–7) is an example of combination of material like that in Lk and Jn, the words, "The days will come," being comparable to Lk 17:22, and, "you will seek me (and) you will not find me," being identical with Jn 7:34.

§313. Whether this material which has such close parallels in Mt, Lk, and Jn is actually derived from those canonical Gospels is, of course, not absolutely certain. Theoretically, it could be derived from a parallel tradition or from a tradition upon which the canonical Gospels also drew. Whether that is the case in any or all instances can be the subject of more detailed investigations than we here undertake. We may note, however, that in at least occasional instances the saying in the Coptic text is almost exactly the same as in the canonical Gospel. Saying 54 (Plate 90, 23–24), for example, reads:

> Jesus said: Blessed (μακάριος) are the poor,
> for yours is the kingdom of heaven.

This is identical with Lk 6:20, only with the use of "the poor" (instead of "you poor") and of "the kingdom of heaven" (instead of "the kingdom of God") from Mt 5:3. Where the similarity to the canonical material is so great it is reasonable to suppose that the Coptic Gospel has drawn directly from the canonical sources. In far more instances the material in the Coptic Gospel exhibits differences from the canonical parallel. In some cases these differences appear to be due to literary or homiletic reasons. For example, the parable which constitutes Saying 57 (Plate 90, 33—91, 7) is probably just a compressed form of Mt 13:24-30, in which the sequence of events is made more difficult to follow by the omission of what would correspond to verse 26 in Mt. Contrariwise in Saying 64 (Plate 92, 10–35) the parable found also in Lk 14:16-24 (cf. Mt 22:2-10) is expanded by the introduction of four excuses instead of the three found in Lk, and by other touches, none of which appears to have any claim to originality over against the canonical version of the parable. In many cases the differences in the material in the Coptic Gospel appear to be due to a rewriting of the canonical material in terms of Gnostic ideas. For example, Saying 86 (Plate 95, 34—96, 4) is virtually identical with Mt 8:20 = Lk 9:58, save that after the words, "to lay his head," come also the added and noncanonical words, "and to rest." Here, in what might otherwise appear to be an entirely inconsequential addition, we have the word "rest," which occurs also in other passages in the Gospel according to Thomas (Saying 51 Plate 90, 7–12; Saying 60 Plate 91, 12–22), and which plays an important role in Gnostic doctrine (§§110, 241) where it often has a meaning equivalent to salvation itself. Where the materials are, thus, basically like those in the canonical Gospels, and the differences are such as could correspond with the interests of the Coptic Gospel, we may judge that the canonical Gospels are indeed the source. If it is desired to investigate the present problem (§§312–13) of relationship to the canonical Gospels further it may be suggested that Sayings 20, 26, 31, 41, 46, 55, 65, and 96 are particularly worthy of consideration. But provisionally, on the basis of the brief investigation above, we may conclude that all of this type of material has been drawn by the Coptic Gospel directly from the canonical Gospels and rewritten as desired.

§314. Finally we must be concerned with materials which occur in the Coptic Gospel according to Thomas and, as far as we know, do not have parallels or relationships elsewhere. Insofar as they, too, bear traces of Gnosticism we may assume that they originated in the same environment which was responsible for the other Gnostic traces in this Gospel. This would be true, for example, of Saying 67 (Plate 93, 19–20), which is difficult to translate and understand but which is at any rate typically Gnostic in its use of the concept of "the All" (cf. §300). But some of the sayings which are unknown and unparalleled elsewhere are not necessarily and explicitly Gnostic in character, and it is in relation to these that the question can best be raised as to whether the Coptic Gospel according to Thomas preserves any materials from outside the canonical tradition which deserve to be considered alongside that tradition. Perhaps half a dozen sayings come into consideration in this regard. They are the following:

§315. Saying 28 (§297), of which the Greek version is available in OP 1 (Text 64 §226), begins, indeed, with what may be a docetic statement ("in flesh I appeared"), but as a lament it may be compared with Mt 17:17 = Mk 9:19 = Lk 9:41 and with Mt 23:37-39 = Lk 13:34-35. Furthermore the pain of soul which is expressed (Lines 17-18 in the Greek text) is akin to the "travail of . . . soul" of the Servant in Is 53:11, and the description of those who "are blind in their heart and do not see" (Lines 20-22 in the Greek text) can recall Is 6:9. The parallelism of statements may suggest a Semitic background. Therefore at least part of this saying may be old material.

§316. Saying 77 (§300), of which the Greek version is provided by OP 1 (Text 66 §228), also concerns us at this point only in part, namely, in the words which read, in the Greek, "Lift the stone and there you will find me; split the wood and I am there." In the Greek these words are prefaced by a statement (Lines 24-28 in the Greek text) to which Saying 30 (§299) in the Coptic text appears to be equivalent, but which is so difficult to interpret in either the Greek or the Coptic that it may here be left out of account. Also in the Coptic Saying 77 there is an introductory statement (Plate 94, 23-26) which we have recognized as Gnostic (§300), which we may also leave out of consideration here. The particular saying which we have quoted again just above is, however, couched in a typically Semitic form, that of synonymous parallelism, and can be taken as conveying a simple promise, quite devoid of Gnostic elaboration. In connection with the saying, Ec 10:9 has sometimes been cited: "He who quarries stones is hurt by them; and he who splits logs is endangered by them." These are hard and dangerous forms of labor; to the follower of Jesus engaged in such labor his presence is promised.

§317. Saying 82 (§311), available also in Latin in Jerome's translation of Origen (Text 86 §283), reads, "He who is near me, is near the fire; he who is far from me, is far from the kingdom." Antithetic parallelism is evident here, which is Semitic and often found in canonical sayings of Jesus. In Lk 12:49 Jesus speaks of the fire which he came to cast upon the earth (cf. Sayings 10 and 16 in the Gospel according to Thomas), and in Mk 9:49 says that every one will be salted with fire. The issuance of a stern warning is also characteristic in his canonical teaching. It has also been suggested that Ignatius of Antioch may allude to this saying when he writes (*To the Smyrnaeans* 4, 2): "And why have I given myself up to death, to fire, to the sword, to wild beasts? Because near the sword is near to God, with the wild beasts is with God."

§318. Saying 97 (Plate 97, 7-14) is translated as follows:

> Jesus said: The kingdom of the [Father] is like
> a woman who carries a jar
> full of meal and goes a long way.
> The handle of the jar broke;
> the meal streamed out behind her on the road.
> She did not know, she had noticed no
> accident. After she came into her house,
> she put the jar down, she found it empty.

This is a relatively simple, direct parable, introduced much as are parables in the Synoptic tradition, e.g., Mt 13:31, "The kingdom of heaven is like . . ." The peril of inattention and unnoticed loss is stressed, a teaching well enough in harmony with the teaching of Jesus otherwise in the Synoptic Gospels about the value and the possible loss of the kingdom.

§319. Saying 98 (Plate 97, 15-20) reads thus:

> Jesus said: The kingdom of the Father
> is like a man who wished to kill
> a great man (μεγιστᾶνος). He drew
> the sword in his house, and ran it through the wall,
> in order to know whether his hand was strong enough.
> Then (τότε) he killed the great man (μεγιστᾶνος).

This also is introduced in the manner of a Synoptic parable (§318), and conveys a lesson much like that in Lk 14:31f.

§320. Saying 102 (Plate 98, 2-5) reads:

> Jesus said: Woe to the Pharisees (Φαρισαῖος)! For
> they are like a dog sleeping in the
> manger of oxen; for he neither (οὔτε) eats
> nor (οὔτε) allows the oxen to eat.

The expression of woe to the Pharisees and others like them or associated with them is familiar in the Synoptic Gospels, e.g., in Mt 23; and the particular woe in Mt 23:13 = Lk 11:52 conveys much the same idea as the present saying. The comparison with the dog in the manger was probably already proverbial, and was used at any rate by Lucian in the second century (*Timon* 14: "like the dog in the manger that neither ate the barley herself nor permitted the hungry horse to eat it"). Lk 12:54-55 probably illustrates the incorporation of popular Palestinian sayings in the teaching of Jesus; the parallel in Mt 16:2b-3, not found in Codex Sinaiticus and Codex Vaticanus, illustrates the introduction of additional proverbial lore at a later stage in the tradition.

§321. If any material has been preserved in the Gospel according to Thomas which is independent of the canonical tradition and should be considered along with that tradition in the search for historical records of the life of Jesus, it would seem most likely that it would be found in the half-dozen sayings just cited (§§315–20). Of these, Greek or Latin versions are available for three in OP 1 and in Origen (Text 64 §226; Text 66 §228; Text 86 §283); for the other three we depend upon the Coptic rendering. A lament (§315), a promise (§316), a warning (§317), two parables (§§318–19), and a woe (§320), is what the sayings contain. Such subject matter is not unlike what is otherwise best attested for the teaching of Jesus. Yet the occurrence of these materials in a document which is generally Gnostic in character makes it necessary to continue to place at least a question mark over against even these six sayings.

## 2 / *The Gospel According to Mariam*

*Literature:* cf. above §122; Walter C. Till, *Die gnostischen Schriften des koptischen Papyrus Berolinensis 8502* (TU 60 V, 5). 1955; R. McL. Wilson, "The New Testament in the Gnostic Gospel of Mary," in NTS 3 (1956–57), 236–43; GGSB 65–68.

§322. We turn next (cf. §281) to Berlin Papyrus 8502, the fifth-century Coptic codex which has already been described (§122), and which is available in German translation by Till. Since the first six pages of the manuscript are lost, the text begins in the midst of a work of which that much is lost. This work continues then from Page 7, Line 1, to Page 19, Line 5. There at the end (Page 19, Lines 3–5) in a colophon is the title, *peuaggelion kata Marihamm*. The personal name here is written Mariham elsewhere in the text. This is presumably the same Mariham, Mariam, or Mariamme, whom we meet elsewhere (§§190, 241, 243, 271, 309, 327), who is probably to be identified with Mary Magdalene. Therefore we have here the Gospel according to Mariam, i.e., Mary Magdalene. From Page 17, Line 5 in this codex to Page 17, Line 20, and again from Page 18,

Line 5 to the end (Page 19, Line 5) we find a text which is very close
to the Greek text of Rylands Papyrus 463 of the early third century
(§§240–43). Therefore the Coptic document is probably the translation of a Greek work of at least as early a date as that.

§323. At the broken beginning of the Coptic text (Page 7, Lines
1ff.) it appears that the question is being asked whether or not matter
(ὕλη) will be saved. To this the Savior (σωτήρ, cf. §241) replies, not
with complete clarity, that all natures will be resolved again into
their own roots; and then admonishes, as frequently in the Synoptic
Gospels (Mt 11:15, etc.), "He who has ears to hear, let him hear."
Then Peter acknowledges that Christ has now explained all things to
them, nevertheless goes on and asks a further question about sin, to
which the Savior makes answer. After that (Page 8, Lines 12ff.) the
Blessed One (μακάριος), as he is now called, gives a sort of farewell
salutation and commission which is woven together out of words
which echo a number of canonical Gospel sayings. From this farewell
salutation and commission and from the fact that the Savior goes
away immediately afterward (§324) we gather that the setting is in
the post-resurrection period. The words of the Blessed One are:

> Peace (εἰρήνη) be with you. My peace (εἰρήνη)
> receive you. Take heed that no one
> leads you astray (πλανᾶν), saying:
> Lo, here! or Lo,
> there! For (γάρ) the Son of man
> is within you. Follow
> him! Those who seek him, will
> find him. Go therefore and preach
> the gospel (εὐαγγέλιον) of the kingdom.

For the language that is used, note the following comparisons: "Peace
be with you," Lk 24:36; Jn 14:27; 20:19. "Take heed, etc.," Mt 24:4
= Mk 13:5 = Lk 21:8. "Lo, here, etc.," Mt 24:23, cf. Mk 13:21;
Lk 17:23. "The Son of man is within you," Lk 17:21 (which speaks
of the kingdom of God rather than the Son of man). "Seek" and
"find," Mt 7:7 = Lk 11:9. "Go therefore and preach," Mk 16:15;
"the gospel of the kingdom," Mt 4:23; 9:35.

§324. Then (Page 9, Lines 5ff.) the Savior went away and the
disciples grieved and gave fearful consideration to their commission,
saying, "If even he was not spared, how shall we be spared?" At this
juncture Mariham stood up and admonished them to overcome their
irresolution, saying, "But rather (μᾶλλον δέ) let us praise his greatness,
for he has prepared us and made us into men" (cf. §309). Peter then

(Page 10, Lines 1ff.) said to Mariham, "Sister, we know that the Savior (σωτήρ) loved you more than the other women," and asked her to tell them the words of the Savior which she knew but which they had not heard. Mariham accordingly began to tell them how she saw the Lord in a vision (ὅραμα). He explained to her that it is not the soul (ψυχή) nor the spirit (πνεῦμα) but the mind (νοῦς) which is between the two, which sees the vision.

§325. At that point we reach the place in the codex where Pages 11 to 14 are missing. At Page 15, Lines 1ff., Mariham is evidently continuing to recount the revelation which the Savior gave her, and is describing the ascent of the enlightened soul past various powers. To them the soul speaks triumphantly. On Page 16 and in Lines 19–21 it says:

> My desire (ἐπιθυμία)
> has come to an end, and ignorance
> is dead.

On Page 17 and in Lines 4–7 the soul concludes:

> From this time on
> I will attain rest (ἀνάπαυσις) in the
> time (χρόνος) of the season (καιρός) of the Aeon (αἰών) in
> silence.

Here we are at the point where Rylands Papyrus 463 (§§240ff.) begins. The Greek sentence is only partially preserved (Text 74 Lines 1–2 §240), and in comparison with what is preserved the Coptic text is somewhat divergent. In the Coptic text there is no equivalent to τὸ λοιπὸν δρόμου, "the remainder of the course," and the words καιρός and χρόνος are reversed in order. Nevertheless it is evidently the same essential statement that is preserved in both texts, and this has to do with the completion of its course by the soul and the attainment in the opportune season and in the duration of time and in the supernatural Aeon of that rest in silence which is the ultimate goal of the Gnostic. That the balance of this Gospel continues to speak in Gnostic terms has already been sufficiently shown in consideration of the Greek text (§§240–43).

### 3 / The Sophia of Jesus Christ

*Literature:* cf. above §122; Walter C. Till, *Die gnostischen Schriften des koptischen Papyrus Berolinensis 8502* (TU 60 V, 5). 1955; Hans-Martin Schenke, "Nag-Hamadi Studien II: Das System der Sophia Jesu Christi," in ZRGG 14 (1962), 263–78, and "Nag-Hamadi Studien III: Die Spitze des dem Apokryphon Johannis und der Sophia Jesu Christi zugrundeliegenden gnostischen Systems," in ZRGG 14 (1962), 352–61.

§326. Next (cf. §281) we turn to the work which extends from Page 77, Line 8 through Page 127 of Berlin Papyrus 8502 (§122). The title *tsophia niesous pechristos* stands at the beginning (Page 77, Line 8) and in a colophon at the end (Page 127, Lines 11–12). The name of Jesus Christ is abbreviated I̅s̅ X̅s̅ at the beginning and I̅η̅s̅ X̅ρ̅s̅ at the end. The word σοφία may either be translated "wisdom," or left untranslated as Sophia, since in Gnosticism we hear both about the "wisdom" which is spoken in a mystery (§105), and also about Sophia who is a great Aeon (§§110f.). There is also a copy of the same work among the Nag Hammadi manuscripts. In the listing in Table 11 (§126) it appears as the fourth item in Codex III. In this manuscript the work is entitled The Sophia of Jesus Christ in the superscription, and The Sophia of Jesus in the colophon. Since this manuscript is not yet published our references will be only to the Berlin Papyrus, but the Nag Hammadi copy is said to present a very similar text.

§327. Furthermore, from approximately Page 88, Line 19 to Page 91, Line 15 the text of Berlin Papyrus 8502 is recognizably the same as that of OP 1081 (§§246–48). The Oxyrhynchus Papyrus is badly damaged at the beginning and end, but in Line 5 (Text 77 §246) the mention of "the things that are incorruptible" corresponds to similar language in the Berlin Papyrus, Page 89, Line 3; and in Line 48 (Text 78 §247) mention of the "unbegotten" (ἀγέννητ[ος]) corresponds with the same word (ἀγένητος) in the Berlin Papyrus, Page 91, Line 13, where it can be seen that the speech has to do with the unbegotten Father. Between these points where the Greek is preserved the Coptic follows it quite closely; where the Greek is missing the Coptic makes it possible to ascertain, with probability, what stood there. Of particular interest is the discovery that in the section extending from Page 89, Line 20 to Page 90, Line 1 of the Berlin Papyrus, corresponding to Lines 24–25 of the Oxyrhynchus Papyrus, it is none other than Mariham (§322) who asks the question of Christ. Since OP 1081 comes probably from the early part of the fourth century (§246), the Sophia of Jesus Christ may probably be dated at least as early as the third century. Since it is throughout, in typical Gnostic style (cf. §323), a conversation of the risen Savior with the disciples which is presented, we can, for our purposes, dispense with further consideration of this work.

## 4 / The Apocryphon of John

*Literature:* cf. above §§122, 127; Walter C. Till, *Die gnostischen Schriften des koptischen Papyrus Berolinensis 8502* (TU 60 V, 5). 1955; LCGP I, Plates 47, 1—80, 9; GGSB 69–85; Martin Krause and Pahor Labib, *Die drei Versionen des Apokryphon des Johannes im Koptischen Museum zu Alt-Kairo.* Abhandlungen des Deutschen Archäologischen Instituts Kairo, Koptische Reihe, 1. 1962; Hans-Martin Schenke, "Nag-Hamadi Studien I: Das literarische Problem des Apokryphon Johannis," in ZRGG 14 (1962), 57–63, and "Nag-Hamadi Studien III: Die Spitze des dem Apokryphon Johannis und der Sophia Jesu Christi zugrunde-liegenden gnostischen Systems," in ZRGG 14 (1962), 352–61; Andrew K. Helmbold, "The Apocryphon of John," in JNES 25 (1966), pp. 259–72.

§328. The foregoing works (§§282–327) are those which, at the present stage of discovery and research, have been found in Coptic papyri and also, at least fragmentarily, in Greek papyri, namely, the Gospel according to Thomas, in a Nag Hammadi manuscript (fourth or fifth century) and in Oxyrhynchus Papyri 654, 1, and 655 (second and third centuries); the Gospel according to Mariam, in Berlin Papyrus 8502 (fifth century) and in Rylands Papyrus 463 (third century); and the Sophia of Jesus Christ, in Berlin Papyrus 8502 (fifth century) and in Oxyrhynchus Papyrus 1081 (fourth century). In view of this evidence it may be presumed that much other of the Coptic literature also rests back upon Greek originals, although those have not, at least as yet, been recovered. With special probability this may be assumed for the works contained in Berlin Papyrus 8502 since, as we have just seen, the Greek originals of two of these have already been found. Two other works are contained in the same Papyrus (§122), the Acts of Peter, which is outside the area of our present concern; and the Apocryphon of John, of which brief mention is here to be made. There are also no less than three copies of the Apocryphon of John in the Nag Hammadi manuscripts (Table 11 §126, Codex II, No. 1; Codex III, No. 1; and Codex IV, No. 1).

§329. In comparison of the four copies of The Apocryphon of John thus available, namely, the one in Berlin Papyrus 8502 and the three from Nag Hammadi, it has been established that there is a shorter version represented by the Berlin text and in Codex III, and a longer version found in Codex II and Codex IV. As far as the shorter version is concerned, it begins in Berlin Papyrus 8502 on Page 19 at Line 6, immediately following the colophon of "the Gospel according to Marihamm," and without a superscription of its own. At the end (Page 77, Lines 6–7) it is supplied with a colophon, reading *papokruphon niōhannēs*, i.e., The Apocryphon (ἀπόκρυφον, probably meaning, Secret Book) of John. In Codex III from Nag Hammadi, the first four pages are missing, but the title is put on the *verso* of a prefatory sheet and then the text begins on Page 5, Line 1, at a point corresponding to Page 24, Line 6, of the Berlin papyrus. Thereafter the text in Codex III runs parallel to that in the Berlin papyrus, except that Pages 19 and 20 are missing, all the way to the end where (Page 40, Lines 10–11) it too has a colophon with the same title.

§330. The text in the Berlin Papyrus, available in German translation by Till and in English by Grant, begins (19, 6) by telling how John, the brother of James—these beings the sons of Zebedee—went up to the Temple one day where he met a Pharisee named A[.]manias. The Pharisee asked where his Master was, and John replied that he had returned to the place from which he came. Then the Pharisee reproached John, saying, "Through error (πλάνη) this Nazoraean (Ναζωραῖος) has led you astray (πλανᾶν)." Thereupon John went away to the mountain, in a desert place. With grief in his heart he asked (20, 8–14):

How (πῶς) then was the Savior (σωτήρ) appointed (χειροτονεῖν), and why was he
sent into the world (κόσμος) by his
Father who sent him? And
who is his Father? And of what
nature is that Aeon (αἰών) to which
we will go?

Then John sees a vision. A child appears to him, who at the same time has the luminous form of an old man. This one, who is eventually (45, 6) called Christ, promises (22, 3ff.) to reveal all things to John, and he proceeds to do so in a long discourse which continues uninterruptedly until (45, 6) John breaks in with a question.

§331. The Father of All, it is explained (22, 20ff.), is an incomprehensible Spirit (πνεῦμα, 23, 3), describable mainly in negatives, and his imperishable Aeon (αἰών) exists in rest and reposes in silence (26, 7–8). The Spirit saw its own image (εἰκών), however, in the pure water of light which surrounded it, and its thought (ἔννοια) became active (27, 1ff.). So Barbelo came into existence, who is the First Thought (ἔννοια), the Image (εἰκών), and the Virginal (παρθενικόν) Spirit (27, 18ff.). From Barbelo was born Monogenes (μονογενής = Only-Begotten), or Christ (30, 1ff.). Out of the light which is Christ came four emanations (32, 19ff.), namely, Charis (χάρις = Grace), Synesis (σύνεσις = Understanding), Aesthesis (αἴσθησις = Perception), and Phronesis (φρόνησις = Prudence). Charis is connected with the first great light, Harmozel (33, 8ff.), where the perfect (τέλειος) man, Adam, is established (35, 5ff.). In the second light, Oroiael, is the abode of Seth, the son of Adam (35, 20ff.). In the third light, Daueithe, are the souls of the saints, who are the descendants of Seth (36, 2ff.). In the fourth light, Eleleth, are the souls who repented only belatedly and thus finally came to know their fulfillment (36, 7ff.). Connected with the fourth light, also, was Sophia (σοφία), the Aeon who in ignorance gave birth to an imperfect work, a monster, whom she named Ialdabaoth (36, 16ff.). This is the First Archon (ἄρχων) (38, 14f.). He joined himself with Unreason (ἀπόνοια) and created the firmament and material world and the powers and angels who rule over it (39, 5ff.). When he saw all this creation and all these angels beneath him, Ialdabaoth, now (41, 6f.; 42, 10f.) called also Saklas, became boastful and, using the words of Ex 20:5 and Is 45:5, said: "I am a jealous God; besides me there is no other" (44, 14–15). Thereupon the Mother, i.e., Sophia, began (ἄρχεσθαι) to be "moved" (ἐπιφέρεσθαι) (Gen 1:2 LXX) because she recognized her deficiency.

§332. Up to this point the Apocryphon of John is almost certainly the source employed by Irenaeus in his account (cf. §113) of the Barbelo-Gnostics in *Against Heresies* I 29. Summarizing the doctrines of this group of Gnostics, Irenaeus tells about the Father who cannot be named, the Aeon called Barbelo, and the four emanations, Charis, Synesis, Phronesis, and (varying one name) Thelesis (θέλησις = Will), who are associated with the four great lights. Also he tells about

Sophia, and the work of the First Archon, and closes the account with the arrogant declaration of the latter: "I am a jealous God; and besides me there is no other." Also in *Against Heresies* I 30 Irenaeus tells about the great role of Ialdabaoth in the doctrine of the Sethians. Since in *Against Heresies* I 29 Irenaeus so plainly uses a source very much like the first part of the Apocryphon of John (Berlin Papyrus 8502, approximately 22, 17—44, 18, and parallels in the three Nag Hammadi codices), we can date the Apocryphon of John in its original and presumably Greek form at least as early as the time of Irenaeus, i.e., c. 180 or earlier.

§333. At the point reached in our summary of the Apocryphon of John (Berlin Papyrus 8502, 45, 6), John breaks in with a question to Christ concerning the significance of the word "moved" (ἐπιφέρεσθαι), which had just been used (45, 1) concerning the Mother, Sophia. From here on through the balance of the book there are increasingly numerous questions by John. As the revelation progresses we are told of the creation of man (49, 2ff.). Like the perfect man (§331), in whose image he was made, he too was called Adam. Although seven Powers (ἐξουσία) and three hundred and sixty angels (ἄγγελος) took part in making him, this creature remained unmoving (50, 15ff.) until Ialdabaoth breathed into him his spirit (πνεῦμα) which was the power he had from the Mother, i.e., from Sophia (51, 17ff.). Then a formation (πλάσις) was made out of earth, water, fire, and wind (πνεῦμα), which really means out of matter (ὕλη), darkness, desire (ἐπιθυμία), and the opposing spirit (ἀντικείμενον πνεῦμα), and this material body became the fetter and the tomb of the man (55, 3ff.). The man was then (55, 20ff.) placed in Paradise (παράδεισος), but the delight (τρυφή) of this place was only a deceit (ἀπάτη). The blessed (μακάριος) Father, however, is a compassionate benefactor, and had sent the Thought (ἐπίνοια) of Light, called Life (ζωή, the name of Eve in Gen 3:21 LXX), as a helper (βοηθός, Gen 2:18) for the man (52, 17ff.). At the present juncture this power, i.e., the Thought of Light, was brought forth out of the man and made into a formation (πλάσις) with a female form (μορφή) (59, 6ff.), and this was Eve. Ialdabaoth realized that these two withdrew from him, and his angels drove them out of Paradise (61, 7ff.). Then Ialdabaoth looked upon the virgin (παρθένος) who stood at the side of Adam, and with her he begot two sons (62, 3ff.). These were Yahweh (ἰαυε) and Elohim (ελωειμ). Yahweh had a face like a bear, and was unrighteous. Elohim had a face like a cat, and was righteous. These two have been known ever since as Cain and Abel.

§334. Then (63, 2ff.) Adam begot Seth, and this one had the same substance (οὐσία) as himself. Therefore the Mother sent the spirit (πνεῦμα) to Seth and his descendants to awaken them out of lack of perception and out of the wickedness (κακία) of the grave (i.e., of the body), so that they may attain to holy perfection (63, 16ff.). Concerning these Christ says (65, 3—66, 12):

> Those upon whom the spirit (πνεῦμα) of
> life descends, after they have
> bound themselves together with the power, will be
> saved and will become perfect (τέλειος); and they
> will become worthy to
> ascend to those great lights; for (γάρ) they will
> become worthy to purify themselves with them
> from all wickedness (κακία) and from the
> temptations of iniquity (πονηρία), in that they
> aim at nothing but (εἰ μή) the
> incorruptible assembly, and
> they strive (μελετᾶν) for it without (χωρίς)
> wrath, envy, fear,
> desire (ἐπιθυμία), and satiation. They will not
> be affected by all of these things
> nor (οὔτε) by anything
> except only (εἰ μή τι) the
> flesh,
> which they make use of (χρῆσθαι) while they
> wait in expectation
> for the time when they will be led forth and
> will be received (παραλαμβάνειν)
> by the Receiver (παρα-
> λήμπτωρ) into the dignity of the
> eternal, imperishable life
> and calling; whereby they endure (ὑπομένειν) all
> things and bear all things,
> so that they
> may pass through the contest for the prize (ἆθλον) and
> inherit (κληρονομεῖν) eternal life.

So they will attain to the place of rest (ἀνάπαυσις) of the Aeons (αἰών) (68, 11–13). But those souls (ψυχή) which have not known the All will have to be placed repeatedly in fetters, i.e., undergo new incarnations, until at last they attain knowledge and are saved (68, 13—69,

13). With certain other disquisitions the revelation concludes. Then (76, 7ff.) John is told to write down what he has received, and a curse is expressed upon anyone who gives out this information in exchange for a gift or food or drink or clothing or anything else. "He (i.e., Christ) gave him (i.e., John) this mystery (μυστήριον) and forthwith disappeared from him. And he (i.e., John) came to his fellow disciples (μαθητής) and began (ἄρχεσθαι) to tell them what had been said to him by the Savior (σωτήρ)" (76, 15—77, 5). So the Apocryphon comes to its end in the Berlin Papyrus, and the colophon follows (77, 6–7) with the title.

§335. A longer version of the Apocryphon of John, it has been said (§329), is found in Codex II and Codex IV from Nag Hammadi (cf. Table 11 §126). In Codex II the Apocryphon of John extends from Page 1, Line 1, to Page 32, Line 9, with the title at the end (32, 7–9). As may be seen in the photographic reproduction (§127), the text is fragmentary in the earlier pages but excellently preserved in the latter pages. In much-damaged Codex IV the Apocryphon of John runs from Page 1, Line 1, to Page 49, Line 28, with the title at the end (49, 27–28). By comparison of Codex II and Codex IV the following four lines of introduction can be reconstructed:

> The doctrine and the words of the Savior (σωτήρ). And he re-
> vealed these mysteries (μυστήριον) which are hidden in a
> silence . . . and he taught them
> to John, who gave attention.

After that the text continues, as in the Berlin Papyrus (§330), with John's encounter with the Pharisee in the Temple, and the subsequent vision and revelation. At occasional points additional sections are included, as compared with the shorter version. In Codex II the longest of these begins on Page 15, Line 29, and extends through Page 19, Line 12. This is at the point of the making of the man, Adam (§333), and much more detail is given concerning the powers which worked in this creation, demons (δαίμων) as well as angels (ἄγγελος), until the psychic (ψυχικός) body (σῶμα) was brought into order. Reference is also made (19, 10) to the Book of Zoroaster for additional details. At the end Codex II and Codex IV conclude in the same way as Codex III and Berlin Papyrus 8502. Further details of the text need not concern us here, nor the unsolved question of the relative priority of the longer and shorter versions. It is plain that the Apocryphon of John is a treatise of Gnostic type. Like many other works of this type, it aims to answer the questions of how this evil world came into being, and how the soul may rise out of it to salvation.

Compounded as it is out of uninhibited speculations, it has very little to do with Jesus in history.

## 5 / The Gospel of Truth

*Literature:* cf. above §127; H.-Ch. Puech, G. Quispel, and W. C. van Unnik, *The Jung Codex, A Newly Recovered Gnostic Papyrus, Three Studies,* ed. by F. L. Cross. 1955; Michel Malinine, Henri-Charles Puech, and Gilles Quispel, *Evangelium Veritatis, Codex Jung f.VIII^v–XVI^v (p. 16–32)/f.XIX^r–XXII^r (p. 37–43).* 1956; LCGP I, Plates 9, 10, 6, 5; Walter Till, "Das Evangelium der Wahrheit," in ZNW 50 (1959), 165–85; Kendrick Grobel, *The Gospel of Truth.* 1960. Michel Malinine, Henri-Charles Puech, Gilles Quispel, and Walter Till, *Evangelium Veritatis, Codex Jung F.XVII^r–F.XVIII^r (p. 33–36).* 1961; Johannes Munck, "Evangelium Veritatis and Greek Usage as to Book Titles," in ST 17 (1963), 133–38; Sasagu Arai, *Die Christologie des Evangelium Veritatis.* 1964.

§336. Among the Coptic papyri in our field of investigation we have dealt first with the three works (§§282–327) of which Greek sources have actually been found, namely the Gospel according to Thomas, the Gospel according to Mariam, and the Sophia of Jesus Christ. The Gospel according to Thomas is one of the papyri from Nag Hammadi which date probably in the fourth or fifth century (§125), but it rests back upon materials found in Greek in the second and third century Oxyrhynchus Papyri 654, 1, and 655 (§306). Therefore it seems probable that other of the Nag Hammadi documents also derive from early Greek originals. The Gospel according to Mariam and the Sophia of Jesus Christ are found as Coptic works in the fifth-century Berlin Papyrus 8502 but have been shown to rest back upon Greek originals preserved fragmentarily in the third century Rylands Papyrus 463 and the fourth-century Oxyrhynchus Papyrus 1081 (§328). Therefore it was judged probable that the Apocryphon of John in the same Berlin Papyrus also had a similar early source. Three copies of the same work also exist in the Nag Hammadi papyri, where the example of the Gospel according to Thomas had made the same assumption of early Greek sources probable. Upon investigation of this Apocryphon we found that it was almost certainly used as a source by Irenaeus (§332), therefore must have been available in the second century and presumably in the form of a Greek book. With consideration of the Gospel according to Mariam, the Sophia of Jesus Christ, and the Apocryphon of John we completed notice of Berlin Papyrus 8502 insofar as it contains Gospel-type materials. With consideration of the Gospel according to Thomas and the Apocryphon of John in the Nag Hammadi papyri we have, of course, only begun to notice that very large body of literature (§126). Our task in this area is necessarily limited, however, by the fact that as yet only a few of the documents have been edited and become available for study (§127). Our task is also voluntarily limited by concern for Gospel-type materials and for such of these as have the greatest likelihood of being based on relatively early sources. Therefore we have yet to take up of the Nag Hammadi papyri only the Gospel of Truth, which may have been mentioned by Irenaeus and would therewith belong in the second century (§338); the Gospel according to Philip, whose affinities of thought point to the second or third century (§359); and a Work without a Title in Codex II, which probably goes back to a Greek original that would at least be earlier than the present Coptic text (§369).

§337. The Gospel of Truth is found in Codex I of the Nag Hammadi manuscripts (Table 11 §126). The first work in the Codex is a Letter of James, which extends from Page 1, Line 1, to Page 16, Line 30.[1] Then the Gospel of Truth begins at Page 16, Line 31, and extends to Page 43, Line 24, while several other works fill out the rest of the codex to the end. Most of this codex is in Zurich (the Jung Codex), but there is a small gap as far as the Gospel of Truth is concerned. The pages are carefully numbered by the scribe in Greek characters at the top, and after Page 32 (Lambda Beta) the next page is Page 37 (Lambda Zeta). The pages missing in Zurich are in Old Cairo, and appear in Pahor Labib's photographic reproduction of parts of Codex I (LCGP I) as Plates 9, 10, 6, and 5. Here there are two errors in the page numbering. Plate 9 is Page 33 and has the correct number, Lambda Gamma. Plate 10 is Page 34 but is incorrectly numbered Lambda Epsilon (35) instead of Lambda Delta. Plate 6 is Page 35 but is incorrectly numbered Lambda Vau (36)

---

[1] In this work the author calls himself James (although which James is not explicitly said) and tells how he and Peter were summoned by the Lord, five hundred and fifty days after the Resurrection, for special instruction. The saying, "Save yourself," is given twice, which could be the same saying quoted by Theodotus, according to Clement of Alexandria (Text 6 §140). W. C. van Unnik in VC 10 (1956), 149–56.

instead of Lambda Epsilon. Plate 5 is Page 36 and is correctly numbered Lambda Vau.

§338. While we have already called the work presently under discussion the Gospel of Truth, it actually bears no title in either superscription or colophon. It begins, however, with these words: "The Gospel (εὐαγγέλιον) of Truth is joy. . . ." Since an ancient book was often known by its opening words, it seems proper enough to take "The Gospel of Truth" as the title of this work. Therewith we are reminded of the identical title cited by Irenaeus (*Against Heresies* III 11, 9) as that of a writing which was, in his time, comparatively recent. As we have already noted (§114), Irenaeus says that this writing was in use among the followers of Valentinus and, although called a "Gospel," actually agreed in no way whatsoever with the Gospels which had been handed down from the apostles. This description by Irenaeus of the writing to which he referred agrees very well with the work which lies before us in the manuscript from Nag Hammadi. The doctrines set forth in the latter are in general of the sort promulgated by the Valentinians (§§107ff.), and the work is certainly not a Gospel in the canonical sense. In fact the Gospel of Truth is not even a Gospel of the type favored among the Gnostics, of which we have seen examples in the Gospel according to Mariam (§§322ff.), the Sophia of Jesus Christ (§§326ff.), and the Apocryphon of John (§§328ff.), in which the risen Savior, seen sometimes in a vision, converses with the disciples and imparts esoteric teachings to them. The present work is rather an address or homily in which a teacher (Valentinus himself?) explains the nature of the "truth" in Gnostic terms. As a work of this sort it falls largely outside the area of our concern, and it will suffice to describe the contents briefly, following for the translation of the Coptic Malinine *et al.*, and Grobel.

§339. The author begins, as we have seen (§338), by saying that the Gospel of Truth is joy, and goes on (16, 32ff.) to say that this joy is experienced by those who have grace from the Father of Truth to know him who came forth from the Pleroma (πλήρωμα), who is immanent in the thought and mind (νοῦς) of the Father, and who is called the Savior (σωτήρ). On the other hand, those who are ignorant of the Father experience anguish and terror and live, as it were, in a fog in which no one can see (17, 10ff.). In that fog, error (πλάνη) prepares its works and forgettings (17, 30ff.). But in Jesus Christ (thus named for the first time in 18, 16) Gnosis appeared in order that forgetting might be destroyed and the Father be known (18, 4ff.). For that reason error became angry with him and he was nailed to wood (18, 21ff.). This is, of course, a reference to the crucifixion and, a little farther along, where the same language about being nailed to wood is used, there is explicit mention of the cross. In the latter place (20, 25–27) the author quite unmistakably echoes Col 2:14, using for the "handwritten document" (χειρόγραφον) "with its ordinances" (τοῖς δόγμασιν), the substantially synonymous words, "deed" or "testament," and "edict" or "disposition" (διάταγμα), the latter meaning in particular the total provisions of a will:

> He was nailed to wood, he
> fastened the deed of disposition (διάταγμα)
> of the Father to the cross (σταυρός).

§340. Recurring evidently to the public ministry of Jesus, the author says (19, 17ff.) that he (i.e., Jesus) made himself a guide and proclaimed the word in the midst of a school. Then (19, 21ff.) there came those who were wise (σοφός) in their own opinion, and put him to proof (πειράζειν), but he confounded them and, so, they hated him for they were not truly wise. Whether or not the "school" is a synagogue, the "wise" are evidently the Pharisees and their associates, whose testing of Jesus is described with the same Greek verb (πειράζειν) in Mt 16:1 = Mk 8:11; Mt 19:3 = Mk 10:2; Mt 22:18 = Mk 12:15, etc. Over against the wise come "the little children to whom belongs the Gnosis of the Father" (19, 28ff.) and they, like the babes who are contrasted with the wise in Mt 11:25 = Lk 10:21, receive the revelation. As it is put here (19, 34ff.), there is revealed in their hearts the living Book of the Living (cf. Phl 4:3; Rev 3:5), which was written in the thought and mind (νοῦς) of the Father. Indeed (22, 3ff.) if a person has Gnosis it is shown that he is a being from on high. If he is called, he hears, responds, and turns to him who calls him, in order to reascend to him. To those who are such the author says, "You are the children of the understanding of the heart" (32, 38–39), and to them he gives ethical exhortation (33, 1–8) which echoes the language of the canonical NT as we indicate:

> Strengthen the foot of those who
> have stumbled, and stretch out your
> hands (Mt 8:3 = Mk 1:41 = Lk 5:13) to those who are sick;
> feed those who are hungry (Mt 25:35), and to those who
> are weary give rest (Mt 11:28);
> lift up those who wish
> to arise (Mt 13:25 = Mk 5:41 = Lk 8:54; Jn 5:8); awaken those
> who are asleep (Rom 13:11).

"If strength does this way," the author adds (33, 9–11), "it becomes even stronger."

§341. Continuing this theme, and continuing to incorporate many allusions to the canonical NT in his language, the author admonishes (33, 30ff.) his readers to do the will of the Father (Mt 7:21; Mt 12:50 = Mk 3:35 = Lk 8:21), "for (γάρ) the Father is kind (Lk 6:35), and what is of his will is good (Rom 12:2)." The kindness and mercy (Eph 2:4, etc.) of the Father are also stressed in connection with the chrism or anointing (Ac 10:38) which is described at a later point (36, 17ff.). This anointing is for those who "return," and "the chrism is the mercy of the Father." "Those whom he anointed, these are those who are perfect." "He is good (ἀγαθός)" (Mt 19:17 = Mk 10:18 = Lk 18:19), it is reiterated (36, 35ff.), and he knows his plantings (Mt 15:13) and has planted them in his paradise (παράδεισος), which is his place of rest. It is, in fact (42, 21ff.), in him who rests that they rest, and the Father is in them and they are in the Father (Jn 17:21). Finally (42, 41ff.), using the first person singular for the first time, the author testifies that he himself has sojourned in the place of rest but, having had this experience, deems it unfitting to say anything more about it. But (ἀλλά) (43, 2ff.) he will be in this place in order to devote himself at all times to the Father of the All, and to the true brothers over whom hovers the love (ἀγάπη) of the Father. Thus, with only a few more words, the author brings to a close this remarkable homily in which language so frequently allusive to the canonical NT expresses a Gnostic view of life, yet a Gnostic view which here, at any rate, is not elaborated with all the speculative detail reported by Irenaeus for Valentinus and his followers (§§109ff.).

## 6 / *The Gospel According to Philip*

*Literature:* cf. above §127; LCGP I, Plates 99, 29—134, 19; Hans-Martin Schenke, "Das Evangelium nach Philippus," in TL 84 (1959), 2–26; E. Segelberg, "The Coptic-Gnostic Gospel according to Philip and Its Sacramental System," in *Numen* 7 (1960), 189–200; R. McL. Wilson, *The Gospel of Philip.* 1962; C. J. de Catanzaro, "The Gospel according to Philip," in JTS 13 (1962), 35–71; Walter C. Till, *Das Evangelium nach Philippos.* Patristische Texte und Studien, ed. by K. Aland and W. Schneemelcher, 2. 1963; Martin Krause, Review of *Das Evangelium nach Philippos* by Walter C. Till in ZKG 75 (1964), 168–82; Andrew Helmbold, "Translation Problems in the Gospel of

Philip," in NTS 11 (1964), 90–93; W. C. van Unnik, "Three
Notes on the 'Gospel of Philip,' " in NTS 10 (1964), pp. 465–69;
Eric Segelberg, "The Antiochene Background of the Gospel of
Philip," in *Bulletin de la Société d'Archéologie Copte* 18 (1965–66),
pp. 205–23.

§342. The Gospel according to Philip (cf. §336) is contained in
Codex II from Nag Hammadi (§126 Table 11), where it follows
immediately after the Gospel according to Thomas (§§282ff.) and
extends from Page 51, Line 29, to Page 86, Line 19. In the photographic edition by Labib (LCGP I), however, it extends from Plate
99, Line 29, to Plate 134, Line 19, and it is customary (e.g., Till, *Das
Evangelium nach Philippos*, 5) to cite the text in terms of the latter
manner of designation, i.e., from 99, 29 to 134, 19. The text was
divided by Schenke (see the *Literature* above) into one hundred and
twenty-seven sayings, and this division is preserved with very minor
alterations by Till. Therefore we follow these divisions too, as found
in the edition by Till. The sheets of the manuscript are quite well
preserved in their upper parts, but damaged at the bottom and the
damage is progressively worse in the later portions of the text. Two
translations of the Coptic are available in German, by Schenke and by
Till, and two in English, by Wilson and by Catanzaro.

§343. The work has no superscription at the beginning, but in a
colophon at the end of the last line of text and in the line following
(134, 18–19) has the title: *peuaggelion pkata philippos*, equivalent to
Greek, τὸ εὐαγγέλιον κατὰ Φίλιππον, and English, "The Gospel according to Philip." The fact that in Codex II (§342) this work, so entitled,
follows immediately after the Gospel according to Thomas may be
explained as being in accordance with the tradition found in the
Pistis Sophia (§383), where Jesus charges Philip, Thomas, and Matthew to write down what he says and does (Chapter 42), this arrangement being intended to fulfill the requirement of Dt 19:15 for two or
three witnesses to provide adequate evidence. The existence of a
Gospel of this name is also attested by Epiphanius. In *Pan. haer.*
XXVI 13, 2–3 (GCS 25, 292–93) he cites a Gospel "fabricated"
(πεπλασμένον), as he says, in the name of the holy disciple Philip,
which was in use among the Gnostics. In it, according to the excerpt
given by Epiphanius, Philip said that the Lord had revealed to him
what the soul (ψυχή) must say in its ascent to heaven and what
answer it must give to each of the powers above, namely: "I came
to know myself (ἐπέγνων ἐμαυτήν) and gathered myself together
(συνέλεξα ἐμαυτήν) from all places, and I did not sow children to the

Archon, but I rooted out his roots and gathered the scattered members, and I know you who you are (οἶδά σε τίς εἶ, cf. Mk 1:24 = Lk 4:34); for I am of those who are from above (ἄνωθεν, cf. Jn 3:3, 7, 31)." And thus, according to the Gospel, as Epiphanius continues the excerpt, the soul is set free (ἀπολύεται). But if it be found that it has become the parent of a son it is held below (κάτω) until it is able to retrieve its own children and bring them back to itself. This is the excerpt given by Epiphanius, and it is obvious that it presents a typically Gnostic view of the ascent of the soul, made possible through knowledge. This passage does not occur, however, in the copy of the Gospel according to Philip found at Nag Hammadi and, if this is the work to which Epiphanius refers, he must have had a somewhat different copy of it. A somewhat similar statement is reported to be in the Sacred Book of the Great Invisible Spirit from Nag Hammadi (Codex III No. 2 Table 11 §126),[1] but this work has not yet been made available in publication.

§344. In general the Nag Hammadi text of the Gospel according to Philip consists of a series of "sayings" of varied length and little recognizable order. Philip himself is named and quoted only once (Saying 91, Plate 121, 8ff., cf. §350), several sayings of Jesus, canonical (§360) and uncanonical (§§361–64) are quoted, and some other persons and events in the canonical Gospels are mentioned (§350). Perhaps the most distinctive emphasis is upon the sacraments and upon what is evidently a Gnostic interpretation of the same. In what follows, when the text is quoted at any length the lines will be made to correspond with the lines of the Coptic text, and the translation will follow the German translation by Till.

§345. The text begins at the bottom of Plate 99 (Lines 29ff.) with Saying 1 which is not well preserved and is scarcely intelligible. It is only evident that it uses comparisons connected with the making of a Hebrew proselyte to illustrate something else. Saying 6 (100, 21–24) also has to do with Hebrews. It reads:

> When we
> were Hebrews (ἑβραῖος) we were orphans (ὄρφανος).
> We had our mother. But (δέ) when we
> became Christians (χριστιανός) we had father and mother.

This seems to say that the author, and perhaps his readers, had come out of a Jewish background. In Gnostic and particularly in Valen-

[1] Doresse, *The Secret Books of the Egyptian Gnostics*, 225.

tinian doctrine (§§109–11) it was from the Aeon Sophia that the material universe derived. So from the Gnostic point of view it was perhaps Sophia who was their mother and upon whom alone they depended when they were still only Hebrews. As a different clue to the possible interpretation of Saying 6, we have in Clement's extracts from the Valentinian Gnostic, Theodotus (cf. §140), a statement (*Excerpts from Theodotus* 68 GCS 17, 129) in which our state when we were children of the female alone (ἦμεν τῆς θηλείας μόνης τέκνα), as if from a shameful union (ὡς ἂν αἰσχρᾶς συζυγίας), and were imperfect and childish and foolish and weak and formless, and were like abortions (ἐκτρώματα), is contrasted with our state when we have been formed by the Savior and have become children of a husband and a bridechamber (ὑπὸ δὲ τοῦ σωτῆρος μορφωθέντες ἀνδρὸς καὶ νυμφῶνος γεγόναμεν τέκνα), i.e., are like legitimate children. Although this statement, too, is hardly without obscurity, it seems to embody the same figures of speech as the passage in the Gospel according to Philip, and there can be little doubt that in each case the concluding description is intended to apply to the Christian Gnostic. Sophia, it may be added, is explicitly mentioned elsewhere in the Gospel according to Philip: in Saying 36 (107, 31—108, 1) which is badly preserved; in Saying 39 (108, 10–15) where her other name, Echamoth (= Achamoth §111) is given; and in Saying 55 (111, 30—112, 5) where she is called the mother of the angels. The last designation agrees with the Valentinian description (Irenaeus, *Against Heresies* Ⅰ 5, 2) of Achamoth as the mother of the Demiurge, and the Demiurge as the creator of seven heavens (cf. §111), which they affirm, Irenaeus says, to be intelligent and speak of as being angels.

§346. There is another passage in the Gospel according to Philip, however, which also speaks about the mother and the father. It, too, is clearly Gnostic and symbolic in its language, but it does not necessarily imply such a highly mythological background as has been suggested above (§345) for Saying 6. This other saying is No. 110 (125, 15–35). It begins with the affirmation that the man who has the knowledge (γνῶσις) of the truth is free (ἐλεύθερος), and adds that the free man does not sin, for he who commits sin is the slave of sin. Here we have, evidently, a rephrasing of Jn 8:32 (which is quoted almost exactly in Saying 123, Plate 132, 8–9), followed by an almost exact quotation of Jn 8:34. Then comes the statement to which we refer, namely (125, 19–20), "The mother is the truth (ἀλήθεια), but (δέ) the knowledge (γνῶσις) is the father." Shortly after that in the same saying comes the ethical admonition (125, 26–29):

But (δέ) he who has become free (ἐλεύθερος)
through the knowledge (γνῶσις) is a servant on account of love
(ἀγάπη) to those who have not yet been able to receive
the freedom ([ἐ]λευθερία) of the knowledge (γνῶσις).

The emphasis is of course heavily upon knowledge, as is characteristic
of Gnosticism (§92). Similarly in Saying 115 (127, 18–30) there is
added to the Pauline (1 Cor 13:13) trio of virtues, namely, faith,
hope, and love, yet a fourth, which is knowledge, and to it is accorded
the climactic position. The husbandry of the world, it is observed in
this passage, is possible through four things (εἶδος), through water,
earth, wind (πνεῦμα), and light. The husbandry of God also operates
through four things, through faith (πίστις), hope (ἐλπίς), love (ἀγάπη),
and knowledge (γνῶσις). In the balance of the passage the comparison
is carried out, but there are gaps in the text and we cannot reconstruct
it for certain. The earth is faith, in which we take root. The water is
hope, through which. . . . The wind is love, through which we grow.
But (δέ, introducing the climax) the light is knowledge, through
which. . . . In terms of the agricultural sequence employed in the
comparison we may guess, but without complete certainty, that the
text said, at the point where there are gaps, that through water =
hope we are nourished, and through light = knowledge we ripen,
or bear fruit, or come to the harvest.

§347. If the writer has come out of a Jewish background and con-
siders that the Hebrews have a status very inferior to the Christians
(Saying 6 §345), he also contrasts the poor state of the Gentiles with
that of the Christians. Saying 4 (100, 15–18) states the contrast in
this way:

A Gentile (ἐθνικός) man
does not die, for (γάρ) he has never lived in order that (ἵνα)
he die. He who has believed (πιστεύειν) in the truth has
lived, and he is in danger (κινδυνεύειν) of dying.

Since a Gentile, this says, has never really been alive anyway, he
cannot die, because he cannot lose what he does not have. Conversely
a believer has life, therefore he could lose what he has, presumably
by relapse from his belief. Apart from the truth (as known to the
Christian Gnostic) all mankind, of course, is in a pitiable condition.
The soul (ψυχή) is a precious thing, but it has gotten to be in a worthless body (σῶμα) (Saying 22, Plate 104, 20–26). The Archons (ἄρχων)
or world rulers, wanted to deceive (ἀπατᾶν) man, since (ἐπειδή) they

saw that he has a relationship or kinship (συγγένεια) to the things that are truly good; therefore they took the name of the things that are good and gave it to the things that are not good (Saying 13, Plate 102, 18–31). The Archons, of course, thought that they were acting through their own power and will, but it was actually the Holy Spirit (πνεῦμα) who worked (ἐνεργεῖν) secretly in everything through them as he wished (Saying 16, Plate 103, 14–22).

§348. In this "Gospel," where not very much organization is recognizable (§344), the connection between "sayings" often seems to be on the basis of association of ideas or catchwords. Of this there may be an example at the present point, where Saying 16 (§347) mentions the secret working of the Holy Spirit through the Archons and then Saying 17 (103, 23–36) goes on to discuss the affirmation of some that Mary conceived from the Holy Spirit (πνεῦμα). Here the only discernible connection between the two Sayings is the mention in each of the Holy Spirit. Although this affirmation of "some" was presumably based upon Lk 1:35, the author combats the idea. He asks: "When did a woman ever conceive from a woman?" This argument presumably rests upon the representation of the Holy Spirit as a feminine power (§167). The author also says: "Mary is the virgin (παρθένος) whom no power (δύναμις) defiled." The contrast implied here is probably with Eve. Justin Martyr (*Dialogue with Trypho* 100) already contrasts Eve, who had been a virgin but "conceived the word of the serpent" (τὸν λόγον τὸν ἀπὸ τοῦ ὄφεως συλλαβοῦσα), with the Virgin Mary, who "received faith and joy" (πίστιν δὲ καὶ χαρὰν λαβοῦσα). As for the developed Gnostic speculation concerning the seduction of Eve, we have already (§333) seen an example of it in the Apocryphon of John, where Ialdabaoth is the one who takes Eve. In a later Saying (No. 82, Plate 119, 3–15), where the author professes to utter a mystery (μυστήριον), he speaks of Jesus (Line 12) and seems to present his Sonship quite literally by saying that "the Father of the All united with the virgin (παρθένος) who came down." So, he adds, "his body (σῶμα), which came into being on that day, came out of the bridal chamber (παστός), as one who came into being from the bridegroom (νυμφίος) and the bride (νύμφη)." Here, since it is "the Father of the All" who acts, the bridal chamber, also called (in Line 7) "the great bridal chamber," may be nothing less than the Pleroma (§109) itself. Again in Saying 83 (119, 16–21) the author compares the manner of origin of Adam and of Christ. Adam came into being from two virgins (παρθένος), he says, namely, from the Spirit (πνεῦμα) and from the virgin (παρθένος) earth. This is a plain allusion to Gen 2:7, where God formed man of dust from the earth and then breathed into his nostrils the breath of life. It was because of this, the Saying concludes, that Christ was born of a virgin (παρθένος), in order that he might set in order the fall which took place at the beginning.

§349. In Saying 19 (104, 3–13) and Saying 47 (110, 6–17) the names Jesus, Christ, Nazoraean (Ναζωραῖος), and Nazarene (Ναζαρη-νός), are discussed. "Jesus," it is said, is a hidden name, but "Christ" is a revealed name. The point seems to be that "Jesus" is simply transliterated and not translated in various languages, but "Christ" is translated from Hebrew and from Syriac (it is the latter language which the author mentions at this point) into Greek as "Christ" and into the tongues of many other peoples according to (κατά) the language of each. Without any explanation at all, it is said that Nazara is the truth (ἀλήθεια). Interestingly enough the name of "Jesus Nazaria" ('Ιησοῦ Ναζαρία) is given by Irenaeus (*Against Heresies* I 21, 3) in a list of invocations used by the Marcosians (§113), and is translated by Irenaeus as meaning "Savior of truth" (Σωτὴρ ἀληθείας). It is still not evident, however, in what language the word Nazara would be found with this meaning.

§350. Some other references to the life and work of Jesus occur, apparently quite at random, in the Gospel. Christ came in order that he might ransom some, save others, and redeem others (Saying 9, Plate 100, 34—101, 14). He brought bread from heaven (Saying 15, Plate 103, 6–14, cf. Jn 6:33). He appeared to his disciples (μαθητής) in glory upon the mountain (Saying 26, Plate 105, 28—106, 14, cf. Mt 17:1ff. = Mk 9:2ff. = Lk 9:28ff.). There were three who walked with the Lord at all times; these were Mary his mother, and her sister, and Magdalene, this last one being called his companion (κοινωνός) (Saying 32, Plate 107, 6–11). If Jn 19:25 is to be understood as naming just three women at the cross, then the sister of the mother of Jesus was also named Mary, as was Magdalene. In that case each of the three women mentioned in Saying 32 was named Mary. The saying concludes, however, as the text stands, with a slightly different observation: "For (γάρ) Mary is his sister and is his mother and is his consort." Here the name of the sister of Jesus (as well as the name of the sister of his mother) is Mary. This fact can neither be verified nor disproved in the canonical Gospels since there (Mt 13:55 = Mk 6:3) the brothers James, Joses, Judas, and Simon are mentioned by name, but the sisters (in the plural) are mentioned but not named. Epiphanius, however, who describes the brothers and sisters as children of Joseph by a previous marriage, names not only James, Joses, Symeon (or Simon), and Judas, but also two daughters, Mary and Salome (*Pan. haer.* LXXVIII 8, 1; 9, 6 GCS 37, 458, 460; cf. *Ancoratus* 60, 1 GCS 25, 70, where the present text has Anna and Salome). In Saying 91 (121, 8–15) it is stated on the authority of Philip the apostle (ἀπόστολος) (§344) that Joseph the carpenter (cf. Mt 13:55) planted a garden of trees (παράδεισος) because he had need (χρεία) of wood for his craft (τέχνη). He is the one who made the cross (σταυρός) out of these trees, and thus it was his seed that hung on that which he had planted. "His seed was Jesus, but (δέ) the plant is the cross (σταυρός)."

§351. Before Christ, Saying 70 (116, 17–22) declares, some came out from where they were no longer (οὐκέτι) able to go in, and they went in where they were no longer (οὐκέτι) able to come out. In a Gnostic framework of thought this can mean that souls came out of the Pleroma and cannot get back in, and entered the world and cannot get out. But (δέ) Christ came and brought out those who had gone in, and brought in those who had gone out. By the same Gnostic interpretation this can mean that he delivered souls from the world, and reintroduced them to the divine realm. In the darkness, Saying 56 (112, 5–9) points out, there is no difference between a blind man and a man who can see, for neither one can see anything. But whenever (ὅταν) the light comes, then (τότε) the one who sees will see the light, and the one who is blind will remain in the darkness. Furthermore, as Saying 44 (109, 20–35) observes, in the natural world one indeed looks at an object, the sun for example, without becoming that object, but in the spiritual world one becomes what one sees. Therefore these affirmations become valid: "You saw the Spirit (πνεῦμα), you became Spirit (πνεῦμα). You saw Christ, you became Christ. You saw [the Father, you] will become Father." Another way of stating what Christ has made possible is found in Saying 74 (117, 4–8). On the one hand (μέν) we are born through the Holy Spirit (πνεῦμα), but (δέ) on the other hand we are born again through Christ. Presumably the first birth is natural birth, but even at this point the Holy Spirit might be thought of as the agency of the birth of the soul, for we remember (Saying 16 §347) that the Holy Spirit worked secretly in everything, and (Saying 22 §347) that the soul, although imprisoned in a worthless body, is itself a precious thing. Likewise, as Saying 48 (110, 17–26) points out, a pearl (μαργαρίτης) retains its same value whether it is thrown in the mud (βόρβορον) or anointed with balsam oil (ἀποβάλσαμον) and, even so, the sons of God have value in the eyes of their Father wherever they are. As for being born again through Christ (Saying 74), this is presumably the spiritual rebirth of Jn 3:3. There (Jn 3:5) the reference to being born "of water and the Spirit" suggests that the rebirth is connected with baptism as well as with the gift of the Spirit. In Saying 74 baptism is not mentioned, but elsewhere in the Gospel according to Philip it has considerable prominence (§352).

§352. Saying 68 (115, 27–30) is somewhat damaged in the papyrus, but begins with a statement about "The Lord" and "everything in a mystery (μυστήριον)." Perhaps it said that he "did" or "made" or "brought" or "worked" everything in a mystery. At any rate there follows simply a short list of five items which appear to be the sacraments recognized by this author. The first item is "a baptism." This is designated by the word βά[ππ]ισμα which, in the form τὸ βάπτισμα, means literally "that which is dipped," but which is the regular word for "baptism" in the canonical NT (Mt 3:7; Mk 1:4; Lk 3:3, etc.) and in early Christian writers (e.g., II Clem 6:9). In Greek the verb βαπτίζειν means to dip under, i.e., to baptize, and the verb βάπτειν means to dip under, with one specific meaning, frequently found, to dye. A figure of speech which probably originated in a play on these words is found in Saying 43 (109, 12–20). Here it is noted that good dyes perish only with the things that are dyed in them, i.e., last as long as they do. But God's dyes are immortal, therefore those who are dyed with them are immortal. "But (δέ) God baptizes (βαπτίζειν) those whom he baptizes (βαπτίζειν) with water." Saying 101 (123, 21–25) speaks of "living water" (as does also Did 7 in connection with baptism), presumably meaning running water, and says that it is a body (σῶμα). Then, in a way perhaps reminiscent of Gal 3:27, the author says that "we must put on the living man," and describes the one who goes down to the water as unclothing himself "in order that (ἵνα) he may put this one on." Sayings 59 (112, 22–29) and 109 (125, 7–15) also speak about going down "into the water," and confirm the picture of the baptism as an immersion. Saying 59 also insists that if anyone comes up out of the water without having received anything, and still says, "I am a Christian (χριστιανός)," he has the name at interest, i.e., he has just borrowed it, and is subject to having it demanded of him. But if he receives the Holy Spirit he possesses the gift (δωρεά) of the name, and whoever has received a gift (δωρεά) does not have it taken away from him. In connection with the name of Christian, Saying 49 (110, 26–35) is also of interest. Although damaged, it reads in part:

If you say, "I am a Jew,"
no one will be moved. If you say, "I am a
Roman (ῥωμαῖος)," no one will be disturbed (ταράσσεσθαι). If you
say, "I am a Greek (ἕλλην), a barbarian (βάρβαρος),

a slave, [a] free man ([ἐλεύ]θερος)," no one
will be troubled. [If] you [say], "I am a Christian (χριστιανός)," . . .

At this point the papyrus is too badly damaged to restore with certainty, but it is probable that a contrast is intended with the previous
sayings which evoke no disturbance, and that some expression followed here concerning the disturbance, and presumably the hostility,
which were aroused by mention of the name of Christian.

§353. The second item in Saying 68 is "a chrism." Here the word
is χρῖσμα. This word is used, e.g., in Ex 29:7 (LXX) and in Josephus,
*Ant.* III viii 3 §197, for oil for anointing, i.e., an ointment or unguent.
It is also used, then, for the act or the fact of anointing, as, e.g., in
Jn 2:20 ("you have an anointing from the Holy One"), and in Jn 2:27
("his anointing teaches you about everything"). According to Saying
75 (117, 8–14) there is necessity for baptism in light as well as in
water, and "the light is the anointing (χρῖσμα)." Saying 92 (121,
15–19) mentions the olive tree from which the anointing oil (χρῖσμα)
is made, so the ceremony was probably performed literally. Saying 95
(122, 12–22) declares that the chrism (χρῖσμα) is superior to the
baptism (βάπτισμα). The reason given is that it is on account of the
chrism (χρῖσμα) that we have been called Christians (χριστιανός) and
that he has been called Christ. Tertullian also describes anointing
as following upon baptism, and connects the name Christ with the
chrism. Writing *On Baptism* (7) he says:

> After this, when we have issued from the bath (*lavacro*),
> we are thoroughly anointed with a blessed unction, (a practice
> derived) from the old discipline, wherein on entering the
> priesthood, men were wont to be anointed with oil from a
> horn, ever since Aaron was anointed by Moses. Whence Aaron
> is called "Christ," from the "chrism," which is the unction;
> which, when made spiritual, furnished an appropriate name to
> the Lord because he was "anointed" with the Spirit by God
> the Father.

It is of course correct that the Hebrew word Messiah means
"anointed" and is translated into Greek as Christ, and in Lev 4:5, 16
"the anointed priest" is, in the LXX, ὁ ἱερεὺς ὁ χριστός. Chrism is also
important in the Gospel of Truth (§341) and the Work without a
Title in Nag Hammadi Codex II (§368).

§354. Like the two preceding items (§§352–53) the third item in
Saying 68 is also a sacrament of the church in general as well as of
the Gnostics in particular. This is "a eucharist." The word is

εὐχαριστία. As a name for the Lord's Supper (1 Cor 11:20) it comes from the word εὐχαριστήσας ("when he had given thanks") in the narrative of the Last Supper (Mt 26:27 = Mk 14:23; Lk 22:17; 1 Cor 11:24), is found in 1 Cor 10:16 according to some manuscripts including the ninth century Codex Boernerianus, and is used in the *Didache* (9:1, 5) and by Justin Martyr (*Apology* I 66) in their descriptions of this observance.

§355. The fourth item in Saying 68 is "a redemption." A Greek word is not used here, but the corresponding term would presumably be ἀπολύτρωσις. The latter term is used by Irenaeus (*Against Heresies* I 21, 4; cf. §113) as he tells how some of the Marcosians, in place of water baptism, pour oil and water on the heads of initiates, and wish this to be "the redemption." But in Saying 68 "redemption" is listed in addition to baptism, not in place of it, therefore the situation does not seem to be quite the same as that described by Irenaeus. Also the description of the act by Irenaeus would make "redemption" similar to chrism, but again in Saying 68 both chrism and redemption are listed as separate items. Since a separate sacrament of "redemption" is not mentioned elsewhere in the Gospel according to Philip, it is not possible to determine more exactly what this item in Saying 68 connotes.

§356. The fifth item in Saying 68 is "a bridechamber." The Greek word is νυμφών. As we have seen (§113), it is also used by Irenaeus as he describes rites of the Marcosians. He writes (*Against Heresies* I 21, 3):

> For some of them prepare a bridechamber (νυμφῶνα) and perform a mystical rite (μυσταγωγίαν) with those who are being perfected (τελειουμένοις) (i.e., being initiated), pronouncing certain invocations (μετ᾽ ἐπιρρήσεών τινων), and they affirm that it is a spiritual marriage (πνευματικὸν γάμον) which is celebrated by them, after the likeness of the unions above (τῶν ἄνω συζυγιῶν).

In the Gospel according to Philip the "bridechamber" seems to be very important. This term, or a synonym of it, occurs in some of the longest passages in the book, and appears with increasing frequency toward the end and climax of the work. One or another of the several terms expressing the idea occurs in Sayings 73 (117, 1–4), 76 (117, 14—118, 4), 79 (118, 17–22), 82 (119, 3–15), 124 (132, 14–23), 125 (132, 23—133, 29), 126 (133, 29—134, 4), and 127 (134, 4–18). In Sayings 73, 79, and 82 the word is παστός rather than νυμφών, and may be translated "bridal chamber." In Greek ἡ παραστάς is anything that stands beside, and the shortened form of the same word, ἡ παστάς, means the porch in front of the house, then the part of the house next the porch, and then an inner room or bridal chamber. Finally ὁ παστός is the equivalent of the last meaning in the preceding series, and signifies a woman's chamber, specifically a bridal chamber. It is used in this sense in the Greek translation of Ps 19:5 (LXX 18:5), "as a bridegroom (νυμφίος) coming out of his chamber (ἐκ παστοῦ αὐτοῦ)." The same meaning of "bridal chamber" is guaranteed in Saying 82 by the appearance in the same Saying of the bridegroom (νυμφίος) and the bride (νύμφη). In Saying 82, as we have already noted (§348), "the great bridal chamber" is probably nothing less than the Pleroma itself. In Saying 68, however, the "bridechamber" stands in a sequence of items including baptism, etc., is therefore like the others undoubtedly a sacrament performed among the group for whom the Gospel according to Philip is written, presumably the same group whose "bridechamber" rite Irenaeus describes in the passage quoted just above. Both from the references just cited in the Gospel according to Philip where the chamber in question is both that of an earthly sacrament and of the heavenly Pleroma, and from the description by Irenaeus where the spiritual marriage simulates the unions above, it may be concluded that this sacrament is intended to celebrate and prefigure on earth what is to be enjoyed in ultimate entry into the Pleroma. In this respect the Gospel according to Thomas seems to embody something of the same idea when in Saying 75 (§309 n. 1) entry into the kingdom is synonymous with entry into the bridal chamber. In Saying 76, although it is fragmentary, the bridechamber seems to be accorded the highest place among the sacraments, for we read in part: "Baptism (βάπτισμ[α]) is the holy house. . . . The holy of the holies is the bridechamber (νυμφών)." In Sayings 124, 125, and 126 the word employed is ὁ κοιτών, "bedchamber." It is the holy in the holy (Saying 124, Plate 132, 22–23); it has invited us within (Saying 125, Plate 133, 20–21). In Saying 127 the word νυμφών is used once again, and it is said that, "If anyone becomes a son of the bridechamber, he will receive the light." This light must be received in this place, i.e., in this world, otherwise it will not be possible to receive it in the other place, i.e., in the other world. He who does receive the light cannot be seen or detained by the hostile powers (cf. Saying 77, Plate 118, 5–9, where the "powers" [δύναμις] are explicitly mentioned; and Saying 106, Plate 124, 22–30), nor can anyone trouble (σκύλλειν) him even if (κἄν) he lives as a citizen (πολιτεύεσθαι) in the world (κόσμος).

§357. Even as it is necessary to obtain the light already in this world (Saying 127 §356), so also the resurrection is to be laid hold on even now. In Saying 63 (114, 7–23) it is stated: "While (ὡς) we are in this world (κόσμος) it is fitting for us to acquire the resurrection (ἀνάστασις) for ourselves." Concerning the Lord those are in error (πλανᾶσθαι) who say that he died first and then rose, for (γάρ) actually he rose first and (then) died (Saying 21, Plate 104, 15–29). Presumably such an argument could be advanced on the basis of such a saying of Jesus as that in Jn 11:25, "I am the resurrection." Similarly (Saying 90, Plate 121, 1–7) those who say that men will die first and (then) rise are in error (πλανᾶσθαι). "If one does not first receive the resurrection (ἀνάστασις) while he is alive, he will not receive anything when he dies." Essentially this seems to teach that the resurrection will not be a future experience unless it is already a present experience, but it could also be explicated in terms of the position of Hymenaeus and Philetus in 2 Tim 2:18, who held that the resurrection was past already. Returning to Saying 63, the statement about the appropriateness of acquiring the resurrection already in this world continues: "in order that when we lay off the flesh (σάρξ) we may be found in the Rest (ἀνάπαυσις) and not walk in the Middle (μεσότης)." In the description by Irenaeus (*Against Heresies* I 7, 1) of Valentinian doctrines as set forth by Ptolemaeus we have already noted (§111) that in the final outcome of all things, on the one hand the material will be annihilated, on the other hand the spiritual will enter the Pleroma, but the psychic will remain, together with the Demiurge, in the shadow and void of the Middle. If the author of the Gospel according to Philip writes in terms of Valentinian thought, it is understandable that a final destination in the Middle would be undesirable to him. As for the desirable goal, it is of course the Rest (cf. also Saying 82, Plate 119, 13–15) which is so frequently spoken of in Gnostic writings (§§110, 241, 313, 325, 331, 334, 341, 374).

§358. As for the stripping off of the flesh, in this same saying (No. 63 §357) it is clearly the equivalent of dying (cf. 2 Cor 5:4 §§236, 304). Because of this view that to die is to be unclothed of the flesh, there are some who fear lest (μήπως) they should rise naked, and the author addresses himself to this problem in Saying 23 (104, 26—105, 19). Because of this these people wish to rise in the flesh (σάρξ), but the author points out that it is actually those who wear (φορεῖν) the flesh (σάρξ) who are naked, and he quotes with evident agreement 1 Cor 15:50 in the form: "No flesh (σάρξ) [and blood will] inherit (κληρονομεῖν) the king[dom of God]." He goes on, however, to consider the implication of Jn 6:53, which he quotes in the form: "He who shall not eat my flesh (σάρξ) and drink my blood, has no life in him." The flesh of Christ, he explains, is the Word (λόγος), and the blood is the Holy Spirit (πνεῦμα), and the person who has received these has food (τροφή) and drink and (probably) clothing (this last word is somewhat uncertain in the text, but Mt 6:25 helps to confirm that these three items should go together). With this much established, he then animadverts upon the view of those who say that the flesh will not rise. The argument is somewhat obscure, and at first glance appears to contradict the author's own position at the beginning of the Saying, where he criticizes those who wish to rise in the flesh. Now he criticizes also the one who says that the flesh will not rise. Even as the flesh of Christ is the Word (as was established just above), so there is a Word (λόγος) which is in the flesh (σάρξ) and, therefore, "it is necessary to rise in this flesh (σάρξ)." Difficult as it is to understand what the author is trying to say, perhaps he is trying to formulate a view something like Paul's view of the "spiritual body" (σῶμα πνευματικόν) (1 Cor 15:44), which envisions neither the resuscitation of a corpse nor the continuance in immortality of a "naked" soul.

§359. Such, then, is something of the nature and doctrine of the Gospel according to Philip, a rather miscellaneous collection of longer and shorter Sayings, manifesting many affinities with Valentinian Gnosticism as known in the quotation from Theodotus (§345) by Clement of Alexandria, and in the citations of material from the Marcosians (§§349, 355–56) and from the followers of Ptolemaeus (§357) by Irenaeus. Presumably, therefore, although the work is available only in the relatively late papyrus (fourth or early fifth century, §125) from Nag Hammadi, it goes back in its original form to some such time as is indicated by these affinities of thought, i.e., to the second or third century.

§360. In the survey above (§§345ff.) we have already noticed much use of the canonical NT by the Gospel according to Philip. Pauline thought is reflected, for example, in Saying 23 (1 Cor 15:50; §358) and Saying 115 (1 Cor 13:13; §346). The Fourth Gospel is used in Saying 15 (Jn 6:33; §350); Saying 23 (Jn 6:53; §358); Saying 74 (Jn 3:3; §351); and Saying 110 (Jn 8:32, 34; §346). The Synoptic record is drawn upon for the Transfiguration, as already noted (Saying 26; Mt 17:1ff. = Mk 9:2ff. = Lk 9:28ff.; §350), and also in a number of other cases. Saying 69 (115, 30—116, 17) quotes (116, 10–12) Mt 6:6 in the form: "Go into your room (ταμεῖον, the same word as in Mt), shut your door (and) pray to your Father who is in secret." Saying 72 (116, 26–37) quotes (116, 26–27) Mt 27:46 = Mk 15:34 in the slightly variant form: "My God, my God, why, Lord, hast thou forsaken me?" Saying 111 (125, 35—126, 11) makes plain reference to Lk 10:34 in stating (126, 7–9) that, "The Samaritan gave nothing to the wounded man except (εἰ μή) wine and oil." Saying 122 (129, 34—130, 26) probably alludes (130, 21–23) to Mt 15:27 with the remark: "Let them be nourished from the crumbs that fall from the table (τράπεζα, the same word as in Mt), like the dogs." Saying 123 (130, 26—132, 13) quotes (131, 12–13) Mt 3:10 = Lk 3:9 in the words: "Already (ἤδη; this Greek word and the one following are the same as in Mt and Lk) the ax (ἀξίνη) is laid unto the root of the trees." Saying 126 (133, 29—134, 4) is fragmentary but begins (133, 29–31) with what must be a quotation of Mt 15:13, at least the following words being plain: ". . . plant . . . my Father in heaven plants . . . pull out." The canonical Gospels certainly used are Mt, Lk, and Jn. Mk stands in parallel with Mt in the quotations in Sayings 26, 72, and 122. In Saying 122 the wording follows Mt rather than Mk; in Sayings 26 and 72 either Mt or Mk could have been used but, since there is a predominance of use of Mt otherwise, it is probable that here too it is only Mt which is used.

§361. There are also several noncanonical sayings, attributed to "the Lord," in the Gospel according to Philip. Saying 18 (103, 37—104, 3) reads:

> The Lord said to the disciples (μαθ[ητής . . .
> ] come indeed (μέν) into the house
> of the Father, but do not take, and also do not (οὐδέ)
> carry away in the house of the Father.

While there could be a reminiscence here of the "Father's house" of Jn 14:2, the saying is unique and also quite opaque in meaning.

§362. It will be remembered that Saying 16 (§347) asserts that the Holy Spirit worked through the Archons without their knowing it. In similar fashion Saying 34 (107, 18–27) says that the saints are actually served by the evil (πονηρόν) powers (δύναμις), for the Holy Spirit (πνεῦμα) makes them blind and they do not realize whom they are serving. Then the Saying continues (107, 23–27):

> Because of this a disciple (μαθητής) asked (αἰτεῖν)
> the Lord one day for a
> thing of the world (κόσμος). He said to him:
> Ask (αἰτεῖν) your mother, and she will give you
> from what belongs to another (ἀλλότριον).

Since the Holy Spirit is mentioned in the earlier part (107, 20) of this Saying, and since the Spirit may readily be thought of as feminine (§167), we may judge it probable that the "mother" in the saying attributed to the Lord is also the Holy Spirit. That which "belongs to another" is also, in the connotation of the Greek word, that which is strange, alien, or foreign. If the disciple who begs for something which is of the world, is to make his request of the Holy Spirit and to receive from that source something which is really foreign to himself, then perhaps we have here an expression of the Gnostic sense of estrangement from the world.

§363. Saying 57 (112, 9–12) reads:

> The Lord said: Blessed (μακάριος) is he who is
> before he came into being. For (γάρ) he who
> is, was and will be.

The word blessed is of course characteristic of canonical sayings of Jesus (Mt 5:3, etc.), otherwise the saying has no apparent relationship to the canonical teaching of Jesus. Instead it is very similar to the opening sentence in Saying 19 (Plate 84, 17–25) in the Gospel according to Thomas. The latter saying appears to contain canonical material (§312), particularly in the statement, "these stones will serve (διακονεῖν) you," with which we may compare Mt 4:3 = Lk 4:3. But the opening sentence (Plate 84, 17–18) is, in a short form, the same beatitude as in Saying 57 in the Gospel according to Philip. It reads: "Blessed (μακάριος) is he who was before he came into being." In both forms, in the Gospel according to Thomas and in the Gospel according to Philip, the beatitude is no doubt to be recognized as a Gnostic statement of the pre-existence and future destiny of the individual soul.

§364. Saying 97 (122, 24–36) is very badly preserved. It begins:

> Well (καλῶς)
> did the Lord say: Some went into the
> kingdom of heaven laughing and came out

Beyond this, too few consecutive words are preserved to make restoration possible with confidence. The real import of the complete saying must therefore remain at best conjectural.

§365. Of the foregoing noncanonical sayings of Jesus in the Gospel according to Philip (§§361–64) at least two (Sayings 34 and 57 §§362–63) seem unquestionably Gnostic in character. As far as can be judged about the other two (Sayings 18 and 97 §§361, 364), which are fragmentary, there is nothing pointing to early character or much similarity to canonical tradition, and nothing precluding the supposition that they too, like Sayings 34 and 57, and like so much else as well in the Gospel according to Philip, have been formed in an environment permeated by Gnosticism.

## 7 / A Work Without a Title in Nag Hammadi Codex II

*Literature:* cf. above §127; LCGP I, Plates 145, 24—158 at the end; Alexander Böhlig and Pahor Labib, *Die koptisch-gnostische Schrift ohne Titel aus Codex II von Nag Hamadi.* Deutsche Akademie der Wissenschaften zu Berlin, Institut für Orientforschung, Publication No. 58, 1962.

§366. In Codex II from Nag Hammadi (§§126–27 Table 11) there stands in fifth place after the Apocryphon of John (§§328ff.), the Gospel according to Thomas (§§282ff.), the Gospel according to Philip (§§342ff.), and the Hypostasis of the Archons, a writing which is commonly called A Work without a Title. In Codex II it extends from Page 97, Line 24, to Page 127, Line 17. In the first volume of the photographic edition by Labib (LCGP I) the first part of the work begins at Line 24 on Plate 145 and extends through Plate 158; in the second volume of the same photographic edition, which is yet to appear, the second part of the work is to extend from Plate 159 through Plate 175, Line 17. It is customary to cite the text in terms of these Plate and Line numbers, i.e., from 145, 24 through 175, 17. There is also a fragment of another copy of the same work, corresponding to 145, 24—146, 5, in Nag Hammadi Codex XIII. Immediately preceding the beginning of the work, on Plate 145, Lines 22–23, there is a title, "The Hypostasis of the Archons," but this is a colophon to the preceding work, and the title applies to it. At the end of our work (175, 18), and separated from it as well as from what follows by horizontal lines, there is also a title, but this reads, "The Exegesis concerning the Soul," and belongs according to content to the following work. The work presently under consideration remains, therefore, "A Work without a Title." As far as the present manuscript is concerned, it must belong, like the other Nag Hammadi manuscripts, to the fourth or early fifth century (§125). Like the other manuscripts, also, the text contains many Greek words, and was probably translated out of an earlier Greek form of the work. Where we quote the text the German translation of Böhlig and Labib is followed.

§367. This work begins (145, 24–29) with a statement by the author that both gods and men, i.e., all intelligent beings, hold that there was nothing in existence prior to Chaos, but that the author himself will prove that this view, although so widely held, is erroneous. With this introduction we gather that this work will be a tractate in cosmogony and, indeed, such it is. Since Hesiod writes in his *Theogony* (116), "Verily at the first Chaos (Χάος) came to be," the author is actually challenging the most widely held view of the origins of things in the Hellenistic world. To do so and to build up his own picture he draws upon elements derived from Hellenic, Hellenistic, and Egyptian sources, as well as from the OT, late Judaism, and Christianity. The result of this syncretism is a description of the course of events in the universe, mythological in character, shot through with typical Gnostic motifs, and elaborately detailed beyond anything which we have encountered yet. Precisely because this is the nature of the work, it will not concern us at length.

§368. To begin his argument against the priority of Chaos, the author observes (145, 30—146, 2) that there is universal agreement (συμφωνεῖν) that Chaos is darkness. That means, however, that it goes back to a Shadow (146, 2–3), and a Shadow is something secondary. One must seek, therefore, for what is primary and prior to the Shadow. The Shadow came to be out of a work (ἔργον) which existed from the beginning (146, 3–5). In the immortal realm there was a dual being who, in view of what happened, may be called Pistis Sophia. Out of Pistis there overflowed, as it were, an image which was named Sophia (146, 13–14). Through Sophia a work (ἔργον) came to pass (146, 14–15), and a curtain (παραπέτασμα, cf. καταπέτασμα, Mt 27:51 = Mk 15:38 = Lk 23:45, etc.) was established as a separation between men and the immortal world (146, 22–23). In the events which follow, Gnostic figures with which we are already familiar, and many others which we have not yet met, come on the scene. There is the Archon Ialdabaoth (148, 1ff.) who thinks himself the only god, and creates heaven and earth (148, 29—149, 9). There is the feminine partner of Ialdabaoth, Pronoia Sambathas, and the other Archons, Iao, Sabaoth, Adonaios, Eloaios, Oraios, and Astaphaios, and their feminine partners (149, 9—150, 11), and many other powers (δύναμις) and demons (δαίμων). There are cherubim from the OT (Ezk 10) to carry the throne of Sabaoth (152, 31ff.), and Eros (ἔρως) from Hellenism (157, 2, etc.), and the Phoenix (φοῖνιξ) from Egypt (169, 35ff.). There is Paradise (παράδεισος) (158, 2ff.)

with its trees (158, 6—159, 8), including the tree of immortal life (158, 7ff.) which makes the souls (ψυχή) of the saints immortal (ἀθάνατος), the tree of knowledge (γνῶσις) (158, 24ff.) whereby the souls (ψυχή) are awakened from the sleep of the demons (δαίμων), and the olive tree (159, 2ff.) which is of high importance because of the practice of anointing (χρῖσμα). There is the great angel (ἄγγελος) who is named Light-Adam (156, 2—157, 1), and the Adam whom the Archons made but could not bring to life (162, 29ff.). Then (163, 30ff.) Sophia sent her daughter, Zoe (ζωή) who is named Eve, and she commanded Adam to live and he did, wherefore she is called the mother of the living (Gen 3:20). So all of these and many more play their parts, until the cosmic disturbances of the new Aeon ensue (174, 4ff.) and, finally, all the entities in the cosmos return whence they came. "For (γάρ) it is necessary that each go to the place (τόπος) from which he has come. For (γάρ) each will reveal his nature (φύσις) through his action (πρᾶξις) and his knowledge (γνῶσις)."

§369. Such a work is obviously compounded out of many elements, and it is difficult, at least at the present point, to say how early the Greek form from which the Coptic is presumably translated (§366) might have been. In 162, 1–4 the Powers (ἐξουσία) name the man θηρίον, which can mean a wild animal in general or, specifically, a snake, as in Ac 28:4. The interpretation (ἑρμηνεία) of this name is then given as "the Instructor." "For (γάρ) they found that he was wiser than (παρά) them all." The last comment is almost certainly an allusion to Gen 3:1 where, in the Hebrew, "the serpent was more subtle than any other wild creature," and, in the LXX, "the serpent was the wisest of all the wild animals" (ὁ . . . ὄφις ἦν φρονιμώτατος πάντων τῶν θηρίων). Therefore, although the relationships of Adam, Eve, and the serpent have been made far more complex than in Gen, it is evident that the serpent is accorded a place of special emphasis. This could suggest a connection of the present work with the Ophites, who were known already to Irenaeus (*Against Heresies* I 30; §113) and to Origen (*Against Celsus* VI 24 and 28). Yet the relatively early date which such a connection would suggest might not be correct for the work as a whole, which brings together materials from so many different sources (§367).

§370. As for specifically Christian materials, they can hardly be said to play any predominant role in the present work, and the place of Jesus Christ is, in fact, minimal. He appears in 153, 26ff., where he is said to be patterned after the Savior (σωτήρ) who is above in the Ogdoad (cf. §§105, 109). He sits on a glorious throne (θρόνος) at the right hand of Sabaoth (§368), while the Virgin (παρθένος) of the Holy

Spirit (πνεῦμα) sits on a corresponding throne (θρόνος) at the left, a sort of Trinity thus being constituted. Again in a second passage (162, 16–17), "Sabaoth and his Christ" are mentioned, and that is all.

§371. There is also relatively little use of the canonical Gospels which can be recognized. In 173, 17–19 the Logos says: "There is nothing hidden that is not revealed, and what was not known will be known." This is a rather brief version of a saying of Jesus found in somewhat variant forms in several places in the Synoptic Gospels (Mt 10:26; Mk 4:22; Lk 8:17; 12:2). In the Synoptic form of the saying the revealing of the hidden is yet in the future; here it is already present, presumably in accord with the Gnostic emphasis upon the present attainment of saving knowledge. In 172, 11–13 there is mention of "the little blessed ones (μακάριος)" who are not strange to the Gnosis, for (γάρ) the entire Gnosis is in an angel (ἄγγελος) who is revealed to them. This could reflect the "little ones" and "their angels" of Mt 18:10. Incidentally, at this point Lines 12–15 are repeated in Lines 15–18, evidently due to homoioteleuton. In the description of cosmic upheaval (§368) there is mention of earthquake (173, 34) as in Mt 24:7 = Mk 13:8 = Lk 21:11; the sun and moon are darkened (174, 10–11) as in Mt 24:29 = Mk 13:24, cf. Lk 21:25; and the disturbance of the sea (θάλασσα) (174, 9) could reflect Lk 21:25. While Mk appears in some of these Synoptic parallels, there is no place where Mk is necessarily the only source, as is the case with Mt and Lk, and it is probable that only Mt and Lk are used of the Synoptics. In 148, 17 the reference to what came into being through the Word, no doubt presupposes Jn 1:1-3. As for any other historical information about Jesus and his teachings than what is in the canonical Gospels, it seems unlikely that such was preserved in a work which stands as far from earliest Christianity as this one does.

## 8 / Other Coptic Papyri

### (A) THE LETTER OF THE APOSTLES

Literature: Hugo Duensing, Epistula Apostolorum. KT 152. 1925; HSNTAE 126–55; Manfred Hornschuh, Studien zur Epistula Apostolorum. Patristische Texte und Studien, ed. by K. Aland and W. Schneemelcher, 5. 1965.

§372. There are, of course, other Coptic papyri which might be considered but, for the most part, they fall outside the limits of time or of character within which we have undertaken to focus our inquiry (§281). It should suffice, therefore, to take up one more example here, namely, the Letter of the Apostles. The Coptic text of this work was discovered in 1895 by Carl Schmidt on fifteen leaves of papyrus in the Institut de la Mission Archéologique in Cairo. Another fifteen leaves of the same work are missing. The date of the Coptic manuscript is probably in the fourth or fifth century, but like many other of the Coptic texts it probably rests back upon an earlier Greek original. A fuller version of the text, including extensive portions missing from the Coptic at the beginning, in the middle, and at the end, is found in Ethiopic translation in Oriental Manuscript 793 of the British Museum and certain other manuscripts, all of which are said to be not earlier than the eighteenth century. There are also a few fragments of a Latin translation, in which part of a title is preserved, with the word *epistula*. At the beginning of the Ethiopic version there is mention of "how Jesus Christ revealed the letter of the council of the apostles." From these facts it is supposed that the full title in Latin was *epistula apostolorum*, the Letter of the Apostles. From this title the work might seem not to belong within our purview at all, and the available manuscripts are of course relatively late. Nevertheless the character of the work is such that we will give a brief description of it.

§373. At the point (Chapter 7) where the extant Coptic text begins it is said that Cerinthus and Simon have come to walk through the world, but they are enemies of our Lord Jesus Christ. Simon has already been mentioned (§100). As for Cerinthus, Irenaeus says (*Against Heresies* I 26, 1) that he was educated in the wisdom of the Egyptians. He taught that the world was not made by the primary God but by a lower Power. He represented Jesus as the son of Joseph and Mary. Christ came down upon Jesus after his baptism, and departed from him again before he suffered. In another passage (*Against Heresies* III 3–4) Irenaeus tells on the authority of Polycarp that John, the disciple of the Lord, went to the bath in Ephesus and, seeing Cerinthus within, rushed out, exclaiming: "Let us flee, lest the bath fall, for Cerinthus, the enemy of the truth, is within." Eusebius (*Ch. Hist.* III 28; IV 14, 6; VII 25, 3) quotes Gaius of Rome (c. 200) and Dionysius of Alexandria (c. 250) to the effect that Cerinthus taught that the kingdom of Christ will be an earthly one. Because of these false teachers, Simon and Cerinthus, the present work is set forth to bear witness "that the Lord is he who was crucified by Pontius Pilate and Archelaus between the two thieves" (9).

§374. The finding of the empty tomb and the seeing of the risen Christ are described next. Both Peter and Thomas touch the risen

Christ, and Andrew ascertains that his feet touch the ground, the latter point being important because the foot of a ghost or demon does not touch the ground (11). So he was truly risen in the flesh. Christ then promises to reveal to the disciples what is above heaven, and in heaven, and their Rest (§357) that is in the kingdom of heaven (12). The ensuing revelation (13f.) tells how Christ came down through the various heavenly spheres and entered into Mary in the guise of the angel Gabriel. Not infrequently as the revelation continues, items are woven in from the canonical tradition and also modified as desired. At one point (17) Jn 10:38 is quoted with the addition of the word "wholly" to make as strong as possible a statement of the unity of the Son and the Father: "I am wholly in my Father and my Father in me." Again (18) Jn 13:34 is quoted exactly: "A new commandment I give to you, that you love one another"; and shortly after that Mt 5:44 = Lk 6:27, "Love your enemies," is combined with a negative formulation of Mt 7:12 = Lk 6:31, "and what you do not wish that men would do to you, that do you also to no other one." As for the disciples, Christ promises (21) that, as the Father has awakened him from the dead, in the same manner they also will rise. On their part, they ask him various questions, and a considerable part of the revelation proceeds in dialogue form. Christ himself has descended to Lazarus (Lk 16:23) and preached to the prophets (27); now he commissions the disciples to preach to the twelve tribes and to the Gentiles (30). They say (40) to him: "Lord, in all things you have taught us and pitied us and saved us, that we may preach to those who are worthy to be saved, and that we may obtain a reward with you."

§375. If this work is intended to oppose the teachings of Gnostics and heretics such as Simon and Cerinthus (§373), it has itself absorbed ideas which those teachers promulgated as may be seen, for example, in the descent of Christ through the various heavenly spheres (§374). Also it has adopted the very form, so favored in Gnostic circles, of a conversation between the risen Christ and his disciples, in which to set forth its teachings. The freedom with which the historic tradition is dealt with, under these circumstances, is such that it is difficult to suppose that this document has preserved any materials additional to those derived from the canonical Gospels which should be considered as comparable to them.

# 6 / Coptic Parchments

## 1 / Codex Askewianus

*Literature:* G. R. S. Mead, *Pistis Sophia.* 1921; George Horner, *Pistis Sophia.* 1924; Carl Schmidt, *Koptisch-gnostische Schriften* I (= GCS 13), 1905; 2d ed. by Walter Till (= GCS 45), 1954; 3d ed. by Walter Till (= GCS 45), 1959.

§376. Most of the Coptic parchments are later than most of the Coptic papyri (§§206, 281), and it will suffice now to mention only a few of the oldest of these. The first was acquired in 1773 by the English collector, Anthony Askew, whence it is known as Codex Askewianus. In 1785 it was purchased by the British Museum, where it is numbered as Ms. Add. 5114. The codex consists of leaves of vellum about eight and one-half by six and one-half inches in size, written in double columns on both sides. Among the Coptic manuscripts the double columns are unusual, since more often there is only a single column of text. There were originally one hundred and seventy-eight leaves, of which one hundred and seventy-four remain. The pages are numbered, and the four missing leaves were those with page numbers 337–44. The language is Sahidic, with some influence of Fayumic (§83). The writing is the work of two scribes, and the script is assigned probably to the second half of the fourth century. The text was divided into one hundred and forty-eight chapters by Carl Schmidt in his original edition, and we cite the text by these chapter numbers and also by the pages as found in the third edition of the same work by Till (see the *Literature* above). The translation of such passages as are given follows the German translation in the same work.

§377. The text of Codex Askewianus is divided into four sections. The first book, as we may call it, comprises Chapters 1–62, extends from the beginning to the first column of Page 114 of the manuscript

(81 in Till), and has no title at either the beginning or the end. The second book, comprising Chapters 63–100, begins with the first column of Page 115 of the manuscript (82 in Till) and extends to the first column of Page 233 (162). Extending above both columns on Page 115 (82) is a title which was probably added later: The Second Book (τόμος) of the Pistis Sophia. At the bottom of the first column on Page 233 (162) is a subscription which was written at the same time as the text. It reads: A Part (μέρος) of the Books (τεῦχος) of the Savior (σωτήρ). The immediately following portion of text, identified as Chapter 101, and extending from the second column on Page 233 (163) to the second column of Page 234 (164), appears to continue the argument of the foregoing book at the very point where it is interrupted by a question of Andrew (Chap. 100, Page 158 in Till), and it may have been inadvertently omitted there and then copied in here. If that is correct then the third book, comprising Chapters 102–35, begins with the first column of Page 235 of the manuscript (164 in Till) and extends to the first column of Page 318 (231). This book has no title at the beginning but has a subscription at the end which is identical with that at the end of the second book. The fourth book, comprising Chapters 136–48, begins with the second column of Page 318 of the manuscript (232 in Till) and extends to its end in the second column on Page 354 (254). No title is provided for the fourth book at either the beginning or the end. Finally on the other side (*recto*) of the last leaf (254 in Till), an additional short excerpt from some source has been copied in by a later hand.

§378. The analysis of the contents of Codex Askewianus indicates, it is generally agreed, that the first three books are the three parts of one continuous work, and the fourth book is a separate work. Both works are full of Greek words, and may well be translations of Greek originals. Both works exhibit the typical form of a Gnostic Gospel with which we are now familiar, i.e., they purport to contain revelations given by Christ to his disciples in conversation with them after the resurrection (§149).

§379. The work contained in the fourth book, which must remain nameless in the absence of any title (§377), begins (Chap. 136, Page 232 in Till) with reference to the fact that "our Lord Jesus" was crucified (σταυροῦν) and raised from the dead on the third day. At that time his disciples (μαθηταί) gathered around him. Jesus stood with them and prayed to the Father, but his prayer was an incantation filled with magical words such as are found in Egyptian magical papyri (§97): αεηιουω· ϊαω· αωϊ· ωϊα· . . . σαβαωθ. Then (Page 233) the universe was moved, and they found themselves in an aerial (ἀέρινος) place (τόπος) which Jesus (now also called Aberamentho) identified as the places (τόποι) of the way of the Middle (§111). Jesus then launched upon the explanation of many mysteries (μυστήριον) (Chap. 137, Page 234). When he divulged the imperishable (ἄφθαρτοι) names of the Archons (Page 235), the disciples professed themselves the most blessed of all men to have learned such great wonders (Chap. 138, Page 235). From then on many of them spoke up individually, Mary (i.e., Magdalene, cf. §190), Salome, Peter, Andrew, Thomas, Bartholomew, and John, and asked him questions to which he replied with further extended teachings.

§380. From the titles already (§377) noted in it, the work contained in the first three books (Chapters 1–135) of Codex Askewianus could be called the Books (τεῦχος) of the Savior, or the Books (τόμος) of the Pistis Sophia. The former title appears twice in the extant manuscript and was probably written in at the same time as the text, therefore may be the original title. Originally, also, the word τεῦχος is the designation of a roll of writing material, rather than of a codex, and may be preserved from a time when this work was written on rolls of papyrus. The divisions between the first three books of the codex do not fall at any particularly obvious dividing points as far as content is concerned, but the first book, the second book, and the third and fourth books combined are respectively of about the same extent as far as size is concerned; therefore the entirety may once have been distributed in three papyrus rolls, the third of which was filled out by the copying in of a separate work just to complete the roll, namely, the untitled work contained in the fourth book of the codex. As for the latter title mentioned above, the fact that it was written into the manuscript later, and the circumstances just outlined, make it unlikely that it was the original title. It is, in fact, appropriate only to a certain extent, for Pistis Sophia is prominent in the account up through Chapter 82 (Page 118 in Till), but not after that. Nevertheless, "Pistis Sophia," rather than the less distinctive "Books of the Savior," is the title by which the work contained in the first three books of Codex Askewianus is most commonly known.

§381. In contrast with the fourth book in Codex Askewianus (§379), where the revelation takes place immediately on the day of the resurrection, i.e., the third day after the crucifixion, here at the beginning of the first book (Chap. 1, Page 1 in Till) we read that after Jesus was raised from the dead he spent eleven years with the disciples (μαθηταί), and in his discourses with them taught them only as far as the places (τόποι) of the first commandment and as far as the places (τόποι) of the first mystery (μυστήριον). In their ignorance of greater mysteries still, the disciples sat on the Mount of Olives—while Jesus sat a little distance away—and spoke to one another of how blessed (μακάριοι) they were, beyond (παρά) all men, to have had everything revealed to them. Then (Chap. 2, Page 3) "on the fifteenth of the moon in the month Tybi, which is the day on which the moon becomes full," a great event took place. On that day, when the sun came out on its course (βάσις), a great power (δύναμις) of light came after it. This light-power descended (Chap. 3, Page 4) upon Jesus and gradually enveloped him altogether. Then (τότε) Jesus ascended or (ἤ) flew into the heights. There were great disturbances and all men, including the disciples (μαθηταί) thought: "Perhaps the world (κόσμος) will be rolled up together." But as the disciples sat and wept (Chap. 4, Page 4), at about the ninth hour of the following day the heavens opened and they saw Jesus coming down in immeasurable light. He reassured them (Chap. 5, Page 5), saying: "Be of good cheer; it is I; be not afraid" (Mt 14:27 = Mk 6:50). Upon their question (Chap. 6, Page 5) as to where he had gone, he promised that from then on he would speak to them plainly (παρρησία) and tell them about everything from the beginning (ἀρχή) of the truth (ἀλήθεια) all the way unto its completion.

§382. Proceeding (Chap. 6ff., Pages 6ff.) with the promised revelation, Jesus tells how he journeyed through the various spheres (σφαῖρα). When (Chap. 29, Page 25) he came up to the curtains (καταπετάσματα, cf. §368) of the thirteenth Aeon (αἰών) he found the Pistis Sophia beneath the thirteenth Aeon (αἰών), sitting all alone, grieving (λυπεῖσθαι) and mourning. It seems (Chap. 30, Page 27) that Authades, the third of the three thrice-powerful (τριδύναμοι) rulers of the thirteenth Aeon, hated her because she aspired to the light which is higher than she. So (Chap. 31, Page 28) all the material (ὑλικοί) emanations (προβολαί) of Authades enveloped her, and the great light-power with the countenance of a lion devoured her light-powers (-δυνάμεις). Her matter (ὕλη) was driven down to Chaos (χάος) and became an Archon (ἄρχων) there, with the countenance of a lion, half fire and half darkness, i.e., none other than Ialdabaoth (§113). In her desperation Pistis Sophia expressed her first repentance (μετάνοια) (Chap. 32, Page 28), in which she cried (Page 30); "Rescue me out of the matter (ὕλη) of this darkness." Only after her thirteenth repentance (μετάνοια) (Chap. 57, Page 71) was the time fulfilled (Chap. 58, Page 72; Chap. 60, Page 76) that she should be brought up out of Chaos (χάος). Christ sent a light-power to lead her up, and (Chap. 64, Page 85) all her own light-powers recognized each other and gathered themselves together again. So she became once again as she was before. Among her proper companions, the twenty-four Invisibles (ἀόρατοι) (Chap. 81, Page 115; Chap. 82, Page 118), she praised the Savior (σωτήρ) and said: "I will sing this hymn (ὕμνος) to the Light, for it has saved me and has rescued me out of the hand of the Archons (ἄρχοντες), my enemies."

§383. The elucidation of these mysteries proceeds for the most part in dialogue form, with various ones of the disciples asking questions and also being inspired by Jesus to set forth explanations themselves. Those who speak (citing only the point of their first appearance in such role) are Mary Magdalene (Chap. 17, Page 16, and most frequently), Philip (Chap. 22, Page 19), Peter (Chap. 36, Page 36), Martha (Chap. 38, Page 38), John the Apostle (Chap. 40, Page 41), Andrew (Chap. 45, Page 48), Thomas (Chap. 46, Page 51), Matthew (Chap. 49, Page 55), James (Chap. 51, Page 60), Salome (Chap. 54, Page 65), and Mary the Mother of Jesus (Chap. 59, Page 75). Among all of these, Mary Magdalene and John are given a pre-eminent place. Jesus says (Chap. 96, Page 148): "Mary Magdalene and John, the virgin (παρθένος, which can be used of a not-married man), will surpass all my disciples (μαθηταί) . . . and they will be on my right hand and on my left." Three others, however, are chosen as the ones to write down the revelations which are given, namely, Philip, Thomas, and Matthew (§343). Jesus says (Chap. 42, Page 44; cf. Chap. 43, Page 45): "Listen, Philip, you blessed one (μακάριος), that I may speak with you, for you and Thomas and Matthew are the ones who are commissioned, through the first mystery (μυστήριον), to write all the discourses which I say and do, and all the things which you will see." This, it is pointed out a little later (Chap. 43, Page 45), fulfills the injunction of Moses (Dt 19:15) which says that only on the evidence of two witnesses, or of three witnesses, shall a matter be established. "The three witnesses are Philip and Thomas and Matthew."

§384. As the disciples themselves participate in the conversations they quote a number of the canonical Psalms of David (Chap. 33, Page 32, etc.), and five of the apocryphal (= pseudepigraphical) Psalms of Solomon (Chap. 58, Pages 73–74, etc.). Jesus, as we have seen (§381), occasionally speaks in the language of the canonical Gospels, and the disciples also quote sometimes from these sources. For example, at the point where the history of the Pistis Sophia comes to an end (Chap. 82, Page 118; cf. §380), Mary Magdalene introduces the further conversations by recalling (Chap. 83, Page 119) a saying which Jesus had once uttered to them, namely, "Seek, that you may find, and knock, that it may be opened to you. For (γάρ) every one who seeks will find, and to every one who knocks it will be opened" (Mt 7:7–8 = Lk 11:9–10). Then she asks some questions about this saying, and this provides occasion for Jesus to proceed with certain explanations. Finally, near the end of the work (Chap. 134, Page 228), the Savior (σωτήρ) himself quotes to Mary Magdalene a saying which he had once uttered to the disciples: "Be like the wise money-changers (τραπεζῖται), take the good, reject the bad." This is a noncanonical saying of Jesus which we have already encountered (Text 9 §143). It is the only example of such material preserved in the present work.

§385. The two works (§378) contained in Codex Askewianus are probably of Egyptian origin. In the work contained in the fourth book we have noted the use of magical words such as are found in the Egyptian magical papyri (§379). This work also introduces other un-mistakably Egyptian ideas, such as the moon-ship (Chap. 136, Page 233), and in its discussion of the punishments of various sins con-demns an obscene rite (Chap. 147, Page 251) which is like a practice described by Epiphanius (*Pan. haer.* 26, 4, 5ff. GCS 25, 281) among the Gnostics of Egypt. In the work contained in the first three books of Codex Askewianus we have observed the dating of the Ascension on the fifteenth day of Tybi (§381). This date is stated in terms of the Egyptian calendar[1] and is equivalent to January 10. According to Clement of Alexandria (*Stromata* I 21, 146 GCS 52, 90)[2] some of the Basilidian Gnostics celebrated the baptism of Jesus annually on this same day (τὴν πεντεκαιδεκάτην τοῦ Τυβὶ μηνός). The develop-ment of ideas in the two works suggests perhaps a third-century date for them: the fourth book may belong to the first half of the third century; the first three books may have been written in the second half of the third century. So elaborate is their unfolding of Gnostic doctrine, and so extensive is their preoccupation with the supposed experiences of Jesus in supramundane realms, and with his revela-tions about those realms, that we may consider the above sketch of their contents adequate for our purposes.

[1] FHBC 29, §49, Table 8.
[2] FHBC 249, §393.

## 2 / *Bodleian Ms. Copt. d 54*

*Literature:* W. M. Flinders Petrie, *Gizeh and Rifeh.* 1907, 2;
W. E. Crum, "Coptic Anecdota: I. A Gnostic Fragment," in
JTS 44 (1943), 176–79; Paul E. Kahle, *Bala'izah, Coptic Texts
from Deir el-Bala'izah in Upper Egypt.* 1954, I, 473–77.

§386. In 1907 the British School of Archaeology in Egypt under
W. M. Flinders Petrie excavated at Deir el-Bala'izah, a site about
twelve miles south of Asyut on the edge of the desert on the west side
of the Nile. A large body of Coptic manuscripts, written on papyrus
and on parchment, was found, comprising fragments of perhaps three
thousand texts. Some of the manuscripts mention the monastery of
Apa Apollo, or of Apa Pouli, which may be the name (or names) of
this monastery. If it took its name from Apa Apollo, this could be a
monk by that name who is said to have been expelled from the
Pachomian monastery of Pbow (§79) in the time of Justinian, and
to have founded two monasteries.[1] In this case the monastery was
founded in the sixth century, and it probably came to an end soon
after A.D. 750, the beginning of the 'Abbasid caliphate, when many
of the smaller Coptic monasteries disappeared. In 1908 the manuscripts were placed in the Bodleian Library, Oxford.

§387. Among the manuscripts just described (§386), the first of
two texts (cf. §389) with which we will be concerned is identified as
Bodleian Ms. Copt. d 54, and it is sometimes referred to simply as the
Bala'izah Gnostic Fragment. This manuscript consists of a leaf of
papyrus, about six and one-fourth by four and three-fourths inches in
size, written in a single column of text on either side, and two additional fragments also written on both sides. The large leaf has page
numbers on either side, 41 on the *recto*, and 42 on the *verso*. The
language of the text is Sahidic (§83), the characters may be described
as square uncials, and the script is judged to belong to the fourth
century. Numbering the lines of text on the three pieces consecutively, and apparently allowing for a few gaps, text Lines 1–6 are on
one side (*recto?*) of the smallest fragment (a), Lines 8–12 on the

---

[1] Kahle, *Bala'izah* I, 19.

other (*verso?*); Lines 14–33 are on the *recto* (Page 41) of the large leaf (b), Lines 35–56 on the verso (Page 42); and Lines 58–73 on the *recto* of the other fragment (c), Lines 75–91 on the *verso*. Insofar as we quote the text we follow the English translation by Crum, as corrected by Kahle (see the *Literature* above).

§388. On the first fragment (a) only portions of words can be read but, by supplying missing letters, the words "the body ($\sigma\tilde{\omega}[\mu a]$)," "naked," and "without sin," can be recognized. Already the vocabulary sounds like that of Gnosticism, and this is confirmed on the large leaf (b) where the first incomplete sentence ends (Line 18) with the name of Sige ($\Sigma\iota\gamma\acute{\eta}$ = Silence), who is a great Aeon in the Valentinian system (§§109f.), and the next sentence reads: "For ($\dot\epsilon\pi\epsilon\iota\delta\acute{\eta}$) all they that (were) in the heavenly Paradise ($\pi\alpha\rho\acute{\alpha}\delta\epsilon\iota\sigma\sigma$) were sealed in silence." Then, beginning at Line 27, we find: "Lo, I have explained ($\dot\epsilon\rho\mu\eta\nu\epsilon\acute{\upsilon}\epsilon\iota\nu$) unto you, O John, concerning Adam and Paradise ($\pi\alpha\rho\acute{\alpha}\delta\epsilon\iota\sigma\sigma$) and the Five Trees, in an intelligible ($\nu\sigma\epsilon\rho\acute{\sigma}\nu$) allegory ($\sigma\acute{\upsilon}\mu\beta\sigma\lambda\sigma\nu$)." To this the one addressed replies, beginning in Line 35 at the top of the *verso:* "When I, John, heard these (things), I said: I have made a good beginning ($\breve{\alpha}\rho\chi\epsilon\sigma\theta\alpha\iota$, $\dot\alpha\rho\chi\acute{\eta}$); I have completed knowledge ($\gamma\nu\tilde{\omega}\sigma\iota s$) and a hidden mystery ($\mu\upsilon\sigma\tau\acute{\eta}\rho\iota\sigma\nu$) and allegories ($\sigma\acute{\upsilon}\mu\beta\sigma\lambda\sigma\nu$) of truth, having been encouraged ($\pi\rho\sigma\tau\rho\acute{\epsilon}\pi\epsilon\iota\nu$) by Thy love ($\dot\alpha\gamma\acute{\alpha}\pi\eta$)." On the remainder of the leaf there is a question about Cain and Abel. On the other fragment (c) there is something on the *recto* about the explanation which has been given to John concerning Noah and his ark ($\varkappa\acute{\iota}\beta\omega\tau\sigma s$) (Line 72), and on the *verso* a somewhat better preserved text which mentions (Lines 80f.) Melchizedek and quotes Heb 7:3 concerning him. It is evident that we have here a portion of another "Gospel" of the well-known Gnostic type in which Christ communicates revelations, usually after his resurrection, in conversation with a disciple or disciples. As far as it extends, there is nothing here which adds to historical knowledge concerning Jesus.

## 3 / *Other Coptic Parchments*

### (A) BODLEIAN MS. COPT. G 8

*Literature:* Paul E. Kahle, *Bala'izah, Coptic Texts from Deir el-Bala'izah in Upper Egypt.* 1954, I, 403–4.

§389. While there are other Coptic texts on parchment as well as on papyrus (§372), it seems unnecessary to extend the survey further. For a single example, but one that is already beyond our limits of time (§281), we may mention one more manuscript from among those found at Deir el-Bala'izah (§386), namely, Bodleian Ms. Copt. g 8. This is a leaf of parchment about three and three-quarters by three and one-quarter inches in size. The text is in a single column of fifteen lines on each side. The characters are rather heavy, square uncials, and are judged to belong to the sixth century. As far as it is preserved, the text gives an address, evidently by Christ, although he is not named in the extant portion, to his angels on the subject of the fall of the devil. He says (Lines 1ff.) to the angels (ἄ[γγ]ελος) that he has chosen them and revealed to them all of his mysteries (μυστήριον) from the beginning of the creation (κτίσις) until now. From this revelation they know that "it is arrogance which has cast the devil (διάβολος) forth out of his office (ἀρχή)." Presumably quoting Mt 8:12; 22:13; and 25:30, it is also said that he was cast forth "into the outer darkness" because of arrogance, and this same trait is called the mother of every sin. With the warning that, "He, therefore, who will not humiliate himself among you is a devil (διάβολος)," the fragment breaks off. Although it is so brief that more can scarcely be learned about it, this is presumably the fragment of an apocryphal Gospel, and it may be judged to be of Gnostic type, insofar as it conveys a revelation which must be that of the risen Christ rather than some record out of the earthly ministry of Jesus.

# Conclusion

Sufficient statement has been given already (Preface, Introduction, §§130, 206, 281) of the intended limits of this study, according to which we have fully reached the point of conclusion. In conclusion it is unnecessary to recapitulate all the materials which have been assembled in the foregoing pages. They stand there in the order which we have given them, readily accessible for every kind of consideration and subject to the judgments of those who wish to consider them, judgments which may or may not agree with those stated, sometimes provisionally and always, it is hoped, with openness to further light, in the course of our study. Suffice it to recall that the texts looked for were those of Gospel-type materials outside the canonical Gospels, whether found in the form of quotations in other early sources, or in the form of actual manuscripts or fragments thereof. These were arranged generally in the order of their relative antiquity, as far as rather positively ascertainable from the sequence of authorities making the quotations or from the probable dates of the extant manuscripts. The oldest texts available in Greek (and a few in Latin) were set forth in the original language and numbered to make them readily noticeable as Texts 1–86. For other texts, generally later and farther afield, including those in Coptic, the presentation of the materials on the basis of the translations available in various modern languages seemed adequate. Whether in them all there is, finally, anything which may stand on a par with the materials about Jesus Christ in the canonical Gospels, and in what the value of the extra-canonical materials consists, are questions on which, doubtless, each student will make his own decision. Certainly there is much that reveals later modification and speculation. Yet even here the modification and the speculation reflect in their own way the very great impact in human history and human thought of the life of Jesus.

# Indexes

# INDEX OF SCRIPTURAL REFERENCES
All references are to sections (§§) of this book.

# GENERAL INDEX

All references are to sections (§§) of this book. See also the analytical Table of Contents and the cross-references in the text.